A CANADIAN WOMAN'S
HEALTH GUIDE

TAKING CHARGE

BY

TAKING CARE

MARILYN LINTON

MACMILLAN CANADA
TORONTO

Canadian Cataloguing in Publication Data

Linton, Marilyn
Taking charge by taking care : a Canadian woman's
health guide

Includes index.
ISBN 0-7715-7382-0

1. Women – Health and hygenie – Canada. I. Title.
RA778.L55 1996 613'.04244'0971 C96-930954-6

Macmillan Canada wishes to thank the Canada Council, the Ontario Arts Council and the Ontario Ministry of Culture and Communications for supporting its publishing program.

Cover and text design: Counterpunch/Linda Gustafson

Macmillan Canada
A Division of Canada Publishing Corporation
Toronto, Canada

1 2 3 4 5 00 99 98 97 96

Printed in Canada

ACKNOWLEDGMENTS

I would like to acknowledge the following people who have helped me in this project: Vena Eaton for doing a terrific job in helping to compile the book's resources; Anne Rochon Ford for her work in the areas of pregnancy and childbirth, reproductive technologies and disabilities; Sam Linton for her contributions to the exercise portion of the book; and Tanya Linton's contributions to a portion of the chapter on reproductive health. Thanks too to Marian Hebb for her wise counsel and Chris Parkinson for his patient computer tutoring. Colleagues at the *Toronto Sun* who helped this book along one way or another include Trudy Eagan who supported the series of health supplements that led up to the book's idea, Julie Kirsh, Joanne Richard, Sandy Naiman, Rita DeMontis, and Alan Shanoff – my thanks to them and the many consumers who shared their health stories with me.

This book is intended as a background reference only, not as a medical guide or a manual for self-treatment. It is not intended as a substitute for any treatment prescribed by your doctor. However, the book owes much to the contributions of dozens of doctors and health care professionals (through individual interviews, some of which ran in my *Toronto Sun* health articles, or from workshops, lectures or conferences). In particular, thanks to the staff at Women's College Hospital in Toronto and to Dr. Donna Stewart for her informative and important ongoing Women's Health Series at Toronto Hospital. Finally, on the publishing side, thanks to Bob Dees, Loral Dean, Liba Berry and Macmillan's Nicole de Montbrun.

FOREWORD

For more than eighty years, Women's College Hospital has been an incubator for new ideas and new ways of teaching and providing care for women at each stage of their lives. This commitment to the care of women and their families and the development of research and education in women's health has given Women's College a unique and critical leadership role – not only in Canada but throughout the world.

This tradition continues with the establishment of The Centre for Research in Women's Health, a joint effort of Women's College Hospital and the University of Toronto. For years, women's health issues have been largely ignored by researchers. And yet, women constitute 52 percent of Canada's population. The Centre for Research in Women's Health is working to bridge this gender gap by welcoming the participation of researchers dedicated to giving women's health issues the attention they deserve.

With this book, author Marilyn Linton has made a great contribution to women's ability to take charge of their health care by making informed choices—a cornerstone of the mission of Women's College Hospital. A team of Hospital advisers has reviewed her wide-ranging research and advice. We look forward to working with Marilyn on all future editions of *Taking Charge by Taking Care* in a cooperative effort to present the most current information on women's health care issues.

Taking Charge by Taking Care will be an excellent addition to any Canadian woman's library.

K. Ann Kerwin, Chair, Board of Directors,
Women's College Hospital Foundation

Macmillan Canada wishes to acknowledge the support of Women's College Hospital, an academic health centre affiliated with the University of Toronto, and the following advisers, all of whom gave generously of their time to review this book:

Mary M. Addison, R.N., M.S.W., C.S.W.   Mary Neill, B.A., M.E.D., R.N.
James Ruderman, M.D., C.C.F.P.   Sandra Messner, M.Sc., M.D., C.C.F.P.

CONTENTS

TO OUR HEALTH: A BOOK TO HELP CANADIAN WOMEN BE THE BEST WE CAN BE!

This is not a book about disease, and the women you will meet here are not victims. This is a book about health and how to get the best for yourself. It's also about the dozens of inspiring women we have to thank for heightening our awareness of health issues in Canada.

Why has women's health become such a hot topic in the nineties? Because we're discovering that as women, we have unique health needs. Because we finally feel entitled enough to ask tough questions, to seek second opinions, to question our treatment, to challenge the experts. Because as women, we feel empowered to take our place beside our physicians as partners in our health care.

Why a Canadian book on women's health? Because although plenty of information is available on the subject, there's no book that gives you expert opinion on the subject of women's health from the perspectives of both physicians and the women who are consumers of health care in this country. This book marries the two perspectives .

SO WHAT'S IN THIS BOOK?

In this book, you'll find up-to-date information on the top women's health issues in Canada. Each health topic includes a personal guide to prevention, risk factors, medical treatment and a detailed resource list: recommended books, videotapes, audiotapes, support groups, foundations, women's health centres and survivors' organizations across the country.

You'll find answers to important questions such as: How safe is tamoxifen, the breast cancer drug? How do I decide whether or not to take HRT? How do I find a midwife? What can I do about chronic fatigue? How do I help a friend who has an eating disorder? What can a massage do for me that a stiff drink can't? What's the latest word on carpal tunnel syndrome? What's the route to go if my partner and I are infertile but want to try the new reproductive technologies? How can I start a health-sharing group in my community? What can I do if my family tree reveals branches of ovarian cancer? Should I have cosmetic surgery? How do I get enough calcium without gaining weight? What's the true story on women and AIDS? These are only some of the hundreds of women's health questions discussed within these pages.

This book will give you sound information from medical experts, but it will also give you what medical books can't – a collection of personal stories straight from the hearts of survivors.

How to Use This Book

Taking Charge by Taking Care is divided into two parts. Part One is about health today and the contemporary Canadian woman. In this section you'll find up-to-date information about the women's health movement in Canada and how you're a part of it. You'll learn how to build your health team, how you can develop your own personal risk profile and how to be the best you can be through setting exercise goals, reducing stress and tailoring your diet to achieve optimum health. Part Two is divided into fifteen chapters, each devoted to a top women's health issue, and each organized as follows: the first section provides facts about that chapter's health topic and explains why it is a women's health issue. The second section of each chapter in Part Two is your guide to staying healthy and reducing your risks, whether it's learning about breast health or the latest in how-to-stop-smoking research. The third section directs you to more information through recommended resources.

The ideas contained here will give you both an overview and a detailed update about a large number of women's health issues; however, it won't give you the last word on every subject. There are great books on the market that cover individual subjects comprehensively; breast cancer, migraines, heart disease and pregnancy, to name but a few. You will find many of these books recommended as further reading. Use *Taking Charge by Taking Care* as a resource in itself, one you can refer to according to your needs or interests. I hope you will turn to it the way you would to a good friend, for reassurance, sound advice and reliable information.

GOOD HEALTH AND THE CANADIAN WOMAN OF THE NINETIES

CHAPTER 1

CANADIAN WOMEN'S HEALTH CARE IN THE NINETIES

WOMEN'S HEALTH COMES OF AGE

Why are the late 1990s a significant time for women's health? One reason is the shift from the emphasis on women as reproductive vessels to women as people. The narrow reproductive focus of the fifties broadened in the sixties thanks to the women's movement fight for greater reproductive rights in everything from contraceptive options to abortion clinics and family-centred maternity care. Over the past five decades, we have rethought the traditional doctor-patient relationship and in the process we have learned more and more about our bodies. Books like the Boston Collective's *Our Bodies, Ourselves* (updated, 1992) reshaped women's thinking forever by empowering them to take charge of their health.

A series of women's health tragedies – the terrible fallout of thalidomide, a sleeping drug withdrawn in Canada in the 1960s after it was found to cause limb deformities in the fetuses of women who had taken it during pregnancy; diethylstilbestrol (DES), a hormonal drug formerly used to treat the threat of miscarriage but abandoned when it was discovered that the daughters of women who had consumed it developed cancer; the Dalkon Shield, an IUD that caused infertility and pelvic disease; the overprescription of mood-altering drugs such as Valium; faulty breast implants – woke women up. We started to question routinely prescribed drugs and treatments and standard dicta about women's diseases. Until the fall of 1993, when a group of women volunteers working with the Heart and Stroke Foundation of Ontario decided to make women and heart disease a women's health issue, women were unaware that heart disease is the number-one killer of Canadian women. These women volunteers talked to women who'd had heart attacks after being told their symptoms were merely indigestion. They realized that women health consumers need to be made aware that women present heart disease symptoms differently from men, and that traditionally, women have been treated less aggressively. Thanks to these volunteers, the heart-attacks-don't-just-happen-to-men message is out there today.

And then came the tide that washed over us all as our awareness of breast cancer grew. It seemed as if breast cancer started in the eighties! It didn't, of course, but who spoke openly of it until then? Ditto for ovarian cancer. Until comedian Gilda Radner went public about the disease we knew very little about it.

We've come a long way over the past couple of decades, but even today, talking about our bodies is a problem for some women. When interviewing the daughters of immigrant women about breast cancer, for example, I learned that many of their mothers felt shame touching their own breasts, never mind talking about breast health.

SHOULD WOMEN'S MEDICINE BE A SPECIALTY?

Some people feel that women's health will only receive the attention, research and funding it deserves when women's medicine is established as a specialty like geriatrics or pediatrics. Female physicians in the United States who have been especially committed to this cause include Dr. Karen Johnson, an assistant clinical professor of psychiatry at the University of California at San Francisco. "To paraphrase Virginia Woolf," Dr. Johnson says, "we need a home of our own."

Whether women's medicine needs a specialty of its own or whether women's needs can be better addressed under the current system is an ongoing debate throughout North America. But women's health is definitely carving out a niche in Canada. In Toronto, Women's College Hospital (WCH) now offers two-year fellowships for doctors to study women's health. A one-year training program in women's health is now available at Queen's University in Kingston, Ontario. In 1989, the federal government established the Royal Commission on New Reproductive Technologies to help women and men understand and deal with the implications of new and powerful technologies related to human reproduction. In the fall of 1994, Canada's minister of health Diane Marleau announced the formation of five Centres of Excellence for women's health across the country. Every province now has women's health centres that are either community-based or hospital-housed. Support and information groups on everything from anorexia nervosa to violence against women exist throughout Canada. A national, federally funded breast cancer initiative addresses prevention, early diagnosis, treatment and follow-up care. And in the spring of 1995, Dr. Donna Stewart was appointed to the University of Toronto chair in women's health at the Toronto Hospital – the first hospital in the world to establish and appoint a chair in women's health for the development and support of research and education. Shortly thereafter, Dr. Steve Narod, part of the team that discovered the first breast cancer gene a few years back, was appointed to the Canadian Breast Cancer Foundation Chair at Women's College Hospital and the University of Toronto.

Gender Bias in Medicine

According to the Genesis Research Foundation, 85 percent of Canadian women will have a female-specific health problem during their lifetime. Yet only 3.5 percent of Canadian medical research funding is devoted to women.

I first heard about gender bias in medicine at a breakfast meeting at Toronto's Women's College Hospital. wch chief of medical staff affairs, Dr. Bev Richardson, told the audience that medical studies and drug trials have traditionally not included women or minorities. "Yet women consume 70 percent of the health care dollar," she said.

Arguments against including women as subjects in drug trials include cost and legal liability for fetal damage. But many experts dismiss this argument as patriarchal: if we exclude all women from drug trials to protect the few who might become pregnant, aren't we putting the lives of all women at risk? Besides, many women choose not to exercise their reproductive rights. Since there are many Canadian women who cannot get pregnant or are unlikely to get pregnant, the argument that no woman should be included in a drug trial because of potential fetal damage doesn't hold water. Dr. Donna Stewart believes we must get more data on how various drugs affect women specifically. Other authorities believe that drug companies who want to sell drugs to women have a responsibility to test those drugs first on women. If things don't change, drug companies may find themselves faced with lawsuits from women using drugs that have been tested only on men.

Many Canadian physicians believe that guidelines about who should be included in research studies are overly protective and exclusive. "The point is, if you don't do research on women, you actually expose them to more risk in the clinical setting," Dr. Richardson says. Women as patients are always part of the research *results*, she points out.

When women learn that research has been largely conducted by men on men and has benefitted mostly men, we feel a profound sense of betrayal. The most common example is an American aspirin study done on 22,000 men, the results of which were released in 1988. Because that study, called the Physicians' Health Study, looked at men only, we don't know yet whether aspirin affords women the same protection it affords men in preventing heart disease. What an important piece of research this would be, considering that heart disease is the leading cause of death for Canadian women! Other gender bias examples seem as bizarre as they are unjust. For example, in cholesterol drug research, three out of four trials used male subjects only, yet 50 percent of prescriptions for cholesterol-lowering drugs are written for women over the age of 60.

We now know that women's bodies metabolize drugs differently than men's. Sex hormone levels affect some drugs – not just alcohol but also lithium and diazepam. We've learned that drugs affect the sexes differently because women's hormonal levels fluctuate: we have to factor in pregnancy, lactation, contraceptive drugs and hormone replacement therapy, along with the fact that women have more body fat and less muscle than men.

The United States has a better record than Canada in the gender bias arena. In contrast to the meagre 3.5 percent Canadian medical research allots to women, the United States spends 15 percent. A $625 million 15-year study is under way at the U.S. National Institutes of Health which will study 160,000 women to research cancer, heart disease and osteoporosis. At the National Institutes of Health (NIH) in Bethesda, Maryland, new regulations state that no research applications will be funded in which women and minorities are not included. Many of the changes have been given the stamp of law. Says NIH spokesperson Dr. Virginia Cain: "There are now offices of women's health in several federal agencies in the U.S."

No such requirements exist in Canada at present. However, the Medical Research Council in Ottawa has recommended that a policy be developed to ensure the inclusion of women as research subjects. "The bottom line is it's in place elsewhere," says Toronto Hospital's director of women's health Dr. Donna Stewart. "In Canada we need to put our house in order."

THE HEALTH CARE CRISIS: HOW IT AFFECTS WOMEN

Stories about massive cuts in government spending on health care have become a familiar news staple in recent years. Hospital closures and cutbacks in every province are so predictable they rarely enjoy front-page newspaper coverage anymore. In Alberta, a major teaching hospital rations angioplasties because its program is way over budget, and new mothers have to pay for "extras" such as tissues during their hospital stay. In early 1996, officials estimated that 20,000 more jobs would be chopped from Ontario hospitals.

According to Deloitte & Touche's Health Care Services Group, Canada's health care financial issues include limits in both federal and provincial funding, pressure on industry to reduce costs and constraints on transfer of costs to consumers. At the same time, additional funds are required for new technologies and drugs, operational and financial information systems and the maintenance of properties and buildings. An excellent way to cut costs long term, the accountancy firm says, is to focus on disease prevention.

A nationwide poll released in the spring of 1995 by Toronto's Women's College Hospital indicates that Canadian women are very concerned about what they expect will be a decline in the quality of health care over the next five years. Cutting the fat in the medical system may be necessary, but we need to make sure women are not shortchanged in the process. (Consider the revolving-door deliveries in today's hospitals: women who have given birth are virtually pushed out the hospital door within hours. While the standard five-day stay of 20 years ago may be unnecessary, recent reports show that too-short hospital stays may endanger the emotional and physical health of both mother and baby.)

The more we know, the more we can improve and protect the system we have. Indeed, we're probably more aware of the serious fiscal pressures on the Canadian health care system than we are of our own individual health issues. Says Kathleen McDonell, a Canadian women's health movement activist, in the winter 1993 issue of *Ontario Medicine* : "Women have been and will continue to be in the forefront of movements for the change of the health care system. We are working towards a radically new kind of system, one that respects the integrity and self healing capacity of the body, one that acknowledges our right to make our own choices, one that sees health as a complex fabric of social, economic and environmental influences rather than a purely medical concern."

Why Every Woman Should be Concerned about Health Issues

Women have traditionally been nurturers and caregivers, but today our involvement in health concerns has assumed a new urgency. "Women's health is really an issue whose time has come," said Dr. Judith Kazimirski to a gathering celebrating Women's Health Day in March 1995.

"Fifty-two percent of the population of Canada are women," the Nova Scotia family physician and president elect of the Canadian Medical Association continued. "They are strong members of society. They are strong members of the workforce. They care for families. They care for children as well as developing their own careers, and many of them hold down more than one job. Many women are single heads of households and we need to remind ourselves that when a woman's health fails, often the family's health fails as well."

Women are indeed the gatekeepers of their families' health. Toronto family physician Dr. Carolyn Bennett conducted an informal survey in which she noted how often her male and female patients asked her questions for someone other than themselves. Most women, she says, came in and had a question about their sick mother/daughter/secretary. Her male patients did not ask such questions. Bennett's conclusion? Women just look after everybody.

To continue to "just look after everybody" as we struggle to cope with our pressure-cooker lives, we must learn to look after ourselves better.

CHAPTER 2

HEALTH CARE IS NOT ABOUT DOCTORS ONLY: A TEAM APPROACH TO GOOD HEALTH

The Doctor-Patient Team

Surveys show that one of the most difficult health care problems for women is dealing with their family doctor. For many women, the doctor-patient relationship is troubling because of an imbalance of power; over and over again, we hear how doctors patronize and talk down to women. Certainly any woman over 40 has had at least a few experiences with doctors who called her "dear" and whose attitude implies, "Don't worry about a thing . . . just take these pills and leave the rest to me." But ask women what they want from a doctor and you'll hear "to be heard and understood." Ask women what they *don't* want and you'll hear "to be told it's all in my head."

A 1995 nationwide survey of Canadian women and their health revealed that more than 50 percent are very satisfied with their family doctor, 26 percent are somewhat satisfied, 3 percent are neutral, and 17 percent are either somewhat dissatisfied or very dissatisfied. The survey indicated that the gender of the doctor is not an issue. What's important is his or her attitude.

"Women are not passive consumers," says Dr. Carolyn DeMarco, a British Columbia health specialist and educator who has been involved in both traditional western and complementary medicine. "I've found them to be active participants in their own health lives." DeMarco says that patients teach her a lot: "Doctors today can't possibly know everything and frankly they're better off saying that. They can say to a patient, 'I don't know, but I'll try and find out or refer you to someone who does know.' The information is exploding."

"I believe that women originally came to the health table believing that doctors and patients were a team," Dr. Carolyn Bennett, a Toronto physician who works out of Women's College Hospital's Family Practice Health Centre told me. "I now think women should be captains of that team with the general practitioner as coach. The final decision should be left to the patient." One of the things Bennett advocates is doctors and patients talking on a first-name basis. "If you are Betty, being introduced to Dr. Ego, is this a partnership?" she asks. "I hardly think so!"

How to Choose a Doctor

By the time most of us reach adulthood, chances are we've tried several different doctors as we search for the right doctor-patient fit. Much of this searching tends to be hit-and-miss.

So how do you find a doctor who's skilled and competent, can communicate well and whose relationships with his or her patients are based on respect? Here are some points to consider and some questions to ask yourself before settling on your next doctor:

- While doctor-shopping is discouraged, there's no reason to stick with the first doctor you find. Gather recommendations from friends, co-workers, neighbours or others whose opinions you value; ask another doctor. Ask these people why they recommend the physician. Check with your local or regional hospital: many have family practice or women's health clinics and doctors who work out of these clinics may take on new patients.

  Once you find your doctor, you'll then have to interview him or her in order to determine the fit of your health philosophies and communication styles.
- Take into account your lifestyle fit with this person. For instance, is his or her office location convenient to you? Do you sense he or she is poorly organized and so may keep patients waiting unreasonable lengths of time on a regular basis? Ask what kind of backup he or she leaves behind in the event patients have an emergency: with hospital emergency departments cutting back and closing, hearing a recording from a doctor's office that says, "If you have any problem, go to your nearest emergency" just isn't good enough. Some doctors now practise in a group and, if that's the case, do you have confidence in his or her associates? Does he or she return your phone calls, if not promptly then within a reasonable time?
- Is he or she up-to-date in both information and attitude? For instance, does the doctor realize that heart disease may present differently in women than in men? Does he or she speak of menopause as a disease or deficiency in which women lose their femaleness? What's the doctor's attitude towards breast lumps: every one should be further investigated? Or leave it and see? When you're troubled by symptoms that don't go away (like a rash, for instance), does

he or she keep insisting it's nothing or does the doctor ask for a specialist's opinion to satisfy both of you or to rule out possible illnesses?

- Does the doctor spend enough time with you during your appointment? Or do you constantly feel rushed out? We've all had the experience of waiting more than an hour for a doctor's appointment that took less than 15 minutes. Dr. Carolyn DeMarco says that most doctors work on 15-minute appointment schedules. "I tell women you can't go into a ten-minute appointment with a long list of questions. Try to book a longer appointment if you think you need one. And a doctor should sometimes be able to say to you, 'You know, I can't answer all these questions right now; we'll have to book a longer appointment, but we will do them.'"

- Does this doctor have an affiliation with a hospital that you'd choose to go to? What is the hospital's specialty or specialties?

- Can your family physician coordinate your care? In other words, can he or she make appropriate referrals to a nutritionist, psychologist, women's centre or medical specialist? Does the doctor take note of a specialist's report and discuss it with you, or does the report get shoved in your file while he or she says nothing to you?

- What do you sense of his or her medical philosophy? Does the doctor say it's "all in your head," or are you listened to, understood and your medical needs reasonably attended to? Does he or she consider you a whole person, or just a collection of body parts? Is he or she pill-happy: do you feel pills are pushed at you at every turn? How open is he or she to discussing alternative or complementary treatments?

- Does this person believe in preventive care? If you're a smoker, does he or she encourage you to quit (and try to offer help)? How supportive and helpful is this doctor regarding diet and exercise? Is he or she aware of the need to inform patients about lifestyle diseases such as skin cancer and STDs? Is the doctor happy to offer you literature on these and other illnesses?

- Does he or she know you as a person, or try to? Is he or she aware of your name, type of work, potential stresses?

Your Doctor Needs Your Help

Your doctor's appointment. It's your body and your right to know what's happening to it. So start by preparing for your doctor's appointment:

- Jot down your symptoms and your concerns (for instance, headaches more painful and appearing more often than usual) and try to provide as much

information on the symptoms as possible (for instance, headaches appear when weather changes).
- Include in your report how you've been managing your symptoms (for instance, write down the names of the over-the-counter pain relievers you have tried, and which work and which don't).
- Make sure you know the names of all the medications you're taking and mention them during your appointment.
- Be well versed in your medical history (you had headaches even in childhood – but you recall that when you were pregnant your headaches went away) and your family's history (your father suffered migraines).

There is no dumb question, so ask your doctor to explain things in language or terms you can understand. However, educating yourself is the key to improving communication between you and your doctor.

"There's often not enough time for your doctor to tell you everything," says Dee Taylor, a Burlington, Ontario, psoriasis patient. "If you belong to a support group, you can get additional information." Taylor developed her own coping strategies for managing her condition and now shares them with other psoriasis patients through workshops. "People today are recognizing they're more responsible for their health," Taylor says. "They're meeting with each other and sharing information. Now doctors are also finding that if you put 50 people in a room, they can tell 50 people the same information that they in their offices would only be able to tell one person."

How to be a responsible patient

- Part of being a responsible patient includes following up on things that a lot of us expect our doctors to do for us.

  For instance, when I asked a friend what her cholesterol levels were, she told me she didn't know, her doctor had never checked them as far as she was aware. Ditto with her blood pressure. Doctors do have a responsibility to give us regular and thorough physical examinations, but we also have a responsibility to make sure that our blood pressure is checked regularly and that our blood cholesterol levels are in the healthy range. If we're aware of our family's health history, we can also talk to our doctors about possible screening tests: for example, women with a familial history of bowel cancer should definitely ask their physicians which tests they recommend at what age and why.
- Patient responsibility includes being aware of your body changes.

  Obvious changes such as a breast lump should signal that a medical investigation is needed, but so should other body changes that are troublesome, that seem odd or are just different. One of the highlights of the spring 1995 meeting of the American Academy of Dermatology was the claim by dermatologists that primary-care physicians and patients often trivialize skin problems such as lesions, rashes, bumps, sores and pigment changes. Several serious diseases other than skin cancers signal their presence via skin changes. Diagnosing skin problems properly may mean earlier detection and lives saved.

• Adults often forget immunizations. We make sure our kids have the right shots, but we need to know if we're up to date on our own.

Your doctor, of course, should be aware of your immunization schedule – but so should you. For instance, if you have a contaminated wound and require emergency assistance, you will need to know the date of your last tetanus booster. Ask your physician about booster shots for polio, tetanus and diphtheria, and, if you're a woman of childbearing age, talk to your physician about rubella immunization. Other immunizations to discuss with your physician include flu shots, hepatitis B shots and any immunizations recommended for destinations in your travel plans.

• When it comes to surgery, asking questions (even asking for a second opinion) is especially important.

We've all read stories about women in some parts of the country having more of certain kinds of surgeries than women in other parts of the country. Recently, there are a lot of questions being raised about cesarean sections and hysterectomies, for example. Faced with a medical condition for which surgery is recommended, women need to be especially well informed about their bodies as well as the choices available to them.

Among the questions to ask your doctor are the following:

• Is there an alternative to this surgery, and if so, what is it and what are its consequences?
• Is there a less invasive type of surgery that can be done than the one being suggested and if so, what are its pros and cons?
• What are the risks that accompany the recommended surgery?
• What benefits will I feel and what improvements to my health can I expect as a result of the recommended surgery?
• How much pain is associated with the surgery and what is a typical recovery profile for this type of operation?
• What would happen to me if I chose not to have this surgery?

YOUR MEDICAL CHECKUP: WHAT TO EXPECT

A standard medical examination first involves the history-taking, the process by which a physician learns from you your symptoms as well as your past health profile – your number of pregnancies, menstrual history, risk-associated behaviours such as smoking and alcohol consumption, previous problems such as a thyroid disorder, and current symptoms or complaints.

As he or she asks these questions, your doctor is also assessing your physical appearance, to see whether you are pale or flushed, whether your skin seems healthy, whether you seem relaxed or worried.

The physical exam follows, in which the physician looks at, feels and listens to various parts of your body in order to assess your health or illness. A physical examination includes *percussion* (that's when the chest is tapped and the vibration felt and heard), *auscultation* (that's when the stethoscope is used to listen to lung and heart sounds) and tests for *tendon reflexes* in which a mallet is used to tap a stretched tendon. Physicians also use *palpation* in which they feel for signs of swelling, tenderness or the enlargement of organs. Usually, a *urine sample* is requested and a *urinalysis* done to determine, among other things, potential kidney disease, diabetes or urinary tract infection.

You and your doctor will decide on whether or not you should have a complete physical examination annually. Generally, experts in women's health advocate that women have the following as part of their regular physical examination:

• *Cardiovascular checkup*
This includes listening to your heart, a discussion about a heart-healthy lifestyle and how to attain it, and noting and following up on any symptoms such as chest pain or breathlessness. You and your doctor may decide to review your cholesterol through an analysis of your blood. Some physicians believe that ECGs *(electrocardiograms)* should be part of a physical checkup in women (and men) after the age of 40 and they also make sure their patients have a base-line ECG done earlier so that it can be used for comparison. Every checkup should include a blood pressure check – one a year from your teens to about age 40 if you have no heart disease risks and are not taking oral contraceptives, twice or more if you're older, take oral contraceptives, have a personal history of high blood pressure or your physician has recommended it for reasons other than the above. A healthy reading is less than 140 systolic over less than 90 diastolic. The instrument with a Velcro cuff that your doctor pumps up then

deflates in order to get your blood pressure reading is called a *sphygmo-manometer*.

• *Blood work*

When your physician takes blood samples, he or she may have the lab analyze them for a variety of reasons. Blood tests can be *hematological* (this includes looking at the blood's components to determine, among other things, blood clotting function, your blood count and your particular blood group); *microbiological* (if you've had a nasty virus, your doctor may ask the lab to identify your blood's microorganisms so as to determine how to best treat you); or *biochemical* (these tests measure blood gases, levels of potassium or glucose.) You or your physician may have specific concerns and use certain blood tests to zero in on a particular issue, be it the functioning of your thyroid, a test for HIV, an evaluation of your kidney function, the presence of anemia or an analysis of your blood cholesterol.

• *Cancer screening*

There are three or four cancers women should be screened for on a regular basis, more if you've had a family history of certain others.

1 BREAST: While you should perform breast self-examination (BSE), you should also ask your doctor to examine your breasts. You should have a mammogram yearly after the age of 50, earlier if you have a family history of breast cancer.

2 SKIN: Skin cancer is something both you and your physician can look for, you to check regularly for signs of changed moles, your physician to identify suspicious or potentially precancerous skin conditions.

3 GYNECOLOGICAL: An annual Pap smear can help screen for cervical cancer. Your physician can also inspect your vulva for cancers that can appear there. If you have symptoms, or if you are in a high-risk group, your doctor may want you to be screened for ovarian cancer. If you are experiencing abnormal uterine bleeding or other symptoms, your physician may want to perform an endometrial biopsy to check for endometrial cancers.

4 LUNG: If you smoke, live with a smoker or work in an environment that's unhealthy to your lungs, and if you have symptoms of possible lung disease, your doctor may want you to have a lung X ray or sputum test.

5 OTHERS: Many doctors suggest that women with a familial risk of colon

cancer (or with a personal history of polyps or ulcerative colitis) undergo a colonoscopy every three to five years to screen for colon cancer; a digital rectal examination is routinely done by many physicians.

• *Pelvic Health*
Most women have annual pelvic examinations to check for any abnormalities of the uterus and ovaries. Sometimes doctors recommend a transvaginal ultrasound to detect changes in the lining of the uterus and the ovaries that might suggest problems.

• *Bone Health*
Early detection may prevent the fractures caused by osteoporosis, the bone-thinning disease. Women who are menopausal (especially those who are small-boned and have a familial history of the disease) often have a bone scan to measure their bone density, detect low bone mass and diagnose osteoporosis.

DR. CAROLYN DEMARCO'S WOMAN'S HEALTH BILL OF RIGHTS AND RESPONSIBILITIES

In her book *Take Charge of Your Body*, Dr. Carolyn DeMarco introduces an excellent woman's health bill of rights and responsibilities. It's reprinted here with her permission in the hope that each of us can learn from it in our journey towards becoming better health consumers:
• I have the right to be treated as an equal human being.
• I have the right to be listened to and have my problems taken seriously.
• I have the right to an explanation that I can understand in my native language (using a translator if necessary) on any questions concerning my health care.
• I have the right to know the choices I face in getting treated for any health problem, and to have the possible side effects of any drugs or surgical treatments clearly explained.
• I have the right to choose the types of treatment I prefer from among the options offered to me by my doctor.
• I have the right for normal events in my life, such as pregnancy and menopause, not to be treated as diseases requiring treatment.

- I have the right to request a second opinion on any major surgery or health decision.
- I have the right to refuse any drug or surgical treatment.
- I have the responsibility to become knowledgeable about my body and how it works.
- I have the responsibility to learn as much as possible about my health problems so I can make informed choices.
- I have the responsibility to look after my diet, reduce stress, exercise and relax on a regular basis.
- I have the responsibility to avoid pressuring my doctor into giving me drugs when I don't need them.
- I have the responsibility to prepare my questions for my doctor beforehand and schedule adequate appointment time to discuss them.
- I am ultimately responsible for my own health care, using my doctor as a resource rather than an authority.

BUILD YOUR OWN HEALTH TEAM: REMEMBER, YOU'RE PART OF IT TOO

One hundred years ago, the general practitioner was most people's one and only doctor. He (and almost all doctors *were* men) was the person who set your broken arm, delivered your baby, tended your pneumonia and diagnosed your chicken pox. Today, although GPs still provide a complete range of medical services, many – particularly those in large cities – refer patients to specialists for complaints such as arthritis, heart disease, asthma, breast lumps, high-risk pregnancies, chronic sinus infections, even certain headaches. Some hospitals offer special services such as menopause, sleep, pain or fracture clinics. Today's GP, in other words, may have to be as much facilitator as practitioner.

"When I use the term 'team' it may refer to a general practitioner, a chiropractor and an acupuncturist," says Dr. Carolyn DeMarco. "If my patient needed ongoing psychotherapy, then her team would include a psychotherapist or psychologist." Your health team will probably build as you age. This doesn't necessarily mean seeing more health specialists because you're sick. A commitment to better nutrition, for example, may encourage you to seek help from a dietitian or nutritionist. In other words, your health team is unique to you.

Your growing health team may also include complementary medicine specialists such as a registered massage therapist, chiropractor, acupuncturist and nutritionist.

While traditional western medical specialists often pooh-pooh complementary therapies, more and more of their patients do not. Chances are, someone in your circle of family and friends sees a complementary therapist as well as a traditional doctor, or includes natural therapies (like taking evening primrose oil for premenstrual syndrome (PMS), menopause or chronic fatigue syndrome) along with prescription drugs for other conditions. It is becoming an increasingly mainstream trend to include complementary therapists in the health team. Last summer, for example, massage and shiatsu therapists toured with figure skaters across North America to help them avoid injuries.

Dr. Carolyn DeMarco likes the term *complementary* "because you'd be crazy to throw away all of western medicine." But she advises caution: "Someone may be calling himself a holistic healer and (only) have a six-month course from somewhere." Be sure to check the training of complementary therapists, she says. And choose carefully, as you would any professional, "by quality, experience, reputation – and lack of sexism."

Alternative therapies such as homeopathy are fully accepted in many countries outside of North America. Canada is slow to embrace homeopathy but a movement is building to have it included in mainstream medicine. For instance, in Winnipeg, homeopath Leelamma Nielsen opened a clinic in 1994 even though homeopathy is not licensed in Manitoba. In Quebec, almost 100 health care providers formed a group whose aim is to integrate homeopathic medicine into general medicine. Dr. Ginette Varin, a Quebec general practitioner, told the *Medical Post* that the organization, Regroupement pour l'Homéopathie Médicale (REM) was founded because of the number of patients coming to physicians, dentists and pharmacists wanting homeopathic treatment. Dr. DeMarco says that in Britain nearly 50 percent of doctors refer patients to homeopaths, while in France there are homeopathic pharmacies as well as regular ones. In the last few years, some Canadian pharmacies have begun selling homeopathic remedies.

MDS AND MORE: THE HEALTH CARE SPECIALISTS

Persons authorized to call themselves doctors in Canada include medical doctors (general practitioners and specialists such as oncologists and psychiatrists), dentists, optometrists, chiropractors and psychologists. Here is a brief list of some specialists in the health care field, both traditional and complementary:

• *Acupuncturist*
Acupuncture is a branch of Chinese medicine in which needles are inserted into a

patient's skin at certain points (called meridians or channels) to treat various disorders or to treat ill health caused by a blockage in one or more of the meridians. Acupuncturists must be licensed physicians in some provinces; in others, they are licensed as nonmedical practitioners. Check with the Acupuncture Foundation of Canada before visiting an acupuncturist to make sure the practitioner is licensed.

• *Cardiologist*
This medical specialist's area of expertise is cardiology, the study of the function of the heart and the investigation, diagnosis and medical treatment of disorders of the heart and its blood vessels, including hypertension and atherosclerosis. If surgery is necessary, the cardiologist will probably refer the patient to a cardiovascular surgeon.

• *Chiropodist*
A health care professional, but not a medical doctor, who has completed a three-year diploma course and who assesses, treats and manages acute and chronic foot-care problems.

• *Chiropractor*
Chiropractors use manipulation to restore or maintain health, or to relieve certain types of back, neck and joint discomfort. In Canada, they have completed a four-year diploma program from one of two chiropractic colleges in Toronto, Ontario, and Trois Rivières, Quebec. They can diagnose and treat conditions concerning the spine, muscle and nervous system, but are not allowed to prescribe drugs or perform surgery. The Canadian Medical Association does not accept any scientific basis for chiropractic treatment of diseases such as cancer and heart disease. There are about 4,000 doctors of chiropractic in Canada.

• *Dentist*
Doctors of dentistry work in general practice and provide a wide variety of dental services, from filling cavities to cleaning teeth, fitting bridges and extracting teeth. Within dentistry there are several specialized branches including *periodontics* (the treatment of disorders such as gum disease) and *orthodontics* (the management and movement of improperly aligned teeth to straighten them and improve their function). *Dental hygienists* complete a certified postsecondary course which allows them to perform such services as scaling teeth and equip them to educate patients in teeth and gum health.

- *Dermatologist*

A medical specialist whose areas of expertise include the skin, nails, hair and its diseases and disorders.

- *Dietitian/Nutritionist*

A registered dietitian or nutritionist has a degree from a certified postsecondary program in nutrition; a dietitian has also completed a dietetic internship at a hospital. While dietetics is not a medical specialty, a dietitian works in a hospital setting (or, like a nutritionist, in private practice or in a clinic) to help patients with their dietary needs, be it lowering fat intake or adjusting to a special diet as required by a diagnosis of, say, diabetes.

- *Endocrinologist*

This physician specializes in diseases and disorders of the endocrine glands and the hormones they secrete. People with suspected thyroid disorders or diabetes mellitus may be referred to an endocrinologist by their general practitioner.

- *Family practitioner/General Practitioner (GP)*

About 50 percent of practising physicians in Canada are family physicians or general practitioners; they are certified by the College of Family Physicians of Canada. A physician in Canada may practise under either the family practice or general practice designation; "family physician" will eventually replace the term GP.

   This nonspecialized medical doctor offers continuous and comprehensive medical care, according to the Canadian Medical Association's definition.

- *Gynecologist. See obstetrician/gynecologist.*

- *Gastroenterologist*

A medical specialist of the digestive system (the mouth, esophagus, stomach, intestines, colon, liver, gallblader and pancreas) and the diseases and disorders affecting it.

- *Hematologist*

This medical specialist studies and treats all aspects of blood disorders, including anemia and leukemia.

- *Herbalist*

Though herbal medicine (the treatment of symptoms through specific plants, their leaves or roots) has been used by various cultures for centuries, it's not medically recognized, nor is it endorsed or its practitioners certified or regulated. Naturopathic doctors are skilled in the administration of herbal remedies; part of their training includes botanical medicine.

• *Homeopath*
This is a nonmedical practitioner who uses homeopathy, a system of alternative medicine used by the British royal family and millions of people in Europe and South America. Homeopathy, which is legal in Canada but unlicensed, uses homeopathic remedies that are generally dilutions of natural substances from plants, minerals and animals which match different symptom patterns and act to stimulate the body's healing response. In homeopathy, patients are given minute doses of medicines that in a healthy person would bring on symptoms similar to what the medicine is prescribed to treat, the theory being that the sick person's natural defence system is stimulated into healing by these substances.

• *Internist*
An internist is a specialist in the diagnosis and nonsurgical treatment of diseases of the internal organs; most internists further specialize in diseases of a particular organ system such as cardiology or dermatology.

• *Midwife*
A midwife is a nonmedical specialist who provides care and information during pregnancy; assists with and supervises labour and delivery; and cares for both mother and baby after birth. Midwives are recognized in some provinces, and there are a few hospitals in Canada that allow midwives to be part of the delivery team.

• *Naturopath*
Naturopathy is a form of complementary or alternative medicine that believes that disease is due, in part, to the accumulation of waste products and toxins in the body. Naturopaths believe that good health is *natural* health – the avoidance of anything artificial or unnatural in the diet or environment. Naturopaths have completed a four-year diploma course from the Canadian College of Naturopathy where they learn acupuncture, clinical nutrition, botanical medicine, physical therapy (including manipulation of the spine) and homeopathy. A doctor of naturopathy uses the initials N.D. after his or her name. Naturopathy is regulated in some provinces (Ontario, British Columbia, Manitoba and Saskatchewan). Elsewhere, its legislation is under consideration.

• *Neurologist*

This medical specialist studies and treats disorders of the nervous system including pain control, migraines, headaches, multiple sclerosis and Parkinson's disease. Where surgery may be indicated, a neurologist might refer a patient to a neurosurgeon.

• *Nurse*

There are more than 220,000 registered nurses in Canada, most of them women, and all of whom have graduated from a certified provincial postsecondary nursing program. Some people trained in nursing care specialize in certain areas such as emergency care or psychiatric nursing. Today, there are also nurse practitioners in some provinces: these people provide some services previously performed only by physicians, such as ordering tests.

• *Obstetrician/Gynecologist*

Most obstetricians are also gynecologists – medical specialists who study and treat all aspects of reproductive health including pregnancy, prenatal, childbirth and postnatal care, as well as all aspects of pelvic health and disease.

• *Oncologist*

This medical professional is a physician specializing in the study and treatment of cancer.

• *Ophthalmologist*

Ophthalmologists are physicians who specializes in the care of the eyes.

• *Optometrist*

This health care professional diagnoses disorders and diseases of the eyes and visual system and prescribes or provides treatment such as eyeglasses and contact lenses. (An optician dispenses eyeglasses or contact lenses according to the prescription of an optometrist or ophthalmologist.)

• *Orthopedic Surgeon*

An orthopedic surgeon specializes in the branch of surgery concerned with disorders of the bones, joints and their associated muscles, tendons and ligaments. Orthopedic surgeons (or orthopods as they're known in the hospital community) perform a wide range of surgeries, from hip replacements to setting broken bones, and treat diverse bone, joint and muscle disorders, from arthritis to slipped disks.

• *Pharmacist*

A pharmacist is a licensed, trained health professional who has completed a four-year university degree in pharmacology. He or she prepares drugs and dispenses them according to a doctor's prescription and provincial regulations. More and more, pharmacists are ensuring that patients have adequate information about both prescription and over-the-counter drugs, including possible interactions and side effects.

• *Physiotherapist*

These health professionals have expertise in relieving, alleviating and managing pain and injury. Registered physiotherapists work in a variety of health care settings, from sports and recreational centers to hospitals and rehab clinics.

• *Podiatrist*

A doctor of podiatric medicine (DPM) specializes in the diagnosis, prevention and treatment of foot disorders. DPMs take a four-year course, after which they get a provincial license.

• *Psychiatrist*

Psychiatrists are medical doctors who specialize in the study, prevention and treatment of mental illness, emotional and behavioural problems. Within psychiatry there are a number of subspecialties, including geriatric and child psychiatry, and a number of treatment specialties, including feminist therapy and psychoanalysis. (Some family physicians, psychologists and social workers also do therapy: always check the individual's accreditation before beginning treatment).

• *Psychologist*

A psychologist has completed the scientific study of mental processes, which include everything from memory to thought, perception to learning, and intelligence to personality. A psychologist may specialize in a particular area such as counselling, intelligence testing, behavioural psychology or educational processes. He or she usually has a Ph.D. and may be addressed as Doctor.

• *Psychotherapist*

Anyone who counsels can call themselves a psychotherapist, so make sure you check the person's credentials before you start treatment. All medical doctors (including psychiatrists), psychologists and social workers are trained to do psychotherapy. This is one area of the counselling sciences that professionals would like to see better regulated.

• *Radiologist*

This medical specialty includes the use of X rays, ultrasound, mammography, computerized tomography scanning (CAT scanning), magnetic resonance imaging (MRI) systems and radioactive tracers to diagnose, investigate and treat diseases.

• *Registered Massage Therapist*

The basis of massage therapy is the manipuation of the tissues, primarily with the hands, for remedial purposes. Massage therapists are trained in numerous specialized techniques to treat soft tissue pain and disability as well as to provide preventive care. Registered massage therapists work in collaboration with physicians, chiropractors, physiotherapists and other health care professionals in private practice, rehab clinics or health clubs.

• *Surgeon*

A surgeon is a physician who specializes in treating disease, injury or other disorders by operative surgery (as opposed to treatment by drugs or diet modification). Surgeons may be general surgeons performing a variety of operations, from appendectomies to tonsillectomies, or they may specialize in specific areas of surgery such as cosmetic, orthopedic or gastrointestinal surgery.

• Other complementary therapies include *aromatherapy* (the enhancement of body, mind and spirit with aromatic oils); *hypnotherapy* (lifestyle and behaviour modification through hypnosis); *iridology* (the analysis of health through the examination of the iris of the eye); *reflexology* (applying finger pressure to specific body points on the hands and feet); and *shiatsu* (a Japanese healing art some call acupuncture without needles).

BUILD YOUR HEALTH KNOWLEDGE: START YOUR OWN HEALTH INTEREST GROUP

A few years ago, about 15 women in Collingwood, Ontario, got together with Helen Forrest, a public health nurse in this community of 12,500. "With a list about a mile long," they brainstormed about their individual and collective needs regarding health care issues and formed a public education group called the Women's Health Interest Group. You could do the same in your community: start by talking to someone from your local public health department. Once your group has formed and has decided on a topic, plan an evening by inviting a speaker knowledgeable on the topic. (Many of the associations listed in this book offer a speakers' bureau with professionals who are happy to share their information with the public.)

Over the years, the Women's Health Interest Group has explored a number of issues, including menopause and breast cancer, and they've researched osteoporosis, nutrition, smoking and health care costs for future workshops. The no-hierarchy group works on the team approach, researching, organizing and hosting women's health care events for the community at large. The women said they wanted something that would allow them to learn, and they got what they wanted because they did it for themselves!

The fact that the community's male physicians were not amused at the women's idea at the beginning didn't stop them from growing bigger and bigger (hundreds now come out for events). "People are taking more ownership," says Helen Forrest. "They're really trying to get all the information to do what is best for them and not accept just the professional advice." Adds Rosemary Hahne, one of the women in the group: "Women are doing a lot more reading than before. Women are more informed and want to be."

Three cheers for the go-for-it women of Collingwood, Ontario!

CHAPTER 3

KNOW YOURSELF: HOW YOUR FAMILY TREE AFFECTS YOUR HEALTH

LEARN YOUR PERSONAL RISK FACTORS

Talking about risk factors is something our parents and grandparents rarely did. We must learn our personal risk factors. It's a good thing to know, for example, that our high blood pressure and a family history of heart disease puts us at increased risk for heart disease. It's a good thing to know because we can then do something about it: we can work on important lifestyle changes, and consult our physicians about treatment.

Sometimes risk factors are misunderstood. For instance, the one-in-nine statistic that relates to breast cancer risk doesn't mean what most of us think – that one in nine of us will get breast cancer. Instead, it means that one in the nine of us *who live to be 85* will get breast cancer. Quite a difference.

Risks, in health as in other things, have to be assessed carefully. To illustrate, many women believe that they're more likely to die of breast cancer than heart disease. The truth is, heart disease kills more women annually. But so powerful are the risk statistics surrounding breast cancer that a 1993 Gallup survey of 1,000 women revealed that 82 percent believed that breast cancer causes more deaths than diabetes (wrong: it's the opposite). Even some women with diabetes believe their chances of dying from breast cancer are higher!

Risks are an integral part of our health lives and women in particular are attuned to risks. We live with risks every day – whether it's the risk of a complication with a pregnancy or the risk of brittle bones once our estrogen levels drop. But risk statistics, thrown at us daily through a variety of sources, are confusing.

Don't become a slave of statistics. Assess your risks individually. This is very easy today because every health association can provide you with all you need to know to determine your very own risk profile. Here's a typical the-more-you-have, the-more-you-are-at-risk checklist for osteoporosis, from a 1990 Toronto workshop called Menopause and You. Check which points apply to you:

- Race: White or Oriental
- Early menopause before the age of 40, either naturally or ovaries surgically removed
- Small-boned
- Slender or underweight
- Fair-complexioned
- Family history of osteoporosis
- Chronic stress or illness
- Poor diet, particularly a high-fat one lacking calcium and Vitamin D
- Low calcium intake
- High caffeine intake
- High alcohol intake
- High protein intake
- Sedentary lifestyle
- Smoking

HOW GENES AFFECT YOUR RISK PROFILE

Discovering your own genetic inheritance is one of the keys to taking charge of your health, especially if you are predisposed to a disease like cancer. Knowing you're at risk for certain cancers can lead you to make lifestyle changes and demand closer medical surveillance; the result can be earlier detection of the disease at a more curable stage. In her book *How Healthy Is Your Family Tree?* New York author Carol Krause expresses the importance of knowing your family medical tree because of her own family's cancer history: her mother died of ovarian cancer and she and two sisters were diagnosed with the disease; her father died of prostate cancer and five aunts and uncles lost battles to cancer.

Krause's book explains how genes are passed on to us and then shows us how to make our own family medical tree. Since many of us do not have enough information to fill in the medical details of all our relatives, Krause suggests trying to find missing information through death certificates and medical records.

"A family history of ovarian cancer – especially if two or more first-degree relatives had it – is the most important risk factor," says Dr. Joan Murphy, head of gynecology and gynecologic oncology at the Toronto Hospital, which runs a Family History of Ovarian Cancer Clinic. "If you had 100 women in your family tree and only one had ovarian cancer, you are theoretically less at risk than if you have had only one female in your family and she died of ovarian cancer."

Since common cancers such as ovarian, breast, endometrial and pancreatic cancers have some inheritance links, there's every reason to try to fill out the branches of your own family medical tree. But there's also evidence to suggest that if we don't exactly inherit faulty genes, we may inherit predispositions to certain illnesses such as heart disease, diabetes and thyroid disorders. The nature versus nurture argument also applies to lifestyle-induced diseases such as alcoholism.

Educate Yourself: Build Your Own Health File

Dr. Carolyn DeMarco says her favourite kind of therapy is bibliotherapy – reading to find out information. But reading to find out information can be confusing. There seem to be so many conflicting studies. Coffee, for example, has bounced back and forth between good, bad and no-harm-done for the past 20 years. In the end, we're forced to come to our own conclusions.

One way to find your way through the maze of studies and opinions is to try building your own health file to help you determine whether something is low-risk, increased risk or high-risk to you personally. A few more tips:

- Try to determine if the information source is reliable and if the information itself is accurate. All research is supposed to be unbiased, but that depends on how you define bias: ask yourself who was funding the research for the study, assess the reputation of the hospital, foundation, association or clinic reporting the health news and note how many people were actually studied and how.
- Read the information carefully and look for buzzwords or euphemisms that don't quite tell it like it is. Phrases such as "may be linked to" or "may promote" or "in some people" don't offer real proof. Weigh what you read carefully. Was the report based on a small, short study or a more impressive large one involving thousands of people over a long time?
- Pay attention to the real risks that affect you and that you can control. If you're allergy-prone, for instance, learn all you can about managing and avoiding your allergen.

To reduce your general risk profile, try the following:

- Drink only moderately; stop smoking; exercise regularly; eat a low-fat high-fibre diet; follow safe-sex guidelines; get regular physical and dental checkups; follow guidelines for safety in the street while walking, driving or cycling; keep your immunizations up-to-date and your blood pressure and cholesterol levels healthy.

- Consider your partner's habits and how they may hurt your health: second-hand smoke and sexually transmitted diseases are only two of someone else's lifestyle habits that can affect your health directly and, especially in the case of secondhand-smoke, the health of your fetus and child. Studies show that if your partner abuses alcohol, the risk of domestic violence is increased. Moreover, if your partner is stressed or unstable, you and your family are at risk.

Your guide to women's health newsletters

A Diabetic's Friend, 1615 Dundas St. E., PO Box 70632, Whitby, ON L1N 2K0 (905) 666-9932.

A Friend Indeed: for women in the prime of life. PO Box 515, Place du Parc Station, Montreal, PQ H2W 2P1 (514) 843-5730.

Action, Canadian Association for the Advancement of Women and Sport and Physical Activity, 1600 James Naismith Dr., Gloucester, ON K1B 5N4 (613) 748-5793.

Health News, University of Toronto, Faculty of Medicine, Medical Sciences Bldg., University of Toronto, Toronto, ON M5S 1A8 (416) 978-5411.

Herizons, PO Box 128, Winnipeg, MN R3C 2G1 (204) 774-6225.

John Hopkins Medical Health Letter, Health After 50, PO Box 420179, Palm Coast Florida, 32142 (904) 446-4675.

Montreal Health Press, PO Box 1000, Stn. G, Montreal PQ H2W 2N1 (514) 282-1171.

Wellness Letter, University of California, Berkeley, Subscription Department, PO Box 420148, Palm Coast Florida, 32142.

Women's Health Matters, Women's College Hospital, Subscription Department, 76 Granville St., Toronto, ON M5S 1B2 (416) 323-7322.

Women's Health Office, published 10 months/year by Women's Health Office, McMaster University, Health Science Centre, 2B11-1200 Main St. W., Hamilton, ON L8N 3Z5 (905) 525-9140.

CHAPTER 4

PREVENTION IS THE BEST MEDICINE: THE FOUR PILLARS OF GOOD HEALTH

I. EATING WELL

THE NEW NUTRITION

Many people find the subject of nutrition a cauldron filled with confusing facts and conflicting studies. A few examples: nuts are generally bad for your heart health but an excellent source of Vitamin E (which some studies show have a heart-health benefit); milk is an excellent food and necessary to fight osteoporosis, yet 44 percent of Canadians are not eating the recommended number of servings of milk products (women who are afraid of milk packing on the pounds should try skim milk, it's even higher in calcium); and with enough studies done to fill a zillion coffee tins, don't even try to figure out whether coffee is considered an okay drink or something to be avoided.

When a study comes out saying green tea protects against esophageal cancer, green tea sales do go up – but becoming a nutrition groupie and changing one's diet to reflect the implications of the latest study is a recipe for disaster.

My own nutritional plan may sound old-fashioned: I simply follow Canada's Food Guide to Healthy Eating, choose a few of the study conclusions I feel fit my own body's needs (I'm a great believer, for instance, in the benefits of Vitamins C and E) and allow a little room now and then for the occasional treats that dietitian Rosie Schwartz says are vital to everybody's eating plan. (What Schwartz tries to teach is to trust your taste buds: taste that chocolate chip cookie and if it's not a ten out of ten, don't eat any more. When you discover the chocolate chip cookie that's a true ten, you'll enjoy every morsel, feel no guilt about consuming it, and it will do very little damage to your nutritional balance sheet, as long as you eat them on special occasions, one at a time.)

But I, too, feel betrayed by contradictory research. And I think Canada's Food Guide to Healthy Eating could be rewritten to better reflect real serving size (for instance, why is one serving of fruit equated to 1/2 cup of juice, an amount nobody drinks?). And I think the United States has us beat in both product nutrition labelling and low-fat supermarket choices.

Generally speaking, however, I find today's nutritional climate exciting and vital. Never before has good, solid nutritional information been more readily available, and never before have the experts in this field been more approachable. Moreover, a fall 1994 report by the National Institute of Nutrition reported that Canadians' awareness of nutrition is at an all-time high: 87 percent of people surveyed recognize the benefits of lower fat and higher-fibre diets and consider nutritional issues important to the foods they choose to eat.

This is an area in which women can really take charge by taking care. Here, then, is a mini-guide to help you navigate today's nutritional waterways:

How to Interpret Canada's Food Guide to Healthy Eating

Different people need different amounts of food but the real key to healthy eating is to eat a variety of foods in moderation. This is the message that underlies Canada's Food Guide. See the accompanying Canada Food Guide to Healthy Eating and check your food intake against it to ensure that you're meeting your nutritional needs. But read it carefully: many people find the guide a little confusing (one cup of spaghetti, for instance, is really two servings of grain products. To help simplify the guide's serving sizes, the Dairy Bureau of Canada (1981 McGill College Ave., Ste. 1330, Montreal, Quebec H3A 2X9) offers a free pocket serving sizer and food guide that helps you figure out what exactly Canada's Food Guide means by a serving of meat, fish or poultry. Here are its basics:

- A whole thumb equals about 25 g of most cheeses, so two thumbs equal a serving.
- A thumbtip only (from the top of the thumb to the first joint) equals a teaspoon. Three thumbtips equal a tablespoon, about the amount of milk you'd put in your coffee. About 50 thumbtips equal one serving of milk.
- A palm (the area of your hand, without the fingers and thumb, that a palm reader would read) equals a serving of meat, fish or poultry.

- A fist equals a cup. A fist would be 1 1/2 servings of yogurt. A fist size of l greens would be a serving of lettuce.

HEALTH CANADA'S RECOMMENDED
DAILY NUTRIENT INTAKE FOR WOMEN

- 16 to 19 years: 2,100-2,200 calories; 1200 mg of calcium; 42 g of protein; 15 mg iron.
- 29 to 49 years: 2,000-2,100 calories; 700 mg of calcium; 44 g of protein; 13 mg of iron.
- 50 to 74 years: 1,900-2,000 calories; 800 mg of calcium, 47 g of protein; 8 mg of iron.

Pregnant and breastfeeding women need to eat a variety of foods from a balanced menu; refer to Canada's Food Guide to Healthy Eating. If you're a vegetarian, talk to your nutritionist or doctor to ensure you're getting the right protein requirements your and your baby will need. Pregnant women need 30 mg iron daily, breastfeeding women need 15 mg; pregnant women and lactating women should increase their calcium intake to 1,200 mg a day.

NUTRITION PLUS FOR WOMEN: THE TOP TEN EXTRAS

Eat according to Canada's Food Guide to Healthy Eating *and* pay special attention to the following nutritional elements that may be lacking in many women's diets:

1. *Calcium*

Most adult women need 700 mg a day, but lactating, pregnant, postmenopausal and adolescent women need more, from 800 mg to 1,200 mg.

Gwen Chapman of the University of British Columbia's School of Family and Nutritional Sciences wrote a review on the eating habits of teenage girls for the National Institute of Nutrition's fall 1994 *Review*. In her article, Chapman points out that teenage girls, concerned about body image, may lower their calcium intake, thus putting themselves at risk for osteoporosis later in life. She also points out that despite concerns over body image, fat intakes are still higher than recommended in the diets of teenage girls, and iron and energy intakes, as well as calcium, are too low.

2. *Folic Acid (Folacin)*

Green leafy veggies, nuts, grains and organ meats such as kidney and liver are excellent sources of this nutrient, which helps keep red blood cells healthy and has been linked to the prevention of birth defects. Folic acid helps protect women against cervical dysplasia, which is a precancerous change in the cells of the cervix. Pregnant women should make sure they're getting the required amount: a daily intake of anywhere from 180 to 195 mg for adult women.

3. Vitamin B12

Vegetarians and women trying to cut down their cholesterol intake or lose weight sometimes lack this vitamin, essential for both the manufacture of healthy red blood cells and the synthesis of haemoglobin. Vitamin B^{12} helps prevent pernicious anemia, and may also protect against heart disease. Sources include meats, milk products, eggs, liver and fish.

4. Iron

Since iron is essential in producing the oxygen-carrying haemoglobin in our red blood cells, a shortage of this nutrient can lead to fatigue. "Iron-deficiency anemia is one of the most common nutritional deficiencies in North America, identified in many endurance athletes, especially women," says dietitian Fran Berkoff in *Power Eating*, a book she coauthored with Barbara Lauer and Dr. Yves Talbot. Red meat is still an excellent source of iron, so vegetarians and dieters may be at particular risk of deficiency. Other sources include fish, green leafy vegetables, nuts and beans. Women need about 8 to 13 mg a day.

5. Vitamin C

Some call Vitamin C the supervitamin because the nutrient is present so abundantly in the vegetables often touted as the most healthy: citrus fruits, broccoli, cabbage, strawberries and peppers. Vitamin C is an essential vitamin: it works to promote healthy gums, capillaries and teeth while aiding iron absorption. Unlike Vitamins A, D, E and K, which are fat-soluble and can be stored in the body, Vitamin C is a water-soluble vitamin and remains in the body for only a short time and so must be consumed daily. The lack of Vitamin C in the diets of early seafarers and explorers caused the dread disease scurvy (a painful and potentially fatal disease marked by poor healing, hemorrhages, bruising, bleeding gums and the loosening of teeth).

Vitamin C is probably best known as the vitamin that is supposed to prevent colds when taken in large quantities. Dr. Linus Pauling's book *Vitamin C and the Common Cold* (1970) claimed that megadoses of the vitamin would prevent colds or shorten their duration. Although several studies since have found that large doses of Vitamin C do not prevent colds, millions still believe it can either prevent a cold or shorten its life.

Some physicians recommend about 30 mg a day, but others, such as Dr. Carolyn DeMarco, recommend a larger dose. In her book *Take Charge of Your Body*, DeMarco recommends as natural therapy, a natural Vitamin C supplement containing bioflavonoids (500 to 1,000 mg three times a day) for the mood swings, irritability and insomnia that sometimes accompany menopause.

6. *Vitamin E*

There's increased interest in Vitamin E because of studies showing that it may help protect against heart disease. It's also a vitamin star of the nineties because it seems to protect the lungs from damage by pollution. An antioxidant (an agent that appears to neutralize free radicals that damage cells), Vitamin E is essential for normal cell structure and is found in all the body's tissues. Nutritional sources for Vitamin E include polyunsaturated oils, nuts, meat, egg yolk, wheat germ, cereals and leafy green vegetables. The average adult woman needs about 6 mg a day, more if she's pregnant.

7. *Beta Carotene*

Another antioxidant that helps neutralize the free radicals that can destroy healthy cells, beta carotene is a nutrient that the body converts to Vitamin A, the vitamin that helps prevent night blindness. Current interest in beta carotene, however, is based on conflicting studies that show it may be a factor in reducing the risk of certain kinds of cancers, particularly of the lung and colon; other studies, however, report that too much beta carotene increases the risk of some cancers. Fruits and vegetables contain naturally occurring substances called phytochemicals which may help shield cells from disease, and beta carotene is one of these substances. Beta carotene is contained in dark green and deep yellow and orange vegetables and fruit. The richest source of beta carotene is carrots. Perhaps eating a carrot a day will keep the doctor away.

8. *Fibre*

Recently, upping fibre in our diet has taken a back seat to cutting fat, but it's a mistake to underestimate the value of a fibre-rich diet: it helps to speed elimination as well as protect the body from disease. A good fibre-rich diet includes between 25 and 35 g of fibre a day. One cup of cooked kidney beans contains about 12 g, a cup of broccoli about 5 g, an ounce of bran cereal about 9 g. Fibre is actually the undigestible part of plants and there are two types: water-insoluble fibre (from wheat bran, whole wheat and the skins of fruits and vegetables), which is thought to be an excellent method of guarding against colon cancer; and water-soluble fibre (from fruit, beans and oats), which seems to lower blood lipid levels and thus, it's thought, protect against coronary artery disease. Some people add 100 percent wheat bran (the kind you'd buy to make bran muffins from scratch) to their breakfast yogurt or juices. You can also use wheat bran as a filler in meat loaf or other ground-meat dishes. One tip: a fibre-rich diet also requires that you drink plenty of fluids to aid the fibre in doing a more efficient elimination job.

9. *Zinc*

Studies show that women underconsume this mineral. One reason may be that it's mostly found in animal products (meats, liver, eggs), nuts, seeds and dairy products – many of the foods that women avoid for fear of gaining weight. Zinc assists the immune system by playing a key role in cell growth and repair; it's involved in the functioning of the hormone insulin; and it also helps to heal wounds. Some studies suggest that a low level of zinc in pregnant women can lead to fetal abnormalities.

10. *Water*

Nutrition consultant Susie Langley calls water "the forgotten nutrient." Water carries many soluble substances (oxygen, hormones and nutrients) to tissues and cells via the bloodstream; it helps prevent constipation; it's essential as a lubricant (water is the basis of saliva and other mucous secretions throughout the body); and it's essential to a healthy metabolism. Langley says that when nutritionists talk about total fluids in a diet, they mean water, juice and milk – not soda pop, wine or tea. How much water is recommended? Six to eight glasses a day are necessary to maintain proper hydration levels in women who are healthy and not on any special diets.

THE SKINNY ON FATS: NOW WE COUNT FATS THE WAY WE USED TO COUNT CALORIES

Fats are the culprits of the nineties just as sugar was in the sixties and seventies. Research done in the last 30 years shows pretty conclusively that obesity and a high-fat diet contribute to several illnesses, including cancer and cardiovascular disease. Today, people with a high blood cholesterol level are advised to cut down their intake of fats as a matter of course. Indeed, aiming for a 30 percent diet of fat (instead of the nearly 40 percent consumed by most North Americans) has become everybody's goal regardless of individual risks. We're all counting fats today the way we used to count calories.

But the issue of fat in our diet is not so simple: not only has fat become an obsession to many (fear of fat has become an obsessive-compulsive disorder, experts say) but there's also a great deal of confusion surrounding fat issues. The common-sense answer to fear of fat, say nutritionists, is to cut back on fats in a simple way without driving yourself crazy (unless you're on a medically supervised fat-reduction diet). Examples: switch to skim milk, choose low-fat cheeses, try low-fat or no-fat yogurts or ice creams, remove the skin from chicken and go easy on the sauces you add to your pasta.

Other fat tips:

1. There are many different kinds of fats but they are all equally high in calories. The equality stops there, however. Some dietary fats (such as butter) are associated with increased risk of coronary artery disease: these are the fats we try to avoid.

2. In their book *Eat Well, Live Well* (1990) Calgary dietitian Helen Bishop MacDonald and Toronto food consultant Margaret Howard break fats down into saturated, polyunsaturated and monounsaturated.
   - Saturated fats (the villains) are those that are solid at room temperature, the authors say, "plus (by some quirk of nature) coconut oil and palm kernel oil." Sources include milk fats, egg yolks and animal fats. A diet rich in saturated fats can increase your blood cholesterol level; studies show clear links between elevated blood cholesterol levels and atherosclerosis (or clogged arteries) in humans.
   - Polyunsaturates are liquid at room temperature. They include safflower, sunflower, corn and soybean oils.
   - Monounsaturates, also liquid at room temperature, are found in nuts, canola and olive oils.

   Though a heart-healthy diet is one that is low in saturated fats, one of the best ways of lowering your blood cholesterol level is to cut back on *all* fats – saturated and nonsaturated.

3. Dietitian Fran Berkoff offers this easy way to calculate your fat intake: a gram of fat contains 9 calories, so if you eat 2,000 calories a day, your fat intake should be 66 g. That's 30 percent of 2,000 calories, which is 600 calories; then 600 calories divided by 9, which is 66 g. Most adults need between 50 and 80 g of fat per day. For most women, a diet of about 65 g of fat daily – or about 12 teaspoons of fat – is equal to about a 30 percent fat diet. Another way to calculate your daily fat intake is to remember that about six teaspoons of fat are built into your everyday eating patterns through the fat that is already present in foods such as meat, milk and cheese. The other six are fat you consciously add (for example, butter, salad dressings, olive oil or hidden fats used in cooked and baked goods).

4. Trans fatty acids (TFAS) are the latest worry of both nutritionists and consumers. Though they have similar properties to those of saturated fats (raising the so-called bad cholesterol in our blood and lowering the so-called good cholesterol) trans fatty acids are hidden in that they're not directly listed on Canadian food labels. TFAS are formed when vegetable oils are processed through a method called hydrogenation. The way to spot trans fatty acids in foods is by looking for the word *hydrogenated* among the ingredients listed on a food label. "Hydrogenated vegetable oil" or "partially hydrogenated vegetable oil" indicate the presence of trans fatty acids, says Dr. Julie Conquer, Department of Nutritional Sciences at the University of Guelph. "A product that is rich in fat, especially trans fatty acids, may at the same time have a label that – correctly – states the food is 'low in saturates' or 'cholesterol free.' " Conquer's advice to determine the amount of TFAS: simply subtract the sum of the individual fats from the total fat content on a label. Personally, I find it easier to avoid these fats altogether.

5. How do the oils stack up? The oils, from lowest in saturated fats to highest in saturated fats, are as follows: canola, safflower, sunflower, corn, olive, soybean, peanut, cottonseed, lard, palm oil, butter, coconut oil. On any food label that says it's a vegetable oil and contains no cholesterol, do the trans fatty acid check by subtracting the sum of the individual fats from the total fat content listed. Also remember that only animal products contain cholesterol but some plant products such as coconut oils are still saturated fats!

6. What's in a label? Every few months or so, Toronto dietitian Fran Berkoff teams up with cooking-school teacher Bonnie Stern in a course called Delicious and Nutritious at the Bonnie Stern Cooking School in North Toronto. In addition to cooking up some delicious recipes, students are given great tips on how to read labels:
- "Light" can mean anything from light in color or texture to light in calories.
- When a label says "low cholesterol," the food can't contain more than 3 mg cholesterol per 100 g of food and it must be low in saturated fats – but it still can have a high total fat content.
- When a label says "low fat," it means the food can't contain more than 3 g of fat per average serving. (But be sure to check what that average serving is; also check to see how many calories the product contains, as low fat does not mean that the food is also low in calories.)

7. Are we on our way to no-fat heaven? We've all heard about new fat substitutes that promise to transform our favourite treats into guilt- and fat-free pleasures. At the heart of this food transformation is a substance called olestra, which is a chemical

synthesis of sugar and vegetable oil that adds the fat taste to foods fried in it without adding fat to the person eating it. Though approved for use in the United States, olestra is not yet available in Canada and may never be. Though foods fried in the substance are fat-free, there's concern that people who ingest it may suffer side effects, some of which are known and some of which are not yet known. In some people, olestra has caused "leakage" or diarrhea-like symptoms and intestinal gas. Apparently it also impedes the absorption of essential nutrients; hence, foods fried in olestra will have to be fortified with vitamins.

How to Get Off the Dieting Rollercoaster

Many, if not most, women regularly think of dieting or are on a diet. A University of Manitoba study of 20,000 people across Canada reported that as many as 40 percent of women are trying to lose weight at any given time (compared with 25 percent of men). The same study showed that 30 percent of women aged 19 to 74 are obese. But though dietitians repeatedly tell you that diets don't work, whether or not they work really depends on your interpretation of what a diet is. If a diet is an unhealthy eating pattern that makes you feel deprived and hungry, then the diet won't work. But if it's teaching you how to eat more healthily, chances are it will work.

Conventional wisdom is that counting calories is an ineffective way of losing weight. But if you're not aware of how many calories you consume in a day, you may become frustrated when you try to lose weight. Each individual has different caloric needs, but as a general rule, a woman in her twenties needs 2,100 to 2,200 calories a day; and a woman in her thirties and forties needs to consume 2,000 to 2,100 calories a day. By the time a woman reaches her fifties, her caloric requirements drop to between 1,900 to 2,000 calories a day.

Many people believe that we are overweight because we simply eat too much and don't exercise enough. A Rockefeller University study reveals that to maintain a 10 percent weight loss, you have to eat 200 to 300 fewer calories a day, or burn an equal number of calories by exercising. Since consistently eating less is difficult for many (and may be unhealthy for some), experts suggest the healthier alternative: get out and move more!

The Body Mass Index (BMI)

Just how much should you weigh? Weight charts can be misleading but the most sensible to date is the Body Mass Index (BMI). Rather than obsess over a particular number, the BMI assumes that bodies come in all shapes and sizes and that the best method to help determine whether or not you need to lose a few pounds is to determine your BMI. To calculate it, you divide your weight in kilograms by your height in meters squared. Follow this formula:

1. Translate your weight in pounds into kilograms by dividing your pounds by 2.2. So a woman weighing 150 pounds would weigh 68.18 kilograms.

2. Take your height measurement and translate it into inches. If you're five foot five inches, you would be 65 inches tall.

3. Take your height measurement in inches and divide that number by 39.6 or the number of inches in a meter. By dividing 65 by 39.6, you'd get 1.64.

4. Multiply the number from step three by itself to get your height in meters squared. In this example it is 1.64 times 1.64 equals 2.68.

5. Divide your weight in kilograms by your height in meters squared for your BMI. In our calculation that would be 68.18 divided by 2.68 for an answer of 25.4.

So throw away your bathroom scale and get out your calculator. Or check the chart on page 314. If your BMI is lower than 20 or higher than 25, you're not in the healthy weight range.

Getting Ready to Lose Weight

When planning to lose weight, try planning for it in a methodical way, much as you might plan a trip. Recent research from the University of Rhode Island suggests that successful changes of all kinds depends on an individual's going through three stages before getting to the action stage. Applied to dieting, this means going through the three stages before actually changing your eating patterns.

• Stage 1 begins with your wish to change (this is a good time to research various weight-loss methods and to ask yourself why you really want to lose weight).

• Stage 2 is the assessment or contemplation stage: you begin by recording how much you eat and exercise on a regular basis. This way you can establish a baseline for yourself, so that you can work up to real change.

• In Stage 3, you prepare by making a few very small changes. Like the Chinese proverb that says a thousand-mile journey begins with a single step, you substitute milk for cream in your coffee and take the stairs instead of the elevator up three floors. By the time you reach Stage 3, you can come out of the closet and tell your friends and family that you are about to go on a diet. When you announce that the leopard is about to change her spots and prepare for the process through these various stages, the spots indeed can change.

Other research from the University of Scranton on people who had made New Year's resolutions to lose weight showed that those who stayed on track for months after their resolution believed in their ability to change, did not indulge in self-blame and avoided wishful thinking: "I wish I'd lose 20 pounds so I could be happier and more successful."

HOW TO CHOOSE A WEIGHT-LOSS PLAN

Carefully, that's how. Dietitian Susie Langley notes that a diet that reduces or eliminates one of the four food groups below the amounts recommended by Canada's Food Guide to Healthy Eating may harm your health. "And so can a plan that is too low in calories," she says. The National Eating Disorder Information Centre in Toronto reports that 95 to 98 percent of people regain weight lost through dieting within two to five years. In addition, the weight gained back is mainly fat.

Evaluate Your Weight Loss Program: A Checklist

Check with your physician before beginning any diet. Toronto's Food Facts Network suggests you use the following checklist to evaluate a weight-loss program. If you can't answer yes to each of the following, perhaps you should look for another program:

- Does the program encourage me to select a variety of foods in the recommended daily amounts from each of the four food groups of Canada's Food Guide to Healthy Eating?
- Does the program recommend a gradual weight loss of less than one kilogram or two pounds per week?
- Does the program promote exercise and increased activity in everyday life?
- Does the diet provide at least 1,200 calories a day for women?
- Do the food choices suggested reflect my likes, dislikes, lifestyle and income level?
- Does the program avoid requiring me to buy special products, supplements and/or injections?

TIPS ON HEALTHIER EATING: HOW TO GET ON-TRACK

The Ontario Ministry of Health offers plenty of healthier eating tips in *Healthy Weights*, a booklet that focuses on a new way of looking at your weight and health. Rather than thinking of forbidden foods when you're on a diet, start changing your food habits by following some of these steps:

- Zap your taste buds with nonfattening flavours such as lemon juice, garlic, mustard, herbs, and spices such as curry powder and salsa.
- Don't cut out, cut back instead. Eat smaller portions, especially of meat.
- Always think of lower-calorie or lower-fat substitutes when you're cooking. For instance, skim milk instead of cream, or low-fat yogurt instead of full-fat yogurt or sour cream on a baked potato or in a dip.
- Switch your mealtime thinking by eating more starchy foods such as potatoes, pasta, rice and beans – filling but low in fat.
- If you're on the run (or looking for an alternative to a restaurant lunch), try a convenience or grocery store for fresh fruit, yogurt, juice and breads such as bagels.
- Best choices for a main restaurant meal include grilled meats or fish, poached fish, roast chicken, pasta or a fruit salad plate. Salads can be ordered with the dressing on the side or a slice of lemon. Avoid dishes with rich sauces – or ask for them to be served on the side so you can control your intake.

2. KEEPING FIT

WHAT CONSTITUTES REASONABLE EXERCISE?

Picture this: Barbara is 40 years old. Like many Canadians her age, she tries to do it all. She has two small children, a husband and a house. She has a full-time, five-day-a-week job. The few hours between dinner and the kids' bedtime are a tornado of driving, cooking, eating, washing, cleaning and story-reading. Once the kids are in bed, Barbara scrapes herself off the floor and walks the dog. Not just around the block, but a brisk 45-minute jaunt. Besides being bonding time with Fido, the exercise clears her mind.

Believe it or not, most fitness experts would agree that Barbara is getting enough physical exercise. Our ideas about what constitutes exercise is changing in the nineties. Sure, Barbara isn't pumping iron at a glitzy health club, or running flights of stairs (though, in fact, she probably is!). The point is, Barbara's typical day, which includes walking the dog, lifting toddlers and lugging groceries, means she is leading an active lifestyle. And an active lifestyle can be just as healthy as a scientific high-tech workout program.

As any woman will tell you, sticking to a rigid workout routine just doesn't work. True, we should all be able to make exercise a priority. But in the whirlwind that is Barbara's life – and the lives of most Canadian women – how many people have the time to drive to a fitness club, change clothes, work out to Madonna, shower, change again and drive home? It would take at least two hours out of our already overpacked day.

Many fitness experts have realized this by now. All they really have to do is look at enrollment numbers. "Our busiest month is January," says Leslie Kozlowski, health and wellness director of the Vancouver YWCA. "Getting fit is a number-one New Year's resolution. But by the end of January, half of the people have dropped off. Women often use the excuse that they just don't have the time to exercise. It's really unfortunate that's happening, because not only are women not getting that solid half hour of cardiovascular activity that they need to stay in shape, but they're also not getting away from the havoc of their lives and releasing stress." Kozlowski maintains that 80 percent of sickness and disease is caused by stress.

That's where active living comes in. "We're seeing a shift away from exercise as it's traditionally known (the Jane Fonda, go-till-it-hurts kind), to exercise that is more casual and spiritual," says Kozlowski. Programs such as speed-walking, yoga, meditation and massage therapy are more popular than ever before. While they're not purely cardiovascular in nature, they encourage relaxation and are another form of stress release. "If you don't have any time or money, it's better than nothing," she adds.

In 1992, the federal government launched its Active Living Campaign. It was designed to encourage Canadians to walk to the corner store. Active living is all about walking instead of driving, doing instead of watching. But old habits die hard. Many women still don't believe they are "getting a workout" unless they are dripping gallons of sweat, or marching to an aerobics instructor's bark. It's true that in a perfect world, trainers and academics agree that maintaining a high-intensity, aerobic, heart-pumping activity for at least 20 minutes three times a week will benefit the heart immensely, because it is a muscle that needs to be used. But this philosophy, if it stands in the way of more prosaic exercise like walking to the corner store instead of driving, must change. "You cannot wait until you have a problem. You have to start exercising while you are healthy and young. It will help prevent disease later in life," says Kozlowski.

And she's right. Research continues to prove, unequivocally, the benefits of exercise. Exercise builds muscle strength and endurance, improves our body's flexibility, and helps keep our coordination and balance systems finely tuned. Without physical activity, we gradually experience a decline in our ability to perform physical functions requiring any effort: that's why when we're out of shape, running up a flight of stairs can make us feel breathless.

Because heart disease is the number-one killer of Canadian women, improving circulation and toning your heart muscle are probably the best benefits of regular exercise. Sedentary people have almost two times the risk of sustaining a heart attack than exercisers do. We don't need a study to tell us that regular exercise is a good way to keep our weights within a healthy range. Yet another bonus: some studies suggest regular exercise increases your sexual drive and performance.

And the research doesn't stop there. Recent reports from the U.S. National Cancer Institute suggest that about four hours of exercise a week may reduce the risk of premenopausal breast cancer by about 58 percent. The thinking is that exercise diminishes the breast's exposure to hormones by changing the length of the menstrual cycle or by smoothing out hormonal peaks. The study's leader, Dr. Leslie Bernstein, explained it this way: "We already know that you ought to maintain a regular exercise program, based on the reduction of heart disease, adult onset diabetes, osteoporosis and colon cancer. The possible reduction in breast cancer just adds greater fuel to that."

How Should You Exercise? Let Us Count the Ways

When listing the many benefits of regular exercise, remember to include increasing your sense of self-esteem, says fitness expert Mary-Danielle Cifelli, who owns Real Results, a Toronto fitness and wellness company. Cifelli recommends any exercise that is weight bearing, including walking, running, jogging, and low-impact aerobics. And she sings the praises of weight training: "It increases your basal metabolic rate, and it tones, tones, tones!" she says. "Basic 2 1/2 pound weights will do. You don't have to lift a lot of weight. It's the repetition that counts."

And while we're counting, consider the following list of activities:

1. *Walking*
Walking is the most popular exercise activity in Canada. Trend watchers attribute the increase in popularity to women and aging baby boomers who, as the media reminds us constantly, have started to turn 50.

Menopausal women have a lot to gain from this simple one-foot-in-front-of-the-other exercise. Not only does it improve blood circulation, it can improve hormonal circulation. It's also a workout for the mind and spirit. A good walk can calm you down from a busy day. Just ask Jennie Sheps, a 78-year-old walker who founded

Ontario's North York Senior Walkers. Rain or shine, Sheps leads a weekly walking group of about 120 people who range in age from 55 to 89. They walk for about an hour. Sheps also helped found several of the province's shopping mall-walking programs.

Walking is an exercise you can do almost anywhere – as hundreds of Canadian women demonstrate daily, briefcases in hand and Reeboks on their feet.

2. *Ergonomics*

The perfect way to ensure that your body gets the attention it deserves would be to exercise at work. That's why a number of Y's across the country have begun offering ergonomics workshops. Ergonomics is the latest buzzword in the corporate world. The workshops teach people how to relax and reduce stress while they're at their workstation. People learn proper breathing techniques and posture; small stretches they can do at their desk or during a meeting. "Two years ago, everyone would have laughed at the idea," says Leslie Kozlowski. "But today, these workshops are full. And 90 percent of the participants are women!"

3. *Aquafitness*

Dr. Clifford Rosen, director of the Maine Centre for Osteoporosis Research and Education, underlines the importance of exercise for reducing bone loss. His exercise of choice is underwater exercise classes. Rosen's study of 35 exercising women showed that doing small underwater movements was a type of resistance training that worked the body against gravity and maintained the skeleton. The icing on the cake is that water exercise is easy on your joints because you're getting an extra lift. You are less prone to injury because of the cushioning effect of the water around you. This also makes it the exercise of choice for pregnant women and seniors.

Toronto's Grace Lawrence has become Canada's aquafit queen. The 76-year-old senior has taught water workouts for more than 30 years and is the author of *Aqua-Fitness for Women*. Water workouts are simple, Lawrence says, and they can burn up to 500 calories an hour. Lawrence teaches four hour-long sessions weekly in the Glendon Campus swimming pool of Toronto's York University. In 1994, she produced a laminated 15-exercise wall-chart version of her water workout (perfect for home or community pools). It's called Aquafitness for Everyone and is available from Activetics Health and Fitness Marketplace. It comes in two sizes, $12.95 and $25.95, and is available by calling (905) 223-3077.

"Aquafitness is huge for women," says Leslie Kozlowski. (She notes that not one male member of the Vancouver Y has signed up for classes.) She, too, talks about the benefits of controlled movements against water, but she says the reason for its popularity is more prosaic: "Most women are really self-conscious about their weight," she explains. With aquafitness, because much of your body is underwater while you're exercising, you're not self-conscious about how you look in your workout wear! "And in the water, you're 80 percent lighter. You feel better, you have more buoyancy," Kozlowski adds. "You don't have to get your hair and your makeup ruined, and, it's a social time."

How to Get Going – and Keep Going

We are social creatures – and it's important to remember the social aspect of exercise. Indeed, that may be the reason that aerobics classes still remain the most popular activities for women. Talking with friends and instructors in health clubs is a good way to make yourself stay with the program. If someone's expecting you to be at a class, you will likely feel committed and more responsible for showing up.

Fitness instructors tell tales of "the disgruntled woman." Women who spend a fortune on a club, buy themselves a tiny spandex bodysuit that would make Jane Fonda's hips look big, sign up for 70 sit-up classes – and then wake up the next morning unable to walk. They hurt, they lose motivation, and they give up. After all, in this age of the superwoman, something's got to give.

One of the best ways to ensure that you stick with a routine at your health club (and to get the most out of what you pay for) is to take it slowly and to do a little research before you join up.

Most women are good at research. We research health care for our families, we research prices, trips and recipes. But when it comes to joining a health club and laying down hundreds of hard-earned dollars, we often jump in headfirst: "Give me that dumbbell, let me at the StairMaster." Hold on, now.

Leslie Kozlowski says the average woman at her club in Vancouver is between the ages of 35 and 45. They are busy women who are making exercise a priority: this is great. But they are also prone to injury. If they do get hurt, chances are they'll stop working out. So, assuming a woman and her doctor agree she's healthy and should start an exercise program, the first thing she should do, says Kozlowski, is sign up for a fitness assessment. It's money well spent. In a fitness assessment, trained instructors monitor cardiovascular activity, measure muscle and fat ratios, height and weight. Many high-tech clubs punch the data into computers, which then produces an exercise routine tailor-made to your desired results, physical requirements and schedule.

Here are a few tips to help you get the most from your personal fitness regimen:
1. Find something you like to do.

One way to find the right fitness fit is to ask yourself the following questions when considering an exercise activity: Will I enjoy it? Will I be able to do it? Can I do it with friends or do I have to go solo? Is there equipment and, if so, is it affordable? Will I need to join a club to do this activity, and if so, is there a facility nearby and is it affordable?

2. Make sure your exercise of choice is something you can regularly maintain.

If you're a stay-at-home mom with a toddler, perhaps the best exercise for you is something you can fit into your regular routine – like a daily mile-long walk with your baby in his or her stroller.

3. Consider exercise videos.

If you can't get out (February in Winnipeg is not walking weather), don't pooh-pooh the idea of using exercise videos. Ask the fitness department of your local YWCA for their picks of the best ones, then set aside a time each day and do your routine at home by yourself or with a couple of friends.

4. Fitness can mean many things. Think variety and think nontraditional.

Don't just consider high-profile types of exercise such as aerobics, tennis or running. Former Peterborough, Ontario, librarian Gwyneth Hoyle was introduced to canoeing by her sons 20 years ago. A grandmother of six, she's an avid tripper who combines her love of canoeing with an interest in the history of Canada's river system. She has co-authored a book on the history of river travel.

Fitness means working on your motor skills, developing eye-hand coordination and keeping up your reaction times. Remember the activities you used to like doing (volleyball? badminton? table tennis? canoeing? skating? sailing? martial arts?) and seek them out. Or try something entirely new: women's hockey is becoming more and more organized across the country, and practically every town, it seems, has its own women's baseball league. Your provincial or municipal department of sports and recreation will help you start a team or hook you up with one that's already going.

5. Think of fitness as fun.

Though Ottawa's Lee-Anne Quinn, a captain in the Canadian Armed Forces, maintains a high level of fitness for her job as an air evacuation flight nurse (her latest posting was on a UN mission to Somalia) she also looks at fitness as fun. A couple of years ago she even got into the *Guinness Book of World Records* for a military event in which a team had to compete (with other military teams around the world) in carrying a stretcher bearing a 140-pound weight for the most miles. Her team won at 271.4 kilometres, making Quinn the first woman in the world to be part of a winning entry in that category. The event took 2 1/2 days. During breaks, they put their feet in a bucket of ice, Quinn says. But her team won, and in the process raised $20,000 for cancer research!

6. Consider hiring a personal trainer.

If joining a fitness class intimidates you, consider hiring a paid "fitness friend." Personal trainers, highly publicized because of their association with celebrities like Madonna, can help anyone get started on her own unique path to fitness. And they can stay with you to encourage you to keep up your motivation and achieve your goals. Check under Fitness in the Yellow Pages, or call your local Y or fitness club for recommendations.

7. Research the wide range of exercises you can choose to attain your goal.

Running is not the only exercise that builds cardiovascular fitness. Look into other aerobic activities like jogging, dancing, cycling, cross-country skiing, aerobics on land and in water, racquet sports, jump rope, rowing, stair climbing, swimming, basketball, brisk walking.

8. Remember what Aesop said: Go slow and win the race.

Exercise is great for physical health. It improves our stamina, maintains a good level of muscle tone and keeps us flexible and agile. But sometimes you can push yourself too hard and too fast. Physical fitness experts say that during exercise you should be able to carry on a conversation: do a talk test to see whether you are comfortably exercising or pushing yourself too hard.

And not many of us can be like TV talk-show host Oprah Winfrey who reportedly does a regular exercise regimen that includes running four miles followed by 45 minutes on a stair climber and 150 sit-ups. Most of us don't have time to spend three hours a day on intensive exercise. But each one of us can fit a little more in if we take it slow and begin to live a more active life. Being able to touch your toes at 50 is great, but the real key to flexibility is in our minds: keeping a positive attitude towards exercise means it is never too late to start and, as our senior role models are teaching us, it's always too early to stop.

CHOOSING A HEALTH CLUB: A CHECKLIST

To make sure you get the most out of a fitness assessment and a health club, ask these questions before you join:

1. What are the fitness and teaching qualifications of the club's staff members?
2. What training do they have in first aid and safety?
3. Is there always a staff member in the workout area to give advice and to show you how to use the equipment properly?
4. Is the equipment in the weight room spread out so that several people

can comfortably and safely use various parts of it at one time?

5. Does the club have a provincially recognized fitness certification?

6. What kind of floor does the gym have? (Beware of concrete floors hidden under other flooring or carpeting. It can be very hard on your knees.) Gym floors should be wood-sprung floors built with coils underneath the wood that give way and are less resistant to your joints.

7. If there is a pool, is there always a lifeguard on duty?

8. What kind of fitness assessment is available? Does the assessment include goal-setting? What kind of follow-up program is in place to ensure you're reaching your goals safely?

3. SMOKING (NOT AT ALL) AND DRINKING (MODERATELY)

SMOKING: THE JURY IS IN

When it comes to smoking, there is simply no debate: countless studies have demonstrated the dangers of smoking and thousands of premature deaths a year are attributed to it. Smoking is a cause of lung cancer, throat and esophageal cancer and cancers of the cervix and bladder. It contributes to respiratory diseases and heart disease. When combined with oral contraceptives, smoking makes women susceptible to stroke. Complications of smoking include osteoporosis, hyperthyroidism, low-birth-weight babies and cataracts, The dangers of secondhand smoke have also been well documented: asthma, an increased risk of respiratory illnesses, and, for newborns, a higher risk of Sudden Infant Death Syndrome (SIDS).

But why smokers smoke is a complex issue. Few people today would admit to smoking just for the pleasure of it. Research shows that women smoke to be social, to stay thin, to defuse stresses and to replace a feeling of emptiness or loneliness. Add to this a layer of advertising that implies – by showing attractive leggy girls in exciting jobs, wearing beautiful clothes – that cigarettes go hand in hand with an enviable lifestyle, and you can understand why women are subliminally seduced by smoking.

Not only are the statistics alarming that show the number of young women who smoke, but oncologists are also reporting lung cancer in women as young as 30. Women may take up smoking because it's something familiar they watched their parents do, because of peer pressure during the formative years of high school and university or because they perceive smoking's benefits to be a form of weight control, social acceptance and stress reduction.

Once hooked, young smokers learn that while smoking may give them a certain social cachet or group acceptance, stopping smoking requires they go solo. Experts say that cigarette smoking is the most addictive of behaviours; they also maintain that quitting the smoking habit is especially difficult for women because we are constantly being given the message that we must be dependent, that we can't go it alone.

But women can and do give up smoking (as interviews with successful quitters in the chapter on smoking demonstrate). And as several women interviewed have pointed out, stopping smoking is the one important health risk factor you can control. To give up smoking is one way you really can take charge and take care of your health. And the benefits of quitting are enormous. The cardiac benefits are almost immediate; your risk of lung cancer and other respiratory ailments decreases right away; you breathe more easily; and you feel better both within yourself and about yourself.

ALCOHOL: MODERATION IS THE KEY

Alcohol is often a hidden addiction, one that even close friends or family doctors may not be aware of. Experts have reported gender differences in the way men and women use and abuse alcohol. Women sometimes use alcohol to replace something that is missing in their lives – the loss of a family member, the emptiness of feeling unfulfilled. Women who feel lonely or depressed sometimes abuse alcohol. And experts say that many women problem drinkers have a history of physical abuse.

Women who drink too much in public are socially condemned much more readily than men who do the same. One female alcoholic told me that she drank alone and in secret because "men can go to a bar and drink all night and be judged by their friends as having a good time. But there are no excuses allowed for women who drink all night in a bar. They're shunned for losing control and criticized for leaving their families. They're judged as unfit mothers and loose women."

Because alcohol is a depressant, women who drink find themselves dug in deeper than they expected. While they may initially drink to alleviate depression, they find themselves more depressed after consuming a few drinks. Research shows that women drink to self-medicate, but the result – instead of burying frightening memories or alleviating stress – is a general dulling of all sensations.

The dangerous effect that alcohol has on a fetus is well known today, but alcohol use can also increase your risk of breast cancer, infertility, hypertension and early menopause. It's a contributing cause of accidents and its empty calories can play havoc with weight control. Prolonged alcohol abuse can lead to cirrhosis of the liver, a potentially fatal disease. These risks, coupled with the fact that the same amount of alcohol does more damage to a woman's body than to a man's (women's livers are more scarred from drinking than men's), makes you wonder why women drink at all.

Social drinking *is* acceptable providing you know when to draw the line and providing you can be honest with yourself about your drinking patterns. Unfortunately, there is no magic number to indicate what constitutes social drinking and what defines problem drinking. Every woman's body is different in the way and rate it metabolizes alcohol. Use this as a rule of thumb: if you consume more than one alcoholic drink every day or two, you are probably crossing the line from social drinking to problem drinking. Chapter 11, which examines alcohol consumption, will help you manage your drinking, should you feel you might be in trouble.

4. PURSUING A BALANCED LIFESTYLE

KEEP STRESS UNDER CONTROL

Balance is the fountain of youth of the nineties. The many benefits of a balanced lifestyle – stress control, a rested body, emotional well-being – are well-documented. Unfortunately, women often lead such frenetic lives that balance can seem as elusive as endless youth. Tough economic times, coupled with career and caregiving demands, make life not only hectic but inherently stressful. Time is become a precious commodity as we run from making school lunches to seeing the school bus off, preparing for a meeting, doing chores at lunch, writing a presentation, checking to see if the kids have arrived home at four, running home to put on dinner, do housework, helping with homework – and the opportunity to do it all again tomorrow. Add the demands of our closest adult relationships, be they relationships with spouses or with aging parents, and it's easy to see why the norm for today's women is stress and fatigue.

Working moms have additional stresses. They are often burdened with a second shift at home, too little help from kids and dad, and, now, cutbacks to daycare. For single moms, there are even more stresses. The relationship between stress and disease is scientifically documented: too much stress can contribute to everything from heart disease to skin rashes, depression and gastrointestinal disorders. Studies also show that stress levels are highest among people who hold jobs where there is heavy pressure to perform but little lattitude for individual decision-making. Many of those jobs are done by women.

Because stress seems a constant today, learning how to control it instead of letting it controlling you is vital to good health. The chapter on mental wellness addresses ways you can help yourself de-stress. Tips include regular exercise (take that daily brisk walk), learning some relaxation techniques (yoga and meditation are back in style), even doing something entirely mindless (like watching a TV sitcom). If stress has already adversely affected your health, you may want to talk to your doctor about biofeedback techniques or psychotherapy.

GET ENOUGH SLEEP

Being tired doesn't always mean you can sleep. After working a ten-hour day, tending to our kids and our partners, our bosses, our parents and even our friends, it's easy to become too exhausted to sleep.

For some of us, turning out the lights seems like yet another demand; falling asleep becomes yet another deadline to meet. For others, sleep does not come easily as their minds race in overdrive revisiting the problems or the highlights of the day.

Studies show that people who are chronically deprived of sleep experience higher rates of depression. Other studies indicate that sleeping less than six hours a night may make you more prone to stroke, cancer and heart disease. Seven to 8 1/2 hours of sleep a night is what most people need.

Falling asleep when your head hits the pillow is not a typical scenario; people who sleep well and are well-rested usually require 15 minutes or so to fall asleep.

The New Approach to Sleep: Sleep Hygiene and Sleep Clinics

Today's sleep experts focus on breaking the watch-the-clock behaviour that gets us into a panic whenever we can't seem to doze off, rather than on prescribing pills. A new body of science called "sleep hygiene" concentrates on retraining the body to sleep. In some sleep clinics, this includes teaching people about how much alcohol or caffeine is wise to consume, completely reviewing their medical and medication history and having them participate in group sessions to share experiences and exchange tips. Relaxation or biofeedback techniques are also taught.

Tips on Getting A Good Night's Sleep

- Whatever you do, experts say, don't count sheep. Says Dr. Paul Draga of Toronto Hospital's sleep clinic: "The new way of thinking is to get patients to get up when they have insomnia. We say don't stay in bed for more than half an hour if you can't sleep. Get up and walk around, or read; then try again. Anxiety builds if you stay in bed. And anxiety does not promote sleep."

- Don't exercise up to three hours before going to bed because it only increases alertness. But do try to include some exercise in your daily routine.
- Don't take work to bed with you. Do try to unwind, but choose light reading or light television rather than intellectually demanding TV or thought-provoking books.
- Don't drink coffee or smoke during the day if you've been experiencing sleeplessness; these stimulants may keep you awake at night. Switch to decaf coffee and herbal teas; and give up smoking.
- Don't drink alcohol late at night. While it may help you to fall asleep, it may disrupt your sleep later on.
- Refrain from drinking fluids after dinner to avoid having to get up in the middle of the night.
- When it comes to food and sleep, think of the Three Bears: too much dinner or too little dinner may contribute to sleep problems; a dinner that's just right is the best!
- Make your bedroom a room conducive to a good night's sleep. Check its temperature – is it too hot or too cold for you? Make sure the mattress is how you like it, preferably a little firm to give your back some support. If light or noise disturbs you, consider getting drapes or blinds that shut out more of the light – and invest in a set of earplugs.

Your Guide to Nutrition Resources

British Columbia Dietitians' and Nutritionists' Association, 852 Fraser St., Ste. 200, Vancouver, British Columbia V5X 3Y3.

Canadian Fitness and Lifestyle Research Institute, 313–1600 James Naismith Dr., Gloucester, Ontario K1B 5N4. (613) 748-5791.

Canadian Association for the Advancement of Women and Sport and Physical Activity, 1600 James Naismith Dr., Gloucester, Ontario K1B 5N4. (613) 748-5793.

Corporation professionelle des dietetistes du Quebec, 4205 rue St. Denis, bureau 250, Montreal, Quebec H2J 2K9.

Manitoba Association of Registered Dietitians, 320 Sherbrook St., Winnipeg, Manitoba R3B 2W6.

National Institute of Nutrition, 265 Carling Ave., Ste. 302, Ottawa, Ontario K1S 2E1 (613) 235-3355.

New Brunswick Associaiton of Dietitians, PO Box 4102, Moncton, New Brunswick E1A 6E7.

Newfoundland Dietetic Association, PO Box 1756, St. John's, Newfoundland A1C 5P5.

NIA (Neuromuscular Integrative Action). A new low-impact exercise. To find out where classes are, call 1-800-463-0066.

Northern Nutrition Association, Box 116,

Yellowknife, Northwest Territories X1A 2N1.

Nova Scotia Dietetic Association, Box 8841, Station A, Halifax, Nova Scotia B3K 5M5.

Ontario Dietetic Association, 480 University Ave., Ste. 601, Toronto, Ontario M5G 1V2.

Prince Edward Island Dietetic Association, PO Box 2575, Charlottetown, Prince Edward Island C1A 8C2.

Saskatchewan Dietetic Association, PO Box 3984, Regina, Saskatchewan S4P 3R8.

BOOKS

Eat Well, Live Well: The Canadian Dietetic Association's Guide to Healthy Eating, Helen Bishop MacDonald and Margaret Howard (Macmillan Canada, 1990).

Good Fat, Bad Fat, Louise Lambert-Lagace and Michelle LaFlamme (Stoddart, 1995).

The Complete Illustrated Book of Yoga, Swami Vishnu-Devananda (Crown Trade Paperbacks, 1988).

The Vitality Cookbook, Monda Rosenberg and Frances Berkoff (Harper Collins, 1995).

Power Eating, Frances Berkoff, Barbara J. Lauer and Dr. Yves Talbot (Comuniplex, 1989).

The Enlightened Eater, Rosie Schwartz (Macmillan Canada, 1994).

Bonnie Stern Simply HeartSmart Cooking, Bonnie Stern (Random House, 1994).

Western Diseases: Their Dietary Prevention and Reversibility, Norman J. Temple and Denis P. Burkitt (Humana Press, 1994).

Your Guide to Exercise and Fitness Resources

Contact your local Y, a reputable fitness club, or any of the following organizations to help you find a sport you love or to help you get on the fitness track. Each organization listed also can bring you up to date on current issues regarding women and sports; they can also provide a speaker for women's groups or high schools who can talk about a specific sport or aboiut the subject of women and sports.

ORGANIZATIONS

CAAWS (The Canadian Association for the Advancement of Women in Sports), 1600 Naismith Dr., Gloucester, Ontario. K1B 5N4 (613) 748-5793

Promotion Plus, 305–1367 West Broadway, Vancouver, British Columbia V6H 4A9 (604) 737-3075

In Motion Network, 409-11010 142 St. NW, Edmonton, Alberta T8N 2R1 (401) 454-4745

52% Solution, University of Regina Faculty of

Physical Activity Studies, Regina, Saskatchewan S4S 0A2 (306) 585-4842

Female Athletes Motivating Excellence (FAME), Ontario Sport and Recreation Centre. 201–1185 Eglinton Ave. E., North York, Ontario M3C 3C6 (416) 426-7183

Alliance des femmes actives, c/o Institut de Leadership, Universite de Moncton, Moncton, New Brunswick E1A 3E9 (506) 8585-4350

CANADIAN WOMEN'S TOP
FIFTEEN HEALTH ISSUES

CHAPTER 5

HEART TO HEART: PROTECT YOURSELF FROM CANADA'S NUMBER-ONE KILLER OF WOMEN

Why is this a women's health issue? Heart disease and stroke account for more than 40 percent of all female deaths in Canada.

What you can do for yourself: Become aware of your health risks, change your diet, exercise properly.

WHAT IS HEART DISEASE?

Coronary artery disease (CAD) is caused by the narrowing or blockage of the coronary arteries which supply blood to the heart muscle. CAD occurs through atherosclerosis – the "hardening" or clogging of the arteries that feed the heart. Clogging occurs because substances called plaque build up in these arteries, cutting off vital blood supply.

WHAT IS STROKE?

Stroke is a potentially life-threatening cerebral vascular catastrophe that damages part of the brain; it can be caused either by an interruption to the brain's blood supply – through a blood clot, for example – or by the leakage of blood through the walls of blood vessels. Depending on where in the body the damage occurs, people who have sustained stroke acquire deficits in loss of judgement, speech or language, or loss of function in one arm, one leg or one side.

PART ONE

The facts: why heart disease is a new issue for women

Choose from the following list the leading cause of death among Canadian women:

- breast cancer
- uterine cancer
- heart disease and stroke

Most women answer breast cancer. But the facts are these:

- Heart disease and stroke account for more than 40 percent of all female deaths in Canada. In 1993, 38,381 women died of heart disease.
- Not only are heart disease and stroke the number-one killer of women in Canada, women are eight times more likely to die of these diseases than from breast cancer.
- At menopause, a woman's risk of death from heart disease and stroke increases four times. One in nine women aged 45 to 64 has some form of heart or blood vessel disease; past age 65, the ratio soars to one in three.

ARE HEART DISEASE AND STROKE INCREASING AMONG CANADIAN WOMEN?

Yes. There are many reasons for this change: an increase in the number of women smoking over the past 40 years; increased longevity for women and as a result a greater risk of cardiovascular disease post-menopause; and such factors as weight gain and an increase in blood pressure as women age.

DO HEART DISEASE AND STROKE AFFECT WOMEN DIFFERENTLY THAN MEN?

Yes. While the rate of heart attacks is about the same for women and men, women have a higher mortality rate after their heart attacks. Studies show that some women don't do as well as men following surgery and that unlike men, they tend to drop out of rehab programs. Women are also more likely than men to be diagnosed with angina – 56 percent versus 33 percent according to findings reported at the 1995 Toronto conference on the Contemporary Management of Cardiovascular Disease. (Angina is a recurring discomfort, usually located near the centre of the chest but also possible in the shoulders and arms, that occurs when the blood supply to part of the heart muscle doesn't meet the heart's needs). However, women are less likely than men to experience sudden death from a heart attack.

And heart disease among men is decreasing. Men today are more aware of the dangers of high cholesterol and take care to watch their weight, eat less fat and exercise more. Men in rehab after a heart attack tend to do better than women; one reason given by experts is that they have women in their lives to support them back to health.

The Bad News for Women About Heart Disease and Stroke

1. Until recently, cardiovascular disease had been labelled a men-only disease.

In 1964, the American Heart Association's public conference focused on how women could help protect their husbands from heart attacks. In movies, television shows and books, men are the ones who have heart attacks while their women stand steadfastly by them.

2. There appears to be a gender bias in the management of heart disease among women.

Women (and their physicians) sometimes attribute their chest pain to "just nerves and stress" and as a result adopt a wait-and-see attitude. Men (and their physicians), in contrast, are very aware of heart disease and men's chest pains are promptly investigated. Most women have heard stories of female friends or acquaintances going to the hospital complaining of chest pains, only to be told they were suffering from stress or indigestion. The pains later proved to be heart attacks.

3. Women tend to report their symptoms six to ten years later than men.

It has been suggested that women tolerate pain more than men and therefore may ignore heart disease symptoms, or judge them not significant and so fail to report them.

4. Some of the heart disease tests on women (exercise stress tests and thallium scans, in particular) are not as reliable as tests on men.

5. Women may have more microvascular heart disease – blockages in the smaller blood vessels that branch off the main arteries, blockages that are difficult to see on ordinary angiograms and thus harder to diagnose than men's heart disease, which tends to be most commonly observed in the large coronary arteries.

6. Women are more likely to have a poorly understood form of heart disease called Syndrome X, thought to be caused by hypersensitivity of the nerves leading to the heart, esophagus and chest and resulting in chest pain similar to angina in coronary artery disease.

7. There is even less awareness regarding women and stroke than there is about women and heart disease.

One reason many women ignore the warning signs of stroke is that in their role as nurturers they tend to put their own concerns second and dismiss or ignore symptoms.

8. As with heart disease, there are gender differences when it comes to the treatment and management of stroke.

Endarterectomy, a surgical procedure used to prevent stroke in patients who have had a transient ischemic attack or a stroke, can reduce stroke risk for men by 50 percent but only by about 16 percent for women.

The Good News for Women About Heart Disease and Stroke

1. Awareness is increasing about women and heart disease. As a result, doctors are becoming more sensitive to what their female patients say, and women themselves are reporting their symptoms earlier.

2. Research into women and heart disease is being conducted in Canada and more women are getting the message that this is *their* disease, too.

3. The picture is improving for female heart disease patients.

At the 1994 Heart and Stroke Foundation of Ontario Contemporary Management of Cardiovascular Disease conference, researcher and cardiac surgeon Dr. Lynda Mickleborough announced that the risk of bypass surgery is no greater for women with coronary artery disease than for men. "In the past, women may have been reluctant to undergo bypass surgery or angioplasty as treatment options for coronary artery disease," she says, referring to earlier beliefs that women were at an increased risk of dying after coronary bypass surgery.

4. More physicians are recognizing that female patients have been underdiagnosed.

At the cardiovascular disease conference mentioned above, Dr. Mickleborough pointed out that women themselves need to be more aggressive in seeking treatments: "If women suffer from classic symptoms such as chest pain, they should be more specific and objective in describing their symptoms to their family physicians."

5. Unlike breast cancer and other diseases, heart disease and stroke are something you can work at to prevent.

Changing the odds so that you'll be less at risk is very much within your control.

QUESTIONS, CONTROVERSY AND DEBATE

WHAT THE EXPERTS SAY: PREVENTION IS FRONT-AND-CENTRE

"Women have to take ownership of the problem," says Dr. Anthony Graham, past president of the Heart and Stroke Foundation of Canada. "Heart disease must become their number one issue." Dr. Graham and many of his colleagues believe that women patients and their physicians have not understood the enormity of the problem and have become distracted by other legitimate women's health concerns such as breast cancer.

Calgary cardiologist Dr. Nanette Alvarez told the *Calgary Sun* that lifestyle issues such as smoking, particularly with young women, cannot be emphasized enough in the prevention of heart disease. It is her view that women with high cholesterol who are heavy smokers risk heart attacks even before menopause, the time when women are most protected.

Although surgery is becoming more common (nearly 16,000 coronary bypasses are performed in Canada annually), cardiac surgeons emphasize that surgery is *not* the answer: "People are becoming very blasé about open-heart surgery," Dr. Stephanie Brister, one of only about ten female cardiac surgeons in Canada, told me after surgery on a woman who chain-smoked. Dr. Brister, who works out of Hamilton Civic Hospitals, says that surgery should never be considered a cure: "It buys you time, hopefully, to fix other things that contribute to your disease."

Prevention is the key to controlling heart disease. "Women really do have to take responsibility for their own health," Toronto Hospital cardiovascular surgeon Dr. Lynda Mickleborough says. "That means not smoking, keeping their weight within a reasonable range, and making certain they're physically active."

PART TWO

Your guide to heart health

1. LEARN HOW TO PREVENT HEART DISEASE AND STROKE

Be smoke-free: Smoking more than doubles the risk of heart attack. If you smoke *and* take oral contraceptives, you more than double that risk. According to the Addiction Research Foundation, four out of five smokers try to quit more than once before they succeed in kicking the habit. There's help out there for you if you're serious about quitting. There are nicotine patches and nicotine gum, hypnosis, acupuncture and great group support programs available across Canada through public-health offices and Y's.

Keep on the move: Eleven million Canadians are physically inactive, yet lack of exercise is the most common major risk factor of heart disease – and the most modifiable. Regular physical activity can lower resting heart rate, blood pressure and blood cholesterol levels, as well as help you maintain a desirable weight. Besides brisk walking, swimming, skating, dancing or cycling, you can simply take the stairs instead of the elevator or walk to the store instead of driving. Every little bit helps: unlike a decade ago when we were told that 30 minutes of intense physical activity was necessary several times a week, the word today is that the effects of exercise are cumulative and that only 10 to 15 minutes of daily moderate activity is required.

Know your blood pressure: Blood pressure is the force necessary to carry blood to all parts of the body and is created by the force of blood pushing against the walls of the blood vessels as it travels through the body. High blood pressure occurs when the pressure becomes too great – and high blood pressure (or *hypertension*) is a key risk factor for heart disease and stroke in women over the age of 35. To keep your blood pressure healthy, engage in daily physical activity, drink less alcohol, maintain a healthy body weight, use less salt in your food, reduce stress and don't smoke.

The normal range of blood pressure is between 100 and 140 for the systolic pressure – the pressure is created by the contraction of the heart muscle and the elastic recoil of the main artery leaving the heart as blood surges through it – and 70 and 90 for the diastolic pressure – the pressure that reflects the resistance of all the small arteries in the body and the load against which the heart must work. Ask your doctor for your numbers.

Give your attitude a makeover: Changing your mind-set to make sure you take charge by taking care is the biggest thing you can do for yourself. That means paying attention and trying to change your lifestyle where it needs changing. Research shows that depression can contribute to mortality following a heart attack; some studies show that women without social ties are more likely to die from heart disease than women with strong social ties. Building a social network – and maintaining it – is very important. So is managing stress. While stress can't be eliminated and is not always a bad thing, it's worth trying to avoid or modify situations in which you feel driven, tense and irritable. (New research shows that the stresses of daily living can bring on chest pain which may lead to some heart problems.) Relaxation techniques, stress reduction and regular physical activity may help you outsmart the stress risk.

Keep your weight in the healthy range: This is a message women should take seriously, but only after discussing with their physicians what that range is. Too often, weight issues lead to eating disorders for women; it's well worth remembering that being seriously underweight incurs as many health risks as being seriously overweight. Statistics indicate that one in three North Americans are significantly overweight, which doubles your risk for cardiovasular disease at any given age. Since obesity may also lead to high blood cholesterol, hypertension and diabetes, your risks then become compounded. The risk of heart attack in diabetic women is more than double that of nondiabetic women of the same age.

Body shape is another risk factor: a study of 5,932 women from Chicago's Women Take Heart project showed that apple-shaped women had a greater risk of cardiovascular disease than pear-shaped women, who tend to accumulate weight on their hips. Results of the Chicago study found that the thinnest women with the most unfavorable waist-to-hip ratios had higher blood pressures, LDL cholesterol (low-density lipoprotein or bad cholesterol) and serum glucose counts than women who were pear-shaped and even heavier in weight. Your waist-to-hip ratio should be <0.85.

Choose heart-smart foods: Ask your physician if you should have your blood cholesterol checked: a healthy level is 5.2 mmol/L or under for an adult 30 years or over. A borderline reading is between 5.2 mmol/L and 6.19 mmol/L; a high reading is over 6.2 mmol/L.

High-fat diets tend to raise blood cholesterol levels, which in turn raises your chances of sustaining a heart attack or stroke. In addition to a healthy cholesterol level, your blood HDL (high-density lipoprotein) levels should be high (the higher, the better your protection) while your LDL level should be 3.5 mmol/L or below.

Some people can only lower their cholesterol through cholesterol-lowering drugs, but most people can do so with diet. Most of us consume about 40 percent of our calories from fat, but today's target is 30 percent. No more than 10 percent of the 30 percent should be in the form of the saturated fats found in meat, poultry, milk, cheese, butter and tropical oils. Choose your fats carefully; polyunsaturated fats (in nuts like almonds and walnuts), fish and vegetable oils such as sunflower and corn oil, as well as monounsaturated fats (in olive, canola, peanut and soya oils) are much healthier choices than saturated fats.

If you're postmenopausal, talk to your doctor about taking estrogen: studies now show that hormone replacement therapy is good for the ticker. Estrogen, or estrogen taken with natural (micronized) progesterone may translate into a 25 percent reduction in heart disease risk. The hormone estrogen helps protect women from heart disease and stroke until menopause, when the amount in the body drops. However, women need to be aware of the dangers associated with a protracted regimen of hormone replacement theory. While estrogen may be good for the heart, taking the hormone over a period of years has shown a definite increased risk of breast cancer; women with liver disease, gallstones, breast or endometrial cancer, undiagnosed uterine bleeding and a history of blood clots or thromboembolisms are usually advised against taking estrogen. (However, some physicians believe that post-menopausal breast cancer patients who have been cancer-free for a number of years might consider estrogen replacement.)

2. LEARN HOW TO RECOGNIZE THE EARLY WARNING SIGNS OF HEART ATTACK AND STROKE

- Pain or discomfort in the chest that comes on with activity and goes away with rest; shortness of breath or unusual tiredness with activity; difficulty doing activities that used to be easy or normal.
- Think of stroke as "a brain attack." Be aware that the first six hours of a stroke are crucial. Drugs such as clotbusters are available and are administered in some hospital ERs within six hours of stroke, thus minimizing and, in some cases, even reversing some of the damage. The trick is to get people to respond to stroke the way they respond to a heart attack. Says Dr. Sandra Black, head of neurology at Sunnybrook Health Sciences Centre and a researcher in stroke outcome, "People know the symptoms of stroke. The issue is they do not act on it. We have to switch their mind-set to regard either a major stroke or a trans ischemic attack (TIA) as a medical emergency."

Is It a Heart Attack? Know the Warning Signs and Act Now

If you experience any of these feelings, tell someone immediately or call for emergency help.
- A vague discomfort in your chest that doesn't go away with rest, or sudden, severe, crushing chest discomfort that may move to other parts of your body.
- Heaviness, pressure, squeezing, fullness, burning, tightness or other discomfort in the chest, shoulder, arm, neck or jaw that doesn't go away.
- Unusual pain that spreads down one side.

- Shortness of breath, sweating or weakness.
- Nausea, vomiting and/or indigestion.
- Feelings of extreme anxiety, denial or fear.

Is It a Stroke? Know the Warning Signs and Act Now

If you experience any of the following problems, whatever your age, treat them as a medical emergency and get to the hospital immediately.

- Sudden weakness or numbness and/or tingling of the face, arm or leg. These signals may be brief.
- Sudden trouble speaking or understanding speech.
- Dizziness, unsteadiness or sudden falls.
- Sudden loss of vision, particularly in one eye, or double vision.
- Sudden severe, unusual headache.

PROFILE

Frances Greenwood-Navon – it can happen to anyone

Heart disease is often the last thing a woman thinks about when she experiences chest pains. Just ask Frances Greenwood-Navon who experienced them a year or so before she collapsed on the street from cardiac arrest. "I figured they were aches and pains from an old bruise I had on an upper rib," says the Toronto financial manager whose cardiac crisis happened in the summer of 1988 when she was 47. "I also had the pain sometimes during exertion but I never attached any importance to it. The thought never entered my mind."

Nor anyone else's. Even when Greenwood-Navon was in hospital recovering from her crisis, doctors were convinced that her cardiac arrest had been caused by something other than heart disease. The small, slim, former ballet dancer had never smoked, had good cholesterol levels and no family history of heart disease. It was only weeks later, after scores of other tests were done, that she had an angiogram which showed major plaque buildup and a blockage.

"A man collapses and blockage is the first thing doctors think of," says Greenwood-Navon. During an awareness-raising breakfast organized by the Heart and Stroke Foundation of Ontario's Women, Heart Disease and Stroke Initiative, she spoke out on the gender bias she experienced. "I learned it can happen to anyone," she says. Greenwood-Navon is back at work today, feeling and looking good. She attributes her heart attack to stress: the year before her crisis she went through several medical crises with other members of her family. She was the caregiver who ran from work to hospital to home when her mother was ill. She doesn't regret a moment of that time and care, but she has learned to pay better attention to herself as a result. She also takes care to educate others: "If there was more education and women could become more aware of heart disease, then perhaps they may better be able to recognize the telltale signs."

Lynn Lanigan – don't ignore stroke's warning signs

Lynn Lanigan of Ottawa, Ontario, shattered another myth about women and illness when she suffered a stroke at age 46. Stroke, a potentially life-threatening cerebral vascular catastrophe, is an occurrence many people associate with men – old men who are unfit and overweight. But Lanigan was fit and healthy (at five foot two, she weighed only 98 pounds at the time of her stroke) and neither smoked nor drank alcohol. We would have described her as living right, a perfect 40-something role model for health.

But Lanigan had ignored two significant body signals that were telling her something was amiss: one signal was high blood pressure. Like many of us, Lanigan hadn't had hers checked regularly and was unaware that she might be in danger. Another signal was transient ischemic attacks or TIAS – fleeting strokes that have the same symptoms as a stroke but disappear in minutes or seconds. In Lanigan's case, she occasionally experienced sudden blinding headaches, accompanied by a feeling of dizziness and numb tingling. But like many women, she was too busy to focus on these symptoms and when they passed, she forgot about them. On the night of her stroke, she did the same: awakening with a blinding headache, her left side tingling and numb, she decided to wait it out. She didn't seek medical attention until the next day. Fortunately for her, her stroke was mild.

PART THREE

Your guide to heart and stroke health resources

Where to Look for More Information, Support, Services and Self-Help About Heart Disease
and Stroke

ORGANIZATIONS

Some of the following organizations, such as your
provincial Heart and Stroke Association, provide a
bounty of educational materials on heart and
stroke, offer programs in CPR and show you how to
fine-tune your lifestyle to prevent heart disease;
others, like the Stroke Recovery Association, can
put you in touch with support groups as well as
provide educational materials.

Canadian Centre for Stress and Well-Being, 141
Adelaide St. W., Ste. 1506, Toronto, Ontario M5H 3L5
(416) 363-6204.

Heart and Stroke Foundation of Canada, 160
George St., Ste. 200, Ottawa, Ontario K1N 9M2 (613)
241-4361. Heart and Stroke Foundation Healthline:
a 24-hour telephone information service, 1-800-
360-1557. Provincial Chapters: British Columbia
(604)736-4404; Alberta (403) 264-5549;
Saskatchewan (306) 244-2124; Manitoba (204) 949-
2000; Ontario (416) 489-7100; Quebec (514) 871-
1551; New Brunswick (506) 634-1620; Nova Scotia
(902) 423-7530; Prince Edward Island (902) 892-
7441; Newfoundland (709) 753-8521.

Stroke Recovery Association, 10 Overlea Blvd., Ste.
292, Toronto, Ontario M4H 1A4 (416) 425-4209.

BOOKS/NEWSLETTERS/ AUDIOS/VIDEOS

Many of the books, videotapes and audiotapes that
explain heart disease focus on how to change your
lifestyle or decrease your risk factors by getting
your weight and cholesterol under control and
exercising more.

Eat More, Weigh Less, Dean Ornish, M.D. (Harper
Collins, 1994)

Heart Health for Women, Felicity Smart and Dr.
Diane Holdright (Thorsons/HarperCollins, 1995).

Home Rehabilitation – If You've Had a Stroke.
Audiotape available from AND Canada
(Association for the Neurologically Disabled of
Canada), 59 Clement Rd., Etobicoke, Ontario M9R
1Y5 (416) 244-1992.

Impact of Stroke Upon Family; The Recovery
Process, Recovery Phase II; Family Involvement,
Recovery Phase III: Bridging the Gap; On the Road
to Recovery; Spouse Survival. Pamphlets from the
Stroke Recovery Association, 10 Overlea Blvd., Ste.
292, Toronto, Ontario M4H 1A4 (416) 425-4209.

Lighthearted Everyday Cooking, Anne Lindsay
(Macmillan Canada, 1991).

Power Eating, Fran Berkoff, Barbara Lauer and Dr.
Yves Talbot, M.D. (Key Porter, 1989).

The Enlightened Eater, Rosie Schwartz (Macmillan
Canada, 1994).

The Heart Care Kit, The Ontario Heart and Stroke
Foundation, 477 Mount Pleasant Rd., 4th Fl.
Toronto, Ontario M4S 2L9 (416) 489-7100.

Simply HeartSmart Cooking, Bonnie Stern
(Random House, 1994).

CHAPTER 6

BREAST CANCER: THIS IS A WAR CANADIAN WOMEN MUST WIN

Why is this a women's health issue? One in nine Canadian women will develop breast cancer in her lifetime.

What you can do for yourself: Be well-informed, do monthly breast self-examinations, have one done by your physician annually, have a yearly mammogram if you're 50 and over, report any changes in your breast to your physician and make sure he or she investigates further.

WHAT IS BREAST CANCER?

Breast cancer usually begins as a clump of abnormal cells. "People have to realize that the cancer is actually the patient's own cells. Some people still think of it as an infection, but it is your own cells out of control that destroy the normal tissue," explains Dr. Roy Clark, a radiation oncologist who has worked with the Princess Margaret Hospital in Toronto, and who now co-chairs The National Breast Cancer Fund. This applies to all cancers. *Cancer,* the word, really means uncontrolled cell growth.

PART ONE

The facts: why breast cancer is women's number-one health fear

A presentation on breast cancer given by Dr. Ian Tannock, chief of medicine at Princess Margaret Hospital, in March 1995, indicated how far we've come and how far we have to go when it comes to this disease. "The risk factors are well known," Tannock began, referring to the familial risks, breast cancer's possible link to a high-fat diet and hormone factors. He ended his speech with the grim fact that the probability of cure when breast cancer has metastasized is still less than 1 percent.

Compared to awareness a decade ago, women today are very aware of breast cancer. Today, breast self-examination pamphlets are available in pharmacies and college dorms and there are breast-screening centres across the country. The 1995 Canadian Women's Health Test, conducted by Women's College Hospital in partnership with Market Vision Research and Searle, revealed that at age 40, one-third or more women reported having had a mammogram in the past 12 months and that 57 percent of Canadian women, 15 years of age and older, reported having done a breast self-examination during the previous two months of the study.

Breast survivor groups such as the Alliance of Breast Cancer Survivors and the Burlington Breast Cancer Support Services Inc. are thriving. More important, their voices are finally being heard: "Professionals will have to give up some of their ownership of the disease," said Sharon Batt, president of Breast Cancer Action Montreal, speaking at a national conference on breast cancer in Toronto in the fall of 1994. "Women with breast cancer are bargaining for more non-interventional, low-tech solutions." A 1993 National Forum on Breast Cancer in Montreal which urged more research into alternatives was followed by survivors' forums and educational exhibitions across Canada.

Some survivors have become activists; others have become authors. Three Canadian women (Ottawa's Penny Williams, Montreal's Sharon Batt and Vancouver's Rosalind MacPhee) have written books describing their personal experiences with the disease. There's also a book by a man, Claire Hoy, whose wife died from the disease. Over the past two years, virtually every Canadian magazine and newspaper has published articles on the subject. Breast cancer survivors have launched services, organizations and businesses to help others. One example is Burlington, Ontario's Pat Kelly, one of the founders of the activist movement in Canada; another is Linda Jackson, who, after her own mastectomy, designed a post-surgery undergarment with prostheses which she now distributes through Ortho Active Appliances in Coquitlam, British Columbia. Artists, too, have explored the breast cancer experience: in the winter of 1995, the Woodlawn Foundation's Joan Chalmers and Barbra Amesbury launched Survivors in Search of a Voice: The Art of Courage, a spectacular travelling art show of 24 works mounted by Canadian women artists in consultation with breast cancer survivors.

The Bad News for Women About Breast Cancer

1. Is Breast Cancer Increasing Among Canadian Women?

Yes. Although breast cancer ignorance is on the way to being eradicated, the disease itself is not being beaten. Doctors are loath to call breast cancer an epidemic, but many women say just that. Consider the following:

- The incidence of breast cancer in Canada has risen from one in 20 a couple of decades ago to one in nine today. Breast cancer has been increasing at the rate of about 1 percent a year from the mid-sixties through to the late 1980s.
- An estimated 5,400 women died from the disease in 1994, making breast cancer the leading killer of women between the ages of 35 and 55. And 14 percent of these deaths occur in women between the ages of 25 and 49, an age group in which women should not be dying.

2. Breast cancer can strike women at any age. (About 1 percent of breast cancers are also found in men).

3. Experts say that most cancers have been in the breast around eight years before they can be detected on a mammogram and ten years before they can be felt as a lump.

4. Experts maintain that the issue today is distant spread of the cancer, not local recurrence or the site at which the lump was originally found. The big problem occurs when the disease spreads to another part of the body: this might be from a very small tumor. "Size of tumor is not a factor," says Dr. Roy Clark. "Cancer is a capricious disease."

The Good News for Women about Breast Cancer

The March 1995 presentation on breast cancer by Dr. Ian Tannock underlined how desperate we are to get to the next stage in understanding and treating this disease. Every month or so we hear of another step towards what might be better prevention or diagnosis of the disease. Here are a few of those:

- Research is ongoing into better detection systems. Mammograms aren't perfect diagnostic devices, but at the moment they're the best we have for women aged 50 to 59 who should have one every year or two. (Experts say that if your mother had breast cancer, your mammography should start ten years before the age at which her disease struck. So, if your mother had breast cancer at age 55, have your first mammogram at age 45.)
- There are several other systems now being used in Canada along with mammography. Positron emission tomography and magnetic resonance imaging

(MRI) are two, though they're extremely expensive and are currently being used to obtain more information on specific tumors. Ultrasounds help doctors distinguish between cysts and malignant growths (mammograms cannot tell the difference).

- New screening methods designed to improve upon mammography are being explored. Moreover, new technology is being developed to help radiologists make the most of mammography readings: computer programs may soon aid in scanning mammograms, perhaps picking up tumors that doctors may have missed.

- Breast cancer can be treated successfully when found early. Some cancers, such as lung and ovarian, kill largely because they're found too late. That's why early detection is key in breast cancer. Fortunately, early detection is also possible.

- Four out of five women diagnosed with breast cancer live at least five years after their diagnosis. Though early detection reduces breast cancer deaths by only 30 percent, it also means an almost 87 percent recovery rate from the disease.

- Clarifying the statistics can only help. Women want to know what these scary numbers really mean! The statistic that one in nine Canadian women will get breast cancer applies to a population of women at the age of 85. So, for every age group, the statistic is different. For instance, at the age of 50, a woman's chances of contracting breast cancer are one in 50.

- Surgery need not be as radical as it was in the past: more than 80 percent of patients in southern Ontario are treated by lumpectomy. Studies show that by adding radiation as a treatment, the incidence of recurrence is reduced from 30 percent to 8 percent.

- Several methods are now used in Canada to improve breast cancer survival. In addition to surgery, there's also adjuvant therapy – the use of drugs to kill cells directly, or hormonal therapy to stop the spread of hormone-receptive cells. "In women under the age of 50, six months of chemotherapy can improve the probability of long-term survival by about 10 percent," says Dr. Tannock. "Removing the ovaries gives similar results in patients with tumors containing estrogen receptors." In women over the age of 50, the drug tamoxifen has been beneficial, he adds.

- Research is ongoing into promising preventives: studies have shown that flaxseed and linseed have anti-tumor effects. Specific breast cancer/flaxseed studies are now under way in Canada.

- Breast cancer and the environment is another area in which there is a growing body of research. There's particular interest in hormone copycats called xenoestrogens (they are in the environment, in susbstances such as DDT and plastics – and they mimic estrogen); the result, some physicians say, is more exposure to estrogen and, thus, a greater risk in getting breast cancer.

- Other research studies suggest a possible link between breast cancer and high levels of sex hormones in postmenopausal women; still others suggest an association (albeit, a weak one) between abortion and increased breast cancer risk.

WHERE DO WE GO FROM HERE?

Most experts agree that we have caught up, in terms of information, at any rate. Now we have to reach beyond awareness, beyond mammography and early detection. What that means, among other things, is that more research money is needed. While breast cancer kills more women than AIDS kills people of both genders, the AIDS community has been far more successful in its fund-raising efforts to date than the breast cancer community.

QUESTIONS, CONTROVERSY AND DEBATE

1. *WHAT THE EXPERTS SAY:* WHERE WE'RE GOING IN BREAST CANCER RESEARCH AND TREATMENT

In the fall of 1994, Dr. Susan Love, a world-renowned breast surgeon, addressed the Canadian Breast Cancer Foundation's Awareness Day in Vancouver on the topic of the future of breast cancer research. "We're sort of stuck in the same old stuff," Dr. Love told me during an interview after her speech. "We're still trying to think of ways to do surgery, radiation and chemo better. Well, I think we have gone as far as we can go with slash, burn and poison. It's just not enough," she said.

Love believes that we should delve further into molecular biology, genetics and the gene/environment interaction. "All cancer is genetic in that it's all screwed-up genes," she said. "Sometimes you inherit the gene that's messed up or sometimes you acquire it." The discovery of the BCRA1 gene was exciting news because it's one of the first inherited genes, said Love. "But since 80 percent of women with breast cancer have no family history, we have to be looking as well at what it is that screws up that gene. Is it pesticides, electromagnetic fields, virus, hormones? We have not a clue."

"Radical surgery is going, going, and will be gone," said Dr. Roy Clark, speaking to the Canadian Breast Cancer Foundation. "Control and management of breast cancer (and all cancers) is a better way to think than cure," he said, adding that most diseases, including diabetes and high blood pressure, are actually managed (through diet and medication) rather than cured. "Can cancer cells be taught to behave?" is the number-one question being asked in research, he said. "Instead of killing the intruder, we are more and more looking at cellular control and reversing the malignant process."

2. DOES LESS FAT EQUAL LESS BREAST CANCER?

A unique Canadian study, being carried out in several cities across the country, and the only one of its kind in the world, aims to find out whether significantly lowering fat intake makes the difference between getting breast cancer and not getting it. The idea that there is a link between breast cancer and diet began years ago when studies showed that women in Japan have significantly lower rates of breast cancer than Canadian women. Because Japanese women traditionally consume diets higher in carbohydrates and lower in fats than women in North American and Europe, it was suggested that the relationship between diet and breast cancer exists, and that incidence of the disease may have something to do with a woman's fat intake.

According to a paper by Toronto's Dr. Norman Boyd, head of the Diet and Breast Cancer Prevention Study (coordinated by the Ontario Cancer Institute and Princess Margaret Hospital), the five-year survival rate of women with breast cancer in Tokyo, where dietary fat intake is low, is about 15 percent greater than that of women from western countries.

Animal experiments further suggest that dietary fat may play a key role in contracting the disease, and the disappointing results of the Nurses Health Study – the eating habits of 89,000 women were surveyed in the United States, but no association between breast cancer and fat intake was found – have convinced many people that more definitive studies on the subject are needed. "The question is still alive and well," says registered dietitian Cary Greenberg, nutrition coordinator of the Diet and Breast Cancer Prevention Study. "The studies in the past tried to describe what people ate, but they didn't try to change what people ate." This study certainly does that. In it, 6,800 Canadian women will be asked to either change or monitor their eating habits for a decade. Half of them will be on a regular diet. Half of them will be put on a fat-restricted diet, where the amount of fat consumed is 15 to 20 percent of their total intake. That's cutting your daily fat intake by half! In Japan, Greenberg explains, the intake of fat is under 20 percent. Even though Canada's Food Guide suggests a fat intake of 30 percent, most of us are eating 35 percent or more.

The study, now under way in Toronto, Hamilton, Windsor, London, and Vancouver, has about 1,850 participants to date. Interested women can make an appointment to learn more by phoning (416) 506-0983. But while anyone is welcome to apply to take part, there are no lineups to do so. One reason may be that for many, cutting fat intake to the extent required by the study is neither easy nor desirable. Cooking for a family and eating out are two big problems, Greenberg admits.

Participants must be between ages 30 and 65 (the average age of women in the study is in the early forties), must not be pregnant or breastfeeding, must not have had cancer and must not have any dietary restrictions. Nor should they have had breast reduction or augmentation. Participants must come in with a mammogram and agree to have one regularly (one of the study's criteria is that participants must have breast tissue that shows up as dense on a mammogram), and they must be within a healthy weight zone.

Lest anyone think this is an easy way of losing weight, Greenberg cautions that weight has nothing to do with the study. Though half the participants are put on a low-fat diet, the displaced calories are made up from fruits and vegetables and grains. "It's not just eating less fat, it's eating less calories from fat," she says. "It's like getting to the same number of calories per day but in a different way." Losing weight, in fact, would only confuse the issue; researchers wouldn't know if the breast cancer link was due to weight loss or to lower-fat intake.

PART TWO

Your guide to breast health

1. ARE YOU AT RISK?

• *Risk factor #1: Heredity*

If your mother or sister has had breast cancer, your risk is increased – even more so if they developed the disease before menopause and/or in both breasts.

All women are not created equal when it comes to developing breast cancer. Hereditary factors have to be examined closely, says Dr. Pamela Goodwin, a medical oncologist and epidemiologist. For instance, having a mother or sister who has or had breast cancer puts you at a higher risk than if a grandmother or aunt had the disease. Dr. Goodwin points out that women should also take into account whether or not the relative with breast cancer had one breast involved or both: if both were involved, your risk is greater, she says. The age at which your relative developed breast cancer is relevant, as well.

The discovery in 1995 of the breast cancer genes BCRA1 and 2 may have implications for high-risk families: some women even consider prophylactic mastectomies, the removal of both breasts. However, women with a breast cancer gene account for only 2 to 5 percent of known breast cancer cases. Women with a genetic predisposition to the disease should talk to their doctors about a possible course of action. Women identified in the high-risk group should ask their doctors about local breast-screening programs for high-risk women. They should see their doctors regularly and make sure any suspicious lump or thickening in the breast is investigated.

• *Risk Factor #2: Age*
The older you are, the more you are at risk. If you're over 50, have regular mammograms and visit your doctor or local breast screening clinic.

• *Risk Factor #3: Later Pregnancy*
Never having given birth to a child or having your first child over the age of 30 increases your risk of developing breast cancer.

• *Risk Factor #4: Early Menstruation and Late Menopause*
Women who began menstruating at an early age (before the age of 12) and who reach menopause at a relatively late age (after the age of 56) have a higher breast cancer rate.

• *Risk Factor #5: Unusual Breast Conditions*
At risk are women with a history of benign breast disease that required biopsy, and/or other breast conditions. (One current study is exploring the relationship between dense breast tissue and breast cancer.)

• *Risk Factor #6: Smoking, Alcohol and Obesity*
Ongoing studies indicate that smoking, consuming more than seven alcoholic drinks weekly and obesity may be risk factors. However, the evidence is still inconclusive.

• *Risk Factor #7: Hormonal Therapy*
Research is under way to determine if there is a link between breast cancer and a woman's taking birth control pills or undergoing hormone replacement therapy for

long periods of time – both because they contain estrogen and because breast cancer is a disease with hormonal connections.

• *Risk Factor #8: Diet*

Diet may or may not be a risk factor. According to Dr. Ian Tannock, it may be difficult to draw valid conclusions from diet studies for some time: "For instance, in countries where they eat a lot of red meat and have a high rate of breast cancer, it wouldn't mean necessarily that red meat causes breast cancer. It might be something totally unrelated like, say, the amount of smoke in the air."

Nonetheless, a high-fat diet and its potential link to breast cancer receives substantial research interest today. Some experts, however, feel that studying the link between diet and breast cancer in women of middle age will tell us less about the disease than studying the link between diet and breast cancer in women in their teens. Other experts, including Dr. Steve Narod, who holds the Canadian Breast Cancer Foundation Breast Cancer Chair at Women's College Hospital, believe that diet will reveal only part of the answer to why women contract the disease.

2. LEARN HOW TO HELP PREVENT BREAST CANCER

"The most often-asked question is, 'Why wasn't my cancer found sooner?'" says oncologist Dr. Roy Clark. "Small tumors are still the most curable, so early detection is really the key."

LEARN BREAST SELF-EXAMINATION (BSE)

It's as easy as one, two, three. And though most women largely regard breast self-examination or BSE as a form of cancer detection, Dr. Susan Love maintains its importance goes far beyond this. "BSE is part of the larger process of getting to know your own body, becoming acquainted with who you are physically," says the California breast surgeon. "Our breasts are as individual as our faces, and what's normal in your breast might be a danger signal in mine."

Recently, some experts have questioned the value of BSE as there are really no scientific studies to support the inference that women who examine their own breasts regularly are less likely to die of breast cancer than those who don't. Fear immobilizes many women (particularly those in high-risk groups) from doing BSE regularly. BSE shouldn't be a search-and-destroy mission, aimed at feeling for the smallest lump – it is really a way of getting to know how your breasts feel on a regular basis so that you can become aware when or if something seems unusual. But experts say that if you don't do BSE, it's very difficult for you to know when something feels wrong if you have no context for what, for your body, is right. "The best tool is still the mammogram," says Dr. Judith Weinroth, medical coordinator of the Ontario Breast Screening Program's Toronto Centre. "But it misses 10 to 15 percent of breast cancers." She knows what she's talking about, having had several lump scares over the years, half of which she has described on her own through regular BSE.

When should you do BSE?

Most health care professionals agree that premenopausal women or women on hormone replacement therapy should examine their breasts at the same time every month. Once again, the point is to get to know what your breasts normally feel like so you can detect any variations from that norm. A week to ten days after your period is a good time to do BSE. That's when breasts tend to be the least lumpy. If you're postmenopausal, and not on hormone therapy, just pick a regular time each month.

When should you start BSE?

"You should start doing BSE as soon as you're old enough to have breasts," says Dr. Judith Weinroth. "We teach our kids to brush their teeth, why not teach our daughters breast self-examination?" suggests breast cancer survivor Monica Wright-Roberts. By adolescence, young women should be doing BSE on a regular basis. While breast cancer in young women is rare, it can happen.

Have a Mammogram

You have to find the cancer before you can cure it. This is still the most powerful argument in mammography's favour. While recent research concluded that in women aged 40 to 49, screening with mammography did not decrease breast cancer death rates over a seven-year period, it also showed that even in this age group mammography helped detect cancers in their earlier stages.

Dr. Nancy Wadden of the Toronto Hospital says there's "lots of conflicting evidence" about whether women under the age of 50 should seek mammograms. Mammography, on average, detects 85 percent to 90 percent of breast cancers in women aged 50 and over. Early detection is important for increased survival.

In the summer of 1995, a Canadian study showed that mammography may be too costly for the number of lives it saves. But most women and their doctors would like-ly agree that the issue shouldn't be can we afford mammography but rather that we can't afford not to do it. In fact, international studies indicate that breast cancer death rates for women 50 and over could be reduced by up to 40 percent by the use of mammography alone.

A cancerous lump can be as small as a peppercorn. In fact, the average-size lump found by women having regular mammograms is .3 cm. If you get treatment when a tumor is this small, you have a 96 percent chance of being cured, assuming the can-cer is confined to the breast.

Compare the above to the average-size lump found by practising regular breast self examination – 1.3 cm, the size of a small button. Still, if you obtain treatment when a tumor is between 1 cm and 2 cm, you have an 85 to 90 percent chance of cure, assuming the cancer is confined to the breast.

What You Need to Know About Mammography

What is it?

Mammography is an X ray of the breast used to screen for breast cancer or to learn more about a breast abnormality found on a physical exam. It is performed by an X ray technician or radiologist and is read by a radiologist specifically trained in mam-mography.

Mammography is used for screening, to monitor the breasts of an apparently healthy woman and to make sure her breast tissues are healthy. It is also used for diagnosis, to investigate a lump or other problem in the breast.

There is a difference between screening and diagnostic mammography. In the former, two different views of each breast are routinely done; in the latter, more or particular views of the breast may be requested.

What is the X ray procedure?

The mammography machine, which costs anywhere from $70,000 to $120,000, is about the size and shape of a refrigerator with a couple of shelves on it each about the size of a magazine. You stand up against the machine while a technician places your breast between the two plates and compresses it. This is uncomfortable, but only lasts a few seconds until the picture is taken. Two views are taken of each breast, top to bottom and side to side.

Who should have a mammogram and how often?

All women aged 50 and over, every year or two. Women with a high familial risk of developing the disease should have their first mammogram ten years before the age of the earliest cancer in their family. So, if your mother had breast cancer at 50, you should have your first mammogram at 40. Any woman of any age with symptoms of breast disease, such as a lump, discharge from the nipple, swelling or pain, should consult her doctor. While in most cases these symptoms do not indicate breast cancer, the doctor may still suggest mammography.

Can mammography miss tumors?

Yes. In younger women who normally have denser breast tissue, it's more difficult to pick up cancers via mammography. Between 5 and 10 percent of all cancers are not picked up by mammography. That is why it's important for women of all ages to do breast self-examination monthly and to report any lumps or abnormalities to their doctors immediately.

Is mammography safe?

Yes, because modern equipment uses very low doses of radiation and the benefits of breast screening outweigh the risk or harm from the X ray. However, women should check with their doctors to make sure the equipment used is up-to-date and delivers the least possible radiation dose. Having the X ray done at a breast-screening centre helps to ensure that the equipment is safe and that the results are accurately interpreted.

3. COPING WITH BREAST CANCER

Getting a Diagnosis

If either a mammogram or physical examination suggests the possibility of breast cancer, a doctor will order a biopsy as a diagnostic tool to confirm the cancer before treating it. One biopsy method uses a fine needle to draw out some liquid or material from the suspicious site in order to have it tested for malignancy by a pathologist; the procedure, almost painless, may be done in a doctor's office.

A second biopsy method is through surgery in which the lump or part of it is removed and sent to a lab where it is analyzed for breast cancer. (If you're concerned about a lump that your doctor insists is nothing, exercising your right to a second opinion is a good idea.) Some doctors, including Dr. Ian Tannock, believe that any lump should be biopsied if it's been in the breast more than two weeks.

If the Diagnosis is Breast Cancer, What Happens Next?

If cancer has been confirmed, doctors want to conclude on the type. If the cancer cells remain within the confines of the duct or lobule, the cancer is called in situ (meaning confined to that site.) Once the cancer has penetrated through a cell's basement membrane, the cancer is called invasive.

Some cancer cells travel to the underarm lymph nodes and other distant parts of the body to form metastasis (secondary spreading cancers.) If the lymph glands and blood vessels have conveyed the cancerous cells to other parts of the body, the primary tumor may not be the main problem.

The type and size of tumor, the presence of cells in the lymph nodes and the possible metastasis are all taken into consideration in order to classify the tumor in a system called staging, an important tool in measuring risk and choosing treatment. One of the factors upon which prognosis is based is whether or not there are nodes involved and, if so, how many. "If your nodes are not involved," says Dr. Tannock, "your 20-year survival rate is about 70 percent. If one to three nodes are involved, the survival rate is 30 to 40 percent."

The stages go from I, in which the tumor is small, the lymph nodes are not involved and there's no metastasis, to IV, in which the cancer has spread to a site distant from the original tumor. "It's the distant disease that kills the patient," says Dr. Roy Clark.

Even a small breast cancer that's barely detectable on a mammogram may have been growing many years; it's possible that tiny clumps of cancerous cells from it have spread via the blood and lymph system before the breast tumor is finally found. That's why systemic treatment of the whole body, through chemotherapy or hormone therapy to kill escaped cancer cells, is often done along with localized surgery and/or radiation.

Getting Treatment: Ask Questions, Then Some More

Finding a lump, having it investigated for breast cancer, having the lump or your breast surgically removed, and following through with prescribed treatment thereafter usually means you'll be involved with a series of doctors.

Your family doctor is the first person you'll probably consult about your breast. He or she will examine your breasts and make arrangements for a mammogram, if necessary. If you need surgery, be sure to ask your family doctor to refer you to a specialist in breast lumps. Don't be afraid to ask questions about anything you don't know.

Questions to Ask Your Surgeon

- Do you prefer one type of surgery over another. If so, why?
- Will I require a local or general anaesthetic? What are the side effects of this?
- Will I be hospitalized, and, if so, how long?
- What are the steps towards recovery from this operation?
- What kind of scarring should I expect?

Questions to Ask Your Oncologist (Cancer Specialist)

- What type of breast cancer do I have?
- At what stage is the breast cancer I have? (Be sure you understand "staging" as it applies to your cancer.)
- What treatment are you recommending and why?
- What are its risks and side effects?
- What would happen if I chose not to have this treatment?
- How long will this treatment take?
- Where and when would I have this treatment? How often?
- What other medications might I be taking with this treatment?
- Would I consult you if I get other illnesses while I'm on this treatment, or would I go to my family doctor?

Remember, you are part of a medical team involved in your care. Ask questions! And while none of us likes to doctor-shop, experts say we must exercise our right to a second opinion if we feel we need one. (Breast cancer patients advise taking someone along to your appointments. That person can offer support and can take notes so you don't forget some of the things discussed after you've left the doctor's office.)

UNDERSTAND BREAST CANCER TREATMENTS

Here are some of the breast cancer treatments in use in Canada today:

• *Lumpectomy*
This surgery, which is also called a partial mastectomy, wide excision, segmental mastectomy and quadrantectomy, removes the lump and part of the surrounding tissue. Benign tumors are treated by lumpectomy alone, but when a tumor is malignant, surgery also includes the removal of the lymph nodes from the armpit area. This is usually followed by radiation and sometimes chemotherapy.

• *Modified Radical Mastectomy*
This surgery involves removal of the breast and underarm lymph nodes.

• *Radical Mastectomy*
The removal of the breast along with underarm lymph nodes and the muscles of the chest wall is performed less often today.

• *Radiation Therapy*
High energy X rays are used to kill cancer cells and shrink tumors. It is believed that when used in conjunction with a lumpectomy, the success rate of this treatment is comparable to that of a mastectomy.

• *Chemotherapy*
The administration of drugs given to kill cancer cells that have shed from the original tumor and travelled to other parts of the body.

• *Hormone Therapy*
Some of the cells that form malignant tumors are stimulated by estrogen, a hormone that passes through the blood. If a breast tumor has an estrogen receptive cell, patients may be given an estrogen blocker such as the controversial drug tamoxifen. (See Questions, Controversy and Debate below). Familiarize yourself with the debate, then discuss with your doctor whether or not this is the drug for you.

QUESTIONS, CONTROVERSY AND DEBATE

WHAT THE EXPERTS SAY: THE DEBATE ABOUT TAMOXIFEN

Some doctors believe tamoxifen is a wonder drug that will save millions of lives. Others say it simply substitutes one disease for another. The drug definitely results in shrinkage of breast tumors, and it's involved in a Canadian trial of high-risk women to determine if it can even prevent breast cancer. So why the controversy?

When data suggested that patients on tamoxifen had almost a threefold increase in chances of developing endometrial cancer, the drug was suspended by law for a time.

However, Dr. Lavina Lickley, chief of surgery at Women's College Hospital, stands firm on her commitment to the drug. She is using it for WCH's Breast Cancer Prevention Trial on high-risk women who have not yet developed the disease. As principal investigator for the study, she believes the potential benefits of the drug outweigh the potential risks. "It's the single best drug for breast cancer," says Dr. Lickley, explaining that it helps improve patients' chances for survival.

But while some oncologists agree with her, others feel that the drug shouldn't be given to high-risk patients who have no evidence of breast cancer: "It's a matter of philosophy," she says of the drug's associated risks. "Everyone has to answer for themselves. But some people feel that no risk (at all) is acceptable."

The controversy centres around tamoxifen's association with an increased risk of a patient's developing endometrial cancer. "This is definitely a risk," she says. "But the prognosis is much better and more predictable. If you had to choose a cancer to get, you'd choose endometrial over breast."

Dr. Adrianne Fugh-Berman, a Washington-based general practitioner who has continuously opposed the U.S. Tamoxifen Prevention Trials, takes the opposite view. In Toronto in the summer of 1994 at a workshop sponsored by the Alliance of Breast Cancer Survivors, she cautioned that the drug merely substitutes one disease for another and in doing so is just not good medicine for healthy patients. Moreover, she and other doctors report that the type of endometrial cancers associated with this drug are particularly aggressive.

Tamoxifen was developed about 30 years ago as a contraceptive but failed miserably in this capacity. Research then showed it to be an anti-estrogen on breast tissue. (Some breast cancer tumors are hormone-receptor positive and these tumors benefit from the drug.) "It appears to work in part by attaching to the estrogen receptor," explains Dr. Lickley. It also appears to promote anti-growth factors and suppress-growth factors. The fact that it seems to keep new cancers from developing in the other healthy breasts of breast cancer patients is the reason that it is being further explored as a possible preventative against breast cancer. Even if it is an effective cancer treatment, few patients or doctors are prepared to call it a miracle drug. Dr. Lickley admits that she doesn't know whether or not the drug will make a good prophylactic. "But I do know it's the only drug that currently has promise," she says. Tamoxifen is being taken by approximately 100,000 breast cancer patients in North America. Says Dr. Lickley: "It's very well tolerated."

Beyond the breast cancer front, the drug appears to maintain bone density in postmenopausal women and reduce the risk of cardiac events. "Originally, everyone expected that as an anti-estrogen, tamoxifen would give you worse bones and heart. But to everyone's surprise, it seems good for both," says Dr. Lickley. Some people report that the drug increases libido, too.

There are side effects, however: hot flashes, blood clots, depression, nausea, eye problems and loss of memory, to name a few. And there are the documented cancer risks plus the fact that tamoxifen is most effective on post menopausal women.

AN EXPERT'S OPINION: BREAST RECONSTRUCTION IS AN OPTION, BUT IT'S NOT FOR EVERYONE

When Dr. John Semple talks about breast reconstruction being an option for women who've had a mastectomy, he likes to underscore that word: *Option.*

For some women, he says, the choice is easy: a breast prosthesis that can be worn for balance and the desired visual effect. For others, the choice is more difficult and more painful: surgery.

Down this road there are three further choices: removal of the other breast (some women choose this prophylactic route because, in part, it's a good bet against a second occurrence of breast cancer); an implant (despite the recent publicity, they are still a choice for many women); and, Dr. Semple's specialty, reconstruction of the breast that was removed.

The Women's College Hospital plastic surgeon uses the patient's own tissue if at all possible. The result is no rejection problems, a low complication rate of less than 5 percent, and a guarantee of no recurring cancer in the reconstructed breast since the tissue it's made from is not breast tissue. The tissue (the skin, fat and small amount of muscle) comes from what's discarded after a tummy tuck, Dr. Semple says. Nipples can also be fashioned from tissue or tattooed on.

At Women's College Hospital, the operation is often done at the same time as the mastectomy: "The result of this is that the patient doesn't have to go through the whole grieving process of losing one's breast," Dr. Semple says. Neither does she have to endure more than one operation.

The technique used is complex. Called the transverse rectus abdominus muscle (TRAM) flap, the operation is performed by a team of two surgeons and takes a minimum of two hours. In the United States, the procedure would cost between $15,000 and $20,000. In Canada, medicare covers costs up to $10,000 to $15,000.

Breast reconstruction is being done much more than it used to be. One reason is that many women who've had a mastectomy experience a body-image crisis: with this operation, they get a breast back and a tummy tuck, though they have to live with a large horizontal scar across their abdomen.

Some women choose not to undergo reconstruction surgery, particularly women who've already had a mastectomy and are ready to get on with their lives, even if it means living with only one breast. And since chemotherapy and radiation often follow surgery for breast cancer patients in Canada, the idea of reconstruction surgery around the same time may strike some women as just too much to cope with at once. While the procedure can be performed by most plastic surgeons at most major hospitals in Canada, Dr. Semple feels that one reason more women don't choose it is that they don't know about it. "It also has to be appropriate from the operating surgeon or oncologist's point of view. We feel it should not interfere with a person's treatment," he says.

Breast reconstruction can still be performed months or years after a mastectomy. But Dr. Semple cautions that not everyone is a suitable candidate for the surgery: women must be otherwise well, and nonsmokers. Both surgeon and patient have to agree that reconstruction is a reasonable way to go, he adds.

Your Prescription for Breast Health

1. Do BSE monthly.
2. Have a clinical exam done by a physician annually.
3. Have a mammogram every year or two after age 50. Discuss with your doctor your risk profile to determine whether or not you need a mammogram before the age of 50.
4. Report any breast lumps, changes or thickening to your doctor immediately.

Darlene Betteley – your body is your house

Darlene Betteley had one 38D breast left after her mastectomy eight years ago. Following her surgery, she tried a variety of prostheses and found nothing that worked well enough for her. "I was not a happy camper," Betteley told me. "I did not like myself. I was not content with my body image. When I undressed at night and looked in the mirror, I was unhappy. I was dealing with one, and none!"

Betteley chose to have her one remaining breast removed. Her reason was not solely prophylactic (though that was a worry, she admits). She chose this alternative because she felt that her remaining large breast made everything from exercising to dressing well extremely difficult.

After having the second mastectomy, the Kitchener, Ontario, woman performed many hours of volunteer work for her local Reach for Recovery program, a group of breast cancer survivors that helps new breast cancer patients. Then something unusual happened: Betteley received a call from her convenor who told her that the society had decided that she should stop volunteering for the Reach to Recovery breast cancer program because of her decision not to wear any prosthesis.

Betteley resigned, but her daughter Cathy Caron wrote the society, chastising them for their judgemental and discriminatory policy. We've always been told that cancer can be beaten, Betteley told me, but the message she was hearing was that cancer must be hidden. After her local newspaper got wind of the incident, Betteley was reinstated as a volunteer and has since received several public apologies for the shortsightedness of the society. "Life is health after cancer," Betteley told me. "Your body is your house. If you're going to have something done, get all the quotes in and decide for yourself. I've certainly learned to use the word *lobby* as a result of this experience."

Penny Robertshaw – sharing her experience with other women

A mastectomy in 1992 changed Penny Robertshaw's life. The Edmonton breast cancer survivor discovered a desperate need to share survivor stories with women under the age of 40: "I've made it a personal priority to share what happened to me with young women in hospitals," Robertshaw told me. "I tell them, 'I went through what you went through and I am still here.' It's a message of hope."

To show others and herself that she faced up to breast cancer, Robertshaw recorded her personal journey with photographs. She took pictures of herself from her biopsy right through to her mastectomy. Then, when she heard about the Survivors in Search of a Voice art project, she contacted Edmonton artist Jane Ash Poitras and asked that Poitras include her in her multimedia work in progress which was to be both a monument to breast cancer survivors and a memorial to those who'd died.

Robertshaw took her photographs to Ash Poitras. Then she took off her top to show the artist her scar. "The way my scar is, I can see my heart beating," Robertshaw says. "This means a lot to me, so I showed it to Jane. I think my scar is beautiful and unique and I wanted to show Jane that this is what it is really like to have cancer."

Ash Poitras then took her own photo of Robertshaw's mastectomy. She incorporated it into the piece she made for the art show, which toured cross-country. Robertshaw is delighted to share her scar with the rest of Canada. The surgery changed her whole life, she says. "I have decided to become a risk taker and I never was. I decided to start living some of my dreams. All across the country I find a sisterhood with women and it isn't just breast cancer. I hear these women saying, 'I am the most important person now.' Maybe I too am a slow learner. I celebrate every day, now."

PART THREE

Your guide to breast cancer resources

Where to Look for More Information, Support, Services and Self-Help About Breast Cancer

ORGANIZATIONS

The Canadian breast cancer network is vast. There are many organizations, too many to compile a comprehensive list. The following selection offers information and access to support groups, counselling and workshops.

Breast Clinic, British Columbia Women's Hospital, British Columbia's Women's Hospital and Health Centre, 4500 Oak St., Vancouver, British Columbia V5H 3N1 (604) 875-2424.

Vancouver Hospital & Health Sciences Centre, 855 W. 12th Ave., Vancouver, British Columbia V5Z 1M9 (604) 875-5000.

Canadian Breast Cancer Network, PO Box 45115, 2482 Yonge St., Toronto, Ontario M4P 2H0 (905) 731-6821.

Canadian Breast Cancer Foundation, 790 Bay St., Ste. 1000, Toronto, Ontario M5G 1N8 (416) 596-6773.

National Cancer Institute of Canada, 10 Alcorn Ave., Ste. 200, Toronto, Ontario M4V 3B1 (416) 961-7223.

Ontario Cancer Institute/Princess Margaret Hospital, 610 University Ave., Toronto, Ontario M5G 2M9 (416) 924-0671.

Willow, 785 Queen St. East, Toronto, Ontario M4M 1H5 (416) 778-5000.

Canadian Cancer Society, National Office, 10 Alcorn Ave., Ste. 200, Toronto, Ontario M4V 3B1 (416) 961-7223. Information lines: Ontario 1-800-263-6750; British Columbia 1-800-663-4242; Quebec 1-514-255-5151.

Bayview Support Network, Toronto Bayview Cancer Centre, 2075 Bayview Ave., North York, Ontario M4N 3M5 (416) 480-6898.

Breast Cancer Action Support and Resource Centre, Billings Bridge, PO Box 39041, Ottawa, Ontario K1H 1A1 (613) 736-5921.

Burlington Breast Cancer Support Services Inc., Burlington Mall, 2nd F., 777 Guelph Line, Burlington, Ontario L7R 3N2 (905) 634-2333.

Cancer Information Services, (905) 387-1153; 1-800-263-6750.

Ontario Breast Screening Program; for information on current screening sites, call (416) 946-4450.

The Henrietta Banting Breast Centre, Women's College Hospital, 60 Grosvenor St., Toronto, Ontario M5S 1B6 (416) 323-6225.

Wellspring, 81 Wellesley St. E., Toronto, Ontario M4Y 1H6 (416) 961-1928.

Breast Cancer Action Montreal, 257 Villeneuve West, Ste. 5, Montreal, Quebec H2V 2R2 (514) 276-4575.

The National Breast Cancer Fund, PO Box 122, 169 The Donway West, Don Mills, Ontario M3C 2R6 (416) 544-8487.

PROSTHESIS/FASHION/BEAUTY

The Canadian Cosmetic, Toiletry and Fragrance Association's Look Good ... Feel Better. A free national program for cancer patients to learn beauty techniques that camouflage the side effects of treatment while boosting self-esteem. Bilingual services from 9 a.m. to 5 p.m., weekdays. 1-800-914-5665.

Softee Comfort Form: Post-surgery garments by Ladies First Inc., distributed by Ortho Active Appliances Ltd., 103-250 Schoolhouse St., Coquitlam, British Columbia V3K 6V7 (604) 520-3414; 1-800-663-1254. Montreal, (514) 363-3029; 1-800-363-3029; Toronto, (416) 466-9665; 1-800-361-5241.

Linda Lundstrom Limited mastectomy fashion, 1-800-665-4632.

Newsletters

Breast Cancer News, Alliance of Breast Cancer Survivors, 20 Eglinton Ave. W., Box 2035, Toronto, Ontario M4R 1K8 (416) 487-9899.
Cancer Connection, Ottawa Regional Cancer Clinic, 190 Melrose Ave., Ottawa, Ontario K1Y 4K7.

Ontario Breast Cancer Network Newsletter, BBCSS, Burlington Mall, 777 Guelph Line, Burlington, Ontario L7R 1B1.

Women and Breast Cancer. A newsletter. New Brunswick Advisory Council on the Status of Women, 95, rue Foundry St., Ste. 207, Moncton, New Brunswick E1C 5H7 (506) 856-3252; 1-800-332-3087.

Books/Reports

Some of the following are books with a medical focus, while others are written by survivors from a more personal perspective. Each provides an important picture of breast cancer today.

Picasso's Woman, Rosalind MacPhee (Douglas & McIntyre, 1994).

Breast Cancer: Unanswered Questions, a report from Health and Welfare (Queen's Printer, 1992).

Dr. Susan Love's Breast Book, 2nd ed., Dr. Susan Love (Addison-Wesley, 1995).

Getting Better – Conversations With Myself and Other Friends While Healing From Breast Cancer, Anne Hargroove (Compacare Publisher, 1988).

If It Runs in Your Family – Breast Cancer Reducing Your Risk, Mary Dan Eades (Bantam, 1991).

My Breast – One Woman's Cancer Story, Joyce Wadler (Addison Wesley, 1992).

Side By Side: A Workbook for Breast Cancer Caregivers, Monica Roberts. Available through the Canadian Breast Cancer Foundation, Ontario Chapter (416) 596-6773.

We're All in This Together: Families Facing Breast Cancer, Irene Virag (Andrews and McMeel, 1995).

What You Need to Know About Breast Cancer, booklet by the Burlington Breast Cancer Support Services, Inc., Burlington Mall, 777 Guelph Line, Burlington, Ontario L7R 3N2.

Audios/Videos

A New Breast Self-Examination Video, the Ontario Cancer Institute/Princess Margaret Hospital. Available to organizations and educators, in English or French, for a nominal charge.

Cancer Confidence and You, a video and workbook, and other material available from Look Good . . . Feel Better, CCTFA Foundation, 5090 Explorer Drive, Ste. 510, Mississauga, Ontario L4W 4T9.

Up Front – Sex and Post Mastectomy Woman, Linda Dackman (Viking, 1990). Addresses a subject many try to avoid.

Voices in the Night: A Cancer Companion, Joy S. McDiarmid, Dawn M. Holman and the Recovery Resource Centre, producers. Call 1-800-268-0009. Other audiotapes available: Early Breast Cancer, Diagnosis and Questions and Choices.

CHAPTER 7

SMOKING: QUIT OR FACE THE CONSEQUENCES

Why is this a women's health issue? Every 35 minutes, a Canadian woman dies as a result of smoking. And lung cancer recently replaced breast cancer as the number-one cancer killer of Canadian women.

What you can do for yourself: Make up your mind to quit and do it. There are lots of new therapies and programs to help you stop smoking.

SMOKING: THE MOST ADDICTIVE HABIT IN THE WORLD

Nicotine is the most addictive chemical substance in the world and cigarette smoking is the most difficult drug habit to break. Its addictiveness is so potent that 85 percent of smokers are not ready to commit to stopping. And when smokers do make up their minds to stop, it typically takes five to ten years until they go for a full year without a cigarette.

PART ONE

The facts: why smoking is an urgent women's health issue

More Canadian women than men smoke today, and the illness and death statistics reflect this tragic fact. Female death rates from lung cancer have quadrupled since the late sixties. In contrast, the incidence of lung cancer among men under the age of 50 has stablized over the last few years.

One in six smokers, male and female, will die of lung cancer. Every day, 42 Canadian women – one every 35 minutes – dies as a result of smoking, either from heart disease, cancer or lung disease. In the late sixties, the lung cancer rate was six per 100,000 women; in 1994, it was 24 per 100,000. That translated into 5,600 Canadian women who died of lung cancer in 1994. Lung cancer has now surpassed breast cancer as the number-one cancer killer of Canadian women (in 1994, 5,400 women died of breast cancer).

WOMEN SMOKE FOR DIFFERENT REASONS THAN MEN

Tobacco is the drug of choice for a lot of people, regardless of gender. But unlike men, for whom that first cigarette is often equal to that first beer in a kind of rite-of-passage experience, women use tobacco for different, often surprising, reasons. Dr. Cathy Cervin, a family physician in Dalhousie University's family medicine department, explains that many women use smoking as a tool to try to manage their stress, anger, loneliness, shyness or discomfort.

Studies done by Dr. Helen Batty at Toronto's Women's College Hospital also show that busy working women use smoking as a way to create a break for themselves: a cigarette break gives them permission to stop what they're doing to grab some time for themselves. "If you want to legitimize taking five minutes off, you have a cigarette. If you're at home with small children, sitting down with a cigarette is a way of escaping," Batty says. "You can legitimately say to your kids, 'Stay away....I have a lighted cigarette here.'" Perhaps that's why, after working all day, then coming home to the kids, doing chores and making dinner, women savour that after-dinner cigarette so much.

Dr. Cervin has run two smoking-cessation groups for women. During these sessions, Dr. Cervin learned about the various ways women perceive smoking. "The thing that struck me the most was that women seem to develop a relationship with their cigarette," Dr. Cervin says. "The words they used were 'best buddy' or 'your cigarette is there for you.' It was a comfort, they felt an attachment to it. For some women, giving up smoking is akin to the loss of a close relationship."

Other women participating in Dr. Cervin's smoking-cessation groups said they smoked as an expression of rebellion, as excitement, as an expression of risk taking or a way of expressing a nonconformist side of themselves. Some reported that when they felt out of control or angry, they would smoke. "There's also the issue of weight gain," adds Cervin. "Young women start smoking to control their weight, and the thought of gaining is an absolute barrier to quitting."

Feeling better about the way they look is another reason women smoke. "Women tend to wear a cigarette," says Dr. Gerry Brosky, a Nova Scotia physician and vice president of the Canadian Council on Smoking and Health. "Women also use cigarettes to bond with other smokers; they use cigarettes as comfort."

Another reason women smoke: to help them cope with a sense of powerlessness in the workplace. Dr. Helen Batty speculates that pink-collar women workers may use nicotine to help them "keep calm and keep their temper." She explains: "Let's say someone is given an unreasonable demand by their superior. They cope by taking five minutes to have a cigarette, then they keep their job by coming back and doing what was asked. It helps women to maintain the expectations society has of them." And in this day of cutbacks and layoffs, when toeing the line may be crucial to keeping your job, cigarette-smoking must relieve job-uncertainty stress for thousands of Canadian women.

Women also use tobacco to cope with stressful personal situations, including abusive relationships or depression. Caryn Lerman, a psychologist at Georgetown University, Washington, D.C., told USA Today that there's a higher rate of depression among smokers than nonsmokers and that a lot of this kind of smoking is for "self-medicating – to make themselves feel better." There are ongoing Canadian studies on this issue, too.

Smoking is a Young Women's Habit

Eighty percent of women smokers begin smoking while they're in their teens, and two out of five women in their twenties smoke.

Dr. Frances Shepherd, an oncologist, professor of medicine at the University of Toronto and mother of a twenty-something daughter, speculates that weight control has a lot to do with the reason teen women smoke. "Perhaps we should start appreciating the more full-bodied woman as opposed to the skinny model type," she said at a Toronto Hospital educational forum on women and smoking.

In their report Evening the Odds: Tobacco, Physical Activity and Adolescent Women, the Canadian Association for the Advancement of Women and Sport and Physical Activity (CAAWS) examined the disastrous effects of smoking on Canadian female adolescents. They found that when young women pick up the tobacco habit they drop out of physical activity. CAAWS executive director Marg McGregor notes that sport and physical activity can provide the very benefits young women think they are getting from smoking – sensible weight management, independence, status with peers, relaxation, a chance to make or meet friends and, above all, a more positive sense of self-esteem.

THE BAD NEWS ABOUT SMOKING: A LONG LIST OF MINUSES

With the exception of a few head-in-the-sand tobacco industry spokespersons, no one disputes that smoking is inextricably linked with illness and death. The evidence is overwhelming. Consider the following:

1. One in six smokers, male and female, will die of lung cancer: 5,600 Canadian women died of lung cancer in 1994.

2. Women who smoke run a higher risk of other cancers, too. Examples: cervical, pancreatic, bladder and throat cancers.

3. Smokers run a higher risk of having heart attacks, hardening of the arteries (atherosclerosis) and strokes.

4. Women smokers who use birth control pills are ten to 20 times more likely to have heart disease or stroke than nonsmokers.

5. Smokers are more likely to have emphysema, colds, bronchitis and pneumonia.

6. Smoking can cause lower levels of estrogen in premenopausal women. And it wipes out the benefits of estrogen therapy in postmenopausal women.

7. Smoking may make some women less able to get pregnant.

8. The chemicals in cigarette smoke can travel from a mother's blood to the blood of her developing baby resulting in a higher risk of miscarriage, stillbirth, premature birth and lower birth weight.

9. Secondhand smoke increases the risk of heart disease, lung cancer, cancer of the cervix and childhood bronchitis among nonsmokers. And it's linked to several chronic illnesses in children.

10. Other reports link smoking near babies with an increased risk of Sudden Infant Death Syndrome (SIDS). (Results of an American study of women who smoked during pregnancy indicated related deaths from both SIDS and miscarriages or stillbirths.)

11. Some studies show that smoking is associated with a decline in physical function in women 50 and older.

12. Research indicates that some women inherit genes that slow their ability to cleanse their body of the toxins found in cigarette smoke that are linked to breast cancer.

THE GOOD NEWS ABOUT SMOKING

The benefits of stopping smoking are enormous. Here are some of them, courtesy of the Heart and Stroke Foundation of Canada:

1. Within a few hours of quitting, your body starts getting healthier. Within a few days, you'll be able to do more exercise, and your sense of taste and smell should improve.

2. One year after you quit smoking, your odds for having heart disease are halved.

3. The longer you are smoke-free, the more your odds of getting cancer decrease. For example, your risk of developing lung cancer is reduced by 50 to 70 percent after ten years.

4. Your air quality and the air quality of your family improves at once.

5. After 15 smoke-free years, life expectancy is similar to that of someone who never smoked.

6. The benefits listed above apply if you quit, no matter what your age.

So it's never too late to quit.

LUNG CANCER: AN UP-TO-DATE REPORT ABOUT SMOKING'S NUMBER-ONE KILLER

The Bad News: A lung cancer diagnosis often comes too late.

In terms of lung cancer, says oncologist Dr. Frances Shepherd, "women are going in the wrong direction." Lung cancer cases have skyrocketed and incidences of women contracting the disease in their twenties, thirties and forties are more prevalent.

There are two types of lung cancer, small cell and non-small cell. Small-cell lung cancer tumors grow rapidly: on average, small-cell tumors double in size every three weeks. Only one-third of patients have localized disease in the chest, which means that by the time this cancer is found it has often spread to other parts of the body.

Of the non-small cell types, adenocarcinoma (one of the subtypes of non-small cell lung cancer) is on the increase in women, says Dr. Shepherd. "And unfortunately, it often presents with involvement of the organs outside the lungs, at a time when it's not curative." And non-small cell lung cancer is a lethal killer: only 15 percent of people who develop it survive five years or more.

More bad news: Chest X ray screening isn't that effective, says Dr. Shepherd. "It doesn't save lives and it doesn't really pick up more cancers at a stage at which they can be cured." Ditto for sputum analysis.

The Good News: This is one cancer you can prevent.

"Probably 90 percent or more of lung cancers are preventable by stopping smoking," says Dr. Shepherd.

Stopping Smoking: What the Experts Say

When it comes to helping women quit, Dr. Cathy Cervin believes we need to use *anything* that works.

The arsenal at smokers' disposal includes stop-smoking programs (some of them women-centred), educational courses and materials from provincial lung associations, books, pamphlets, hypnosis and acupuncture. Young Nova Scotian women participating in a focus group said they wanted hard-hitting ads that "would grab them by the throat."

Nicotine replacement therapy is highly effective. Studies show and experts claim that the approach at least doubles and sometimes triples the average success rate for stopping. There are now three different transdermal patches on the market, all equally successful.

New thinking on how to get people to stop smoking takes into account that typically, people pass through different stages on their way to quitting, everything from precontemplation to preparation. This process may take months and is vastly different from yesterday's I'm-quitting-tomorrow approach. "Previously you challenged the person to stop," says Nova Scotia's Dr. Gerry Brosky. "Today the emphasis includes talking to people who are not quite ready to stop about the things they enjoy about their smoking and the not-so-good things about it. That final decision to do something about it is actually quite personal. You can't really instil that in them."

Dr. Brosky is one of several physicians across the country trying to motivate his colleagues to become more proactive in getting patients to stop smoking. Dr. Brosky employs a sticker-labelling system that reminds him, via each patient's chart, who is a nonsmoker, who is a smoker and who is a previous smoker. "This sticker system calls attention to the file for the physician," Dr. Brosky says. "It's good because studies have shown that if you train physicians to counsel, they'll do it – but they tend not to remember to do it enough. Reminding is a critical part of applying the knowledge, and the stickers help to remind."

Dr. Fred Bass of the British Columbia Medical Association has spent years trying to convince the province's doctors that helping their patients to stop smoking should be a priority. Now almost one-quarter of the province's family physicians participate in a program spearheaded by Dr. Bass; through closer monitoring of their patients, these physicians believe they can help them work towards breaking the habit. "Stopping smoking is a chronic condition," says Dr. Bass, who is chair of the tobacco and illness committee of the British Columbia Medical Association's Council of Health Promotion. "It takes five to ten years for the typical smoker to finally get to a year without a puff on a cigarette." A survey on the subject revealed that patients want their doctors to prescribe a smoking-cessation program. Dr. Bass urges family doctors to encourage smokers who indicate a desire to stop to work towards final cessation.

PART TWO

Your guide to smoke-free health

TIPS TO STOP SMOKING

- Know why you smoke before you quit. Some people smoke for one reason, others for several. Know your reason and you'll be able to substitute another activity for it more easily. Smoking is built into one's social life, one's physiology, one's coping mechanisms, notes Dr. Brosky. "It's difficult to learn to live without it."
- If you smoke for stimulation (some people report that smoking gives them a physical lift), try to substitute a pick-me-upper such as a cool shower or a brisk walk.
- If you smoke for pleasure, for that relaxed take-a-break sensation that overcomes you occasionally, try finding a healthy substitute (maybe a catnap, daydreaming, a cup of special tea or ten minutes of your favourite music) that you can connect with a feel-good moment.
- If you smoke for stress, try to define the moment you want to reach for that cigarette and substitute deep-breathing exercises, a quick game of squash or a leisurely walk.
- If you smoke to satisfy a craving, try to remember the times you don't crave cigarettes – when you have a sore throat, for instance. The next time you feel you've lost your taste for cigarettes, ride the wave and quit cold turkey.
- If you smoke out of habit, try hard to do activities other than the ones you associate with smoking. For example, if you smoke in bed (which is a fire hazard, anyway) while reading, make sure you read elsewhere and not in bed; if you smoke in your car while driving, switch to public transit or at least try singing when the radio's on; if you smoke while watching television in the living room, take up knitting or crocheting; if you smoke every time you pick up the phone, move your cigarettes and ashtray from the room the phone's in and substitute a doodle pad and pen.

Try asking yourself, "Do I really want this cigarette?" before you light one out of habit. You may be surprised at the ones you actually don't want.

- If you quit cold turkey, the most important thing is to have strategies available to help you handle the urge to smoke when it comes. Plan ahead so the urge doesn't take you over.
- If you mean to quit gradually, begin to decrease the number of cigarettes you smoke two weeks prior to your target quitting day. Each day, carry no more cigarettes than the number you've allowed yourself to smoke that day. While you're weaning yourself from cigarettes, be sure to replace the smoking with other activities. On the day you finally quit, toss out all cigarettes, matches and ashtrays.
- Increase the use of your hands: play cards, knit, garden, do crossword puzzles.
- Don't forget about healthy oral substitutes: carrot sticks, apples, sunflower seeds, licorice roots and chewing gum, for example.
- If you got pleasure out of lighting your cigarette, light candles and incense daily. Savour the moment, the flame and the fragrance.
- Increase your physical activity as you begin to cut down or when you quit cold turkey.
- Avoid, for the time being, situations (and even people) with which you associate smoking: for instance, long dinner parties where people linger and smoke, or the outdoor luncheon patio at the office where the smokers like to congregate.
- Keep in mind the advantages of not smoking – the good health, the money saved, the fresher air.
- Don't be rough on yourself if you don't succeed your first go-round. Dr. Gerry Brosky reports that people go through four to seven attempts at stopping smoking before they learn to live without cigarettes.
- Welcome encouragement and support from friends, family and organizations: it's not easy to stop smoking. Women need individual support, group support and support from friends and family, Dr. Cathy Cervin says. Don't be afraid to accept it.

For Parents Only: A Guide to Nonsmoking for the Family

1. Consider the benefits of being a role model: young women whose parents or older siblings smoke are several times more likely to begin than children of non-smoking families. So if you're a parent, quit.
2. If you find your daughter smoking, tell her gently how you feel about the habit.

Too often, parents who smoke belittle their smoking children with hostile remarks such as, "You should know better. Can't you see how hard it is for me to quit!" Better to tell her you love her but are concerned about her health.

3. Don't be a partner to your daughter's tobacco habit: if she wants money for cigarettes, don't give it to her. Set strict no-smoking rules in your home.

4. Try to bring the smoking issue out in conversation even before your daughter is at the experimental age of nine to 13. The best time to talk to your daughter is long before you find her with cigarettes, or smell it on her clothes.

5. Remember, you're a parent not a police officer. You can voice your concern, even your disapproval, and you can set limits, but sometimes nothing – not even nagging – will make your daughter break the habit. Your teen daughter is beginning to make her own choices and you may not be able to control her decisions.

Loretta Favari – trying to quit is like a roller coaster ride

Any woman who has smoked, tried to quit, then smoked again can identify with Loretta Favari's frustration. The 33-year-old started smoking when she was 16. Her numerous attempts to quit have taught her a lot about her particular triggers. "It's like a roller coaster," Favari says. "You quit two years and you think you have beaten it, then something happens and it triggers it. You think, 'Oh, one won't hurt!' But it does and you start the whole ball rolling again."

Emotional stresses usually trigger her regressions, Favari says. When a roommate left a couple of years ago, she felt a temporary absence in her life. So when she returned home from work each evening, she'd light up to fill the empty space. "I think women have more of an emotional attachment to cigarettes," Favari muses. "When they quit, it's a little like losing a best friend." Socializing with women is a strong trigger for Favari. "Maybe it's a trigger from my past when we used to get together as teen girls and talk and smoke. There were all those pleasurable moments."

What Favari has learned from stopping and starting several times over is the necessity to replace those "pleasurable moments" with other weed-free activities. "One question I've been asking myself is, 'Are there things in my life I can do differently?' I am now trying yoga and tai chi," says the Toronto woman. "I thought if I could put energy into them they could change my life." She has become a member of her local Y and makes sure yoga and tai chi are regular "appointments" in her daybook.

It has taken Favari some time to understand her addiction, but she plans on applying what she's learned to quitting for good this time: "Smoking is a physical addiction. It's also something you do more than eating, if you think about it. It's a habit, an emotional attachment, and when you repeat it 25 times a day, that's pretty powerful."

Joining a smoking support program has made her realize she can't quit by herself. Talking about smoking with other smokers, she believes, is "fundamental" to her quitting. She now realizes that very few people can quit on their first try. But she vows she will stop: "After all, I now know what it is like to be a non-smoker," she says. "I know I can live through quitting." Unfortunately, she has also set up a habit of stopping and starting again. "Now my goal is to stop and get past that two-year record of not smoking."

PROFILE

Donna Walters – "I don't even think about it anymore."

It's been 13 smoke-free years for Donna Walters, after smoking for close to a decade. She was in her late twenties when she made the decision: "I was trying to get into shape and starting to take care of myself. So I guess I was just ready to give it up." Though she had never tried quitting before, she had obviously thought about it for a long time. "It got to the point where I was smoking a pack a day at work. Those were the days you could smoke at your desk. I found I was nervous, jittery, full of tension. I would get a coffee first thing in the morning and have a cigarette with it. I began to notice that my hands quivered for a few hours after. I was getting a little wheezy. It was just affecting how I was performing and feeling."

Her interest in feeling better led her to her local Y-Smoke program (available in Y's across Canada) with its emphasis on fitness, nutrition and stress management techniques. "Quitting was terrible," she recalls. But she complied with the program, which teaches you to monitor your intake by documenting it in a diary, identify your triggers and cut back on the number of cigarettes you smoke. The first step, she says, was to identify which cigarettes she really didn't want: "For me, they were the ones in the middle of the day. If there was nothing going on, I would light up – and for no reason." Eventually, when she got down to two low-tar, low-nicotine cigarettes per day, she decided to give up smoking entirely: "It was ridiculous. It wasn't my usual brand and it tasted terrible – like sucking air."

By the end of the ten-week program, Walters had launched herself into a new lifestyle in which better eating habits and regular exercise had replaced smoking. "Today, I don't even think about it anymore," she says. Her advice to other women who want to quit: "Your personal health is one of the few things you can have some control over. Ask yourself how you can live more healthily. And start thinking about where your smoke is going and who else it might be affecting."

PART THREE

Your guide to stop-smoking resources

ORGANIZATIONS

Contact any of the following groups for information, education and help in locating your nearest stop-smoking support group.

British Columbia Medical Association, 1665 W. Broadway, Ste. 115, Vancouver, British Columbia V6J 5A4 (604) 736-5551.

Action On Smoking and Health, PO Box 4500, 11402 University Ave., 3rd Flr., Edmonton, Alberta T6E 6K2 (403) 492-2344.

Women's Health Clinic, 419 Graham Ave., 3rd Flr., Winnipeg, Manitoba R3C 0M3 (204) 947-1517; TTY (204) 956-0385.

Allergy/Asthma Information Association, 30 Eglinton Ave. W., Ste. 750, Mississauga, Ontario L5R 3E7 (905) 712-2242.

Asthma Society of Canada, 130 Bridgeland Ave., Ste. 425, Toronto, Ontario M6A 1Z4 (416) 787-4050.

Canadian Network on Women and Tobacco (CAN-WAT), c/o Canadian Council on Smoking and Health, 1202–170 Laurier Ave. W., Ottawa, Ontario

K1P 5V5 (613) 567-3050; 1-800-267-5234. Publication: *Taking Control: An Action Handbook on Women and Tobacco* (Canadian Council on Smoking and Health, 1989).

Canadian Cancer Society, 10 Alcorn Ave., Ste. 200, Toronto, Ontario M4V 3B1 (416) 961-7223. Provincial Chapters: British Columbia/Yukon Territory (604) 872-4400; Alberta/Northwest Territories (403) 228-4487; Saskatchewan (306) 757-4260; Manitoba (204) 774-7483; Ontario (416) 488-5400; Quebec (514) 255-5151; New Brunswick (506) 634-6272; Nova Scotia (902) 423-6183; Prince Edward Island (902) 566-4007; Newfoundland (709) 753-6520.

Canadian Council on Smoking and Health, 1000–170 Laurier Ave. W., Ottawa, Ontario K1P 5V5 (613) 567-3050; 1-800-267-5234.

The Tobacco Programs Unit, Health Canada, Jeanne Mance Building, Tunney's Pasture, Ottawa, Ontario K1A 1B4 (613) 957-8333. Publications: *Background Paper on Women and Tobacco* (1987, and update, 1990).

JOURNALS/REPORTS

Catching Our Breath: A Journal About Change for Women Who Smoke, Women's Health Clinic, 419 Graham Ave., 3rd Flr., Winnipeg, Manitoba R3C 0M3 (204) 947-1517; TTY (204) 956-0385.

The Report on Women and Smoking, New Brunswick Advisory Council on the Status of Women, 95 Foundry St., Ste. 207, Moncton, New Brunswick E1C 5H7 (506) 856-3252; 1-800-332-3087.

CHAPTER 8

SEXUAL AND REPRODUCTIVE HEALTH: THE BUILDING BLOCKS OF WOMEN'S WELL-BEING

Why is this a women's health issue? Healthy menstrual cycles are essential to women's wellness; thousands of Canadian women suffer from Pelvic Inflammatory Disease and endometriosis; by the year 2000, nearly half the HIV carriers in Canada will be women; and female reproductive cancers can be the most deadly of all cancers.

What you can do for yourself: Take charge of your body by taking care. Learn that in the age of AIDS, contraception and protection must often go hand in hand. And find out about the latest in reproductive cancer-screening tests.

1. MENSTRUAL HEALTH

"I've got my period." Few of us have ever calculated how often we've said that sentence in a lifetime. But a woman's period isn't only a physiological event that happens to her on a regular basis. It's also a frame of reference she uses for measuring other events in her life: "I remember, because it was right before my period," is something any one of us might say. Marking that day on the calendar when your period starts is something every young woman is taught to do.

Our cycles are a natural and important part of our lives, yet menstruation is still burdened with secrecy, shame, taboos and myths. In some cultures, menstruation is associated with being dirty or being sick; in others, washing one's hair during menstruation or visiting one's friends is discouraged. In still others, menstruation is linked to the moon (the Greek word for moon is *mene*) and it's believed that the lunar cycle and menstrual cycle are one.

Even in North America where we're typically more open on the subject, periods may be regarded by some as uncomfortable, messy and inconvenient. When periods are too close together, we worry. When they're heavier than usual, we worry. When we experience breakthrough bleeding, we worry. It's no wonder that generations of women have referred to their monthly periods as "the curse."

What exactly is a period?

That first menstrual period represents a rite of passage by which a female moves into her reproductive years. The normal menstrual cycle is a complex hormonal cycle that works this way:

At the start of the menstrual cycle, the estrogen in the body causes the endometrium (the lining of the uterus) to thicken in order to prepare the uterus for the possibility of fertilization. Around the middle of the menstrual cycle, ovulation (or the release of an egg) occurs. At the same time, there's an increase in the hormone progesterone, which furthers the thickening of the endometrium with fluid so that a fertilized egg can more successfully implant itself. If pregnancy fails to occur, the production of estrogen and progesterone drops and the thickened endometrium, now not required, prepares to shed itself within 14 days of ovulation. Uterine contractions and vascular constriction within the uterine walls help this process by forcing the menstrual discharge out of the uterus and into the vagina .

That cycle, defined from the first day of bleeding to the last day before the next menstrual bleeding, lasts between 25 and 35 days (The average menstrual cycle is about 28 days). The amount of blood lost when the uterine lining is shed varies from woman to woman and from cycle to cycle. But the average is about 60 ml. The blood itself is made up of a combination of cervical mucus, vaginal mucus, blood and cells shed from the uterine lining.

Your period: Should you chart it?

Charting your menstrual cycle is a good way to get a real sense of what's normal for you. By noting the day of each month your period begins, the kind of menstrual activity you notice that month (heavier than usual) and any accompanying symptoms (bloating), you'll also become aware of changes that could signal problems. A menstrual chart will enable you to pick out patterns that might help you plan pregnancies or alleviate symptoms. For instance, if you notice bloating a week before your period usually begins, you can plan to limit your salt intake during that time. Charting your symptoms may also help your doctor diagnose premenstrual tension or PMS.

What's a normal period?

The average period occurs once a month and lasts three to six days. However, each woman has her own personal menstruation profile. Some women experience short periods and few or no symptoms. Other women may retain fluid and gain weight or experience moodiness, breast tenderness and cramping. Your period also depends on the nutrition you take in and the energy you expend: women who have little body fat as a result of either overexercise or an eating disorder like anorexia nervosa may have delayed periods or even no periods. Illness may also affect your menstrual cycle.

What is considered heavy bleeding?

A heavier flow than is normally expected might involve any of the following: more than three to six sanitary pads or tampons a day during the first few days; episodes of flooding; the passing of large or numerous blood clots; a feeling of tiredness; an increasing number of days of bleeding each month, which may signal menorrhagia, a common condition of excessive menstrual bleeding that should be discussed with your doctor.

What is dysmenorrhea?

Dysmenorrhea means painful periods. Cramps are caused by uterine contractions as they work to shed the lining of the endometrium each month, thus giving you your period. Birth control pills often help alleviate the discomfort, as does anti-inflammatory medication. If your pain is severe and occurs with every period, discuss it with your physician. He or she may want to examine you for other conditions, including endometriosis. Lifestyle changes, such as starting a regimen of regular exercise, may help reduce the incidence of severe cramps. Some women report relief after reducing or eliminating their alcohol or caffeine intake.

What is amenorrhea?

Amenorrhea refers to an absence of menstrual periods. It can be caused by many things, from a thyroid imbalance to a fluctuation in estrogen levels. Excessive skinniness (either as a result of anorexia nervosa or overexercising) can also cause one's periods to stop. Treatments may include weight gain, oral contraceptives or hormonal supplements.

Is PMS real?

Since there is no test to diagnose the condition, doctors disagree as to whether or not PMS is real. Some feel that PMS is just a convenient way to make menstruation seem dysfunctional; others believe it's a biochemical hormonal condition deserving more research. Some doctors tell women that their PMS is "all in their heads"; other doctors, believing in the disease model, medicate women with tranquillizers and water pills.

But arguing over whether or not PMS exists is of little value to women who suffer from it. Only an estimated 10 percent of women do not experience some form of discomfort around the time of menstruation. Reported symptoms include breast swelling and tenderness, weight gain and abdominal bloating, mood swings, food cravings, muscle pain, dizziness, fatigue, an improved sex drive, unexplained crying, disruptive sleep patterns, less alcohol tolerance, loss of control and irritability.

However, only an estimated 5 percent of women suffer from incapacitating symptoms that interfere with work or relationships. Doctors now describe this condition as premenstrual dysphoric disorder or PDD.

Help for PMS

Hormonal changes are a constant in women's lives. While your doctor may want to prescribe certain medications to target specific symptoms (a diuretic for water retention or an antidepressant to reduce mood swings, for instance), you may first want to try less invasive so-called natural treatments. Fine-tune your lifestyle in the following ways to reduce or eliminate your discomfort:

- Eat differently. Avoid salty and spicy foods to reduce the bloating and water retention that often accompanies PMS. Natural diuretics include cucumber, parsley and asparagus.
- Sign off caffeine. Caffeine can contribute to breast tenderness (and breast cysts). Slow down your caffeine intake before eliminating it entirely: sudden caffeine withdrawal may cause headaches and sleep disturbances.
- Take a walk. Many women attest to the benefits of exercise: regular aerobic activity can relieve emotional tension, increase the self-esteem that comes from feeling better about your body and result in fewer or milder cramps.
- Be good to yourself. Eat smaller, more frequent meals; avoid alcohol; try some relaxation techniques such as yoga or massage; consider joining a PMS support group; have on hand a larger-size bra and a few pieces of clothing you can comfortably wear during your PMS days.

- Talk to your physician about the possibility of taking Vitamins E and B[6], and evening primrose oil (some women report less bloating and tenderness).
- Make your PMS work for you: feelings of anger and assertiveness can be used to motivate positive actions, particularly if your PMS includes increased energy levels. Go after that bad debt, finish the business plan for your dream business, design your Victorian herb garden.

2. PELVIC INFLAMMATORY DISEASE (PID) AND ENDOMETRIOSIS

Millions of North American women are affected by these two diseases of the pelvic cavity, and their symptoms are often similar: pain or cramping in the abdomen and abnormal periods, or bleeding or spotting between periods are symptoms common to both. However, the two diseases have other identifying symptoms and treatments that are specific to each. Most important, they each have their own support groups.

PID: Pelvic inflammatory disease is an infection or inflammation of a woman's reproductive organs that can affect the uterus, fallopian tubes, ovaries and the tissues around these organs. It's caused by bacteria which can get inside your pelvis through a variety of ways: when certain bacteria-based sexually transmitted diseases (STDs) remain untreated, they can spread higher inside your pelvis. Bacteria can also infiltrate your pelvis through surgical procedures such as abortions and D & Cs (dilation and curettage, a gynecological procedure in which the lining of the uterus is scraped away). Douching can sometimes be the vehicle for bacterial spread, as can IUD (intrauterine device) insertion.

Though symptoms vary widely, they include pelvic and lower back pain, abnormal periods, frequent or painful urination, and unusual vaginal discharge. There may or may not be fever.

Several tests may be required in order to arrive at a definite diagnosis of PID. The doctor may start with a normal pelvic exam; blood tests (to determine whether you're fighting an infection through an elevation of white blood cells) may be ordered, as may an ultrasound test. If all else fails, a surgical procedure known as laparoscopy confirms PID. Treatment includes antibiotics for infection and/or surgery for abscesses. The consequences of PID include infertility, recurring infection and chronic pain. PID increases your risk of ectopic or fallopian pregnancy.

Endometriosis: This occurs when bits of the endometrium (the tissue lining the uterus) travel up the fallopian tubes and implant in other sites in the pelvic cavity (the cervix, bladder, rectum), causing lesions or nodules, usually noncancerous. What causes this to happen is unknown. When the hormones that trigger the uterus's endometrium to bleed monthly also stimulate the misplaced tissues (these tissues, which are parts of the endometrium, try to shed as if they were in the uterus and therefore bleed every month), scarring, inflammation, cysts and pain can occur. The result can be chronic pelvic pain and painful or irregular menstrual cycles. There seems to be a link between endometriosis and infertility. Ultrasound and laparoscopy, and often analysis of biopsy samples, confirm the diagnosis. Treatment may include anti-inflammatory medication, pain medication, hormone therapy or surgery.

3. FROM HERPES TO HIV: THE SOBER TRUTH ABOUT SEXUALLY TRANSMITTED DISEASES (STDs)

Sexually transmitted diseases have always been with us. But in today's world in which sexual permissiveness uneasily co-exists with fatal STDs such as AIDS, women are more vulnerable than ever.

STDs must be included in every young woman's sex education. And any adult woman who is sexually active needs to be aware of STDs and how to best protect herself.

A recent report from the World Health Organization revealed that there are annually at least 333 million new STD cases worldwide; the report further warned that such infections appear to greatly increase the risk of contracting the human immunodeficiency virus or HIV. We must take responsibility for our own protection. Practising safe sex is at the top of the list.

What Exactly is Safe Sex?

Current guidelines for safe sex include the following:
- Safe: Massage, body-to-body rubbing, masturbation, hugging, kissing.
- Possibly Safe: Wet kissing, hand-to-genital contact with latex or rubber glove, vaginal or anal intercourse with a condom, fellatio with a condom, or cunnilingus with a barrier device.
- Possibly Unsafe: Hand-to-genital contact without a latex or rubber glove, cunnilingus without a barrier device.
- Unsafe: Blood contact (including menstrual blood or sharing needles), oral-anal contact, fellatio without a condom, semen in the mouth, vaginal or anal intercourse without a condom.

What Exactly are STDs?

STDs run the gamut from common infections such as vaginitis, often dismissed as merely annoying, to a host of serious STD s that can lead to pregnancy complications, liver damage, cancer and, in the case of AIDS, death.

If you have symptoms that may be STD-related, seek diagnosis and treatment from your family physician, a gynecologist or a community or hospital clinic for sexually transmitted diseases.

Some STD s you should be aware of:

Chlamydia

An STD not unlike gonorrhea. It too affects the cervix and shows its symptoms through discharge, although women sometimes report no symptoms until the disease has spread. But unlike gonorrhea, which is on the decrease, chlamydia is on the increase, particularly in women under the age of 25. Once diagnosed, chlamydia is often treated with antibiotics. Left untreated, however, chlamydia can cause pelvic inflammatory disease (as can gonorrhea) and infertility. Other organs such as the heart, liver or appendix may also be affected.

Herpes

An estimated one in five Canadians carries Herpes simplex, a common virus infection caused by Herpesvirus 1 and Herpesvirus 2. The former commonly causes cold sores around the mouth; the latter causes sores around the genitals. Since about 50 percent of the people who have herpes present symptoms so mild they may not know they have the disease, this STD has had little attention paid to it in recent years. However, the disease is infectious and though outbreaks of its genital blisters come and go, herpes stays with you forever. The virus never leaves the body, even when the acute infection is gone. Ointments and pills such as Acyclovir or Zovirax help many alleviate the symptoms of the disease. (A North American herpes hotline, based in the United States, can be reached by calling 1-800-478-3227.)

Hepatitis

There are several different types of hepatitis. Each type, however, manifests itself as an inflammation of the liver, with accompanying damage or death of liver cells. The viral form, called hepatitis type B, is classified as a sexually transmitted disease and is on the rise. The virus, which some experts feel is more contagious than HIV, is transmitted through mucus-sharing activities that include semen, vaginal fluid and saliva; the virus is also transmitted through contaminated needles. These can include body-piercing and tattooing needles, as well as needles employed in drug use.

Symptoms include fatigue, nausea, diarrhea, vomiting and, in the second stage of the illness, symptoms typical of liver damage – dark urine, jaundice, and a tender and enlarged liver. Though there is currently no cure for hepatitis B, a vaccine is available. If you engage in high-risk sex, have many partners or are a health care worker, talk to your doctor about the possibility of getting the vaccine.

HIV

Anyone can become infected with the human immunodeficiency virus (HIV) that can cause AIDS, or Acquired Immune Deficiency Syndrome. This life-threatening disease of the immune system (the immune system is the body's internal mechanism for fighting infections) is called "acquired" because people contract it as a result of exposure, experience or behaviour rather than through heredity. It is called "immune deficiency" because the virus that causes AIDS infects and can destroy certain white blood cells that help fight disease. And it is called a "syndrome" because there is not just one sign or symptom but a group of signs or symptoms that identifies that someone has AIDS.

Experts estimate that by the year 2000 nearly half the people infected with the virus in Canada will be women. The virus can affect any woman, regardless of age, race or economic status, and is passed directly from one person to another via blood, semen or vaginal fluids. You risk contracting HIV by having unprotected vaginal or anal sex without a condom or if you use drugs and use a needle of someone who is infected. The HIV infection can also be transmitted from an infected mother to her child either during pregnancy, at birth or, in rare cases, through breastfeeding.

Unlike many viruses, an HIV infection stays in the body forever. However, some people infected with HIV may remain healthy and display none of the symptoms generally associated with AIDS. Testing positive means you've been infected with HIV, but you may not have AIDS and may never develop it.

However, even though you may feel healthy, you can still infect others if you're HIV positive, so practising safe sex is absolutely essential. Women who are infected with the virus face some difficult decisions: whether to have children or terminate a pregnancy (not all fetuses acquire the infection, but about 30 percent do). Breastfeeding can transmit the virus from mother to baby. Some doctors believe that *all* pregnant women should be offered HIV information and testing.

Syphilis

Syphilis is probably the most widely known venereal disease because of the notoriety it's been given in history books. However, syphilis is also a modern-day disease: in fact, the number of syphilis cases increased in Canada between 1981 and 1992. Many people still think of syphilis as a men's disease. However, a 1994 federal public health survey showed that women under the age of 30 have shown the largest increase.

The good news today, however, is that syphilis is easily treated in its early stages with penicillin or antibiotics and can be diagnosed with a blood test. In its early stages, syphilis often presents in a telltale painless sore or chancre; however, some people notice no symptoms at all. In its second stage, which can last for months or years, syphilis presents symptoms that are flu-like or that appear as rashes or swollen lymph nodes. In the final stage, syphilis, if left untreated, can attack major organs such as the ear, eyes and brain, as well as the nervous system.

Vaginitis

If you're a woman, chances are you've had a vaginal infection of some sort in your life. Vaginitis is simply an inflammation of the vagina that can be caused by everything from a hormonal deficiency associated with aging, to an infection. You can contract the condition at virtually any age, although the reasons may vary. A younger woman's vaginitis may be due to an allergic reaction to a spermicidal cream; an older postmenopausal woman's vaginitis may occur because the lining of the vagina has become thin, dry and prone to irritation and inflammation.

Vaginal infection, however, is primarily caused by one of two culprits – the fungus *candida albicans* or the parasite *trichomonas vaginalis*. Treatment for each is specific and different, so it's important that the type be properly diagnosed.

The symptoms of trich (trichomonas vaginalis vaginitis) include itching, irritation and a yellowish green or grey vaginal discharge with a foul odour. Usually contracted through vaginal intercourse, trich can also be passed on through borrowing others' bathing suits, sharing washcloths and toilet seats. Trich is often treated with an antibiotic.

The symptoms of yeast infections (candida vaginitis) include itchiness, redness, irritation and a cottage-cheesy discharge that may even smell like fermenting yeast. Yeast grows naturally in the vagina and is kept under control by the body's normal acidic environment. When some of that acidity is lost in the vagina, however, the yeast thrives and infections occur. Taking antibiotics, eating an excess of sugary foods or hormonal changes within the body can predispose you to yeast infections.

The most commonly prescribed medication are anti-fungal creams, some of which are now available without a prescription.

Venereal Warts

Venereal warts (also called genital warts) are painless soft warts that grow in and around the entrance of the vagina and the anus or can appear on the cervix. They are transmitted by sexual contact and are currently the most common STD in North America. Most affected today are women aged 18 to 35. However, women of any age can contract venereal warts.

The warts are caused by a virus called the human papilloma virus (HPV). HPV can cause the cells on the lining of the cervix to change. This could lead to cancer of the cervix, a potentially life-threatening disease that can be detected early through a Pap test. (Every woman should have a Pap test annually). Several treatments exist for venereal warts. Consult your physician.

4. REPRODUCTIVE CANCERS: WHAT EVERY WOMAN SHOULD KNOW

The XIV World Congress of Gynecology and Obstetrics held in Montreal in the fall of 1994 had little good news about women's reproductive cancers. There are no easy screening methods for endometrial cancers, the Congress reported, and cancer of the cervix, which is a largely preventable disease, accounts for 44 percent of all genital-cancer mortality in women in developing countries. As for ovarian cancer, the fourth most frequent cause of death from cancer in women, the survival rate has not changed in 30 years (according to Canada's Genesis Research Foundation).

Despite this gloomy picture, there are many ways we can minimize our risks of contracting reproductive cancers and keep ourselves healthy. These include education, screening and self-awareness – paying attention and taking action when our instincts tell us something in our body isn't quite right. And sharing what we know with other women is crucially important to all women's health.

Cervical Cancer: Screening and Prevention Go Hand in Hand

Worldwide, 500,000 cases of cervical cancer are reported each year. In Canada, the national average is eight per 100,000 newly diagnosed cervical cancer cases annually. Unlike other cancers that affect women in midlife, young women should especially pay attention to this one. One report put the average age of women with cervical cancer at 28.

The good news: If cervical cancer is detected early, a woman has an 80 percent chance of being cured. And an annual Pap test (a cervical smear test to detect abnormal changes in the cells of the cervix) is the key to cervical health. "The success of the Pap smear is truly inspiring," Dr. Donna Stewart, head of Toronto Hospital's women's health program, said during a seminar on women and cancer at Toronto Hospital in the winter of 1995. The good news is that ongoing research is heading in this direction. Many doctors now believe that the real answer to cervical cancer prevention lies in a future vaccine.

The bad news: Thousands of Canadian women have never had a Pap smear.

Dr. Stewart's accolades notwithstanding (some say the Pap smear's accuracy is 95 percent), the traditional Pap smear is not foolproof. Manual screening can report a normal (negative) Pap smear to be, in fact, abnormal or positive. The reason this happens can be any one of the following:

- the pathologist can make an error;
- the doctor can take the sample incorrectly;
- an infection may obscure the results.

What can we do to protect ourselves against inaccurate test results?

- Computer technology is helping. Three labs in Alberta and Ontario are now using new computer technology called PAPNET to rescan slides deemed negative by a cytotechnician. This technology has caught as many as 50 percent errors.
- Some experts suggest that women planning on having a Pap smear should avoid using birth control foams and jellies, douches and tampons for a few days before the test.

What causes cervical cancer?

In recent years, medical researchers have discovered that cervical cancer is caused by a virus called HPV (human papilloma virus) that is spread by sexual contact. "Barrier" protection (through male or female condoms that protect the cervix) during sexual intercourse would curtail the virus's spread and lower the incidence of cervical cancer.

You are at increased risk of developing cervical cancer if:

- You have multiple sexual partners. (Women who are in a monogamous relationship can also be at risk if their partner, unknown to them, has other sexual partners.)
- You began sexual intercourse early in life. Some gynecologists are calling the incidence of HPV an epidemic among Canadian women aged 15 to 30.
- You smoke or are exposed to a significant amount of secondhand smoke.
- You take birth control pills. One study links an increased risk of a rare form of cervical cancer with the Pill.
- You have a history of herpes simplex or genital warts.
- Your immune system has been suppressed by corticosteroids, kidney transplants or AIDS.

What is a Pap smear?

A Pap smear, named after Greek pathologist George Papanicolaou, is a cervical smear test that aims to detect abnormal changes in the cells of the cervix, which is at the neck of the uterus. Besides functioning as a screen for cervical cancer, a Pap smear also can detect viral infections of the cervix.

How often should women have a Pap smear?

The Canadian Medical Association recommends women have a Pap smear every three years beginning at age 18. Many women, however, prefer to include a Pap smear in their annual medical checkups. Pap smears can be performed by obstetricians/ gynecologists, family doctors and in family planning clinics.

What does a Pap smear show?

A Pap test that comes back from the lab showing abnormal changes in the cells is not an instant cancer diagnosis. Not all abnormal cells are cancerous. Abnormal results can indicate an inflammation or infection, as well as a possible cancer.

If a Pap smear is positive, your doctor may perform a colposcopy (an examination of the cervix with a magnifying device) to check tissues more closely for abnormalities. If the test reveals the presence of mild precancerous cells, your doctor may advise you to watch and wait and have some retesting done. If the test shows moderate to severe precancer (dysplasia), your doctor would probably recommend that the abnormal tissue be removed.

How is cervical cancer treated?

Treatment of cervical cancer usually includes surgery (including LEEP or loop electrosurgical excision procedures) and/or radiation therapy.

A simple blood test is being developed which picks up antibodies to the human papilloma virus and which may detect recurring cervical cancer in women: as the disease progresses, the antibody levels apparently increase.

Endometrial (Uterine) Cancer: Your Risks Increase in Middle Age

Six per cent of all women's cancers come from the endometrium or lining of the uterus. The greatest incidence of endometrial cancer occurs in women between the ages of 45 and 65. It is rare in women under the age of 40.

The good news about endometrial cancer: When it is diagnosed at the early stage, the cure rate is high – a five year survival rate of 83 percent.

The bad news: There is no simple screening test for endometrial cancer, such as a Pap test.

What causes endometrial cancer?

1. The most publicized risk factor for endometrial cancer is taking unopposed estrogen as a treatment for menopausal symptoms. Studies show that taking estrogen alone increases the risk of endometrial cancer; when progesterone is added to this hormone replacement therapy, the uterine lining is shed (through a period) and with it, theoretically, any precancerous cells that may be lining the uterus. This is one reason why Dr. Elaine Jolly, an Ottawa gynecologist, once said that the ideal candidate for estrogen therapy is a woman without a womb.

2. Women who take the drug tamoxifen for breast cancer are also at risk of developing endometrial cancer. Toronto's Dr. Lavina Lickley, chief of surgery at Women's College Hospital, strongly believes that the benefits of tamoxifen for prolonging survival in breast cancer patients outweigh the risks of endometrial cancer: "If you had to choose a cancer to get, you'd choose endometrial over breast," says Dr. Lickley.

3. Other endometrial cancer risk factors:
   - being overweight;
   - never having had children;
   - being postmenopausal;
   - hypertension;
   - diabetes;
   - a family history of the disease;
   - a history of menstrual irregularities or failure to ovulate;
   - having had breast, ovarian or colon cancer.

4. Women with a history of polycystic ovarian syndrome (characterized by scanty or no periods, excessive hair, obesity, infertility and sometimes cysts on the ovaries) may be at increased risk because they often have a high level of estrogen in the body.

What are the warning signs of endometrial cancer?

The major signs of endometrial cancer are:
   - bleeding between periods;
   - excessive bleeding during periods;
   - spotting or bleeding after menopause.

In 90 percent of cases of endometrial cancer, there is abnormal uterine bleeding, from insignificant staining to hemorrhage. However, five percent of women may have no symptoms at all.

How is endometrial cancer diagnosed?
The most effective tests now being used include:
- Aspiration curettage, which collects sample scrapings for microscopic examination and may be done, with a little discomfort, in a doctor's office.
- Transvaginal ultrasound, a painless procedure that measures the thickness of the uterine lining. Transvaginal ultrasound may become the standard diagnostic tool for diagnosing postmenopausal bleeding, due to its simplicity, low cost and effectiveness.
- A Pap test can pick up some endometrial cancers (less than 25 percent).

How is endometrial cancer treated?
Cancer of the endometrium is often treated by a hysterectomy – a total abdominal hysterectomy which includes the removal of both fallopian tubes and both ovaries for women who have completed childbearing. Another treatment is hormone therapy for women who want to keep their reproductive organs. Radiation may also be given if the cancer has invaded the wall of the uterus.

Ovarian Cancer: An Elusive and Devastating Disease
When women learned of the death of comedian Gilda Radner from ovarian cancer, we couldn't believe that her cancer hadn't been detected earlier. But the truth about ovarian cancer is that by the time it's discovered, it has often progressed to a stage where the survival outlook is grim. At the xiv World Congress of Gynecology and Obstetrics in Montreal in the fall of 1994, Dr. Hans Ludwig, a Swiss gynecologist, called ovarian cancer "the great problem in gynecologic oncology."

In Canada, ovarian cancer is the fifth most common cancer among women. About 2,200 new cases a year are reported. In 1995, 1,350 Canadian women died of ovarian cancer.

The good news about ovarian cancer: There's a 70 percent cure rate with ovarian cancers caught at the first stage. And if the disease is caught early, the vast majority of women will survive disease-free for five years.

The bad news about ovarian cancer: Ovarian cancer is devastating because it is frequently well advanced before it is detected. And the survival rate for women with advanced stages of the disease is only 15 to 20 percent. More than 60 percent of women who develop ovarian cancer will die from it.

The survival rate for this fourth largest cancer killer of women (some say it is the most lethal of women's cancers) has not changed significantly in 30 years. The reason is late detection. There is no true screening test that is cheap and accessible; ultra-sounds and annual pelvic exams don't always pick up the presence of the disease; and the symptoms are vague and sometimes even nonexistent.

"These are usually well women and, boom, it's like they run into the wall," says Dr. Joan Murphy, ovarian cancer expert and head of gynecology and gynecologic oncology at the Toronto Hospital. The cancer is often diagnosed at Stage 3. "Its behavior is surreptitious," Dr. Murphy says, explaining that ovarian cancer spreads by seeding itself, shedding malignant cells into the abdominal cavity. "The outlook is bleak for Stage 4," she adds. "By then the cancer is usually advanced and metastasized."

What causes ovarian cancer? And how can women reduce their risks of developing the disease?

Says Dr. Murphy: "There isn't a woman who isn't at risk. By no means is this a rare cancer. Ovarian cancer is common enough to be scary."

The following is known about the disease:

- It rarely strikes black women.
- It's the same gene that causes breast cancer.

But there are plenty of things not known about ovarian cancer, and risk factors seem as elusive as the disease itself.

1. Some studies suggest that taking ovary-stimulating fertility drugs can increase the risk of developing ovarian cancer.

2. Some studies suggest that estrogen replacement therapy taken for at least 11 years increases one's risk of developing the disease by 70 percent.

3. Ovarian cancer predominantly affects postmenopausal women.

4. Risk increases for women who have never had a child.

5. Risk increases for women who are of North American or northern European descent.

6. Risk increases for women who have a history of endometrial, colon or breast cancer.

7. Heredity is the risk factor currently being focused on in Canada. Some experts say that women in affected families have nearly a one in two lifetime chance of developing the disease. "A family history of ovarian cancer, especially if two or more first-degree relatives had it is the most important risk factor," says Dr. Murphy. "There are currently a number of women in Canada who are at greater risk probably because of their family history but who don't know it. That is why it's especially important for women to ask questions of their mothers and grandmothers."

At Toronto Hospital's Familial Ovarian Cancer Centre, patients (under doctors' guidance) make up their family trees to determine their real risks of developing ovarian cancer, and their possible treatment. Other women choose a more controversial path: they have their ovaries removed though there's no sign of disease. New York writer Laura Furman took this radical step and wrote about it in the December 1994 issue of *Mirabella* magazine. She described how she'd lived under a cloud of doom knowing of her mother's premature death from ovarian cancer. Though she took every screening test available and had minor surgery to investigate a suspicious ovarian cyst (it turned out to be normal), she could not shake the fear.

Prophylactic surgery is a valid option, notes Dr. Joan Murphy. But surgery, especially surgery that's not necessary, brings with it its own risks. And once your ovaries are removed, the question then is whether or not to take hormone replacement therapy, which carries other possible risks.

You may be at lower risk of developing ovarian cancer if:

1. You take the Pill. Some studies suggest that the birth control pill protects against ovarian cancer.

2. You had your first child at a relatively late age. Studies point to the fact that the older the mother when she first gave birth, the lower the incidence of ovarian cancer.

What are the warning signs of ovarian cancer?

The symptoms of ovarian cancer are vague. And sometimes there are no symptoms at all. Symptoms may or may not include:

- pelvic pressure;
- low back discomfort;
- feeling full early when eating;
- constipation;
- gas;
- abnormal uterine bleeding.

"It's an elusive disease," Dr. Murphy says. "We're often way behind the eight ball when we find it."

How is ovarian cancer diagnosed?

1. Earlier enthusiasm about a blood screening test called CA-125 has been somewhat dampened now that readings have proved to be often unreliable, particularly in premenopausal women. The test, fairly reliable in postmenopausal women, measures the amounts of a specific antigen (the one associated with ovarian cancer) in the blood: up to 35 as a reading is okay, but 100 is a dangerous level. Unfortunately, other

conditions, including pelvic inflammatory disease and endometriosis, can also raise the levels of this antigen.

2. An ultrasound examination of the pelvis can show a suspicion of ovarian cancer but it is not a totally reliable test.

3. Unfortunately, only surgery confirms ovarian cancer. As a result, women without ovarian cancer sometimes have unnecessary operations, based on an erroneous suspicion of the disease.

How is ovarian cancer treated?

1. Surgery, radiation and chemotherapy are part of the treatment arsenal.

2. The drug currently offering the most hope is Taxol, a very expensive drug whose active ingredient was originally discovered in the late 1950s from natural substances contained in the bark of the Pacific yew tree. Women on a chemotherapy combination of Taxol and cisplatin survive longer than women on non-Taxol regimens.

3. This cancer is probably the one in most need of research, awareness and fundraising. The current goal is to develop a screening test with a high sensitivity and high specificity: one that's cost-effective, noninvasive and leads to early diagnosis.

PROFILE

Sherry Abbott – a survivor of ovarian cancer

I last talked to Sherry Abbott the day before her 36th birthday. The cake she was eating was much more than part of a birthday celebration. It was a treat that also marked five years of being cancer-free. Abbott, the former director of sales promotion and public relations for Revlon Canada, remembers her last cancer treatment. "I remember saying this is the first day of the rest of my life."

In the late eighties, when she had barely turned 30, Abbott was diagnosed with a rare form of ovarian cancer. Typically, by the time it was discovered, it had progressed to her lymphatic nodes (100 of them were subsequently removed) and formed two tumors behind her heart.

Aggressive cancer treatment, which included surgery and 5 1/2 weeks of radiation, left her with a bit of a limp (the stylish Abbott now walks with a stylish cane) but "they cured the cancer," she says.

Abbott's story illustrates what the experts say about this disease: it's elusive and by the time it's diagnosed, it has advanced like a silent army in the middle of the night. Abbott was misdiagnosed for several months before she admitted herself to hospital. She was told she had kidney stones and that she should learn to be patient and wait until the stones passed. After she had lost 20 pounds and had developed a protruding abdomen, doctors began to examine her more closely and carefully.

"Barely a week goes by without a person phoning me and asking me to phone their husband's sister's wife," says Abbott. "In my own way, I'm giving back, sharing a little of my own optimism. You know, you're never really sure what to say. Sometimes you just have to say, 'I know, it's a really terrible feeling' rather than, 'Oh, don't worry, you'll be fine.' You really want to hear, 'I felt that way, too, before it got better. It gets worse, but then it will get better.'

"I remember being in the hospital and feeling just that way. Just before my chemo, one of the nurses took my hand and said, 'You're going to feel terrible. But then you'll feel a little better and later this week a lot better.' That was kind of her to admit that. In the end, you just become more respectful and more appreciative of every aspect of life. You end up with an appreciation for feeling good and enjoying life."

PROFILE

Corinne Boyer – listen to your body

The audience of over 1,000 was stunned to hear Corinne Boyer's story. During a 1994 fund-raising breakfast for Genesis, a Toronto-based women's health organization, Boyer described a roller-coaster ride in which she was told by doctors that nothing was wrong. Yet three times in a period of 15 years, she was diagnosed with cancer – first a malignant melanoma, then breast cancer, and finally ovarian cancer.

The Dutch-born Boyer, wife of former MP Patrick Boyer, spoke up every chance she got with a message that urged women to take charge of their own health. "Each one of us is the best guardian of our health," said Boyer, who passed away in the fall of 1995. But Boyer also illustrates how awareness isn't the only key to paying attention to our health. Acting on what we know, and on what our instincts tell us, counts too. As Boyer told many of us, persistence is a virtue.

Her experiences with cancer underlined the importance of listening to our own bodies. Though a mammogram weeks earlier had revealed nothing unusual and although her doctor had insisted she was fine, Boyer went for a second mammogram after she felt a painful area in her breast while examining it herself. Even though that mammogram revealed nothing, something told Boyer she should not stop her investigation. After all, her mother had died of breast cancer. Investigative surgery later showed up a malignant tumor that required a lumpectomy and radiation to cure.

A few years later, she went for an ultrasound because she experienced some postmenopausal bleeding. It proved to be normal, but her bleeding didn't stop. A second opinion reinforced the first: there was nothing to worry about. Only after she insisted that her oncologist look into her problem further, did another ultrasound confirm her ovarian cancer. It was the disease that claimed her life, but not before she could communicate her message loud and clear: "Don't be passive. Listen to your body." After her death, her husband created the Corinne Boyer Fund for Ovarian Cancer Research. Tax deductible donations to it can be made through Genesis, 92 College St., Toronto, Ontario M5G 1L4

PART THREE

Your guide to sexual/reproductive health resources

AIDS – INFORMATION AND SUPPORT SERVICES

Positive Women's Network, c/o Pacific AIDS Resource Centre, 1107 Seymour St., Vancouver, British Columbia V6B 5S8 (604) 893-2200

AIDS Calgary, 300–1021 10th Ave. S.W., Calgary, Alberta T2R 0B7 (403) 228-0155.

University of Manitoba, Health Science Centre, Winnipeg, Manitoba R3T 2N2 (204) 474-8346.

ACT (AIDS Committee of Toronto), 399 Church St., 4th Flr., Toronto, Ontario M5B 2J6 (416) 340-2437.

Voices of Positive Women, Box 471, Station C, Toronto, Ontario M6J 3P5 (416) 324-8703.

Canadian AIDS Society, 100 Sparks St., Ste. 400, Ottawa, Ontario K1P 5B7 (613) 230-3580.
Canadian Public Health Association, 1565 Carling Ave., Ste. 400, Ottawa, Ontario K1Z 8R1 (613) 725-3769.

Centre for AIDS Services of Montreal, 1168 St. Catharine St. W. Ste. 202, Montreal, Quebec H3B 1K1 (514) 954-0170

AIDS – BOOKS

Bad Blood, The Tragedy of the Canadian Tainted Blood Scandal, Vic Parsons (Lester Publishing, 1995)

Creating Hospice at Home for People Living with AIDS. A manual and video set from the Community Hospice Association of Ontario.

Trial Without End, A Shocking Story of Women and AIDS, June Callwood (Knopf Canada, 1995).

Women and HIV/AIDS: An International Resource Book, Marge Berer with Sunanda Ray (Pandora, 1993).

Women and AIDS Project: Facilitation Guide,
Deborah Handziuk (Women's Health Clinic, 1993).
Women's Health Clinic, 419 Graham Ave., 3rd Flr.,
Winnipeg, Manitoba R3C 0M3 (204) 947-1517; TTY
(204) 956-0385.

Women & AIDS, (Health Canada, 1990), New
Brunswick Advisory Council on the Status of
Women, 95 rue Foundry St., Ste. 207, Moncton,
New Brunswick E1C 5H7 (506) 856-3252; 1-800-332-
3087.

ENDOMETRIOSIS – EDUCATION AND SUPPORT GROUPS

Endometriosis Association, International
Headquarters, 8585 N. 76th Place, Milwaukee,
Wisconsin 53223 (414) 355-2200. The order form
and printed materials list is comprehensive and
accommodates Canadian transactions. Books such
as *Living with Endometriosis: How to Cope with the
Physical and Emotional Challenges* and videos such
as The Choice Is Ours are available, along with articles and collections from previous publications.

Endometriosis Network of Toronto, Inc., PO Box
3135, Markham Industrial Park, Markham, Ontario
L3R 6H5 (905) 591-3963.

Women's Health Clinic, 419 Graham Ave., 3rd Flr.,
Winnipeg, Manitoba R3C 0M3 (204) 947-1517; TTY
(204) 956-0385.

ENDOMETRIOSIS – BOOKS AND NEWSLETTERS

Coping with Endometriosis, Mary Lou Ballweg
(Prentice Hall, 1989).

*Living with Endometriosis: How To Cope with the
Physical and Emotional Challenges,* Kate Weinstein
(Addison-Wesley, 1987).

TENT, a newsletter published three times annually
by the Endometriosis Network of Toronto, Inc., PO
Box 3135, Markham Industrial Park, Markham,
Ontario L3R 6H5 (905) 591-3963.

CANDIDA – EDUCATION AND SUPPORT GROUPS

Candida Research and Information Foundation
(CRIF), c/o INPUT MENTAL Orthomolecular
Society and Canadian Schizophrenia Foundation,
32 Farnview Cres., North York, Ontario M2J 1G4
(416) 733-2117.
Candida Research Information Service (CRIS), 41
Green Valley Ct., Kleinburg, Ontario L0J 1C0 (416)
832-0789.

PID – EDUCATION AND SUPPORT GROUPS

Canadian Pelvic Inflammatory Disease (PID)
Society, PO Box 33804, Station B, Vancouver, British
Columbia V6J 4L6 (604) 684-5704. Collect calls
welcome.

SEXUALITY – BOOKS AND VIDEOS

*The Female Touch: The Complete Book of Lesbian
Sexuality,* Nina Rapi (Pandora, 1995).

Forbidden Love, a video available through the
National Film Board's Gay and Lesbian Video
Collection, D-5, PO Box 6100, Station A, Montreal,
Quebec H3C 3H5 (514) 496-2573.

Lesbian Health Guide, Regan McClure and Anne
Vespry (Queer Press, 1994). Lesbian Health Issues
in Family Medicine: A Forum. Regional Women's
Health Centre and Department of Family and
Community Medicine, University of Toronto, 1993.
Available at the Regional Women's Health Centre,
790 Bay St., 8th Flr., Toronto Ontario M5G 1N9 .

Sex, Sex and More Sex, Sue Johanson (Penguin
Books, 1995).

PMS – EDUCATION AND SUPPORT GROUPS.

Vancouver Women's Health Collective, 175 West 8th
Ave., Ste. 219, Vancouver, British Columbia V5L 2Y7
(604) 736-4234; Helpline (604) 736-5262.

PMS Educational and Support Counselling,
Regional Women's Health Centre, Women's College
Hospital, 790 Bay St., 8th Flr., Toronto, Ontario
M5G 1N9 (416) 586-0211.

PMS Clinic, Women's Health Centre, St. Michael's
Hospital, 61 Queen St. E., 3rd Flr., Toronto, Ontario
M5B 1W8 (416) 867-7427.

PMS – BOOKS/ARTICLES/VIDEOS

PMS: *The Essential Guide to Treatment Options,* Dr. Katharina Dalton and David Holton (A Thorsons Book, 1995).

PMS: A Positive Approach, Women's Health Clinic, 419 Graham Ave., 3rd Flr., Winnipeg, Manitoba R3C 0M3 (204) 947-1517; TTY (204) 956-0385.

"The Selling of Premenstrual Syndrome" (*Ms. Magazine*), is part of package available from the Vancouver Women's Health Collective, 175 West 8th Ave., Ste. 219, Vancouver, British Columbia V5L 2Y7 (604) 736-4234; Helpline (604) 736-5262.

What People Are Calling PMS, 28-minute video, director Haida Paul, producer Jennifer Torrance and Barbara Janes, National Film Board.

Sexual Health, British Columbia Women's Hospital and Health Centre, 4500 Oak St., Vancouver, British Columbia V5H 3N1 (604) 875-2424.

STDS – BOOKS

Les Maladies Transmises Sexuellement (Les Presses de la Santé de Montréal). Available from the Vancouver Women's Health Collective, 175 West 8th Ave., Ste. 219, Vancouver, British Columbia V5L 2Y7. (604) 736-4234; Helpline (604) 736-5262.

Herpes Simplex: The Self-Help Guide to Managing the Herpes Virus, Philippa Harknett (A Thorsons Book, 1995).

Sexually Transmitted Diseases Handbook, (Montreal Press, 1993). Available from Women's Health Clinic, 419 Graham Ave., 3rd Flr., Winnipeg, Manitoba R3C 0M3 (204) 947-1517; TTY (204) 956-0385.

STD Handbook: Sexually Transmitted Diseases (Montreal Health Press, Inc.,) CP 1000, Station Place du Parc, Montreal, Quebec H2W 2N1 (514) 282-1171.

The Truth About Herpes, 3rd ed., Stephen L. Sacks, M.D., (Gordon Soules, 1991). Women's Health Clinic, 419 Graham Ave., 3rd Flr., Winnipeg, Manitoba R3C 0M3 (204) 947-1517; TTY (204) 956-0385.

CHAPTER 9

CONTRACEPTION, PREGNANCY, CHILDBIRTH, AND REPRODUCTIVE TECHNOLOGY: FROM BACK TO NATURE TO NEW FRONTIERS

Why are these women's issues? Women today can choose when, how and where they give birth, but their options and choices, as well as the information available, are exploding. Contraception and protection are more closely linked in an era of dangerous sexually transmitted diseases (STD s); childbirth patterns are becoming both more traditional and more sophisticated as midwives make a comeback and reproductive technology dramatically alters our conventional understanding of parenthood.

What you can do for yourself: Find a contraceptive method that protects your health and fits your body and lifestyle; if you are pregnant, make it your business to stay informed about health issues and birth choices; if you are among the 250,000 Canadian couples who are infertile, learn what you can about the new technologies available to you – and don't wait too long before you begin the process of giving them a try.

CONTRACEPTION AND PROTECTION – TODAY, THEY GO HAND IN HAND

PART ONE

The facts: Contraception has always been a women's issue

WHAT'S NEW IN THE NINETIES

A staggering range of birth control choices is available today. Old favourites like condoms have been improved and there are plenty of virtually foolproof alternatives to the Pill. At a 1994 world congress on women's health in Montreal, Dr. Pramilla Senanayake, assistant secretary general for the International Planned Parenthood Federation – the second largest voluntary organization in the world – likened the contraceptive world of the future to a "supermarket" of choices.

Some forms of contraception are used for more than preventing pregnancy. "Safe sex" has become the mantra of the nineties: sexually transmitted diseases are a fact of everyday life. It's crucial for women today to know what forms of birth control will also protect us from STDs.

But despite the array of birth control methods available to Canadian women, contraception will always remain a very personal choice. What method you use depends on many things: your comfort with your own body, your personal health concerns, how important sexual freedom is to you. Sometimes, trial and error is the best way to find out what's best for you. If you need help, your local Planned Parenthood agency can guide you through the alternatives available.

PART TWO

Your guide to contraceptives

Examine the following major contraceptive methods available in Canada, along with their pros and cons.

I. BARRIER CONTRACEPTIVES

These include any contraceptives that act as a physical barrier in the vagina, preventing sperm from reaching the uterus. Unlike the Pill, barrier contraceptives do not interfere with the body's hormonal balance. The most common barrier contraceptive, the condom, offers excellent protection from STDs.

THE CONDOM

This old barrier method is back in vogue again, not so much because of its birth control success (though it's considered to be 98 percent effective if used correctly; more than 90 percent effective if used with spermicidal foam), but because it is one of the few forms of contraception that will prevent STDs.

Condoms can be found easily and readily in places such as high school bathroom dispensers, convenience stores, doctors' offices, pharmacies and condom specialty stores. They don't require a prescription and can be purchased by men and women at a reasonable cost. And it's socially acceptable today for both men and women to carry them.

Most condoms are made from rubber latex, hence the nickname rubbers. Some men can be allergic to them, but you shouldn't let your partner's allergy to one kind deter you: if you test a few brands, it's likely he will find one that doesn't affect him adversely.

Remember: latex protects – no small advantage in the AIDS era (not to mention the many other STDs). If latex isn't your thing, try skin condoms made from animal intestines (although they're not as effective and they're more expensive).

As for the age-old complaint of men that wearing a condom means they lose sensation during sex: new research is being done on a polyurethane condom that promises to be quite durable and provides more sensation than latex.

The condom's advantages

- It provides protection against disease;
- It's easily accessible;
- It's inexpensive;
- It can be purchased at any age by either sex (it's easy for women to have them handy; this way, they don't have to rely on their male partner to produce them);

- It may be fitted by either the male or the female (some couples include her putting the condom on him as part of their lovemaking).

The condom's disadvantages

- It cannot be reused;
- The package must be kept away from heat (carrying it in your wallet or in your car's glove compartment is *not* a good idea);
- It can tear or break off during intercourse.

THE FEMALE CONDOM

The female condom, introduced in 1995 in Canada, is the only contraceptive that allows women to take charge of preventing infections and have their own form of STD protection.

It is *not* as inconspicuous as the male condom, however. The female condom is a shock to behold at first glance. In fact, it looks looks like an oversize condom for an elephant with a flexible ring at either end. How does a woman use this contraption? You insert it the same way you insert a diaphragm, with the open end resting outside the vagina. This new contraceptive definitely takes some getting used to!

The advantages and disadvantages of the female condom are identical to those of the male condom, with two exceptions: first, because it is made from polyurethane rather than latex, there is less loss of sensation during intercourse (any loss of sensation would be experienced by the woman rather than the man); second, some women complain about the noise (because of its size, there's more sheathing. Think of the sounds a plastic bag up your vagina would make).

THE DIAPHRAGM

Another member of the barrier family, the diaphragm is a rubber dome worn in the vagina throughout sexual intercourse. A diaphragm is a very personal device that requires fitting by your doctor, because every woman's exact shape and size is unique (if you lose or gain more than ten pounds, you'll need a new fitting). A diaphragm should fit perfectly on the vagina, to prevent sperm from entering the cervix. Used with spermicidal jelly, it's 81 to 86 percent effective.

The diaphragm's advantages

- It's reusable;
- It does not interrupt intercourse;
- It's inexpensive;
- It can last up to two years;
- It does not affect the fetus if you become pregnant;
- It provides some protection from STD s;
- It does not change the body hormonally in any way;
- It has few or no side effects.

The diaphragm's disadvantages

- It can be difficult to remove;
- It must stay in the vagina for six to eight hours after sex;
- It requires a good fit to be comfortable;
- It needs to be cleaned after each use;
- It increases the risk of urinary tract infections;
- There may be a slight risk of toxic shock syndrome (Toxic shock syndrome is a severe, potentially life-threatening illness caused by an overgrowth of staphylococcus aureus bacterium in the vagina);
- Unless combined with spermicide and a condom, it offers no protection against STD s.

THE CERVICAL CAP

This rubber cap (it looks like an oversize thimble) fits directly on your cervix inside the vagina.

Like the diaphragm, it must be fitted by your doctor. It can remain in your body for up to 48 hours. If used with spermicide, it is 73 to 92 percent effective.

The cap's advantages

- It can be reused;
- It's inexpensive;
- It has very few side effects;
- It causes no hormonal changes to the body;
- It needs to be replaced only every six months.

The cap's disadvantages

- It can be difficult to remove;
- It requires comfort with one's own body;
- It needs to be cleaned after use;
- Some women experience pelvic pain with it;
- It may contribute to an increased risk of toxic shock syndrome;
- Unless combined with spermicide and a condom, it offers no protection against STD s.

The Contraceptive Sponge

The nonprescription contraceptive sponge is made of a polyurethane foam which contains spermicides and can be inserted into the upper vagina so that one side of it covers the cervix. Like the condom, the sponge is made for one-time use only. It can be inserted just before intercourse or ahead of time and left in place for up to 12 hours after insertion. The difference between it and the condom is that it provides effective birth control protection even if you have intercourse several times after you've inserted it.

The sponge's advantages

- It is easy to use;
- You don't need to be fitted for it;
- It causes very few side effects;
- It creates no hormonal changes in the body;
- It acts as a contraceptive because it is both a barrier and is filled with spermicide;
- Newer versions combine several active ingredients, some of which may help prevent STD s; however, studies are inconclusive.

The sponge's disadvantages

- It can be used only once;
- It is not as reliable a form of birth control as the Pill: although some versions report a 90 percent success rate, failure rates of up to 24 percent have also been reported;
- It may irritate persons with sensitivity or allergy to spermicide or polyurethane;

- It may be difficult to remove;
- It does not provide total protection against STD s.

Lea's Shield

A relatively new female barrier contraceptive device, Lea's Shield was invented by Dr. Shlomo Gabbay for his wife, Lea, who for personal reasons sought an alternative to oral contraceptives. Available without prescription, it's like a combination of the diaphragm and the cervical cap. It fits snugly over the cervix thus preventing sperm from entering the uterus.

Advantages of Lea's Shield

- It can be purchased without a prescription;
- It needs no fitting;
- It can be worn up to 48 hours;
- It has an easy-to-use loop for safe removal;
- It does not affect the body's hormones.

Disadvantages of Lea's Shield

- It does not protect against STD s;
- It requires maintenance – it needs to be cleaned after use and replaced after about six months;
- It requires comfort with one's body;

2. NON-BARRIER METHODS OF CONTRACEPTION

The Pill

In almost any discussion about contraception, the Pill heads the list as the best-known form of protection against pregnancy. When it came onto the market in 1960, the oral contraceptive pill revolutionized birth control. First, it surpassed other methods in terms of reliability: the Pill demonstrated a success rate of 98 percent (some experts attribute the 2 percent failure rate to human error). Second, for the first time in history, it allowed women to take complete charge of their reproductive selves: they could finally plan their families with certainty. Third, the Pill gave women a simple, convenient form of birth control which, coupled with its effectiveness, allowed women to be more spontaneous about their sexuality.

However, the Pill soon revealed a dark side. It carried some potentially dangerous side effects. The high estrogen content in the early versions of the Pill carried with it an increased risk of heart attack, stroke and blood clots in the legs and eyes. Today's oral contraceptives contain far less estrogen (no more than half) than the original Pill, and come in a variety of forms: the combination pill (estrogen and progestin) and the progestin-only pill.

The Pill contains synthetic female hormones (estrogen and progesterone, or progesterone by itself). The addition of these hormones to a woman's system trick the body into believing it is pregnant by switching off the hypothalamus so that ovulation does not occur.

A woman on the Pill takes three weeks of hormones continuously; on the fourth week, she takes no hormones and menstruates; bleeding results because the uterine lining is shed as a result of the hormones being withdrawn. Women on the Pill often experience lighter periods and less cramping; for this reason, it is often recommended to young women who have difficult periods.

The Pill's nearly 100 percent effectiveness, its convenience and the fact that it doesn't interrupt intercourse all account for its continuing popularity.

But its failure today – a major failure – is the fact that it offers absolutely no protection from STD s – including the potentially fatal HIV.

The Pill's advantages

- Many women experience lighter and less painful periods;
- It regulates the menstrual cycle;
- It seems to protect against endometrial and ovarian cancers.
- It clears up acne in some women;
- It allows sexual freedom at any time throughout the cycle.
- Many women experience lighter and less painful periods;
- It regulates the menstrual cycle;
- It clears up acne in some women;
- It allows sexual freedom at any time throughout a woman's cycle.

The Pill's disadvantages

- Women smokers on the Pill are up to ten times more likely to suffer heart attacks and four times more vulnerable to stroke than nonsmoking women not on the Pill.

- It offers no protection from disease;
- It requires a prescription;
- The Pill's effects on the body are systemic: it can influence changes in everything from the gallbladder to our blood pressure to the way our blood clots.
- Some women on it experience weight gain;
- Mild side effects (slight nausea, fluid retention, headaches, spotting, breast tenderness) may occur, especially during the first three months;
- Severe side effects such as extreme headaches, pains in the chest or legs, blurred vision, shortness of breath or depression, sometimes occur; women who experience any of these should stop taking the Pill at once.
- Some drugs (antibiotics, for example) will interact with the Pill.
- Estrogen, in many studies, is linked to breast cancer.

THE MORNING-AFTER PILL

This postcoital method, called the MAP, and defined as birth control after unprotected sex, is considered to be 98 percent effective.

Although it was introduced as an emergency form of contraception for rape victims, now it is more widely used by women who have engaged in a single act of intercourse and do not wish to be pregnant. It cannot be used as an ongoing form of birth control, but it is an occasional choice available to women in Canada.

The morning-after pill (in the United States it's called the emergency contraception pill) is a combination of ethinyl, estradiol and levonorgestrel taken within 72 hours of unprotected sexual intercourse. The high dosage of oral contraceptives essentially works by interrupting the implantation of a fertilized egg into the wall of the uterus.

While it may seem an ideal option, it's not recommended as a long-term form of birth control. It requires a prescription; your doctor will determine whether or not you are a candidate for it.

Advantages and disadvantages of the morning-after pill

The same as those of the Pill, with one difference: this method is emergency contraception only. It is more likely to cause nausea and vomiting, and its long-term dangers have not yet been adequately studied. It will probably not be prescribed if you are on the birth control pill (if, for example, you missed a couple of birth control pills) or if you have various risk factors such as high blood pressure, a history of heart disease or are a heavy smoker. Though nobody wants to recommend the morning-after pill as a routine contraceptive device, too few people realize that it exists.

Intra-Uterine Device (iud)

This small plastic flexible contraceptive device, also known as the coil, is inserted through the cervix into the uterus to prevent pregnancy. About 2.5 cm to 5 cm long, and flat, it is partially wound with a copper wire, and inserted by a doctor during an office visit. The bottom of the iud has a tail of threads that hangs down into the vagina. This allows the user to check to make sure the device is still in place. It works by irritating the uteral lining, which prevents the egg from fertilizing. It has a 93 percent to 96 percent effectiveness rate and once inserted, it will protect immediately.

The iud's advantages

- It is highly effective (93-96 percent);
- It causes no hormonal changes to the body;
- Once inserted, a woman can forget about birth control (the device should be changed by a doctor every three to five years).

The iud's disadvantages

- Insertion can be painful;
- It can cause longer and more painful periods;
- It can cause cramping and breakthrough bleeding between cycles;
- There is an increased risk of pelvic inflammatory disease;
- It needs to be inserted by a doctor;
- Previous iud users may have an increased risk of ectopic pregnancies;
- You need to check the iud's string after each period (to be sure the iud was not accidentally expelled during the period);
- It provides no protection from stds;
- It is not offered to teenagers.

Depo-Provera

Depo-Provera is an injection of the progestogen drug medroxyprogesterone; the injection (in the arm or buttocks) is given by a doctor every 12 weeks. Depo-Provera is available in Canada. It has been approved as a drug but not as a form of birth control, although doctors can prescribe it for this purpose. It is rated 99 percent effective.

Depo-Provera's advantages

- It's 99 percent effective;
- Some women experience very little bleeding, if any at all, during their periods;
- It may reduce the risk of endometrial and ovarian cancers;
- It can be used by some women who cannot take the Pill.

Depo-Provera's disadvantages

- Periods are irregular or nonexistent;
- It needs to be injected by a doctor every three months;
- It offers no protection from STD s;
- It can take up to two years for a woman to become fertile after her last Depo-Provera shot;
- Minor side effects may occur. These can include headaches, dizziness, bloating, breast tenderness, mood changes, weight gain or loss, hair growth or loss.

NORPLANT

This is one of the newer birth control methods. Six small plastic rods are inserted into the upper arm. The rods are progesterone hormones (like Depo-Provera) that stop ovulation, thicken cervical mucus and change the lining of the uterus so that a fertilized egg cannot implant.

Norplant is as effective as the birth control pill and is immediately reversible upon removal. The rods are left in the arm for up to five years, which allows for unplanned intercourse. Initially, this method is not as easy because a doctor is needed to insert and remove the rods from your arm, but the procedure itself takes no longer than 30 minutes.

Norplant's advantages

- It's almost 100 percent effective;
- You can avoid daily contraceptive use;

- It contains no estrogen (estrogen has been linked to an increased risk of breast cancer);
- It's a long-term and reversible option.

Norplant's disadvantages

- You can feel the rods in your arms. However, you probably won't see them unless your arms are very thin or muscular (in which case the rods resemble protruding veins);
- It does not protect you from STD s;
- Your periods may become irregular and unpredictable;
- Minor side effects may occur. These can include headaches, dizziness, nausea, breast tenderness, weight gain or loss, hair growth or loss, and depression.
- Some women have reported difficulties, including scarring, with the removal of the rods (in the United States, some women have even filed lawsuits against Norplant's manufacturer).
- Once the rods are inserted, they're there until your doctor removes them.

THE HYSTERECTOMY: IT'S NOT A RITE OF PASSAGE

In any group of women over the age of 50, it's a good bet that about half of them will have had hysterectomies. This major surgery, which may constitute anything from removal of the uterus only, to the removal of the uterus, cervix and sometimes the ovaries, fallopian tubes, upper vagina and surrounding tissues, is one of today's important women's health issues. Why are so many hysterectomies being performed, women are asking. Surely not everyone who reaches a certain age needs to have one!

Over the last decade, investigations, mostly by consumer groups, reveal that many of the nearly 56,000 hysterectomies performed annually in Canada may not be necessary. Most are done as elective surgery (irregular bleeding, endometriosis and fibroids are among the reasons they're performed), not as a treatment in cancer or other emergency medical reasons. And where you live has a lot to do with whether or not you have a hysterectomy. The Toronto Women's Health Network discovered that women in northern Ontario were twice as likely to have their uteruses removed as women in larger cities to the south. The philosophy of individual doctors tends to affect how many hysterectomies they perform. And teaching hospitals generally perform fewer than nonteaching hospitals.

Generally speaking, the more informed women become about their choices, the fewer hysterectomies are done. Since the surgery is major and recovery from it is lengthy, many physicians and their patients try to wait things out. This depends, of course, on why the hysterectomy is advised. But uterine fibroids, for example, frequently are benign and often may be left alone. Ditto for a uterine prolapse.

Start your own research on the subject by talking to women who have had similar concerns or who have themselves gone through hysterectomies. Read up on the procedure. And ask your physician to discuss with you any new medical or surgical alternatives. For example:

NOT ALL HYSTERECTOMIES ARE THE SAME

- The vaginal hysterectomy allows the uterus to be removed through the vagina. Advantages include a speedier recovery time (three weeks versus six), and avoiding the painful healing process that accompanies major abdominal surgery. No pelvic scars, either.
- Vaginal hysterectomy by laparoscopy involves smaller incisions and a faster recovery than traditional hysterectomies with their substantial scars, hospital stays of a week or more, plus a few months' recovery time. The surgeon makes three small abdominal incisions through which the uterus is cut from the abdominal cavity; the uterus is then pulled out through the vagina.
- Endometrial ablation, a process that involves sheering off the endometrium with an electrically charged hysteroscope, may be an alternative for women who want to reduce long, heavy periods.
- Uterine thermal balloon therapy (UTBT) is a new noninvasive method that uses a ballooon device to destroy the uterine lining in premenopausal women who suffer from excessive uterine bleeding as their hormones change (estimated to be the cause of about 20 percent of all hysterectomies).
- There is also a range of drugs available – from birth control pills to anti-inflammatory agents – that may pertain to your particular diagnosis. One thing to remember: the alternatives to surgery carry their own risks, including infertility (although this may not be a large consideration in a situation where the alternative is hysterectomy).

If in the end your physician recommends a hysterectomy, find out how extensive he or she thinks it should be and the reasons why. For example, some hysterectomies include the removal of the uterus and the ovaries, which then plunge women into sudden, surgical menopause. Often, hormone replacement therapy is prescribed, but estrogen brings with it breast cancer risks. Make sure you know the pros and cons of everything available, from drugs to minor procedures and major surgery, before you make your decision.

And ask the question: what will happen if I don't have this procedure done? Sometimes, the answer helps put things in perspective and makes your decision easier.

ABORTION – THE GREAT DEBATE THAT DOESN'T ABATE

Abortion, the voluntary termination of pregnancy for medical, social or personal reasons, is neither a contraceptive choice nor an easy decision for any woman – even in Canada where abortion has been removed from the Criminal Code and supposedly is a private matter between a woman, her partner and her physician. According to the latest available statistics, 104,403 abortions were performed in Canada in 1993. Though most women's health centres across the country offer counselling to help women determine the right choice for them, the decision to have an abortion will always be difficult. And easy access to abortion still depends to a large degree on where you live.

The issue is complicated by anti-abortion lobby groups which tirelessly campaign, threaten, taunt and oppose abortion on moral and religious grounds. Recently, the ante has been upped to dangerous levels. In the United States, some doctors who perform abortions have been murdered in cold blood. In Canada, abortion clinics have been torched and murders attempted (in British Columbia, recently, a gynecologist was shot at). The threat of violence has forced abortion clinics to install high-tech security systems, and some doctors who perform abortions take elaborate precautions and wear bulletproof vests. All of this has created the kind of environment where no woman wants to find herself.

Anti-choice groups talk about what they believe to be the "rights of the fetus." Pro-choice groups defend the rights of individuals to make their own choices about when or when not to reproduce. Many women do not consider themselves pro-choice activists and may not even choose abortion for themselves, but they respect the rights of other women to make that choice for themselves.

How Abortions Are Performed

At the present time, most abortions in Canada are performed in hospitals because some provinces continue to legislate against abortion clinics. Vacuum aspiration or dilation and evacuation are the methods used.

However, many health professionals are debating RU486, the French drug commonly referred to as the abortion pill because it induces abortion in women who take it. (The pill, in fact a two-pill process taken over a period of days and up to seven weeks after a woman's last menstrual period, is administered under a doctor's supervision.) Though getting clearance for the drug is clouded by politics and pressure from anti-choice groups (both in Canada and in the United States) many people see the abortion pill as a possible solution to the abortion conundrum.

The drug, when licensed, would make abortion a truly private issue between a woman and her doctor. Best of all, it would protect patients and doctors from harassment by anti-choice picketers and, in some cases, the threat of violence or death. So far, however, the federal government and the drug company that manufactures the abortion pill have been unable to work together to legalize it. If both fear reprisals from the anti-choice lobby and choose to ignore the issue, women, once again, will be the losers.

In France, where the drug is available, the pill's manufacturer, Roussel Uclaf, removed RU486 from the market in 1988 due to threats from anti-abortion groups. However, the French government ordered the company to return the drug to the marketplace immediately! The abortion pill, the government said, was "the moral property of women." In France, over 150,000 women have used it.

PREGNANCY AND CHILDBIRTH

PART ONE

A Short History of Giving Birth in Canada

Most women in Canada today have their babies with the help of an obstetrician. This has not always been the case. Historically, in Canada, women gave birth in their homes. This was true in both Canada's native and settling populations. Women usually delivered with the help of a midwife, although in some pioneering communities a family doctor assisted. In some isolated areas, only the husbands attended births because they were the only ones around, particularly in rural areas and amongst hunting-and-gathering native communities.

By the turn of the century, more and more Canadian women, particularly in urban areas, began having their babies in hospitals, with the help of doctors. In the early days of hospital birth, many women died in childbirth due to poor hygiene amongst doctors and surgeons and a lack of understanding about the transmission of infection.

Slowly, with a growth in understanding about the importance of an antiseptic environment for surgery and childbirth, giving birth in hospitals became both more common and more safe. Increasingly, however, the practice was to medicate women during childbirth. In our great-grandmother's time in this country, the norm was to have a woman put to sleep while the baby was delivered by forceps. Many women recall delivering their babies totally unconscious of what was happening. In most hospitals, husbands or other family members were not allowed into labour and delivery rooms until the 1960s.

During the days when "unconscious childbirth" was flourishing, however, a parallel trend was at work: there was growing concern and unrest amongst a number of childbearing women, some labour and delivery nurses and a new group of professionals called childbirth educators. When epidural anesthesia (a freezing of a specific area in the pelvic region, which allows a woman to stay awake for her baby's birth but have the sensation numbed locally where there is the most amount of pain) was introduced, it allowed more and more women to be awake and conscious for the delivery of their babies.

Meanwhile, a growing consumer health movement was teaching the public that they had a right to better-quality health care and that childbearing women specifically had a right to more say in how they delivered their babies.

Out of this growing consciousness, a number of changes occurred in the childbirth world: hospitals began to respond to consumers' demands with more humane practices, more involvement of partners and family members and more liberal policies about when a woman could have her baby with her after the birth. In the 1970s, an underground movement of community-based midwives began to flourish in North America with an increasing number of women choosing to give birth to their babies at home. Examining the childbirth practices in other developed countries, many women and researchers began to question the way childbirth was being handled in North American society. Certain obstetrical practices (such as routine electronic fetal monitoring, episiotomy, or surgically cutting the area between the vaginal opening and the rectum – the perineum, and shaving of the perineal area) were examined by researchers and found to be questionable as routine procedures. Birth centres began to open in the seventies in a number of cities across Canada and the United States. More and more childbearing women became informed about childbirth and knew to ask questions.

The end result has been a swing of the pendulum back to more traditional birth patterns.

Where Births Take Place

1. *The Hospital*
Today, in almost all parts of Canada, most women give birth in a hospital. Until recently, a woman would have her labour in one hospital room, then be transferred to deliver in another room. This is changing as hospitals become more responsive to requests by consumers. A growing number of Canadian hospitals now offer birthing rooms where a woman can go through her labour, deliver the baby and stay there for a while after the baby is born.

Some hospitals contain birth centres which allow you to have the same caregiver for your entire labour and delivery (in contrast with a regular hospital delivery where there may be a change of staff in the middle of your labour).

2. *Birth Centres*
Freestanding birth centres are becoming increasingly popular in a number of provinces. These are usually staffed by a combination of midwives, nurses and doctors, but this varies from province to province. Freestanding birth centres are located in the community and offer a homelike atmosphere, often complete with a lounge and small kitchen for the use of the woman and her helpers. Birth centres are usually within close proximity of a hospital, should a complication arise and a woman need to be transferred there.

3. *At Home*
Another option is to give birth to your baby at home. Most midwives will deliver babies at home. A few doctors will do home deliveries, but this is becoming less and less common. Although many myths abound about home birth, a growing body of solid research shows that for a healthy woman who has had a straightforward pregnancy, a planned home birth with a qualified caregiver is as safe as having a baby in the hospital. If you are interested in considering this option, contact your provincial

midwifery organization. Phone numbers are listed in the Resources section of this chapter. In provinces where midwifery is regulated, or on the way to being regulated, arrangements for backup medical care are in place in the event of a problem. In Ontario, home birth with midwives is now covered by the provincial health insurance plan. In most other provinces, a home birth is only possible when a client pays a midwife directly, that is, out of pocket.

The Status of Midwifery in Canada

The underground midwifery movement in Canada has evolved to the point where the profession has gained renewed acceptance in many provinces. Until very recently, Canada was one of a few countries in the world where midwifery was not a legally recognized profession. Although midwifery was once legal in a number of provinces in Canada, by the 1970s midwives had no legal status anywhere in the country and had been replaced by doctors. In some provinces, many midwives continue to practise. But they are in what has been called "a legal limbo": they are neither legal nor illegal. However, this is changing.

Right now, the status of midwifery changes from province to province. For instance, in British Columbia, legislation recognizing midwifery was passed in March 1995 and a board was established to set up standards of practice, a process for registration and educational requirements. Midwives are also practising in the Northwest Territories and in the Yukon, and a project is under way to integrate Inuit maternity workers into the services offered at a birthing centre in Rankin Inlet. Midwifery is not yet legislated, although many people living in these northern regions recognize its value, considering that 44 out of 60 communities are isolated and only accessible by air travel.

There are still very few midwives practising in Saskatchewan, though the province is currently assessing the need for midwives and the way in which the system might be implemented should it be put in place. In Quebec, women can legally have access to trained midwives. In New Brunswick, a committee has been struck to assess how the other provinces have fared on the midwifery issue.

Ontario is one of the leaders in midwifery services. A woman may opt to use the services of a licensed midwife in a hospital, birth centre or at home and the service will be paid for by the provincial health insurance plan. A four-year baccalaureate program at three accredited Ontario universities trains women to be midwives. Approximately 70 midwives are currently practising and fully funded in the province. A professional college – the College of Midwives of Ontario – was established in 1993 and governs the practices of Ontario midwives in the public's interest.

Only midwives who are registered with the College of Midwives can practise in Ontario.

Though the provinces differ on their support of midwifery and how it can be integrated into the existing health care system, the country's midwifery network is an easy one to tap into. If you're interested in exploring the midwifery issue, contact your provincial association of midwives (listed at the end of this chapter) and discuss the midwifery issue with your doctor or hospital.

"Doulas": Emotional Support During Childbirth

Some women are also helped out in their labour and delivery by a woman who is not trained as a midwife or a nurse but who has training to provide emotional support. These women have traditionally been known as "doulas." Although the word *doula* originated from the Greek term for slave, today a doula is "someone who mothers the new mother." Because our extended families have broken down, new moms are often without that extra pair of hands when they come home from hospital. A doula can provide that extra help, plus important emotional support.

The role is making a comeback in Canada. A doula is not involved in a medical way – she is present at the birth only to provide emotional support. Chapters of Doulas of North America are found across Canada. (For more information, contact the Labour Support Association and Registry listed in the Resources section.) Doulas can be particularly helpful in the post-partum period when you are home with your baby.

PART TWO

Your guide to pregnancy and childbirth

For many women, pregnancy and childbirth is among the most intense and engaging experience of their lives. It can be a time of both joy and sorrow, exhilaration and pain, happiness and frustration. But in spite of these extremes of emotions, one thing seems clear: the more you inform and prepare yourself for the experience, the greater the chance that you will be happy with the way things go, and the greater the chance that your baby will have a good start in life.

Women pregnant for the first time are faced with an array of choices and may feel overwhelmed at first if they have no guideposts to help them in their decisions. This sense of being overwhelmed usually passes if you are able to talk to other women and take full advantage of the knowledge that is available from doctors, nurses, midwives, childbirth educators and by going on a hospital tour. One excellent book in helping you make decisions is *Your Baby, Your Way: Making Pregnancy Decisions and Birth Plans*. This book will guide you through the many options and decisions about what is best for you and your baby.

For Women Only?

Pregnancy and childbirth have long been considered "women's business." In many cultures, deliveries can be only be performed by another woman (usually a midwife) and women are surrounded by women (mothers, sisters, aunts) at the time of labour and birth. In North American society, the customs surrounding childbirth have gone through many changes over the years, and today a woman is just as likely to have her delivery done by a man (usually an obstetrician) as by a woman. In spite of these changes, it is still one experience only women can have. For this reason, women tend to turn to other women for advice – to their mothers, sisters, aunts, other female relatives and women friends.

How You Approach Your Pregnancy Will Influence What Kind of Experience You Have

If you are going through your first pregnancy, you will no doubt hear stories from other women who have already had babies, about their own pregnancy and birth experiences. While you may be inclined to think that you will have the same experience as they did – whether it is a "horror story" of a very complicated birth or the most beautiful birth imaginable – it is important to remember that no two women are the same when it comes to how they go through pregnancy and how they give birth. The vast majority of pregnancies and births are normal (doctors, nurses and midwives sometimes refer to these as "routine"), and yet we tend to remember the negative or frightening accounts we hear from some women.

How you approach your pregnancy and birth will strongly influence the experience. If you approach it as a normal process which the human female body was designed to be able to carry out, this will likely minimize the fear and anxiety you feel at the birth. If you approach pregnancy and birth as a frightening experience fraught with potential problems, this will likely influence your experience in a negative way. Above all else, one of the key lessons women often learn from the experience of childbirth is to trust their bodies. This is not to say that preparing yourself guarantees that things won't go wrong. Things can and do go wrong in childbirth. But it is important not to lose sight of the fact that in most cases, things go just fine. If a complication does arise during your pregnancy or during childbirth, you will likely be referred to an obstetrician – a specialist in pregnancy and delivery – if you are not already seeing one.

The kind of experience you will have with pregnancy and childbirth depends upon:

- your state of health and physical fitness when you became pregnant and how you maintain it throughout your pregnancy;
- how you eat during your pregnancy;
- whether you smoke or drink a lot of alcohol;
- how much rest you are able to get when you are tired;
- your physiology (your body build);
- genetics.

Some of these issues will be examined later in the chapter.

ARE YOU PREGNANT?

A Simple Urine Test

Whether you were trying to become pregnant or suspect you may be pregnant unexpectedly, your pregnancy can be confirmed by a simple urine test within a week to ten days after you miss your first period. You can do this through your doctor, through a clinic or with a home pregnancy test kit which can be purchased at any pharmacy.

Whether you are planning to carry on with the pregnancy or not, it's a good idea to confirm pregnancy as early as possible. If you are planning to continue the pregnancy, the sooner you know the sooner you can begin to care for yourself and the growing baby.

THE THREE STAGES OF PREGNANCY

The better informed you are and the more support you have, the more comfortable you will be about your pregnancy – particularly if it is your first. Once you confirm that you are pregnant, you should sign up for prenatal education classes. These are offered in most communities through hospitals, public health departments and midwifery organizations.

What to Expect During the First Trimester (first 13 weeks)

Nausea or "Morning Sickness"

Some women know or suspect they are pregnant right away, even before a test confirms it. The body quickly begins to go through significant hormonal changes which can influence digestion. In some women, this causes nausea, sometimes called "morning sickness" because it often seems to be worse upon awakening.

Roughly one-third to one-half of all pregnant women experience nausea during their pregnancy. It may last for only a brief time or for several months. Most women get over the nausea once they have passed the first trimester of their pregnancy.

Breast Tenderness and Breast Growth

Another early sign of pregnancy is growth and tenderness in the breasts as they begin to prepare for breastfeeding. In some women, this is significant and requires a bra size change (or two!); in other women, the change is less dramatic.

A Desire to Urinate More Often

As the baby begins to grow, your internal organs will get shifted around. Sometimes, a little extra pressure on the bladder may mean you have the urge to urinate more frequently.

Pressure on Internal Organs

As the pregnancy progresses, you may also have pressure on the lungs (causing some shortness of breath) and on the stomach (which can cause heartburn, particularly towards the end of pregnancy). These are all normal physiological responses to the very big change your body is going through. Many of the books in the Resources section at the end of this chapter offer tips on alleviating these discomforts of pregnancy.

"Eating For Two"

The common expression "You're eating for two!" is absolutely true. The nutrients you take in are passed to the baby through the umbilical cord, aided by the large volume of blood your body produces when it is pregnant. Similarly, the oxygen you take in when you breathe passes through to the baby.

The baby develops at a rapid pace during the early weeks of pregnancy, so your diet *is* important. However, "you're eating for two" does not mean you should double your calorie intake during pregnancy. It means eating wisely, not eating excessively. It is also important to avoid certain medications and substances that may harm the fetus. For more information on eating well during pregnancy, books like *Eating Well When You're Pregnant* (listed in the Resources section) can be helpful.

Vitamin Supplements

There are some vitamin supplements that you might consider taking during pregnancy. Talk to your doctor or midwife about which vitamin supplements you should take. For example, adding folic acid (a key B vitamin) to your diet during your childbearing years and when you are pregnant may help prevent certain birth defects such as spina bifida. Although physicians are unanimous about the value of taking folic acid during pregnancy, they seem split on the value of taking other vitamin supplements. Some prescribe a multivitamin, others just an iron or calcium supplement. Still others believe women can consume enough nutrients by following Canada's Food Guide to Healthy Eating when making their food choices. Discuss all aspects of nutrition with your doctor or midwife as early as possible in your pregnancy.

Prescription Drugs, Tobacco and Alcohol

Consult your doctor or midwife about any prescription medication you may be taking or need to take, and make sure that it is safe to take them. If you feel you need additional information, Motherisk, an information line operated out of Toronto's Hospital for Sick Children, provides helpful advice over the phone. If you have any questions about medications or exposure to other substances during pregnancy, give them a call (see Resources section for phone number).

Tobacco and alcohol can harm the developing fetus and should be avoided or at least restricted when you are pregnant. Smoking is a tough addiction to shake but if you are a smoker, you will be doing your baby a world of good if you quit. If you are having difficulty quitting smoking when you are pregnant, consult your doctor or midwife or seek out someone who managed to quit when they were pregnant and find out how they did it.

Smoking is a hazard that can directly affect the fetus and cause either miscarriages or low birth weights. A baby living in an environment where the people around her smoke can generally expect to have more respiratory illnesses, including asthma. Some studies have even found a possible connection between secondhand smoke and Sudden Infant Death Syndrome or SIDS.

You've probably seen the signs in bars and restaurants warning pregnant women about the adverse affects of drinking. The disorder known as fetal alcohol syndrome, associated with heavy drinking during pregnancy, can cause mental retardation and other neurologic deficits in your baby. However, most studies have failed to correlate fetal alcohol syndrome and an intake of one drink every other day or so. Though most pregnant women wisely choose not to drink (as the old saying goes, better to be safe than sorry), the occasional glass of wine during pregnancy (or if you had a few drinks before learning you were pregnant) is not worth beating yourself up over.

Sexual Intercourse
During pregnancy, the uterus contains an amniotic sac containing amniotic fluid that cushions the growing fetus from falls or bumps the mother-to-be may experience. It also protects the baby during sexual intercourse. Unless your doctor or midwife have counselled against intercourse for a health reason particular to you, it is normal and natural to continue sexual relations right up to the end of your pregnancy.

HOW TO COPE WITH MORNING SICKNESS

- Keep crackers, rice cakes or dry toast by your bedside to eat as soon as you wake up. Peppermint tea also soothes a queasy stomach. If possible, take your time getting up.
- Drink ginger tea (made with fresh grated ginger) upon awakening. Ginger tea throughout the day can also be helpful. You can buy powdered ginger in capsule form at most health food stores. Take three or four of these a day with a glass of water.
- Small frequent snacks which are high in protein and complex carbohydrates consumed throughout the day may be better for nausea than 3 regular meals.
- Drink as much water and nourishing fluids (bouillon, nutritious shakes, nonsweetened fruit juices) as you can.
- Some women find extra Vitamin B^6 helps to relieve nausea. Check with your doctor or midwife about the appropriate amount to take.
- Avoid fried and greasy foods, which are much harder to digest.
- "Sea bands" worn on the wrist to prevent seasickness may also be helpful. These can be purchased in marine shops or possibly in your local pharmacy.
- When morning sickness persists, some women have found acupuncture to be helpful.
- If possible, get lots of rest and relaxation. (In some cultures where lifestyles are much more relaxed and less demanding than ours, nausea in pregnancy is almost unheard of!)

What To Expect During the Second Trimester (13th to 28th week)

By the fourth month, nausea (if you experienced it) usually passes. Some women, however, experience the occasional bout of morning sickness into the second or even third trimester. But by then, the risk of complications has decreased considerably. This is when you can expect to begin regular prenatal exams. Depending on your age and risk group, you may also be asked to have various prenatal tests. These may include an ultrasound and blood tests, which, among other things, check your blood sugar levels for the possibility of gestational diabetes.

Some women say this is when they really begin to enjoy their pregnancy. Most women begin to "show" in the second trimester as the growing uterus starts to make the stomach protrude. (The uterus is an extraordinary muscle, most extraordinary in the act of childbirth when its expansion and contraction push the baby out.)

During this time, your total blood volume increases, and by the 27th week the fetus should weigh about two pounds. You'll begin to feel the fetus move – a process some people call quickening. This begins around week 20.

Other things you may experience during the second trimester include:

- Stretch marks. These pinkish, reddish or brownish lines (the color depends on your skin's pigments) may appear across your stomach as your abdominal area begins to stretch. After delivery, they disappear in some women but not in others. Some women claim that applying moisturizing lotion to their abdomens during pregnancy helps alleviate the marks. At this time, the linea nigra, a dark line running down the centre of the abdomen from the bellybutton to the pubic bone, may appear.
- Constipation gets worse because the intestinal muscle is more relaxed than usual. This is the time to up your fibre intake (discuss with your doctor or nutritionist whether you should add a tablespoon or more of wheat bran to your daily diet.) Hemorrhoids may result from constipation or straining during a bowel movement. Plenty of over-the-counter hemorrhoid creams or suppositories are available. Drink lots of water.
- You may begin to experience heartburn during the second trimester. The sensation of heartburn is caused by the relaxation of the sphincter muscle at the top of the stomach, causing more than usual regurgitation of the stomach's contents into the esophagus. Avoid fatty foods, eat slowly, and try not to eat just before bedtime.
- Edema or water retention is experienced by many pregnant women. It results in swollen feet, ankles and fingers (if you're prone to edema, keep your rings off

your fingers!). Talk to your doctor about water retention and limit your intake of salt and salty foods.

• Consult your doctor about the recommended weight gain. A couple of decades ago, women were urged to keep their weight gain under 25 pounds. Today, a 20- to 32-pound weight gain is typically recommended. You may experience the largest weight gain during this period.

What to Expect During the Third Trimester (the 29th week onward)

The main organs, muscles and bones of the fetus have all been formed by the end of the second trimester. During the third trimester, they mature and continue to grow. This is also the time when the baby begins to prepare for birth. The lungs mature and the baby gets bigger and fatter to prepare for entry into the world.

In the third trimester, the baby starts to kick, sometimes so much that it will keep you up at night. Kicking is a good sign; in fact, if you notice a sudden lack of movement over a 12-hour period, contact your doctor immediately, as this may signal that the baby is in trouble. Another sensation you'll experience during this period are Braxton-Hicks contractions, a sign that the uterus is practising for labour. Your abdominal area suddenly tightens up for about 20 seconds, then relaxes. These are not labour contractions. Labour contractions are much stronger and last at least twice as long.

You may find yourself tremendously hungry during these weeks, due to your growing baby's needs. You may also begin to feel large and bulky and, towards the very end, weary of the whole process.

Take Care of Yourself and Prepare for Labour and Birth

The more you can rest and relax, the better prepared you will be for labour and birth. So take every advantage you can of the offers of friends or family to help in your daily routine. Although you will be learning about it in your prenatal classes, it is also a good time to read about the experience of labour and birth and prepare yourself for the different stages. One book many women have found helpful is *What to Expect When You're Expecting*. Other helpful books are listed in the Resources section of this chapter under "The Birth."

Prepare a Birthing Plan – But It's Important to Be Flexible

The third trimester is also a good time to let your doctor or midwife know what your wishes and preferences are for the birth. Some people refer to this as a birthing plan. If you are preparing a birthing plan – and it's not a bad idea to put it in writing –

remember that your choice of birthplace and caregiver will influence what is possible. For example, hospitals have different policies about such things as number of people in the delivery room, maternal discharge dates and so on.

What will happen during a birth and how you will feel and respond is not always predictable, so it is important to be flexible about your plans. Making a birthing plan does make it possible for you to let others know beforehand what your feelings are about certain aspects of the process and if there are special things you would like to have with you or have happen (for example, your partner cutting the cord).

Some things you may want to consider for your birthing plan include:
- your choice of birthplace;
- how long you want to stay at home when labour begins (if you decide to give birth at a hospital or birth centre);
- eating or drinking during labour;
- things you may want to have with you in the birthing room (for example, special music, a camera or personal items from home);
- who you would like to have in the birthing room with you;
- whether or not you want an enema;
- whether or not you want pain medication or external fetal monitoring;
- whether you want oxytocin (a hormone that induces contractions) if your labour is progressing slowly;
- what position you want to be in for delivery;
- who you authorize to make decisions for you if the going gets tough;
- your feelings about cesarean section;
- whether you want to hold the baby immediately after delivery;
- if the baby is a boy, whether or not to circumcise;
- how baby feeding is handled in the hospital and your preferences around that;
- post-partum medication for you or your baby.

The Final Stages of Pregnancy: How Your Body Prepares for Birth
As you enter the final stages of pregnancy, your body begins to prepare for the baby to pass out of the uterus. The cervix starts to soften as you get closer to your delivery date, and when you go into labour, the contractions will help to open (dilate) the cervix so that the baby can get out.

The baby also goes through a number of changes in the last two weeks in order to prepare for its entry into the world. The baby develops a layer of fat for protection in a world without warm, enveloping amniotic fluid. The baby's lungs begin to prepare in order to enable the baby to breathe on its own. And the baby moves lower into the mother's pelvis to prepare for the descent.

Most babies are in the proper position (head first). Some, however – 3 to 4 percent – haven't turned themselves around and come feet or bottom first (called breech position). If your baby is in a breech position, an obstetrician may recommend that you have a cesarean section.

Pre-Labour Contractions

In the final weeks before delivery, before you go into labour, you may begin to experience mild contractions. These are the Braxton-Hicks contractions referred to earlier; they may start any time during the third trimester. Their purpose is to get the uterus ready for the much heavier contractions that come with birth. In the final weeks, you may also experience more vaginal discharge. Some women feel a tremendous burst of energy towards the end of their pregnancy and become very focused on getting things ready for the birth and the period afterwards. You may hear this referred to as "the nesting instinct," as we seem to resemble birds fluttering about gathering twigs and feathers to build their nests before they lay their eggs.

Due Dates

A baby's due date is 41 weeks after the last menstrual period. But some babies come before, some after. Although you will have an expected date of delivery for your baby, remember that a full 75 percent of first pregnancies are not delivered on the due date and many of them are late.

Going into labour before your pregnancy has reached 37 weeks is referred to as "preterm labour." Many babies born preterm do very well with little need for extra attention. Others may need to be kept in a hospital's special nursery for preterm babies until the baby reaches a healthy weight and can manage away from the support of a hospital.

If your pregnancy goes two weeks or more past your due date, it is the policy of many doctors to rupture the membranes of the amniotic sac in order to force the labour to begin. Others have a policy to wait and see up to a certain point – assuming the baby appears to be doing well. One measure of how the post-term baby is doing is the "Non-stress test" described later in the chapter.

Are You Really in Labour? How to Decide

For women who have never experienced labour before, there are a number of signs to help you know that this is probably "the real thing." The cervix has had a protective "plug" covering it for the duration of the pregnancy, and this begins to come out as your body prepares for delivery. You may notice a pink discharge with light signs of blood. For some women, labour begins with the breaking of the waters within the amniotic sac. Women have described this as a "warm gush" of liquid passing through the vagina; in other women, it may just trickle out. Some women's labour starts without the membranes rupturing; in this case, the doctor or midwife may end up rupturing the membranes for you – a simple and harmless procedure.

The contractions of labour are distinctly different in their intensity and regularity from the Braxton-Hicks contractions you may have experienced occasionally towards the end of your pregnancy. Contractions of labour are felt low in the abdomen although some women feel them in their lower back, as well. The intensity increases as labour progresses, and the length of time between contractions shortens. By the time you are into the heaviest part of your labour, the contractions may come as often as 3 to 5 minutes apart.

Birth

When you've reached this stage of your labour, you are beginning to do the hard work of giving birth. (There's a reason it's called labour!) The contractions need to be this intense in order for the uterus to contract enough to force the baby out.

As your uterus is contracting, the cervix is opening wider and wider. From time to time, your caregiver will check how much your cervix has dilated, to see how you're progressing. Often, women dilate very slowly in the first part of labour, and then more quickly as labour becomes more intense. The entire process of reaching full dilation varies from woman to woman and from pregnancy to pregnancy. It can be as short as a few hours and as long as 24 hours (and occasionally, even longer). The average for first-time mothers is between 12 and 15 hours.

When the cervix is fully dilated (10 cm), the baby's head will be very close to the vaginal opening and most women feel a tremendous urge to push. Your caregiver will guide you through this stage, encouraging you to push while you are having contractions, not between them. As the baby's head "crowns" the opening of the vagina, you may experience a strong burning sensation until the head has come out. This sensation is usually intense but brief. Once the head has come out, the rest of the baby's body will follow with subsequent contractions.

Once the baby has been born, the umbilical cord will be cut and the uterus will continue to contract because the body needs to expel the placenta. Within a half hour of the delivery, you will be encouraged to push again, and the placenta (the organ that develops in the uterus during pregnancy and which links the mother's blood supply with the baby's for the mutual exchange of nutrients and oxygen) will be forced through the vagina. The doctors, nurses or midwives will weigh and measure the baby fairly soon after the delivery and check the essentials to make sure all is functioning well. As well, the doctor will immediately look for certain signs of health according to a standard called the Apgar score. The five signs include among other things, her breathing – a weak cry and slow breathing are accorded one point, while a louder, stronger cry scores two points. From seven to ten is a very healthy baby.

TESTS IN PREGNANCY

Modern technology has made it possible for us to know a great deal about how a pregnant woman is doing during her pregnancy and whether the baby's growth and health are progressing as they should. There are a number of tests that can be done during pregnancy. Some are simple and some are more complex. Remember, you do have a say in whether or not you want to have these tests done.

The following questions asked of your doctor may help you decide:
- Why are you recommending this test for me?
- What exactly do the results of this tests show?
- How invasive is this test? To me? To the fetus?
- How common is this test?
- How reliable or accurate are its results?
- What are the consequences of not having this test done?
- Are there alternative methods of getting similar information?

The following are some of the more frequently performed tests in most parts of Canada:

Ultrasound
An ultrasound is used for several reasons:
- to check for size to determine the most accurate due date;
- when a multiple birth (twins, triplets, etc.) is suspected;
- to detect major abnormalities in the baby (it cannot detect all abnormalities).

This test uses high-frequency sound waves which are directed at the uterus and the baby and which create an image on screen of the fetus in the uterus.

Research to date does not show any harmful physical effects of ultrasound, although long-term side effects have not yet been well researched. It is generally accepted that ultrasound should only be used if there is a medical question it can answer, not simply to have a visual record of how the baby is doing.

Amniocentesis
Amniocentesis is used to test a variety of conditions such as Down Syndrome. It is usually done when the fetus is at 13 to 15 weeks gestation.

In this test, a long needle is inserted through your abdomen and into the amniotic sac to collect fluid, which can then be analysed.

Ultrasound is also used with amniocentesis to determine the exact placement of the fetus. This is generally only done on women over 35, who may be at higher risk for developing certain conditions.

If you are having this test done, you may want to speak with a genetic counsellor who may help you understand what the test can and cannot detect and may help you decide your course of action if an abnormality is found. Amniocentesis slightly increases your chance of having a miscarriage, premature labour or bleeding. The more experienced your technician, the better.

Chorionic villi sampling (cvs)
With this test, a small amount of tissue is removed from the placenta between 9 and 12 weeks of pregnancy. This is done either by inserting a thin tube (catheter) through the vagina and cervix to get the tissue or by inserting a long needle through the abdomen to the part of the placenta where the chorionic villi are located. This is a more recently developed technique than amniocentesis and has the advantage of giving the woman information earlier in her pregnancy. It can detect many of the same genetic conditions as with amniocentesis. The rate of miscarriage is slightly higher with this test than with amniocentesis.

Fetal biophysical profile
This test, used late in pregnancy, involves the use of ultrasound to determine how active the baby is, the volume of amniotic fluid, the position of the baby and the placenta (for example, if the placenta is over the cervix, this can be a problem). It is most commonly used if a problem is suspected or if the mother has gone past her due date.

Non-stress test
This is another test mostly used late in pregnancy if a problem is suspected or if a mother has gone past her due date. An electronic fetal heart monitor is used to determine the baby's heart activity as an indication of how he or she is managing. The monitor is kept on for 20 to 30 minutes. At the same time as the monitor is recording heart activity, the mother is also asked to note every time she feels the fetus move.

If you are having this test done, it is important to remember that if the baby is not moving at the time of the test, it may be because he or she is asleep, and not necessarily because there is a problem.

INFERTILITY AND NEW
REPRODUCTIVE TECHNOLOGIES

PART ONE

A short history of the reproductive market – from Louise Brown to the Royal Commission on New Reproductive Technologies.

The birth of Louise Brown, the first child in the world to be conceived and fully gestated through in vitro fertilization, in 1978, marked a turning point in western society's understanding of the possibilities of science in the field of human reproduction. It also marked a turning point in our thinking about definitions of motherhood and what constitutes a family. Phrases like "brave new world" became common in media headlines and casual discussions about test tube babies and surrogate mothers. For the thousands of Canadian couples experiencing fertility problems, Louise Brown's birth gave them hope that they too might be able to have a child of their own.

Since then, thousands of babies have been born in Canada through in vitro fertilization; infertility clinics have sprung up in every corner of the country; and women can now "donate" eggs to other women who have problems conceiving. We may be only a few years away from gene therapy techniques that permit genes carrying specific disorders to be "corrected" before being implanted into the womb. And today, not only can scientists create human life in a petri dish, they can manipulate it. The incredible array of choice now available to women has been called "the reproductive supermarket."

Although the development of these new techniques gives hope to many individuals with fertility problems in Canada, this newfound ability to reshape the course of human life also raises profound questions. Many of these techniques have evolved so quickly and in such a scientific vacuum that the necessary ethical discussions lag far behind.

In response to these concerns, and as a result of significant pressure from a strong lobby called the Canadian Coalition for New Reproductive Technologies, the federal government established the Royal Commission on New Reproductive Technologies in 1989 to do an extensive review of the technologies, consult with Canadians and produce a series of recommendations. Although faced with a series of political and personnel struggles, the commission managed to complete its task, and in the process consulted with close to 40,000 Canadians. The commission's two-volume report, Proceed with Care: Final Report of the Royal Commission on New Reproductive Technologies, was released in November 1993, along with 15 volumes of research studies.

One of the commission's strongest and most hotly debated recommendations was that the federal government establish a federal regulatory commission on new reproductive technologies. Referred to in the report as the New Reproductive Technologies Commission, this body would oversee practice parameters, facility standards, general surveillance, licensing and accreditation, and evaluation of the various technologies. While it remains to be seen whether the federal government will set up such a regulatory body, the level of discussion and debate on new reproductive technologies has now moved to a much more complex and sophisticated level than where it was at the time of the announcement of Louise Brown's birth in Great Britain in 1978.

PART TWO

Your guide to the new reproductive technologies

What are the new reproductive technologies?

Rona Achilles, a Canadian sociologist who has written extensively on the subject, suggests the following classifications when referring to the new reproductive technologies:

- those that inhibit the development of new life (also known as birth control or contraception);
- those that monitor the development of new life (such as ultrasound and amniocentesis);
- those that involve the creation of new life (such as in vitro fertilization, donor insemination and drugs that affect ovulation).

We've already looked at the first two categories, earlier in this chapter and in the preceding chapter. We will now examine the third category – new reproductive technologies that involve the creation of new life.

Infertility is Still a Taboo Topic

When the Royal Commission on New Reproductive Technologies was conducting its public hearings across the country, one of the presenters in the province of Quebec commented: "The vast majority of fertile people cannot begin to imagine the pain experienced by infertile couples and what drives them to seek treatment which offers them hope." True enough. But those of us who have not had fertility problems can at least try to understand the social factors that contribute to it.

Most cultures, including Canadian culture, attach strong importance to the ability to reproduce, to carry on the species. For many men, the ability to reproduce is a sign of their manliness, for women a sign of their womanliness. While these mores may not be topics of everyday conversation they are nonetheless strongly imbedded in western culture. What newly married couple has not had to listen to insensitive though well-intentioned family and friends tease them about when they're going to start a family? How many young girls do *not* absorb the message in their childhood that they will grow up to be a mommy some day?

Many of us never think about how strong those messages are until there's a problem. And even though there are now many new options to help a woman become pregnant, fertility problems still remain a relatively taboo subject in our culture. Part of the reason is that many myths abound about infertility.

What is infertility?

Infertility means that fertility is in some way – perhaps only momentarily – impaired. The technical definition is: a person has tried, with frequent, unprotected intercourse, to become pregnant for more than 12 months.

However, there are myths about infertility that have confused its meaning.

Infertility Myths: From Sterility to Career Women

Myth #1: Infertility is the same as sterility.
Infertility is not the same as sterility. Infertility is defined as the inability to conceive following frequent unprotected intercourse for more than 12 months. Sterility, on the other hand, is the permanent state of infertility. Sterility can also be an imposed state – as in the inability to further conceive as a result of a tubal ligation (the fallopian tubes are sealed or cut to prevent sperm from reaching the egg) or vasectomy (the cutting of the vas deferens, the duct in the male that carries sperm from one testis to the seminal vesicle, so that the semen in the ejaculate will be sperm-free.).

Myth #2: It's all in your head.
Infertile women say how tired they are of being told, "Just relax. You'll get pregnant." Although stress can play a part in some women's ability to become pregnant, no research indicates that if a woman learns to relax, she will become pregnant.

Myth #3: It's the woman's fault.
In fact, men and women are equally responsible for infertility. In about 30 percent of infertility cases, the problem lies with the male; ditto for the female – about 30 percent. And in the remaining 40 percent, the problem is due to both partners.

Myth #4: Women are too career-minded.
One particular myth that has gained popularity in the 1980s and 1990s is that women have brought their infertility upon themselves by being "too career-minded."

Ironically, part of the reason that women have been able to be more sexually active is that modern technology – birth control – has enabled them not to worry about getting pregnant. The Pill and other birth control devices have revolutionized women's choices: women, for the first time in history and in large numbers, have had the opportunity to focus on other things they would like to do with their lives before deciding to have a family. But by a cruel twist of fate, some women find that when they stop using birth control, getting pregnant isn't as easy as not getting pregnant.

But to suggest that a woman has "chosen" this situation consciously is far from accurate. Women frequently put off childbearing because of a realistic fear that if they do not get established in the workforce while they are young, they will never be able to break into it or progress within it. In a perfect world, women would not be penalized for taking time off to have children at a time when their fertility might be less compromised (that is, in their twenties). As the Royal Commission noted, "for many women, the inadequacy of social supports makes it impossible for them to have their children earlier without paying a substantial penalty."

Myth #5: Women were too promiscuous in their youth.
Another recent myth is that infertile women were "too promiscuous" in their younger years. There *is* an ounce of truth in the belief that being sexually active with multiple partners, particularly at a younger age, increases your chances of fertility problems later. The reason is that certain sexually transmitted diseases (sometimes the result of having multiple sexual partners) can lead to pelvic inflammatory disease (PID) which, in turn, can affect a woman's ability to conceive or remain pregnant. However, blaming infertility on early promiscuity is nonsense.

Has the Rate of Infertility Increased in Recent Years?

There is a marked public perception that there has been an increase in infertility in recent years. However, the Royal Commission did *not* find this to be true.

The commission's research found that roughly 8.5 percent of couples in Canada (300,000 couples) who were married or had been cohabiting for at least one year, and who had not used contraception during that period, failed to have a pregnancy. For two years, the rate was 7 percent of all couples.

These figures do not indicate that infertility has increased. Perhaps the perception that infertility has increased is simply the result of people talking about it more. Although still a relatively taboo subject, there is less secrecy than there used to be about infertility. And with the proliferation of technologies to help infertile couples, people may assume that the problem is more prevalent than it actually is.

That said, a recent study of 1,351 sperm donations at a French sperm bank found sperm counts declined from 89 million per ml of semen in 1973 to 60 million in 1992, leading some people to wonder if sperm counts have indeed fallen worldwide in recent years. In another study, the French announced that long-distance truck drivers, whose testicles are crushed close to their bodies because they're unable to shift position, have low sperm counts. According to the World Health Organization, sperm counts have dropped worldwide, and no one seems to know whether stress or environmental pollutants are the cause. However, fertility specialists are quick to remind men (and women) that sometimes quality counts more than quantity. And that most men today have sperm counts at levels high enough to impregnate.

What Causes Infertility?

The Royal Commission on New Reproductive Technologies found that Canadians share the view that more emphasis should be placed on the prevention of infertility than on treating it. Prevention, of course, can only happen when we know what is causing the problem. In the case of infertility, there are many possible causes:

1. *Age*

One of the most obvious causes of infertility is age. As a woman's reproductive system gets older, it is less likely to be able to conceive, carry a pregnancy to term and deliver a healthy baby. Although far from practical for many women, the ideal time for a woman to conceive is in her twenties. The older a woman, the higher the likelihood, too, that she has increased her exposure to other factors that can contribute to infertility. (These factors are discussed below.)

2. *Sexually Transmitted Diseases (STDs)*

As noted above, certain STDs, particularly chlamydia and gonorrhea, can cause fertility problems. The Royal Commission concluded that "STDs are the single most important preventable cause of infertility among women." Specifically, the commission found that "an estimated 20 percent of all infertility among couples can be traced to damage to the female partner's fallopian tubes that has resulted from pelvic inflammatory disease (PID) caused by a sexually transmitted infection".

This finding points to the urgency for educating young women and men about the importance of delaying sexual activity, reducing the number of sexual partners and using barrier methods of birth control. STDs can also contribute to problems in carrying a pregnancy to term and in childbirth itself.

3. *Smoking*

Another preventable cause of infertility is smoking – both in men and in women. It is believed that the chemicals in the smoke inhaled (whether firsthand or secondhand) can have hazardous effects on the hormonal system, testes, ovaries and uterus. Given that one-third of Canadians in their childbearing years (aged 20 to 44) are smokers, more emphasis on smoking-cessation programs, as well as programs and policies to help nonsmokers remain smoke-free, would help decrease the current rate of infertility in Canada.

4. *Exposure to harmful substances in the workplace and in the environment*

Exposure to harmful substances in the workplace and in the environment can also affect fertility. Recent research points to this as a major cause of fertility problems for both women and men. This area is extremely difficult to study because we are exposed to a variety of agents in the environment and the workplace; isolating just one for study is costly and time-consuming. Being exposed to harmful agents can result in irregular menstrual cycles, sperm abnormalities and a reduced interest in sexual activity – all factors that strongly influence fertiltity.

Harmful agents that can negatively influence fertility include:

- a wide range of chemical substances (solvents, medical preparations, anesthetic gases such as nitrous oxide, chemicals used in photocopy machines and other office equipment, and agriculture agents such as fertilizers and pesticides);
- heavy metals such as lead;
- biological agents one may be exposed to in laboratory work.

Some researchers believe that we have barely exposed the proverbial tip of the iceberg about the extent of harm to one's fertility potentially caused by harmful environmental and workplace substances. This sparked the Royal Commission to recommend that "Canada should take the initiative in promoting a worldwide cooperative effort to assemble and analyze existing data, conduct new research, and draw conclusions about potential occupational and environmental hazards that face all of us."

Assisting Human Reproduction

FERTILITY DRUGS

Fertility drugs are the most common form of fertility treatment. Many of these drugs (they belong in the family of hormones) are prescribed outside of the context of infertility clinics by general practitioners and gynecologists.

In Canada, the most popular of this class of drugs are called:

- Clomid (clomiphene citrate); and
- Pergonal (menotropins and human chorionic gonadotropins). These drugs are used to stimulate the ovaries to produce more eggs.

Side effects of these drugs include:

- nausea;
- dizziness;
- anxiety;
- depression;
- mood swings.

More serious, but less common, side effects of the drugs include:

- ovarian cancer;
- blood-coagulation abnormalities (that is, blood clots);
- stroke.

Although some of these drugs have been on the market for a number of years (Clomid has been around for almost 30 years), others are new on the scene. One of the greatest concerns many observers have with these drugs is their unknown long-term effects. Many Canadians haven't forgotten the legacy of drugs like thalidomide and DES or the now very well documented links between estrogen and certain forms of cancer. As Rosanna Baraldi, a doctoral student involved with DES Action Quebec in Montreal notes, "It is important to realize that the long-term effects of a new pharmaceutical product have not been evaluated at the time of marketing."

PROFILE

Shirley and Harriet Simand: the troubling legacy of DES

For thirty years, from 1941 to 1971, the drug DES (short for diethylstilbestrol) was prescribed to hundreds of thousands of Canadian women in the hope that it would help them hold their pregnancy. Many of the women for whom the drug (a strong synthetic form of the hormone estrogen) was prescribed, had a history of miscarriage. However, it was given to some women in the misguided belief that it would make their babies "bigger and stronger."

Shirley Simand of Montreal was one such woman. In 1960, having previously miscarried, her doctor put her on the drug and told her to go home and rest. Unbeknownst to her and to many doctors prescribing the drug, research conducted in the 1950s had demonstrated that DES was no more effective than a placebo (sugar pill) in preventing miscarriage. Far more disturbing was the discovery in the early 1970s that some of the daughters of the women who had taken the drug were developing, at a very young age, a rare form of cancer of the vagina and cervix known as clear cell adenocarcinoma. In 1971, the drug was banned in Canada and several other western countries for use in pregnancy. It continued to be prescribed in Europe and many developing countries for years after that.

When reading about the link to cancer in 1971, Shirley asked her doctor whether the drug he had given her during her first pregnancy was DES. The doctor claimed it was not. In 1981, when Shirley's daughter Harriet developed this rare form of cancer at the age of 20, Shirley asked more questions of her doctor. He continued to say the same thing.

Harriet underwent radical surgery, including a hysterectomy, and withstood two months of radiation therapy because the cancer had spread to her lymph nodes. "My daughter went through menopause before I did," Shirley says.

Most astonishing to Harriet and Shirley was that they could find little information about the drug in Canada and had to look to the United States to learn that a large consumer group, DES Action, had been set up for the victims of this drug. With extraordinary tenacity and a conviction that Canadian women needed to know more about DES and the dangers of ingesting it, Harriet badgered the Canadian government to do something about the cloak of silence surrounding the use of DES. In 1982, she and her mother were granted a small amount of money to set up DES Action Canada out of their basement in Montreal to track the numbers of women who knew or suspected they were prescribed the drug.

Thanks to Harriet's courage in telling her intimate story to the media, the issue finally got some of the attention it deserved in the 1980s, more than ten years after it had been banned for use in pregnancy. Thousands of Canadian women came forward across the country, both the mothers who were prescribed the drug in pregnancy and the daughters who were now suffering ill effects from it. A handful of doctors across the country began to identify themselves as specialists who could screen for problems associated with DES. DES Action chapters began to spring up in 10 towns and cities across Canada providing information, support and medical referrals.

Research conducted subsequent to the link made to clear cell adenocarcinoma found that the offspring were more susceptible to a wide range of problems of the reproductive tract: miscarriage, fertility problems and other abnormalities of the vagina and cervix. Sons too have been affected by their mother's use of the drug, and have experienced problems including fertility problems and a higher incidence of undescended testes. More recently, the mothers who took the drug have been found to be at a higher risk for breast cancer. Because of the range of health problems, and the unknowns about the future of the offspring of the women who were given the drug, those who have been exposed to DES have been strongly encouraged to see a medical specialist (gynecologists for daughters, urologists for sons) who is familiar with the problems associated with DES. The oldest daughters of the women who were prescribed DES are just now going through menopause and it is not yet fully known if they will develop additional problems in an age group when certain forms of female cancers are more prevalent under normal circumstances. Animal research shows that the effects of the drug may also be passed on to subsequent generations. This has not yet been adequately studied in humans.

Since founding DES Action Canada in 1982, Harriet and her mother have received various awards, citations and other forms of recognition for the work they have done on behalf of Canadians exposed to DES. Harriet has a successful law practice in Toronto and continues her work as a consumer health advocate. Shirley continues to work in the DES Action office in Montreal and is involved in efforts to get more women into Canadian politics. To this day, Shirley's obstetrician denies that the drug he gave her in the 1960s was DES – this in spite of the fact that it has now been well documented in the medical literature that young women who contract this rare form of cancer have all been exposed to DES. He also maintains that he lost the medical records relating to Shirley's pregnancy with Harriet, although he has retained all her other medical records.

Harriet and Shirley have used every opportunity to warn the public about the lessons to be learned from the DES story. They have spoken out on the importance of asking questions when you are prescribed a drug and to be wary of taking anything that has not been approved for that use. They have continued to pressure government and medical associations to track the health histories of women and men who have been exposed to the drug. They pressure the pharmaceutical industry for more stringent testing and follow-up of both new and existing drugs on the market. They strongly caution women who are being prescribed other hormone drugs (as fertility treatments and hormone replacement therapy) to think seriously about whether they need it, and not to forget the example of DES. Harriet has commented, "Drug regulation may have improved a bit in this country since the days when DES was prescribed, but I still think we need to be very cautious. No formal body – not the medical profession, not the government and not the medical industry – has made any effort to track the people who were exposed to DES to follow the long-term health consequences. What would make us think things would be any different with the problems associated with fertility drugs?"

ASSISTED INSEMINATION

Assisted insemination (AI) – also known as donor insemination or artificial insemination by donor – is a method of conception that bypasses sexual intercourse and
does not require the presence of a male at the time of conception. The process
involves injecting donated sperm into the vagina of the woman. This can be done in
either a medically assisted fashion (with a doctor in a medical setting, sometimes
known as therapeutic donor insemination) or it can be entirely within the woman's
control (known as self-insemination).

The male who donates the sperm (in most cases, he is paid) may be completely
unknown and anonymous to the mother or couple – or he may be known, depending on the arrangement chosen by the mother or couple.

Assisted insemination traditionally has been viewed by heterosexual couples as a
means of addressing male infertility or as a way of avoiding the risk of transmission
of a genetic disease carried by the male. In these cases, medically assisted insemination tends to be the norm.

Donor insemination is also increasingly used by single lesbians, lesbian couples
and bisexual or heterosexual women who are without partners.

AI is not a complicated technology and as mentioned above does not necessarily
require medical intervention. For many years, lesbians and other women without
male partners have been inseminating themselves (with a needle-less syringe) using
sperm they have obtained from a male friend or relative, or from an anonymous
donor arranged through a third party. One lesbian couple, whose story was recount-
ed in a recent issue of the American magazine *Herizons*, chose to ask the brother of
the woman who would not be carrying the baby, thereby maintaining a biological tie.
One partner in the couple noted, "I certainly learned . . . that this was something you
did not have to invite the state into, or invite the medical profession into at all."

As observed by Dr. Rona Achilles, a noted Canadian expert on the social issues
surrounding donor insemination: "Donor insemination is really more of a social
arrangement than a medical technology."

How are sperm donors screened?

At present, the process by which sperm donors are screened, records are kept and
sperm is stored in Canada for clinical use is not well regulated. The Royal
Commission on New Reproductive Technologies found that "the lack of enforceable
regulation and inadequate monitoring of the practice of AI have the potential to
endanger the health of AI recipients, their partners, and their children."

This is not to say that ethical practices are not followed in many clinics. The Canadian Fertility and Andrology Society requires all sperm to be frozen and stored for at least six months before use. Couples and women interested in artificial insemination should inquire about the length of time the sperm has been frozen and whether or not its donor has been tested for HIV. Couples should also ask about the characteristics of and complete medical history of the sperm donor. In case your doctor retires or dies, it is useful to find out which sperm bank your sperm comes from and what the donor's identifying number is: this may become important if you need to trace the donor for medical purposes.

Secrecy and Assisted Insemination

In contrast with in vitro fertilization (couples often like to proudly announce, "This is our little IVF [or test-tube] baby!"), secrecy is a noteworthy characteristic of assisted insemination. Historically, most women who have been inseminated do not speak to others of a child's origins or tell their children where they came from, particularly in couples where there are male fertility problems.

However, this is much less frequently the case with lesbian couples who have used self-insemination. Research conducted for the Royal Commission found that often lesbian couples not only tell their children but the children sometimes have a direct relationship with the biological father. Where lesbians have used clinics, however, the donor is usually unknown.

IN VITRO FERTILIZATION

In vitro is the Latin term for "in glass." In *in vitro fertilization* (IVF), the glass is the petri dish in which eggs removed from a woman's ovaries are combined with sperm to create an embryo, which is then implanted in the woman's uterus. This may sound straightforward and simple but, in fact, there are many procedures connected to each phase of the process. For example, the man's sperm is usually put through a process called spermwashing to concentrate the more viable sperm. The woman is generally given fertility drugs both to regulate exactly when her body will release the eggs and to force the body to release more than one egg ("superovulate").

The reason for producing more than one egg is to create and implant more than one embryo in the hope that this will increase the chances that one will survive and carry to term. This explains why a high percentage of IVF pregnancies result in multiple births. In Canada, about 39 percent of deliveries from IVF pregnancies are multiple.

The other reason for creating multiple embryos is so that some can be frozen for later attempts, and some can be donated to infertile couples or to research. In cases where too many embryos "take" in the uterus, selective abortion, in which some of the embryos are removed from the uterus, is performed.

In its early days, in vitro fertilization was used only for women who had blocked fallopian tubes. This procedure allowed the possibility of the embryo by-passing the tubes and going right to the uterus. This remains the area in which success rates for IVF are the highest. But overall, the success rates are poor. Why?

First, there are many steps along the way to successful pregnancy where failure occurs in the IVF process. For example, about 80 percent of transfers of the embryo to the uterus do not result in implantation. Based on information collected by the American Fertility Society from both Canadian and American IVF programs, for every 100 attempts at IVF, 13 resulted in a live birth. For those who do go home with a baby (or babies) in their arms, this technology is viewed as a miracle. Nonetheless, one would have to concede that a 13 percent success rate is not very promising for a procedure as costly and risky as IVF.

SURROGATE MOTHERHOOD

Tabloid headlines in the 1980s proclaimed "Women for Hire" and "Wombs for Rent." The practice of one woman agreeing to carry a baby to term for another person is more popularly known as "surrogacy" or "surrogate motherhood."

Preconception arrangements, popularly known as surrogate motherhood, are described in the Royal Commission's report as arrangements "whereby a woman undertakes to conceive and bear a child with the understanding it will be raised by someone else." That someone else is understood to be the commissioning man or couple.

A number of types of arrangements fit this classification of reproduction; what they all have in common is that, unlike adoption, the decision of the gestating mother to relinquish the baby to others is made prior to conception. In the mid 1980s, the celebrated case of Baby "M," in which a birth mother decided she wanted to keep the baby a professional couple had hired her to have, brought the issue of preconception arrangements into full public view. In this case, the gestational mother decided, upon delivering the baby, that she had changed her mind and did not want to surrender the child to the contracting couple. The couple brought the case to court and the gestational mother lost custody of the child.

Preconception arrangements usually fall into two categories:
- genetic gestational arrangements; and
- gestational arrangements.

Genetic gestational arrangements, the most common type, involve inseminating the gestational (or surrogate) mother with the commissioning man's sperm. The insemination can either be done with medical assistance or without. In this instance, the biological mother is the one who carries the baby to term but the social mother is the one who will raise the child.

Gestational arrangements are those in which the gestational mother does not have a biological tie to the child she agrees to carry. Egg from either the commissioning mother or a donor and sperm from the commissioning father or a donor are fertilized in vitro, and then implanted into the womb of the gestational mother.

Couples (and in more rare circumstances, single people) choose this method of having children for a number of reasons, the most common being that the commissioning mother cannot carry a fetus to term. This may be caused by any number of reasons, including structural problems or a preexisting medical condition whereby pregnancy would put the commissioning mother's health at risk. She may have already undergone infertility treatments and found that she simply could not carry a fetus to term. In some cases, the commissioning woman has had a tubal ligation or has gone through menopause.

Deciding When to Stop "Trying"

For many women, deciding when to get off the new reproductive technology treadmill is more difficult than the original decision to get on it. With the emotional roller coaster of infertility treatments, and years of tests, procedures and miscarriages behind them, most women will eventually reach the conclusion that they must bring some closure to this chapter in their lives. This may be because they are simply too tired of being disappointed or because for health reasons they realize it is not wise to keep up the treatments.

Jan Rehner, a professor in the Faculty of Arts at York University in Toronto and herself infertile, has written eloquently about the pain of infertility and about the importance of bringing closure to that piece of her life. In her book *Infertility: Old Myths, New Meanings* (1989), she writes: "Infertility, endured and survived, is about self-knowledge. It is about the knowledge afforded a woman when she is suspended between the familiar expectations of her life and the growing evidence that she will not fit them. Infertility is ultimately a story about the painful reassembling of self, a mending and flourishing that expresses all we still might be, all we have learned to give. . . . It is not a matter of either/or, loss or gain, but of something gained from loss, and the crucial interconnection between the two."

Another Choice: Adoption

Many couples consider the option of adoption at some point in their quest to become pregnant. Some choose to investigate it early in the process, "just in case" they don't become pregnant; others consider it much further down the line, only as a last resort.

There was a time in Canada when the desire for an adopted child could be easily fulfilled. Today, due to improved access to contraception and abortion in Canada, and an increasing number of young women and girls choosing to keep their babies when they unintentionally become pregnant, fewer and fewer babies are available.

PUBLIC, PRIVATE OR INTERNATIONAL ADOPTION?

Whether public or private, adoption agencies maintain specific criteria for adoptive parents and require an extensive home study to determine the suitability of a couple or family. Advocacy groups for gays and lesbians have long fought for the right of gay and lesbian couples to be able to adopt, but only the province of Ontario has passed legislation allowing this to happen in a limited way. Couples over a certain age and single people wishing to adopt have faced similar barriers.

Public adoption

Research on adoption conducted for the Royal Commission on New Reproductive Technologies found that for every child available for adoption through public agencies, eight applicants are waiting to adopt.

Most children available through public adoption (through child welfare agencies such as the Children's Aid Society or a provincial ministry facility) have special needs (physical or emotional disabilities), are older, or have a history that suggests there may be future problems. Because of this situation, and because the waiting list with most child welfare agencies is several years long, couples increasingly are turning to private and international adoptions.

There are some advantages to public adoption, however. One: it provides more support services to adoptive parents. Two: though the waiting list is long, the screening process is excellent. While there may be some professional fees to meet along the way, the prices are by no means as high as those in the private adoption sector. Three: You are adopting a child whose background is fairly well known. That may include his or her birth parents' medical histories and the medical histories of their families.

Moreover, should that child wish to contact his or her birth parents at the appropriate age, the process would be easier and the records more accessible than in an international adoption.

Private adoption

With the exception of Quebec and Newfoundland where all adoptions are coordinated through a public system, private adoption is legal in Canada. Many couples find they are more likely to secure a child by using this route. As well, they face a much shorter waiting list. The biggest disadvantage is the cost: fees average around $5,000 but can be much higher.

International private adoption

More and more Canadian couples are turning to international private adoption. The costs of adopting a child in another country and bringing the child to Canada varies widely. Depending on the country of origin, it can cost anywhere from $6,000 to $30,000. There often are many unknowns with an international adoption (such as the type of prenatal care the birth mother had, the quality of institutional care the child might have had prior to adoption), but many international adoptive parents argue that it is easier than dealing with the red tape of domestic adoption.

Couples adopting internationally must abide both by child welfare laws of the province they reside in, and the adoption laws of the country of origin of the child.

Jan Silverman of the Regional Women's Health Centre in Toronto and the mother of two domestically adopted children comments that if she had to make the decision today – given the present-day difficulties with domestic adoption – she would choose the international route. "I wouldn't spend the emotional time or energy that goes into a domestic adoption. With an international adoption, providing you hook up with a good facilitator, are careful, and do all your homework, you can at least be assured that you will achieve parenting. The same cannot be said about domestic adoption today."

QUESTIONS, CONTROVERSY AND DEBATE

THE ETHICS OF REPRODUCTIVE TECHNOLOGY

Ethicists and others studying reproductive technology have argued that each step in the process is fraught with both ethical and physical health problems. There are many questions:

- What are the long-term health consequences of taking fertility drugs?
- Who decides how many embryos are too many?
- Who owns the frozen embryos if a couple divorces or dies?
- Is it appropriate use of health care dollars to be producing so many multiple birth pregnancies when we know that multiple birth babies tend to have more health problems?

Jan Silverman expresses a note of caution in discussing the multitude of ethical problems that accompany reproductive technologies. "The technology is so far ahead of the ethicists' abilities to deal with them," she observes. "In the work that I do, there is such an assumed acceptance of these various reproductive technologies. But, personally, I have grave concerns about a lot of this."

INTERFERING WITH NATURE: WHERE SHOULD WE DRAW THE LINE?

One of the areas that Silverman and many others are concerned about is the increasing degree of manipulation of otherwise natural processes. One example of this is intracytoplasmic sperm injection (ICSI), which works in cooperation with in vitro fertilization. This procedure, which is aimed at treating male infertility, follows the same process as IVF with the addition of a technique whereby each egg that is retrieved has a single sperm injected into it. This technique can also be used for couples where the man has had a vasectomy, in which case the sperm is extracted directly from the testes through a minor surgical procedure.

Shirley Service, nurse coordinator at the Infertility Clinic at the Foothills General Hospital in Calgary, reports that the waiting list for ICSI is longer than for IVF, and more and more couples are asking for it. "The demand has skyrocketed since we started doing it here," she adds.

Serious Ethical Questions About Commercialism

Although preconception contractual arrangements date back to biblical times, the use of assisted insemination and in vitro fertilization introduces the possibility of eliminating sexual intercourse between the biological mother and father.

Although the "technological" aspects of preconception arrangements are now relatively straightforward, the commercial aspect of such arrangements raises serious ethical questions. These concerns were addressed at the cross-Canada public hearings held by the Royal Commission on New Reproductive Technologies. Although noncommercial arrangements exist (for example, in the case of a woman who agrees to bear a child for her sister who is infertile or cannot carry a pregnancy to term for health reasons), most preconception agreements today have commercial implications.

Often, although not always, a third-party person, known as a broker, is used to organize these arrangements. This may be a lawyer, a physician or other professional who charges a fee for services. In the United States, there are lawyers and physicians whose entire practices focus on facilitating (and hugely profiting from) such arrangements. In some cases, the third-party broker makes as much money on the arrangement as the woman who carries the pregnancy.

The Royal Commission attempted to determine the extent of preconception arrangement activity in Canada. But this is an extremely difficult area to research since much of it goes on in secrecy for fear of litigation. Quebec is the only province in Canada with legislation forbidding the practice of preconception arrangements. In other provinces, the issue falls into a legal limbo: no precedent-setting litigation has taken place in Canada to date.

The Royal Commission discovered private fertility and in vitro clinics in Canada where these procedures are taking place for the purpose of preconception arrangements. However, these clinics or private practices are not legally obligated to report this, so the accuracy of information is questionable.

In 1988, the Law Reform Commission of Canada examined preconception arrangements in Canada. It found that "of the 118 cases of preconception arrangements examined, 42 took place in Canada and 76 involved U.S. agencies. In 13 of the cases involving U.S. agencies, Canadians were serving as gestational women; in 62 cases, the Canadians were commissioning couples; and in one case, a Canadian single man had received a child."

Preconception arrangements are a reality in this country; what is not clear is how widespread the practice is.

SURROGATE MOTHERS: A POTENTIAL FOR EXPLOITATION

The Royal Commission found that the potential for exploitation in this area is tremendous. Research consistently shows that the most economically vulnerable women are the ones most willing to undertake preconception agreements and that women who are financially stable are highly unlikely to engage in them. Moreover, the Law Reform Commission of Canada found that gestational mothers tend to have lower education levels than commissioning couples.

Immigrant women, often amongst Canada's poorest, sometimes act as gestational mothers. This practice has already been documented in the United States, and the Royal Commission was advised on it during its public hearings. This raises serious ethical questions and concerns about whether women truly have a free choice (as advocates of surrogacy proclaim they do) about entering into preconception arrangements. Certainly they do not enter into the arrangements as equal partners with any of the other parties involved.

THE ETHICS OF ADOPTION: ROYAL COMMISSION RECOMMENDATIONS

Because there are many ethically difficult issues involved in the question of adoption, the Royal Commission on New Reproductive Technologies strongly recommended that federal, provincial and territorial governments in Canada jointly undertake a review of adoption in Canada. A review of this nature would address such issues as:
- the relative merits of public and private adoption systems in promoting the best interests of the child and in meeting the needs of the other parties involved;
- access to adoption and barriers to access;
- cost;
- record keeping and disclosure;
- counselling and consent;
- the advantages and disadvantages of interprovincial harmonization of policies, services and practices;
- issues relating to international adoption.

A FINAL WORD ABOUT THE NEW REPRODUCTIVE TECHNOLOGIES

We have seen that an examination of infertility and new reproductive technologies cannot be looked at within the narrow context of which techniques might help which women or couples to have the much-desired babies. After four years of examining the issues, the Royal Commission on New Reproductive Technologies concluded that the rapid expansion of new technologies must be studied within a much broader context. The commission concluded that this context must consider *prevention* of infertility above all. It is infertility that is creating the need for all this "cowboy medicine," as one commentator called it. The only way to avoid this ethical quagmire is to focus society's attention on the prevention of STDs, on prevention of exposure to harmful agents in the workplace and in the environment, on reducing the use of tobacco and on increasing social supports that allow women to have their children (if they so choose) when they are younger.

Those are good thoughts. On the other hand, infertile couples who have conceived thanks to the new technologies are mighty grateful. Still, the need for regulation and monitoring in this new "industry" is urgent. In the summer of 1995, federal health minister Diane Marleau called for a voluntary moratorium on the use of some of the reproductive technologies. It remains to be seen if this is the first step towards regulation. Until there is adequate regulation, that old caveat applies: Buyer, beware!

PART THREE

Your guide to pregnancy resources

MIDWIFERY AND CHILDBIRTH SUPPORT ORGANIZATIONS

In addition to the following, there are countless prenatal courses and postnatal support groups offered through local hospitals and community centres.

Canadian Confederation of Midwives, 132 Cumberland Cres., St. John's, NF A1B 3M5 (709) 737-6528.

Midwifery Association of British Columbia, F-502, 4500 Oak St., Vancouver BC V6H 3N1 (604) 254-0744.

Alberta's Association for Safe Alternatives in Childbirth, Box 1197, Main Post Office, Edmonton AB T5J 2M4 (403) 425-7993.

Manitoba Traditional Midwives' Collective, 14 Michigan Ave., Winnipeg, MB R3T 3V2 (204) 275-6900.

College of Midwives of Ontario, 2195 Yonge St., 4th floor, Toronto, ON M4S 2B2 (416) 327-0874.

The Labour Support Association and Registry (for labour and post-partum support in your area.) 426 Drummond Rd., Oakville, ON L6J 4L4 (905) 842-3385 or (905) 844-0503.

Lebel Midwifery Care Organization of Ontario 2 Carlton St., Ste. 1508, Toronto, ON M5B 1J3 (416) 585-7709.

L'Alliance des sages-femmes de Québec (514) 738-8090.

Association Nova Scotia Midwives, 27 Muriel Ave., Dartmouth, NS B2W 2E4 (902) 434-9882.

Alliance of Midwives and Maternity Nurses of Newfoundland, School of Nursing, Memorial University, St. John's, NF A1B 3V6 (709) 737-6528.

For information about midwifery in the Northwest Territories and Yukon, contact Maureen

Morewood-Northrop, Department of Health and
Social Services, Government of the Northwest
Territories, Box 1320, C.S.T.–6, Yellowknife, NWT
X1A 2L9 (403) 920-3311.

Books

As the number of available books is vast, they are
grouped here according to specific areas of interest
and experience. Along with the following, a selection of books on pregnancy and childbirth can be
found at your local bookstore or library.

I. General

A Complete Book of Pregnancy and Childbirth,
Sheila Kitzinger (Alfred A. Knopf, 1990).

The Pregnancy Sourcebook, M. Sara Rosenthal
(Lowell House, 1994).

*A Guide to Effective Care in Pregnancy and
Childbirth*, Murray Enkin, Marc J.N.C. Keirse and
Iain Chalmers (Oxford University Press, 1989).

Conception, Pregnancy and Birth, Miriam Stoppard
(Macmillan, 1993).

*One Mother to Another: Canadian Women Talk
About Pregnancy and Childbirth*, Winifred Wallace
Hunsburger (Fifth House Publishers, 1992).

The Complete Mothercare Manual. Jerry Shime,
M.D., Sandra Moody, M.D. et al. (Stoddart, 1991).

What to Expect When You're Expecting, Arlene
Eisenberg, Heidi E. Murkoff and Sandee E.
Hathaway (Workman Publishing, 1991).

II. Choices in Pregnancy and Childbirth

*A Good Birth, A Safe Birth: Choosing and Having the
Childbirth Experience You Want*, Diana Korte and
Roberta Scaer (Harvard Common Press, 1992).

*Homebirth: The Essential Guide to Giving Birth
Outside of the Hospital*, Sheila Kitzinger (Dorling
Kindersley, Inc., 1991).

*Mothering the Mother: How a Doula Can Help You
Have a Shorter, Easier, Healthier Birth*, Marshall H.
Klaus, Phyllis Klaus and John Kennell (Addison-
Wesley, 1993).

Painless Childbirth: The Lamaze Method, Fernand
Lamaze (Contemporary Books, Inc., 1984).

*Your Baby, Your Way: Making Pregnancy Decisions
and Birth Plans*, Sheila Kitzinger (Pantheon Books,
1987).

III. Special Circumstances

Having Twins, Elizabeth Noble (Houghton Mifflin,
1990).

*Long Distance Delivery: A Guide to Travelling Away
from Home to Give Birth*, Northwestern Ontario
Women's Health Information Network and the Red
Lake Women's Information Group (Helmsman
Press, 1990).

Losing a Baby. Available for $6.95 from the
Canadian Institute of Child Health, 885
Meadowlands Dr. E., Ste. 512, Ottawa, Ontario K2C
3N2, or phone (613) 224-4144.

*Multiple Blessings: From Pregnancy Through
Childhood, A Guide for Parents of Twins, Triplets or
More*, Betty Rothbart (Hearst Books, 1994).

*Recovering from a C-section: A Comprehensive
Guide to Cesarean Deliveries from Procedure to Post-
Partum to Diet and Exercise*, Margaret Blackstone
and Tahira Homayun, M.D. (Longmeadow Press,
1991).

The Vaginal Birth After Cesarean Experience, Lynn
Baptisti Richards (Bergin and Garvey Publishers,
Inc., 1987).

IV. Special Groups of Women

Birth Over Thirty-five, Sheila Kitzinger (Penguin.
1994).

*Fertility and Pregnancy Guide for DES Daughters
and Sons*. DES Action USA. Available from DES
Action Canada, 5890 Monkland Ave., Ste 203,
Montreal, Quebec H4A 1G2.

*Mother to Be: A Guide to Pregnancy and Birth for
Women with Disabilities*, Judith Rogers and Molleen
Matsumura (Demos Publications, 1991).

*Your Premature Baby: Everything You Need to Know
About Childbirth*, Frank B. Manginello, M.D., and
Theresa Foy DiGeronimo (John Wiley and Sons,
Inc., 1991).

Lesbian Parenting: Living With Pride and Prejudice,
Katherine Arnup (Gynergy Books, 1995).

V. THE BIRTH

Easing Labour Pain: The Complete Guide to Achieving a More Comfortable and Rewarding Birth, Adrienne B. Lieberman (Doubleday and Co.,1987).

The Birth Partner: Everything You Need to Know to Help a Woman Through Childbirth, Penny Simkin (Harvard Common Press,1989).

VI. AFTER THE BIRTH

Post Partum Depression and Anxiety: A Self-Help Guide for Mothers, The Pacific Post Partum Support Society (Grandview Publishing Co. Ltd., 1987).

Rebounding from Childbirth: Toward Emotional Recovery, Lynn Madsen (Bergin and Garvey, 1994).

The First Weeks of Life, Dr. Miriam Stoppard (Ballantine Books, 1989).

The Womanly Art of Breastfeeding, LaLeche League International (Penguin (Plume), 1987).

When Partners Become Parents: The Big Life Change for Couples, Carolyn Pape Cowan and Philip A. Cowan (Harper Collins, 1992).

You and Your Newborn Baby, Linda Todd (Harvard Common Press, 1993).

Your Baby and Child, Penelope Leach (Alfred A. Knopf, 1990).

VII. FATHERHOOD

Birth of a Father, Martin Greenberg (Avon Books, 1986).

Keys to Becoming a Father, William Sears, M.D. (Barron's Educational Press, 1991).

MAGAZINES

Great Expectations: The Magazine for Expectant Parents. Published three times a year and widely available free of charge from physicians, nurses, childbirth educators and midwives. If you are unable to get one from your caregiver or in your community, contact Great Expectations, Circulation, 955 Meyerside Dr., Mississauga Ontario, L5T 1P9, or phone 1-800- 567-8697.

The Compleat Mother: The Magazine of Pregnancy, Birth and Breastfeeding. Quarterly publication available for $12 a year from RR#2, Chesley, Ontario NOG 1LO.

Today's Parent Prenatal Class Guide. An annual publication available for $5.95 from prenatal class instructors or by writing Today's Parent Prenatal Class Guide, Circulation, 955 Meyerside Dr., Mississauga, Ontario L5T 1P9, or phone 1-800-567-8697.

VIDEOS

Comfort Measures for Childbirth (with Penny Simkin). Available from 1100–23rd Ave., Seattle, Washington 98112, or phone (206) 325-1419.

The Use of Water for Labour and Birth. A 23-min. film by Marina Alzugaray U.S. $35. Available from the filmmaker c/o 131 Behr Ave., San Francisco, California 94131.

PART THREE

Your guide to infertility and new reproductive technology resources

ORGANIZATIONS AND SUPPORT GROUPS

Contact the following for referrals to support groups or to keep up on the ever-evolving new reproductive technology scene:

Infertility Awareness Association of Canada (IAAC), 774 Echo Dr. Ste. 523, Ottawa, Ontario K1S 5N8, 1-800-263-2929.

The Adoption Council of Ontario, 3216 Yonge St, 2nd Flr., Toronto, Ontario M4N 2L2 (416) 482-0021.

New Reproductive Alternatives Society. A support and lobby group for parents who have used donor insemination, for donor offspring and for individuals considering donor insemination. BC contact: Shirley Pratton, 641 Cadogan St., Nanaimo, British Columbia, v9s 1t6, (604) 754-3900; Toronto support group chapter: (416) 762-2643

Women's Network on Health and the Environment, 736 Bathurst St., Toronto, Ontario, m5s 2r4 (416) 516-2600

Clinics

If you choose to go the route of infertility treatments, the following clinics specialize in the new reproductive technologies:

University of British Columbia IVF Program, Vancouver, British Columbia, (604) 875-2611.

The Foothills Regional Fertility Program, Calgary, Alberta (403) 284-5444.

University Hospital, Saskatoon, Saskatchewan (306) 966-8033.

University of Manitoba Health Sciences Centre, Winnipeg, Manitoba (204) 787-1961.

Toronto General Hospital, Toronto, Ontario (416) 340-3213.

IVF Canada, Scarborough, Ontario (416) 754-8742.

University Hospital, London, Ontario (519) 663-2903.

Ottawa Civic Hospital, Ottawa, Ontario (613) 761-5177.

L'Institut de Médicine de la Réproduction de Montréal, Montreal, Quebec (514) 345-8538.

Le Centre Hospitalier de L'Université de Laval, Quebec, Quebec (418) 654-2738.

Georges L. Dumon Hospital, Moncton, New Brunswick, (506) 862-4217.

Grace Maternity Hospital, Halifax, Nova Scotia (902) 420-6658.

Grace General Hospital, St. John's, Newfoundland (709) 778-6593.

Books

Adoption in Canada, Michael P. Sobol and Kerry J. Daly (University of Guelph, 1993).

The Canadian Adoption Guide, Judith Wine (McGraw-Hill Ryerson, 1995).
Double Take: A Single Woman's Journey to Motherhood, Kathryn Cole (Stoddart, 1995)

Infertility Among Canadians: An Analysis of Data from the Canadian Fertility Survey (1984) and General Social Survey (1990), T.R. Balakrishnan and R. Fernando. In Research Volumes of the Royal Commission on New Reproductive Technologies, 1993.

Infertility: Problems Getting Pregnant. Available through the Vancouver Women's Health Collective, 1675 West 8th Ave., Ste. 219, Vancouver, British Columbia, v6j 1v2.

Infertility: Women Speak Out About Their Experiences of Reproductive Medicine, Renate Klein, ed. (Pandora Press, 1989).

Misconceptions: The Social Construction of Choice and the New Reproductive and Genetic Technologies, Vol. 1 and 2, Gwynne Basen, Margrit Eichler and Abby Lippman, eds. (Voyageur Publishing, 1993 (Vol. 1) and 1994 (Vol. 2)).

Proceed With Care: Final Report of the Royal Commission on New Reproductive Technologies, Vol. 1 and 2, Ministry of Government Services Canada, 1993.

Uncommon Knowledge: A Critical Guide to Contraception and Reproductive Technologies. Published by Women's Health Interaction and Inter Pares, Ottawa, June 1995. Available for $10 from Inter Pares, 58 Arthur St., Ottawa, Ontario k1r 7b9.

CHAPTER 10

MENTAL WELLNESS: NURTURING AND CELEBRATING YOURSELF

Why is this a women's health issue? One in four Canadian women will suffer severe depression at some point in their lives.

What you can do for yourself: Learn to take care of yourself first, learn the signs of depression and seek help through therapy or medication if necessary.

WHAT IS MENTAL HEALTH?

Health isn't just about strong bones and a healthy heart, it's also about the state of your mind. Mental health means having a sense of well-being, possessing a degree of self-esteem and feeling emotionally on top of things.

WHAT IS MENTAL ILLNESS?

Mental illness is a behavioural, psychological or biological dysfunction associated with some level of distress, suffering or impairment in daily functioning. Among the various kinds of mental illness are mood disorders, anxiety disorders and psychoses.

PART ONE

The facts: why mental health is a women's issue

Mental health issues are women's issues for the following reasons:
  • In the official reporting of mental health problems, women outnumber men.

- Twice as many women have depression as men.
- More women than men are admitted to hospitals for problems related to mental health.
- Women are prescribed mood-altering drugs twice as often as men.
- Women are more likely than men to be dismissed as hysterical.
- Studies have shown that girls enter adolescence with a lower sense of self-worth than boys.

At the Clarke Institute of Psychiatry in Toronto, Dr. Brenda Toner heads the Women's Mental Health Research Program. It became clear to her that although women suffer disproportionately from major depression, eating disorders, irritable bowel syndrome, anxiety, borderline personality disorders, chronic fatigue and fibromyalgia (see Chapter 19), gender has not yet been addressed as a treatment issue.

She told *Toronto Sun* writer Sandy Naiman that she was extremely interested in "what women want out of the mental health care system, what issues in their lives affect their well-being." Psychiatrist Dr. Elaine Borins has also made this point. She believes that women's mental health distresses should be measured differently than men's: the kinds of questions asked to evaluate conditions such as depression are biased towards men, she believes. "Miscarriage, for instance, isn't on the list of significant life events that prove to be stressors."

We hear a lot about mental illness, but why are people not talking about mental wellness, asks Sylvia Hordyski, a nurse therapist at Calgary General Hospital who speaks on mental wellness for the Canadian Mental Health Association. Just as you eat your vegetables when you are not sick, so you also need to take care of your mental health, she says. "Think about who are the three most important people in your life, I ask clients. Women especially rarely put themselves on the list. But unless you are taking care of yourself, you cannot take care of anyone else.If you're looking for love in your life, you cannot love someone else until you love yourself."

Hordyski says women, in particular, have trouble putting themselves first: "If you have $50 and one of your kids needs a new pair of jeans and you need a new bra, I'll bet it's you who goes to work tomorrow hitching yourself up while your kid goes off to school wearing his fifth pair of jeans. We have been taught historically that good people give, give and give. But give too much and you'll soon run on empty," warns Hordyski. "And you can't serve tea from an empty pot."

What Defines the Mentally Well Woman? An Expert's Opinion

Here is Sylvia Hordyski's list of criteria for the mentally healthy woman:

- A mentally healthy woman can differentiate between what she can control and what she can't. "We often spend a lot of time trying to change things that aren't in our control. We waste energy with which we could be doing something that is within our control."
- A mentally healthy woman looks for relationships in which she can receive and give, not just look after somebody or be looked after. "There are no princes or princesses anymore. Only prince-ly and princess-ly type moments. To be healthy, one needs to realize that relationships are about giving and taking, taking and giving."
- A mentally healthy woman realizes she needs to be acknowledged, validated, loved. She will celebrate herself. "We're taught that it's arrogant to say anything positive about ourselves. But why do we have to hide our talents and hope someone else might notice?" A healthy person can also celebrate others. "We're so withholding of praise and compliments. A mentally healthy person can stroke others. A mentally unhealthy person is afraid to because they fear that if they give away something, they won't have enough for themselves."
- A mentally healthy woman is "a person with self-esteem, a person who is able to differentiate between "personal mail" and "dear occupant mail." In other words, when someone is giving them feedback, they have the ability to objectively identify whether this is about their issue or whether the other person is just dumping something. For instance, your boss tears a strip off you. You have to decide whether it is about you or about anybody in your chair. If it's about anyone in your chair, that's 'dear occupant mail,' and you have to let that roll off because you're going to get lots of it in your life."
- A mentally healthy woman knows she needs to be touched. Part of mental wellness is understanding that your needs haven't changed that much over the years. You've grown a larger body but you still need touch. Some people today live by themselves, go to their jobs and go for long times without touching another human body. "We need to share touching, and I don't mean just sexually."
- A mentally healthy woman values herself as a woman but resists conforming to female sex stereotypes. She neither victimizes herself nor allows herself to be victimized. She strives for emotional and economic self-sufficiency.

Self-Esteem: What Does it Have to Do with Mental Health?

Our grandmothers would have called it self-respect, that old-fashioned belief in who we are, what we think of ourselves and how we value ourselves. Some would call it self-worth, that quality that allows us to enjoy a sense of balance and perspective on the rocky roads of life. In the last decade or so, self-esteem has become an issue that women everywhere have been thinking about. Low self-esteem has been blamed for everything from women who stay in abusive relationships to young girls who flee from a commitment to math, from eating disorders to unwanted pregnancies. According to feminist author Gloria Steinem, self-esteem isn't everything. "It's just that there's nothing without it," she says ironically.

But what exactly is self-esteem? How do you get it? And if you have it, how do you know how much of it is enough?

Self-esteem is not something we're born with. It's a quality we develop during childhood that is planted and nurtured by our adult caregivers. Children who are not valued will probably not value themselves and so will lack self-esteem. Everything a child experiences has the potential to enhance or undermine that self-esteem. If she finds positive reinforcement in what she does – playing the piano, for example – her experience will contribute to her sense of accomplishment and self-worth. If the feedback she gets is only criticism and disappointment, her experience will make her feel inadequate, discouraged and will chip away at her self-esteem. If she's compared unfavourably to others around her or judged for the way she looks, if she is told she'll never amount to anything or criticized for what she says and does, she will grow up with a significant lack of self-esteem.

Why have women had to wrestle so much with self-esteem? Probably because we've been socialized to be compliant and a little self-blaming. Studies tell us that most women are dissatisfied with their bodies and faces; women's magazines support (and encourage) the notion that women are desperately in need of help with their relationships; and women constantly struggle to juggle a variety of roles, often putting the needs of others ahead of their own. Add to that list the glass ceiling of the corporate world that makes accomplished women feel passed over and undervalued, and the obsession with youth in our culture that can shake the foundations of self-esteem in older women, and you can see why, as women, we do not come to a sense of self-esteem easily.

In her book *Revolution from Within* (1992), Gloria Steinem writes about coming to her own realization about how self-esteem comes from within, not outside, yourself. "Though the way I'd grown up had encouraged me to locate power almost anywhere but within myself, I began to be increasingly aware of its pinpoint of beginning within."

Steinem's own particular path to claiming the self-esteem she felt was missing was to find her inner child. When she realized that as a child she had been denied a crucial sense of security, she was able to accept her loss and get on with the task of building self-esteem through a journey of self-discovery.

A healthy self-esteem helps us to take charge of our lives. It can enable us to attain goals, to take better care of others and, most important, to nurture and take care of ourselves. With a little attention and time, anyone can reclaim their self-esteem, no matter what their age. Start by surrounding yourself with supportive people who genuinely care for you, learn to recognize and accept your strengths and weaknesses, and begin to please yourself – at least as much as you attempt to please those around you.

PART TWO

Your guide to mental health

1. Stress

Stress is any interference that has an impact on a person's healthy mental or physical well-being. Stress can be both positive and negative and can be the product of anything from a vacation to bereavement. Stress produces a physiological response that increases the production of hormones which, in turn, alter heart rate and blood pressure. Too much stress can cause a wide range of serious health problems, from heart disease to depression.

Stress prepares the body for a "fight-or-flight" response. Some experts feel that women are not well prepared to cope with or act on these responses because most women are socialized to be nurturing, conciliatory and adaptive.

Why is stress a woman's issue?

In the sixties, we heard a lot about the Type A man, at high risk for stress-related diseases. Today, there's also the Type E woman, says Dr. Susan Abbey, a Toronto Hospital psychiatrist with a special interest in women's issues. "She must be everything to everybody. "A man at his desk in a room with a closed door is a man at work," says Dr. Abbey. "A woman at a desk in any room is available." We've all been socialized to some extent to be good little girls and to keep everyone else happy, she says. "We should be asking ourselves, 'Is this desirable and is it even possible?'"

The Type E woman needn't continue down a self-destructive path, Dr. Abbey believes. "It is a problem of how we think and how we behave. [Today] it's most women's struggle in life to not be Type E."

What is burnout?

Burnout is the wearing down and wearing out of energy. It is exhaustion from excessive demands; these demands may be self-imposed or imposed from outside.

Why do women burn out?

Women burn out because of the powerlessness we feel in the face of the conflicting demands that come with independence versus dependence; and the multifarious demands made of us in our many nurturing roles. These often include taking care of growing children and aging parents.

Today, most women work at two jobs – one in the paid workforce and one raising their children and handling the majority of household chores. Dr. Abbey believes that burnout is a condition common to women of the nineties.

LEARN HOW TO REDUCE YOUR STRESS

Here are some ways to be a little kinder to the person who's number one – you!

• *Learn to take care of yourself.*
Dr. Abbey says that women who were raised by mothers who valued and took care of themselves most likely taught their daughters to do the same for themselves. Women who were not raised by such mothers will have to learn what they need to do to keep themselves happy.

• *Try not to be excessively self-reliant.*
"Just remember, there are always people around us who can be helpful to us," says Dr. Abbey.

• *Learn to say no.*
"It's easy to say no when there is a deeper yes burning inside," Abbey says, quoting author Steven Covey, a time-management guru who wrote the bestseller

First Things First (1994). "Think of the three most important things to you this year. Write them out and put them on your phone at work. When someone phones, you will be reminded you have three primary goals that will take your time. This will truly help you to sort out what to say yes and no to."

• *Find out what gives you pleasure and thrills you.*
"Understand your values, be clear about what you must do, prioritize activities, learn to say no and also learn to build pleasure into each day," Abbey says. "Sit down and say, 'What matters to me?' It can be quite sobering."

• *Find out what gives you comfort.*
It may be one Smartie every day. Dr. Abbey suggests making a list of one-minute, ten-minute, 15-minute pleasures. A one-minute pleasure may be closing your eyes and imagining yourself on a secluded white-sand beach. A ten-minute pleasure may be a brisk walk around the block. A 15-minute pleasure may be reading an article while sipping a cup of mint tea.

• *Change your self-talk.*
"If you stop for a moment and try to watch what happens in your mind, you often find a lot of negative thoughts such as, 'I must be stupid.' These are errors in thinking and they also include things such as, 'I must do things perfectly.' Or 'I should be able to accomplish more in a day.' Or 'I should be able to do it all and not feel tired.' Other self-defeating thoughts are: 'I have to please others.' 'I can't relax until I finish what I have to do.' 'I have to prove myself to everyone.' 'I can't be happy unless I have it all.'

Sometimes, just being aware – raising your awareness – of what you're doing is enough to change behaviour.

• *Learn about mental mini-vacations.*
These include things like staring at a favourite postcard on your office wall, treating yourself to a walk to your neighbourhood park, buying yourself a single fragrant rose, two minutes of daydreaming.

• *Take care of your physical self.*
Walk, exercise, practise good nutrition, manage alcohol, cigarettes, coffee or medication, listen to your body, attend to physical problems such as dental care or having your doctor check out a mole that's changed shape. Learn about body therapies such as massage, aromatherapy and yoga.

• *Try relaxation self-control techniques.*
These include the relaxation response, progressive muscle relaxation, guided imagery and meditation.

• *Consider psychotherapy.*
"Know when to ask for help, whether it's for depression, anxiety or an eating disorder," says Dr. Abbey.

2. Anxiety Disorders

The Canadian Psychiatric Association says that people with anxiety disorders may feel irritable and apprehensive, fearing bad things are about to happen to them or their loved ones. Anxiety sufferers may present a number of physical symptoms including shakiness, muscle aches, sweating, cold and clammy hands, a dry mouth and racing heart. Anxiety disorders (from fear of flying to dreading the dentist) affect 5 percent of all people in a lifetime.

Why are anxiety disorders a women's issue?

According to the Canadian Mental Health Association, two-thirds of people suffering from anxiety disorders are women.

Types of anxiety disorders

Panic Disorders
You're at the dentist's and she's just about to get out her drill. You experience a sudden intense fear due to the classic fight-or-flight response. You're having a panic attack. Symptoms include a pounding heart, sweating, shortness of breath, trembling, nausea, light-headedness, a fear of dying or losing control, difficulty in swallowing, hyperventilating, numbness and tingling sensations.

Phobias
You're going to a party that requires taking an elevator up to the 20th floor. You feel terror, dread, panic and even consider not going to the party or trying to walk up instead. You have a fear of enclosed spaces, or claustrophobia.
Common phobias include fear of snakes, of flying and of enclosed spaces such as elevators or tunnels. "You can be afraid of cats, of heights, of blood, you name it," says

psychiatrist Dr. Gail Robinson, director of the Toronto Hospital's Program in Women's Mental Health. "But the fear we're talking about is excessive and unreasonable and the person knows this. The lifetime risk of having any phobia is 10 to 11 percent; in women it is twice as common.

Obsessive-Compulsive Disorder
You can't leave your house without checking to see that the stove's turned off, but you don't check just once, you do it over and over and over again. The Canadian Psychiatric Association says that obsessive-compulsive disorder sufferers try to cope with their anxieties by associating them with obsessions – repeated, unwanted thoughts or compulsive behaviours, or rituals that can get out of control.

Post-Traumatic Stress Disorder
You wake up one night and you find your house on fire. Over the next several months or years, you find yourself startled easily, unable to get a good night's sleep, having difficulty concentrating or completing tasks; you find you have a poor memory. You may also experience anxiety, nightmares, flashbacks and other symptoms of anxiety. According to the Canadian Psychiatric Association, the less anticipated the original trauma was the more severe post-traumatic stress disorder tends to be.

Getting a Handle on Anxiety Disorders

While we all have anxious moments (skidding on an icy highway) and extended, anxious periods of time (studying for final exams), general anxiety disorders are characterized by excessive anxiety and worry for a period of at least six months. If simple relaxation exercises or talking things through with a good friend don't alleviate some of your distresses, it's best to seek professional advice. There are excellent short-term and behavioural therapies (as well as drugs for those who need them) available to help people suffering from anxiety disorders.

3. Depression

The Canadian Psychiatric Association reports that one in four women and one in ten men can expect to develop depression at some point in their lives, although often they will not identify it as depression.

"We get up in the morning, we see the weather and we say we feel depressed. These are everyday stresses, not real depression," says Dr. Robinson. These feelings are what we describe as normal blues.

The seven signs of depression are:

1. A low mood.
2. Changes in appetite – either weight loss or weight gain.
3. Changes in sleep patterns – too much or too little.
4. Decreased concentration and memory.
5. Fatigue or loss of energy.
6. Worthlessness or guilt feelings.
7. Suicidal feelings.

Does Depression Affect Women Differently From Men?

Yes. The psychology of women is one reason women experience more depression and anxiety. Gender differences go right back to adolescence where role conflicts, loss of control and erosion of self-esteem may begin. "If you're a teenage girl interested in the football captain and he's not as smart as you are in math, what do you do?" asks Dr. Robinson. Do you try to play down your smarts, act helpless, find another boyfriend or tell him he'll have to cope with a math brain as his date?

"Young women in the process of forming their identities as they separate from their families may feel depressed. Teen girls who display an assertive attitude risk rejection from their peers and may feel depressed and alone. Dissatisfaction with one's body, a history of family violence or sexual abuse may also contribute to depression in teen women."

Social pressures contribute to women and depression. "Marriage is a very good thing for men," says Dr. Robinson, citing statistics that indicate married men tend not to be as depressed as nonmarried men. "Unfortunately, women who are married have higher rates of depression than men who are married." Add to that the fact that in dual-career households women still do 70 percent of the work, and you can see how social pressures may contribute to burnout and depression.

Other factors that contribute to depression in women:

- poverty and abuse
- loss of a pregnancy (a miscarriage: termination or stillbirth)
- illness or loss of loved ones
- perimenopause: "Women are more likely to feel depressed before menopause [than they are at menopause]," says Dr. Robinson. "They fear what the loss of fertility, role changes, aging and the family leaving the home will be like."

Getting a Handle on Depression

According to surveys, women are more likely to ask for help with depression than men. Seeking professional help for depression is important. There are excellent psychotherapies available; and for serious depression, drugs may be prescribed.

Prozac: A Miracle Drug or a Risk Not Worth Taking?

An estimated 70 percent of prescriptions for antidepressant medications go to women. Though antidepressants help lift many people out of the black hole of serious, sometimes suicidal, depression, some doctors and patients feel they are overprescribed. Women often report that a doctor's first response to their complaints about depression is to write out a prescription for a mood-lifter or "happy" pill.

One of the strongest antidepressant pills around and one of the most widely prescribed is Prozac. An astounding 10 million North Americans have been prescribed this drug. Prozac or fluoxetine is a drug that affects the body's serotonin levels. Serotonin is a neurotransmitter or messenger between our brain cells and is thought to be responsible for certain mood-related functions. Prozac apparently blocks the serotonin buildup in our brains, enhancing our feelings of security and self-esteem.

The long-term effects of Prozac simply are not yet known (it's been in use for less than a decade). Many health care professionals feel that while an antidepressant may help in some cases, it is no substitute for psychotherapy. And Prozac does not work for everyone. Some studies show that it has been no more effective than traditional antidepressants (Elavil or amitriptyline and antidepressant drugs like it have been around since the fifties.)

Prozac's side effects have been underplayed, according to Dr. Peter Breggin, an American psychiatrist who, with Ginger Ross Breggin, wrote *Talking Back to Prozac* (1994). He and many others claim that the seriousness and frequency of the drug's side effects have been dismissed. They say that the side effects include insomnia, nausea, loss of appetite, loss of libido, and, in some cases, violence and suicide. They also question whether it should be so widely prescribed for everything from the management of PMS symptoms to weight control, migraines and as a personality enhancer.

Prozac's advocates, on the other hand, insist that Prozac belongs to a class of drugs that has the fewest side effects of all antidepressants. They say that the backlash about Prozac's serious side effects, including charges of suicide, have less to do with the drug itself than with how doctors have prescribed it. Properly prescribed and carefully monitored, patients should not experience serious side effects, they say.

Clearly, more research is needed. So is a dose of healthy skepticism: anti-depressants may be successful in controlling certain disorders, but miracle cures they're not. Make sure you discuss with your doctor his or her reasons for prescribing this drug and be sure you're aware of the potential side effects before starting a regimen of it.

Helen Hutchinson – "I've stopped trying to be somebody else."

Canadian broadcaster Helen Hutchinson put on a happy face for millions of Canadians while on the air for 30 years. Hutchinson hosted many radio and television shows, including *W5*, *Canada A.M.* and *Hockey Night in Canada*. But when the cameras were turned off, she'd "go home, play the piano and cry."

Hutchinson only began to face her depression in 1987 after a television contract was not renewed and her daughter Megan was diagnosed with the liver disease that eventually claimed her life. "I couldn't get out of bed, I stopped bathing and I couldn't decide what socks to wear," Hutchinson, now in her early sixties, told me several years later. She was in the middle of trying to start a new life by completing a master's degree in library science.

In 1994, Hutchinson was back on the set of *Canada A.M.*, this time as a guest. She told viewers her story in the hope that more people would understand depression, recognize its symptoms and encourage a loved one (or themselves) to seek help. Hutchinson's depression was so all-encompassing that she attempted suicide. Her treatment has included therapy, antidepressants and electroconvulsive therapy treatments.

"I always thought of my depression as a character flaw that could be worked through," Hutchinson told the *Toronto Sun*'s Sandy Naiman. "I never liked myself. I thought I was a fake. But facing this illness has changed me. It's made me more me. I've stopped trying to be something else. I'm resigned and relaxed into who I really am." Today, she's a volunteer patient liaison and advocate at Toronto's Clarke Institute of Psychiatry. In 1994, she was the recipient of their Courage To Come Back Award.

4. Post-Partum Blues

The baby's colicky, you're up at dawn to feed her and you haven't been out of the house for six days. You're tired, cranky, depressed. You've got the post-partum blues.

We tend to think of the birth of a baby as a joyous time," says Dr. Gail Robinson. "So women who don't feel so happy about it don't want to tell anyone." It's not only your time and energy levels that are challenged and altered, she says. "Your body changes dramatically. Any woman's first child is a huge adjustment; it stirs up our old feelings and memories about our own relationships with our mothers." All your relationships change when you have your first child: your relationship with your spouse, your relationship to friends who don't have kids, your relationship with your parents.

How common are post-partum blues?

About 70 percent of new mothers suffer from post-partum blues. They usually begin on day three after the baby is born and they last a week or so, says Dr. Robinson. "This little transition is very normal. New mothers used to be in hospital a lot longer and we could observe them more closely. Now, because they're at home much sooner, it falls to them and those around them to be more aware of what's normal and what's not."

Are post-partum blues the same as post-partum depression?

The blues are normal, but post-partum disorders are not. About 10 to 15 percent of women experience major depression at this time (though it may, or may not, be linked to childbirth). "This is a time when women are most at risk for a major breakdown," says Dr. Robinson.

Unfortunately, symptoms of serious emotional trouble may not be picked up by the mother, her family or even her doctor. "If people broke out in purple spots when they were depressed, life would be a lot simpler," Dr. Robinson says. But depression's symptoms are difficult to diagnose, especially when they can be masked by problems typical to new moms – lack of sleep, feeling cooped up, initial self-doubt in new tasks such as bathing the baby. "What we're talking about, however, is something that goes beyond the normal. Most people feel nervous when they first bathe the baby but then they get less anxious the more experience they have," Dr. Robinson explains. "But if they continue to be very anxious, even though they've gained experience, that may signal something's wrong."

Post-partum disorders may include obsessive-compulsive disorders – checking the baby 20 times to see if he's still breathing, for instance. More severe symptoms include a large loss of weight, lack of concentration, a feeling of confusion. Women can often tell their problems are serious, "but it's a matter of attribution," says Dr. Robinson. "They think, either 'This is normal, everybody feels this way.' or they think, 'I'm a bad mother for feeling this way.' They don't say, 'I'm feeling this way because I've just had a baby and I'm depressed.'"

According to Dr. Robinson, doctors should be more aware of the seriousness of post-partum disorders. Typically, "she [the mother] goes home and is seen six weeks later by an obstetrician and in the meantime she could be developing a full-blown depression." Family physicians should ask themselves: is this more than an adjustment this patient's experiencing? "It could be, on the one hand, an unhappy person taking a while to recover. Or, at the extreme, someone who is at risk of commiting suicide or harming the baby."

Prenatal classes don't focus much on depression. All the time is spent leading up to the event. Yet post-partum depression is one of the complications of pregnancy, says Dr. Robinson. "Spending the first year of your baby's life not being able to enjoy her or unable to cope is not a good introduction to motherhood."

POST-PARTUM BLUES: HERE'S HOW TO HELP

- If you're a friend or relative:

Talk to the new mom about what she's feeling. Allow her to express her negative feelings. Don't say things like, "Bite your tongue. You should feel thankful you have such a lovely baby." If you notice lots of negative thoughts, excessive worry, a chronic lack of sleep, no energy and appetite loss, encourage the new mother to seek treatment. Depression is an illness, not a weakness of character, says Dr. Robinson. Good treatment is available. Don't convey to her that she's bad because she's depressed.

- If you're a new mom:

Be realistic about the sudden drastic changes in your life. You've gone from freedom to being stuck at home within 24 hours. Block off personal time, Dr. Robinson recommends. "Get a relative or neighbour in so you can go for a walk or out with a friend. Just take a break." Watch your rest. If you're breastfeeding, seriously think about supplementing: "Breastfeeding can be exhausting," Dr. Robinson tells us. "Sometimes young mothers need permission to stop it or supplement it."

If you're feeling down, join a support group. Joining a support group will get you out. You can compare notes, get reassurance, and gain perspective from others to determine if you need help. Contact your public health nurse, your hospital or your birthing centre for information on community support groups. Or start your own support group and ask a public health nurse to help you set up a program of speakers to go with it.

5. Suicide

"In our society the topic of suicide is taboo. There is strong reluctance to talk about it openly and seriously," Sharon Barnes, president of the Canadian Mental Health Association, said during a recent campaign by the association to bring the subject of suicide out of the closet.

Myths surrounding suicide include the assumption that it is an attempt at getting attention; in fact, it is a person's cry for help or an attempt to end the pain in her life. Another myth says that suicide is an attempt at avoiding responsibilities; in fact, the person has not found a better way to resolve her problems. "For every completed suicide, there are on average 100 attempts," says Barnes. "Because of the stigma surrounding suicide, as many as 30 percent of suicides are not reported."

In Canada, every three minutes, someone tries to take their own life. The Canadian Mental Health Association estimates that about 8 percent of the Canadian population is directly affected by suicide. The highest suicide rate for women is between the ages of 30 and 49. Many doctors believe that depression causes most suicides.

Some warning signs that a person may be suicidal:
- repeated expressions of hopelessness, helplessness, or desperation;
- behaviour that is out of character, such as recklessness in someone who is normally careful;
- signs of depression (sleeplessness, social withdrawal, loss of appetite, loss of interest in usual activities);
- a sudden and unexpected change to a cheerful attitude;
- giving away prized possessions to friends and family;
- making a will, taking out insurance, or making other preparations for death, such as telling final wishes to someone close;
- making remarks related to death and dying, or an expressed intent to commit suicide.

IS SHE SUICIDAL? HOW TO HELP PREVENT A SUICIDE ATTEMPT

- Talk with the person directly and listen to them without passing judgement.
- Find a safe place to talk and allow as much time as necessary; assure her of your concern and your respect for her privacy.
- Ask her about recent events and encourage her to express her feelings freely. Do not minimize or trivialize the feelings she feels.
- Ask her whether she feels desperate enough to consider suicide. If the answer is yes, ask, "Do you have a plan? How and where do you intend to kill yourself?"
- Admit your own concern, but do not react by saying, "You shouldn't have those thoughts; things can't be that bad."
- Talk about resources that are available (family, friends, crisis centres) to provide support, counselling or treatment.
- Make a plan with the person for the next few hours or days. Make contacts for her on her behalf; if possible, go with her to get help.
- Let the person know when you can be available, then make sure you are. Stay in touch to see how she is doing. Praise the person for having the courage to trust you and for continuing to live and struggle.

The Therapy Dilemma: Should You? And If So, What Kind, Where and From Whom?

Depression and anxiety disorders are real illnesses, Dr. Gail Robinson points out. "Don't blame yourself if you get them. Recognize the signs and go for help." Scientists are studying the importance of brain biochemistry and recognizing the contribution of biochemical imbalances to anxiety and depressive disorders. There are now many anti-anxiety medications, antidepressants, mood stabilizers and other medications to alleviate symptoms.

PSYCHOTHERAPY

And there's psychotherapy in which no drugs are prescribed.

When the young son of a friend of mine was asked by other eight-year-olds in his class why he was seeing a psychiatrist, the child answered, "She's my talking doctor."

Psychiatrists and psychologists may wince at the child's observation, but I think he got to the core of what therapy's all about. "By talking about their thoughts and feelings, people [in therapy] learn things about themselves that they did not previously know or appreciate," writes psychiatrist Karen Johnson in her book *Trusting Ourselves: The Complete Guide to Emotional Well-Being for Women* (1991). "This greater self-understanding allows them to make more informed life choices."

What's the thinking behind psychotherapy?

Psychotherapy operates on the belief that people have the capacity for growth and change, but that a person's growth can become blocked. Think about how "stuck" you can become in a relationship, a job, a pattern of thinking. When growth is blocked and you feel stuck, you may develop symptoms of distress, such as deep depression. "In psychotherapy, that person has the opportunity to explore the ways they or circumstances limit their psychological growth and well-being," Dr. Johnson writes. "By revealing these obstacles, they then have the chance to change those that are within their power to change."

How do you know when you need professional help?

"It comes to a crisis point where life really seems intolerable," explains Dr. Susan Abbey. "Often there's a straw that breaks the camel's back, something that doesn't make sense to the person because they have already been through horrendous things and they know that the 'straw' is something fairly small. They may feel overwhelmed, worried, panicky, have feelings of sadness, feel that nothing whatsoever can ignite a spark for them. Sometimes, for women, the symptoms come out in a bodily way: headaches or constant pain. One woman said she realized she needed to come for help because she'd had a bottle of Tylenol in her office for five years, untouched. Then a new boss came on the scene and she went through it in a month and a half."

Sometimes, a family physician will pick up a cue from you; often a friend or co-worker will notice that you're going through a particularly hard time. Large changes in your life (such as a family member's illness or divorce) can have an impact on your state of mind. But ultimately, the decision to seek help, and follow it through, must come from you. Ask yourself how much your particular distress, be it an anxiety disorder or depression, is affecting your family, work or personal life.

One way you know you're in trouble is by looking for patterns in your relationships and work, says Calgary nurse-therapist Sylvia Hordyski. Questions you might ask yourself include the following:

- What is the longest relationship I've ever had?
- Do I keep hopping from one relationship to another?
- What about my job history? Have I changed jobs because I've been restless, the company's closed, the management hasn't been satisfied with me?
- Am I a content person? Do I have happy moments?
- What kind of home life do I come from? (That has a lot to do with how you feel about yourself, Hordyski says. "Even if we say we're not going to do what our parents did, most of us had 18 years of conditioning. You take part of it along with you.")

Why go to a therapist? Won't talking to a good friend do as well?

Good friends are tremendously important, but most don't have the training to help us sort through a very serious problem or to minimize great distress we may be feeling. Good friends may be good listeners, but a professional therapist is trained to hear not only what the patient says but also what she may *mean* by the words she uses. And as patient, loyal and supportive as good friends are, they can easily get stuck with you when, for the 40th time, they hear you retell your version of your marriage breakup or complain, yet again, about your job. Acknowledging to yourself that you need outside help is often the first step to healing or changing.

"The big thing is that the therapist doesn't have anyone's interest at heart except yours," says Dr. Susan Abbey. "If you're talking to a friend or your partner, in some way they all have an agenda for you. They all have a sense of what would be good for you." With a therapist, she explains, you have the freedom to talk about your needs without worrying that you're going to have a negative effect on your friends or family or that they're going to think less of you when you reveal your secrets or air your dirty laundry. "Therapists are trained to listen, whereas a friend or family member may be thinking more of how they are going to respond to what you say," Dr. Abbey points out. "Also, you can get very stuck by yourself. You know you have problem A you can see solution B and you ask your friends how you can get solution B. Well, a therapist will say I don't know how I can help you get solution B, but why stop there when there's the rest of the alphabet? One woman patient described this insight as a blind having been lifted."

Dr. Arlette Lefebvre, a psychiatrist at the Hospital for Sick Children in Toronto, supports the concept of positive role models for both children and adults. "A good role model is worth one hundred shrinks," she says. Good friends also have been shown to play a part in our maintenance of good overall health. Dr. Sarah Maddocks, a psychologist at Women's College Hospital in Toronto, says that good social support helps a person deal with stress better. According to her statement in the hospital's newsletter, *Women's Health Matters*, caring relationships provide an emotional buffer to help cope with life's ups and downs.

You can't force someone into therapy

"The prognosis for someone who is told they have to come to therapy is very bad because they don't want it for themselves," cautions Sylvia Hordyski. "People usually go when what they're living now becomes too painful. People don't go usually until they're in pain." Hordyski believes it's better to seek help when there are signs that you're either not coping or not dealing with things well.

How To Find a Therapist

Shopping for a therapist isn't quite the same as shopping for a toaster, but it's not that different, either. I advocate the consumer approach. First, get a list of names from friends, colleagues and professionals who you respect, such as your family doctor, your lawyer or member of the clergy. Your provincial psychological or psychiatric association or local hospital may be able to provide you with a list. Remember, at this point, these are names only: you need to do more research into the people them-selves. Here are some tips to finding the right therapist:

- Make sure the person you choose is a qualified, trained therapist. In Canada, these include psychiatrists, psychologists, marriage and family therapists and social workers.
- You may choose to go the route of a self-help group: organizations such as Alcoholics Anonymous have a proven track record and most self-help groups have on their boards a professional consultant such as a psychiatrist, physician or social worker. Some people find group support helpful along with individ-ual therapy.
- You will need to assess potential therapists. To do this, be prepared to set up consultations with them. Be prepared to identify for them the main issue for you as you see it. By all means, listen to what he or she has to say, but more importantly try to evaluate how you feel talking to this person, whether or not you feel you can trust them. Ultimately, you're looking for someone with good qualifications, someone you can talk to and someone with whom you feel a good fit. One caution: some therapists say very little, so if you're the type of person who requires a therapist to do a lot of talking back, tell this to the per-son during your first session. If your gut feeling is that he or she will be too

silent throughout your therapy, you might be happier choosing someone whose techniques are more interactive.

- "When interviewing potential therapists, ask them to describe the school of therapy they practice," advises Dr. Karen Johnson in her book *Trusting Ourselves*. "Many adhere to one, while others are more flexible."
- Discuss fees the first time: some psychiatrists charge only what is covered by health insurance; others tack on an "administrative fee."
- Make sure you understand what type of time commitment is required of you: last winter, two New York psychologists made headlines by offering therapy-to-go for busy clients (the "office" was the back seat of a chauffeur-driven limo). In Canada, therapists don't come to clients, clients go to therapists. Visits can range from four 45-minute sessions each week as in psychoanalysis, to an hour every week or two.

Types of Therapy

There are hundreds of different schools of therapy, and many therapists develop their own approach which integrates different schools of thought.

Brief Therapy

Brief therapy's goals are accomplished in about eight to ten sessions. However, the therapy is not superficial or rushed in any way. The therapy is patient-centred: the patient is viewed as the expert and the physician acts as the facilitator. Dr. Patricia Rockman, a Toronto family physician, explained brief therapy the following way in an August 23, 1995 article in the *Medical Post*: "Brief therapy is a form of psychotherapy that does not treat the patient as a problem. Rather than emphasizing the problem when it is present, as is typical during a medical interview, we look for exceptions to the problem when it is absent. The focus is not on the problem itself, but rather on personal strategies and strengths used by the patient to manage it. Therefore, resolution of the problem is not required. Instead, small changes are negotiated with the patient to improve the situation at hand."

Feminist Therapy

Feminist therapy developed largely in reaction to existing psychological theories which were seen to be male-centred (such as Freud's theory of penis envy). Dr. Brenda Toner of Toronto's Clarke Institute of Psychiatry explains the three basic principles of feminist therapy as follows. First, a consciousness-raising approach is applied: women aren't treated as victims; they are encouraged to take responsibility for their actions.

Second, an egalitarian relationship between therapist and client is fostered: while this doesn't mean that the client and doctor are friends, it does mean that the doctor-client relationship becomes demystified and put on an equal footing; clients are encouraged to trust their experiences. Third, a self-validating approach is used. Women are encouraged to identify their strengths – to value and nurture themselves.

Jungian Therapy

Modelled on the idea formulated by Swiss psychiatrist Carl Gustav Jung (1875–1961), this form of therapy explores ideas shared by everyone in their "collective unconscious." Jung's study of personality focused on the introvert and the extrovert as two basic personality types; for a person to feel whole, one's inner-consciousness must be reconciled with the outer-self. Jungian therapy includes the interpretation of dreams.

Behaviour Modification Therapy

The emphasis on this therapy is trying to change behaviour rather than trying to figure out why it has occurred. Therapists have demonstrated a lot of success using this technique to help patients cope with phobias and anxiety disorders. Using a desensitization model, over time, a person is trained to become less frightened of either flying or heights, spiders or spaces. Techniques include relaxation exercises to help overcome the sensation of shortness of breath that accompanies phobic attacks.

Cognitive Therapy

This form of therapy seeks to help patients become more self-aware. In the therapist-patient relationship, the therapist plays an active role in guiding patients to understand how their view of certain situations may lead them to act negatively or interpret the world as inhospitable. Based on the idea that the way in which we perceive our surroundings and ourselves influences our attitude and behaviour, cognitive therapy encourages the patient to think more positively and to affect her environment in new ways.

Psychoanalysis

Developed by Sigmund Freud, this intensive talk therapy seeks to help the patient explore her unconscious. In these sessions, in which painful memories or feelings are unlocked, the patient usually lies on a couch while the analyst sits out of sight so as not to distract the patient from what she has to say. Taking time (three to five times per week for several years) and money (the sessions are expensive, even though a portion may be covered by insurance), this therapy especially depends on a patient's trust of the therapist.

Violence Against Women: Struggling for Ways to Lessen the Damage

Regina's Ty Hochban, a family physician, wrote a different kind of children's story that went this way:

> Once upon a time there were three little bears. Orsa, his wife Anna, and their child Lungin. They live happily, almost ever after, until an early winter catches them unprepared and their food supplies dwindle.
>
> As a result, the daddy bear takes to drinking Jackberry wine. When, after hibernation, they wake up to find spring is way off, Orsa takes to drink again. He is scared, but he is also a bully. He takes his anger out on his wife and his child, yelling, threatening, and eventually smacking and slapping them both around . . .

Hochban's *Hear My Roar: A Story of Family Violence* (1994) came out of a residency he did a few years before at Newfoundland's Memorial University. Instead of turning in a clinical paper on an obscure subject, he decided to write a book that might be useful to adults and their children. "I wanted to challenge the idea that violence was appropriate behaviour," Hochban says. If you believe the saying that violence begets violence, children who witness it at home will grow up to use their fists to solve problems. "If we're to end family violence," he explains, "we have to start with our children, to show them that violence is never the right answer. We should challenge the idea that violence can be any solution at all. It shouldn't ever even be a choice."

So when the mommy bear sees her child smashing his dolls around, when she notes his constant headaches and tummyaches, she takes him to the doctor. After checking out both symptoms, Dr. Woodland discovers there's nothing physically wrong with Lungin, so he pours mommy bear and Lungin a cup of tea and invites them to chat about their lives. Little by little, Anna's story of abuse comes out, Lungin learns that hitting, shouting and hurting are not acceptable ways to solve problems and the doctor assures Lungin and Anna that they are not to blame for Orsa's violence.

In the tradition of the best fairy tales, this is a lifesaving message told simply. Kids can relate to it, says Shelley Levitz, supervisor of Kids Help Phone. And Anna, the mother bear, is presented not as a pitiful soul, but as a woman of strength and dignity who tries to do the best for her family. It takes her a while, as it does all victims, but she finally leaves her husband and her home for safer shores.

Published in *The Year of the Family*, Hochban's book was a call to action for family physicians. "The book is a reminder to doctors that family violence has to be addressed "because the consequences of it are so great when missed," Hochban says. Treating children affected by family violence is a tall order, he adds. "They love their father, but see him abuse their mother. They love their mother, but feel resentful that she can't stop the violence. Children who are trying to develop in a home that's dangerous and chaotic become fearful. Children shouldn't have to worry about anything except age-appropriate things like their next game of ball or why the sky is blue. They shouldn't have to worry about their mother being beaten so badly she won't be able to care for them."

A CALL TO ACTION: DOCTORS SHOULD INTERVENE MORE

Statistics indicate that three in ten Canadian women, currently or previously married, have experienced at least one incident of physical or sexual violence at the hands of a marital partner. According to Statistics Canada, more than half of the country's 10.5 million women have suffered some form of assault. Dr. Carol Warshaw, a specialist in emergency and internal medicine in Chicago, says that some doctors don't ask patients about abuse for a variety of reasons: a lack of awareness, limited time, the feeling that it's not their role or place, the judgement that discussing it won't do any good anyhow, or simply lack of knowledge about how to ask or help. In addition to obvious assault injuries, battered women present with sexual problems, chronic headaches, gastrointestinal problems and alcoholism.

When doctors don't intervene, Dr. Warshaw says that the injury is treated but the underlying problem is not addressed: "The injury is just the tip of the iceberg." Often, the woman is labelled hysterical and becomes further isolated and locked into the battering relationship. If she is given medication, she may become dependent on the drug or suffer side effects from it that can cause her despair to increase. Drugs are not the answer, Dr. Warshaw maintains. She urges doctors to intervene when they suspect a woman is the victim of abuse.

WHEN YOU KNOW YOUR FRIEND IS HURTING: HOW TO HELP

What can we really do when we think a friend, neighbour or relative is undergoing a crisis involving family violence?
- "Be a good listener," says Barbara Merriam, manager of Health Canada's National Clearing House on Family Violence. "Provide necessary phone

numbers. And if necessary, help the person move into a transition house. Even saying, 'Let me sit beside you while you're making the phone call,' may be a source of strength to someone trying to leave."

- "Assure her she is not alone," says Dr. Carol Warshaw. In the spring of 1995, Dr. Warshaw told an audience attending a Women's Health Day sponsored by Women's College Hospital that friends can reassure a battered woman of many things: that she is not alone, that the violence is not her fault, that help is available, that what happened can't be justified, that she can be treated with dignity and respect and that there are choices she can make.

The Women's Monument: A Marker of Change

The words *Montreal Massacre* are more recognizable to most Canadians than the names of the 14 women murdered on December 6, 1989, at L'Ecole Polytechnique/ Université de Montréal. A group of Vancouver women has pledged to change that. The women, who include Rosemary Brown, chief commissioner of the Ontario Human Rights Commission, and First Nations' artist/curator Doreen Jensen of Surrey, British Columbia, have spearheaded a unique project – the creation of a special monument to honour Genevieve Bergeron, Hélène Colgan, Nathalie Croteau, Barbara Daigneault, Anne-Marie Edward, Maud Haviernick, Barbara Maria Klueznick, Maryse Leganière, Maryse Leclair, Anne-Marie Lemay, Sonia Pelletier, Michele Richard, Annie St.-Arneault and Annie Turcotte, the 14 young women murdered.

Ontario artist Beth Alber's winning design, entitled Marker of Change, will be a circle of 14 five-and-one-half-foot benches of pink Quebec granite, each bench bearing the name of one of the women. Each bench will be designed with a small indentation in it that will collect rainwater, "like a collection of tears," says Alber. The monument will be one of very few pieces of public art made by a woman about the lives of women. The organizers have asked for donations (the monument will cost $390,000). Donors' names will be inscribed in the bricks around the monument.

The organizers point out the enormous waste exacted by violence against women. The names of the women who die yearly at the hands of men must be remembered, they say, not the names of the murderers.

Aruna Papp – "I was scared when I got here. Can we talk?"

Aruna Papp came to Canada from India in 1972 with two small children and an abusive husband. "Different immigrants have different reasons for wanting to come," says Papp, who entered kindergarten in India when she was 11 and seven years later was married off. "I wanted to go to school. Canada was hope."

She got two jobs at York University in Toronto, one as a short-order cook and another as a locker-room attendant. In between the two shifts, her kids would come to the university to have dinner with her. Eventually, she paid students to sit in for her in the locker room while she sneaked off to attend a class.

But while her adjustment to Canada was softened by opportunities to work and to learn, her home life became tougher. Her beatings became regular events. After one particularly horrific incident, she looked around her immigrant neighbourhood in the Jane/Finch corridor and thought: "My God, I wonder if the same thing is happening to any other women here?" She hit the streets and apartments of the corridor, knocked on hundreds of doors and said, in one of the many languages she speaks: "Hi, my name is Aruna. I am new like you. I was scared when I got here. Can we talk?"

She laughs now telling how much tea she drank meeting women like herself. The tea talk eventually evolved into groups for abused immigrant women. "At our first meeting, 156 women came. I only had 30 chairs. They talked about loneliness and depression but, at the beginning, nobody talked about abuse. Slowly, the stories came out. They were horror stories," says Papp. Papp told the women's husbands she was running English classes for their wives. The sessions' first 20 minutes were devoted to the subject so that when the wives returned home, they could say a few new words to their husbands.

Papp eventually left her husband, got a degree in sociology, founded several projects addressing violence in the South Asian community and produced a video on the subject. Today, she still works with abused women in the city's South Asian community. She is remarried and now has another daughter, and a grandchild.

PART THREE

Your guide to women's mental health resources

ORGANIZATIONS

Contact the following organizations to obtain educational materials, for information on support groups. All have access to local counselling services and can help you to obtain either immediate help during a crisis or to locate a therapist.

Greater Vancouver Mental Health Service Society, 800–601 West Broadway, Vancouver, British Columbia V5Z 4C2 (604) 874-7626.

Marital Discord Clinic, Department of Psychiatry, St. Paul's Hospital, 1081 Burrard St., Vancouver, British Columbia V6Z 1Y6 (604) 682-2344.

Mood Disorders Association of British Columbia, 201–2730 Commercial Dr., Vancouver, British Columbia V5N 5P4 (604) 873-0103.

Sexual Assault Service, British Columbia Women's Hospital and Health Centre, 4500 Oak St., Vancouver, British Columbia V6H 3N1 (604) 875-2424.

British Columbia/Yukon Society of Transition Houses, 409 Granville St., Ste. 1112, Vancouver, British Columbia V6C 1T2 (604) 669-6943.

Calgary Women's Health Collective, 223 12th Ave., S.W., Calgary, Alberta T2R 0G9 (403) 265-9590.

Women's Psychological Services, 1301 10th Ave. S.W., Calgary, Alberta T3C 0J4 (403) 228-5594.

Foothills Hospital, Department of Psychiatry, 1403 29th St. N.W., Calgary, Alberta T2N 2T9 (403) 670-1110.

Calgary General Hospital, Department of Psychiatry, Psychiatric Outpatient Services, 841 Centre Ave. E., Calgary, Alberta T2E 0A1 (403) 268-9202.

Suicide Information & Education Centre, 1615-10th Ave. S.W., Ste. 201, Calgary, Alberta T3C 0J7 (403) 245-3900.

Western Canada Behaviour Research Centre, 210–320 23rd Ave. S.W., Calgary, Alberta T2S 0J2 (403) 571-6050.

Mental Health Services, Edmonton Clinic, 9942 108th St., 5th Flr., Edmonton, Alberta T5K 2J5 (403) 427-4444

Provincial Association of Transition Houses, 230 Avenue R. South, Ste. 418, Saskatoon, Saskatchewan S7K 2Z1 (306) 652-6175.

Department of Family Services, 114 Garry St., 2nd Flr., Rm. 201, Winnipeg, Manitoba R3C 4V5 (204) 945-1705.

Klinic: A 24 Hour Sexual Assault Crisis Program, 870 Portage Ave., Winnipeg, Manitoba R3G 0P1 (204) 786-8631.

Society for Depression and Manic-Depression Association of Canada, 1000 Notre Dame Ave., Ste. 4, Winnipeg, Manitoba R3E 0N3 (204) 786-0987; 1-800-263-1460.

Canadian Mental Health Association, Box 2101, The Pas, Manitoba R9A 1L8 (204) 623-7203.

Canadian Centre for Stress and Well-Being, 141 Adelaide St. W., Ste. 1506, Toronto, Ontario M5H 3L5 (416) 363-6204.

Depressive and Manic-Depressive Association of Ontario, 56 Temperance St., Ste. 200, Toronto, Ontario M5H 3V5 (416) 943-0434

Family Abuse Crisis Exchange (FACE): A Work and Interview Clothing Exchange, 2301 Weston Rd., Weston, Ontario M9N 1Z7 (416) 617-7900.

Ontario Friends of Schizophrenics, 885 Don Mills Rd., Ste. 322, Don Mills, Ontario M3C 1V9 (416) 449-6830; 1-800-449-6367.

Ontario Association of Interval and Transition Houses, 2 Carlton St., Ste. 1407, Toronto, Ontario M5B 1J3 (416) 977-6619.

Clarke Institute of Psychiatry, Women's Mental Health Research Program, 250 College St., Toronto, Ontario M5T 1R8 (416) 979-2221.

Mood Disorders Association of Ontario, 40 Orchard View Blvd., Ste. 222, Toronto, Ontario M4R 1B9 (416) 486-8046.

Regroupement provincial des maisons d'héberge-ment et de transition pour femmes victimes de vio-lence conjugale, 5225 Berri, Montreal, Quebec H2J 2S4 (514) 279-2007.

Fédération des Ressources d'hébergement pour femmes violentées et en difficulté du Québec, CP 67, Succ. Longueuil, Longueuil, Quebec J4K 4W1 (514) 674-0324.

L'Association des Dépressifs et Maniaco-Dépressifs, 801: Sherbrooke St. E., Ste. 300, Montreal, Quebec H2L 1K7 (514) 529-7552.

McGill University, Department of Psychiatry, 102-1033 Pine Ave. W., Montreal, Quebec H3A 1A1 (514) 398-4455.

Health Services Association of the Southshore, 90 Glen Allan Dr., Bridgewater, Nova Scotia B4V 3S6 (902) 543-7191.

Nova Scotia Hospital, Community Relations Dept., PO Box 1004, Dartmouth, Nova Scotia B2Y 3Z9 (902) 464-3136.

Transition House Association of Nova Scotia, 169 Provost St., Ste. 310, New Glasgow, Nova Scotia B2H 2P9 (902) 464-3289.

New Brunswick Advisory Council on the Status of Women, 95 Foundry St., Ste. 207, Moncton, New Brunswick E1C 5H7 (506) 856-3252; 1-800-332-3087.

The following national mental health groups pro-vide educational materials on everything from combatting depression to coping with stress.

Canadian Mental Health Association, 970 Lawrence Ave. W., Ste. 205, Toronto, Ontario M6A 3B6 (416) 789-7957.

Canadian Psychiatric Association, 237 Argyle Ave., Ste. 200, Ottawa, Ontario K2P 1B8 (613) 234-2815.

Canadian Schizophrenic Foundation, 16 Florence Ave., North York, Ontario M2N 1E9 (416) 733-2117

Schizophrenia Society of Canada, 75 The Donway West, Ste. 814, Don Mills, Ontario M3C 2E9 (416) 445-8204.

BOOKS/BOOKLETS/ NEWSLETTERS/AUDIO

A Book About Sexual Assault (Montreal Women's Health Press, 1994).

Against Our Will: Men, Women and Rape, Susan Brownmiller (Fawcett Books, 1993).

Dance of Deception: Pretending & Truth-Telling in Women's Lives, Harriet G. Lerner (HarperCollins, 1994).

Grossesse en mauvais termes, a 32-minute. French-language video is available at Riviere-des-Prairies Hospital, 7070 Perras Blvd., Montreal, Quebec H1E 1A4 (514) 328-3503.

Hear My Roar: A Story of Family Violence, Ty Hochban, M.D. (Annick Press, 1994).

Nutrition and Mental Health, a quarterly newsletter from the Canadian Schizophrenia Foundation, 16 Florence Ave., North York, Ontario M2N 1E9 (416) 733-2117.

Sexual Assault: The Dilemma of Disclosure, the Question of Conviction (University of Manitoba Press, 1988).

Singing At The Top of Our Lungs: Women, Love & Creativity, Claudia Bepko and Jo-Ann Krestan (HarperCollins, 1993).

Type E Woman: How to Overcome the Stress of Being Everything to Everybody, Harriet B. Braiker (Dutton, 1987).

The Woman's Comfort Book: A Self-Nurturing Guide for Restoring Balance in Your Life, Jennifer Louden (HarperCollins, 1992).

The Joy of Stress, P.G. Hanson (Hanson Stress Management Organization, 1985).

The Essential Guide to Psychiatric Drugs, Jack M. Gorman (St. Martin's Press, 1991).

Trusting Ourselves: The Complete Guide to Emotional Well-Being for Women, Dr. Karen Johnson (Grove-Atlantic Monthly Press, 1991).

The Seven of Us Survived: Wife Abuse in the South Asian Community, Aruna Papp. Available from Muticultural Community Development and Training, 10 Euclid Ave., Scarborough, Ontario M1C 1J6.

CHAPTER 11

PROBLEM DRINKING AND ALCOHOLISM: WOMEN ARE NOT CREATED EQUAL

Why is this a women's health issue? Alcohol affects women differently from men. Four out of five adult women drink alcohol and women account for 30 percent of all alcohol-related deaths. Few women realize that alcohol affects them differently from men: all things being equal, one drink for a man equals almost two for a woman.

What you can do for yourself: Be aware of your drinking activators; be honest with yourself about your drinking habits. Get a handle on your drinking patterns by knowing yourself better and taking appropriate action when necessary.

PART ONE

The facts: why problem drinking and alcoholism are women's issues

1. ALCOHOL AFFECTS WOMEN DIFFERENTLY FROM MEN.

Women of any age can learn something from Bacchus Canada, an alcohol education program for university students. Bacchus has mounted an excellent awareness campaign to point out that guys and gals are not created equal when it comes to the effects of alcohol on their bodies. In a pamphlet entitled *Women and Alcohol*, Bacchus Canada explains that women may become more intoxicated than men after drinking the same amount of alcohol, even when both weigh the same. The reasons are complex, but include the fact that women generally have less body fluid and more body fat than men and therefore "dilute" the alcohol they drink more slowly than their male counterparts. One drink for a woman is equivalent to almost two for a man.

Women also have premenstrual sensitivity, something men (obviously!) don't have. Studies show that women tend to be affected more by alcohol just before their periods.

Women seem to suffer the severe physical symptoms associated with alcohol consumption sooner than men. Bacchus Canada reports that women experience more serious health problems from alcohol after a shorter history of abusive drinking than men.

Bacchus also points out the connection between drinking and women's increased risk from sexual assault: when one or both people in a date situation are intoxicated, the possibility of a woman being assaulted greatly increases. According to Bacchus Canada, 75 percent of men and 55 percent of women reported drinking or taking drugs prior to a sexual assault taking place.

And women have much to consider concerning alcohol-related risks. For example:

- While moderate drinking appears to be associated with a lower risk of heart disease (it increases the level of good (HDL) cholesterol in the blood), drinking – according to some studies, as little as a drink a day – appears to increase a woman's risk of breast cancer. Research is not conclusive in this area, but there are enough studies to warrant caution.
- Alcohol increases the risk of giving birth to a child with fetal alcohol syndrome, which may include everything from an early delivery and underweight baby to speech and hearing impediments and mental retardation. Because alcohol travels through the mother's placenta to the fetus, alcohol can be toxic to an unborn child.
- Sleep pattern disturbances are common in drinkers.
- Drinking increases the risk of developing disorders of the esophagus, stomach and intestines, all caused by alcohol irritation; some heavy drinkers have heavy, life-threatening bleeding.
- New mothers may be passing alcohol to a child through breastfeeding.
- More than a few drinks a day may damage your liver, an organ you simply cannot live without. Female heavy drinkers appear to develop cirrhosis of the liver more quickly than male heavy drinkers. According to the Canadian Liver Foundation, when you have two or three drinks a day your liver never gets a chance to dry out and the result may be one of several alcohol-related liver diseases.
- Women drinkers have a higher risk of developing osteoporosis.
- Drinkers appear to have an increased risk of contracting some cancers. The reason? According to research, alcohol may be one of the promoters that dam-

age a cell and change it from normal to cancerous; alcohol also depletes your body of Vitamin A, which has a protective effect against several cancers.

- Alcohol adversely affects memory; it may cause brownouts (memory problems such as forgetting where we put our keys) and, with more serious drinkers, blackouts (complete memory loss of a significant block of time).
- Women, in particular, are at risk of dangerous cross-addiction: for example, alcohol and sedatives. Alcohol can have dangerous consequences when ingested with some over-the-counter or prescription drugs.
- Monthly hormonal changes can alter the effect of alcohol. Some women may find alcohol especially difficult to tolerate just before ovulation: they get drunk faster and may feel alcohol's unpleasant aftereffects to a greater degree. Some research indicates that heavy drinking may disrupt the menstrual cycle by lengthening it and increasing the blood flow. Other research suggests that heavy drinking may bring on an earlier menopause.

2. WOMEN DRINK DIFFERENTLY – AND FOR DIFFERENT REASONS – THAN MEN.

Some women are more apt to drink alone and at home than with buddies in a bar, but others drink because of peer pressure to fit into certain groups or situations. Unlike men, many of whom treat drinking as a rite of passage into malehood, many women drink to boost their self-confidence or to loosen their sexual inhibitions. Women may also be invisible drinkers: it's easy to lose count when someone else is paying and pouring – and while many women pay their own way today, there probably are more men buying drinks for women than vice versa.

The fact that some women drink for different reasons than men prompted Dr. Jean Kirkpatrick, a sociologist and recovering alcoholic, to begin Women for Sobriety, a women-helping-women program that's an alternative to Alcoholics Anonymous for both women and men. Like AA, Women for Sobriety encourages its members first to stop drinking and then to work on their own particular problems or triggers. For some women, particularly those who have been sexually or physically abused, the privacy of all-women groups such as this one may be more comfortable than the more public AA.

3. WOMEN DON'T SEEK TREATMENT AS READILY AS MEN

Women tend to be underrepresented in most Canadian alcoholism treatment programs, according to Dr. Bonnie Madonik, director of medical services at Toronto's

Donwood Institute, an alcohol rehabilitation, research and education centre. In one Donwood study, the split was 80 percent male/20 percent female. Women also tend to seek help at an older age than men, says Dr. Madonik: only 12 percent of the women in the study were 18 to 30, compared to 24 percent of the men. The lack of available child care is one reason younger women don't seek treatment.

One powerful motivator for women to seek treatment for alcohol-related problems is sexual or physical abuse. Studies show that up to 80 percent of women who enter treatment are victims of sexual or physical abuse.

PART TWO

To your health: your personal guide to alcohol and sobriety

THE FIRST STEP TO ALCOHOL AWARENESS: KNOW YOUR ALCOHOL ACTIVATORS

In a useful self-help guide to cutting down on drinking called *Saying When*, Dr. Martha Sanchez-Craig, a senior scientist at Ontario's Addiction Research Foundation (ARF), describes drinking "activators" as "situations or events that trigger the desire to drink." Like any other habit, be it smoking or snacking before bedtime, these activators put into motion a chain reaction, the end result of which is that we drink too much.

Some examples:
- All sorts of unpleasant feelings, from anger, to boredom, to a lack of self-confidence, may make some of us use alcohol inappropriately as a coping mechanism.
- There are many pleasurable situations, from sitting down to dinner, to rewarding oneself at the end of a tough working day, that predictably trigger the impulse and desire to drink: it's the happy hour, a way to unwind, a buzz at the end of the day.
- Drinking can become an unthinking habit. This happens to many people who may have started drinking for specific reasons: to cope with pressures, for example, or simply for pleasure.

What's the Difference Between a Problem Drinker and A Social Drinker?

When we think of alcoholics, it's easier to pin the label on a bag lady living on the street than on a vice president of sales. But the facts are these: most serious problem drinkers hold down jobs, have families and contribute to community life. "Alcoholism is not defined by what you drink, how much you drink, when you drink, or how long you have been drinking," writes Dr. Karen Johnson, a California psychiatrist and author of *Trusting Ourselves: The Complete Guide to Emotional Well-Being for Women*. "It has to do with how important alcohol is to you and how your dependence on it affects your life. What is moderate for one person may be far too much for someone else."

The simple ability to say to yourself (and others), "No thanks, I've had enough," may separate a social drinker from a problem drinker.

Any woman who has four or more drinks a day probably has a problem with booze. According to the ARF's Dr. Martha Sanchez-Craig:
- moderate drinkers do not drink daily;
- moderate drinkers do not drink more than 12 drinks a week;
- moderate drinkers do not drink to cope with their problems;
- moderate drinkers do not make alcohol an important part of their recreation activities.

Have You Crossed the Line? Are You in Control of Your Drinking?

Here are some of the warning signs that may indicate you've crossed the line from being a social drinker to a person whose life is being controlled by alcohol:
- You drink at lunch more often than not.
- You avoid parties, events or functions where you think it would be difficult or impossible for you to get a drink.
- You are uncomfortable around people who don't drink.
- You are no stranger to hangovers.
- You suspect you use alcohol to deal with stress or to cover up feelings of anger, joy, fear of failure or worthlessness.
- Alcohol is becoming the centre of life for all your relaxation activities: in other words, if you go for a walk, it's usually essential to end it with a drink.
- You have a pattern to your drinking: ask yourself if you have to have a drink every day at a certain time.
- Drinking changes your personality: do you become more quarrelsome when you're normally easygoing, or do you become the life of the party when you're usually a wallflower?
- Friends and family tell you they're worried about you and your drinking.

TO YOUR HEALTH: HOW MUCH IS TOO MUCH?

There's been plenty of press lately on the health advantages of drinking. Much of the research focuses on evidence that people who drink one or two drinks daily are less likely than nondrinkers to have clogged arteries. But a joint policy statement based on the 1993 International Symposium on Moderate Drinking and Health (endorsed by both the Royal College of Physicians and Surgeons of Canada and the Canadian Medical Association) defines low-risk drinking as not more than two standard drinks per day. And the Canadian Liver Foundation says that more than two drinks a day could scar your liver.

A drink is usually defined as:
- three ounces of fortified wine (such as sherry or vermouth), or
- five or six ounces of wine, or
- 12 ounces of beer, or
- 1-1/2 ounces of 40-proof spirits such as rum or rye.

Four drinks over a period of two hours usually mean unstable movements and clumsy speech for a 120-pound woman and a blood alcohol level indicating you're impaired and shouldn't be driving.

How To (Honestly) Drink Less

Have you tried keeping a drinking diary? A great part of problem drinking concerns denial. So ask yourself: am I being absolutely honest about my drinking?

Some tips:
- Switch to low-alcohol or light beers (their alcohol content is 2.5 percent to 4 percent as compared to 5 percent) or no-alcohol beers and wines.
- Start thinking of liquor in terms of calories. A couple of gin and tonics pack away about 220 calories, calories better spent on a glass of milk and an apple.
- If you're out at a bar or party, try watering your drinks more (order a wine spritzer – half white wine, half water), or setting a pattern of drinking one alcoholic drink followed by a nonalcoholic one, or a drink an hour.
- If you can't break the habit of drinking at a business lunch, try breakfast business meetings.

- If you're hosting a party, don't pressure guests to drink. Have on hand a nonalcoholic beverage such as cranberry juice to offer nondrinkers, and always have plenty of soda or mineral water and lime available.

When hosting a dinner party, make it a point to set a jug of water on the table when you're putting out wine: that way, guests can choose a beverage without feeling conspicuous.

- Don't drink without eating: to cut down your alcohol consumption, order a first course instead of a cocktail at a restaurant.
- Plan your drinking ahead: decide whether you will drink at all before going to a social event and also have your "No thanks, I'm not drinking tonight" strategy planned.
- People who successfully got their drinking under control for more than a year told the Addiction Research Foundation that the two strategies that worked best were: avoiding tempting situations like being with heavy drinkers or going into bars; and carefully monitoring how much booze they were buying and actually drinking.

PROFILE

Bernice Law – "As addicted women we have shared more than we ever felt safe to reveal."

Nova Scotia's Bernice Law has been sober for nine years. She attends Alcoholic Anonymous meetings and has started a peer support group. But she still thinks of herself as an alcoholic in recovery. It never ends, says the woman who drank heavily for 20 years: "I still think of myself as one drink away from going back to the way I was."

Law says there's still a double standard when it comes to men and women alcoholics: "It's still more acceptable for men to drink today. If one of your neighbours is an alcoholic, you're more likely to say, 'Oh, here comes old Jack again; he'll be fine when he sleeps it off.' If his wife came down the street drunk, it would be a different story: It would be 'Look at that! What a disgrace. What about her poor kids and husband!'"

As therapy-intensive as our culture is, Law says there's still a "shame thing" associated with going for help. Especially for women who drink. "If a guy goes in for a checkup, a doctor asks him, 'Do you drink much, Jack?' They rarely ask women that. My doctor doesn't believe I'm an alcoholic to this day." Yet before she started treatment, she drank daily – at first at home in the evening, after her kids were in bed, then all day in local bars.

Law began drinking in her twenties. "I found out early on that I liked to drink a lot and stay out late. I thought my husband would protect me. I thought he'd say, 'Now, don't drink that so quickly, the dance isn't for a couple of hours yet.' But the high gets harder to attain so I would drink at home."

Eventually, Law began facing serious depression, what she calls "the uglies." "I used alcohol for a crutch and I got caught in the addiction," she recalls. "I didn't handle feelings, didn't know I had any I could talk about until I got into recovery."

In addition to attending her local Alcoholics Anonymous, Law became involved with the Pictou County Women's Centre, and, seven years ago, helped found a weekly support group of recovering female alcoholics and drug addicts called Women in Active Recovery.

What began as "kitchen-table talks" among the 11 support group members grew into a conference for recovering women and professional caregivers. A few summers ago, Women in Active Recovery took their show across the province and put on some workshops. They've put on theatrical productions and they've even written a guidebook called *Sharing Our Strengths: Women in Recovery*. It's an excellent resource book chockfull of valuable information on women and addictions, as well as step-by-step guidelines on how to set up a self-help group in your own community.

Here's what Law and her fellow recoverers say in *Sharing Our Strengths* about the reason they chose to form an all-women's recovery group: "As women we have shared more than we ever knew; as addicted women we have shared more than we ever felt safe to reveal."

"It's been neat," Law says, summing up her experience. "And now we're going great guns."

PART THREE

Your guide to alcohol education resources

Where to Look for More Information, Support, Services and Self-Help About Problem Drinking and Alcoholism

ORGANIZATIONS

The following provincial organizations provide information and education. They also can help you to find a treatment program and/or put you in touch with a support group.

Alberta Alcohol and Drug Abuse Commission, 10909 Jasper Ave., Ste. 200, Edmonton, Alberta T5J 3M9 (403) 427-0116.

Poundmaker, N.E.C.H.I., PO Box 34007, Kingsway Post Office, Edmonton, Alberta T5G 3G4 (403) 459-1884.

North Island Women's Services Society, PO Box 3292, Courtenay, British Columbia V9N 5N4 (604) 338-1133.

Women's Post Treatment Centre, 62 Sherbrook St., Winnipeg, Manitoba R3C 2B3 (204) 783-5460.

Addictions Foundation of Manitoba, Family & Women's Centre, 586 River Ave., Winnipeg, Manitoba R3L 0E8 (204) 944-6229.

Action on Women's Addictions, Research and Education (AWARE), PO Box 86, Kingston, Ontario K7L 4V6 (613) 545-0117.

Drug and Alcohol Registry of Treatment (DART), 231 Hyman St., London, Ontario N6A 1N6 (519) 439-0174.

Amethyst Women's Addiction Centre, 488 Wilbrod St., Ottawa, Ontario K1N 6M8 (613) 563-0363.

Addiction Research Foundation, INFO-ARF, 1-800-INFO-ARF or 1-800-463-6273. A hotline with 32 recorded messages in English and French. Includes the Behaviour Change Unit, Women's Day Treatment Program, 33 Russell St., Toronto, Ontario M5S 2S1 (416) 595-6794 or (416) 595-6040. Also Substance Abuse Network of Ontario, Addiction Research Foundation, Modem: SANO (416) 595-6069; Internet: sanohelp@arf.org

Community Older Persons Alcohol Program (COPA), 27 Roncesvalles Ave., Ste. 407, Toronto, Ontario M6R 2K4 (416) 516-2982.

Jean Tweed Treatment Centre, 3131 Lakeshore Blvd. W., Cottage 2, 3rd Flr., Toronto, Ontario M8V 1K8 (416) 255-7359.

Woman's Own Detox Centre. A self-referral or doctor-referral, nonmedical centre. 892 Dundas St. W., Toronto, Ontario M6J 1W1 (416) 603-1462.

Talbot House Detoxification Centre, 14 Deanery Ave., St. John's, Newfoundland A1E 1H5 (709) 738-4980.

Drug Dependency Services, Library, Southcott Hall, 8th floor, Forest Rd., PO Box 8700, St. John's Newfoundland A1B 4J6 (709) 729-0732.

The Self-Help Connection, 63 King St., Dartmouth, Nova Scotia B2Y 2R7 (902) 466-2011.

Women In Active Recovery, Pictou County Women's Centre, PO Box 964, New Glasgow, Nova Scotia B2H 5K7 (902) 755-4647.

NATIONAL ORGANIZATIONS

The following groups provide support, education and information on a national level. Some, like MADD, also lobby to change drinking laws.

Alcoholics Anonymous, 234 Eglinton Ave., E., Ste. 202, Toronto, Ontario M4P 1K5 (416) 487-5591.

Canadian Centre on Substance Abuse (CCSA), FAS Information Service, 75 Albert St., Ste. 300, Ottawa, Ontario K1P 5E7 (613) 235-4048 or 1-800-559-4514.

Canadian Liver Foundation, 365 Bloor St. E., Ste. 200, Toronto, Ontario M4W 3L4 (416) 964-1953 or 1-800-563-5483.

MADD Canada, Mothers Against Drunk Driving Canada, 65076 Mississauga Road, Mississauga, Ontario L5N 1A6 (905) 813-6233 or 1-800-665-6233.

Women for Sobriety: A women's alternative to Alcoholics Anonymous. For information on the program in your location, call the national office in Kitchener, Ontario (519) 884-2395.

Books/Audios/Videos

The following educational resources are recommended for support groups and educators.

An Easy Pill to Swallow, a 29-minute video, director Robert Lang, producer Tom Daly and Arthur Hammond, National Film Board.

Each Small Step: Breaking the Chains of Abuse and Addiction, a self-help workbook available from PO Box 2023, Charlottetown, Prince Edward Island C9A 7N7

Getting Better: Inside Alcoholics Anonymous, Nan Robertson (Fawcett Books, 1989).

Keeping Secrets, Suzanne Somers (Warner Books, 1988).

Lorri: The Recovery Series, a video, National Film Board, Gay and Lesbian Video Collection, PO Box 6100, Station Centre-ville, Montreal, Quebec H3C 3H5 (514) 283-9000.

Many Roads, One Journey: Moving Beyond the 12 *Steps*, Charlotte D. Kasl (HarperCollins, 1992).

Saying When, How to Quit Drinking or Cut Down – An ARF Self-Help Book, Martha Sanchez-Craig. (Addiction Research Foundation, 1993).

Sharing Our Strengths: Women In Recovery, A Guide for Women's Recovery Groups. A starter's manual for self-help groups written by Terri Kilbride and Women In Active Recovery, Pictou County Women's Centre, PO Box 964, New Glasgow, Nova Scotia B2H 5K7 (902) 755-4647.

Women and Alcohol; Sex Under The Influence. Booklets available from Bacchus Canada, PO Box 312, Stn. D, Toronto, Ontario M6P 3J9 (416) 243-1338.

Working Together For Change: Women's Self-Help Handbook. Published by North Island Women's Services Society, PO Box 3292, Courtenay, British Columbia V9N 5N4 (604) 338-1133.

Self-Help: A How-To-Manual. Published by The Self-Help Connection, 63 King St., Dartmouth, Nova Scotia B2Y 2R7 (902) 466-2011.

CHAPTER 12

SAVE YOUR SKIN: PROTECTING AND CARING FOR OUR BODY'S LARGEST ORGAN

Why is this a women's health issue? The incidence of melanoma, the deadliest of skin cancers and more common in women than men, has doubled in the past 15 years; in 1994, 1,450 Canadian women discovered they had the disease and 210 are estimated to have died from it. And women spend millions annually on questionable potions and lotions that promise skin that's younger, smoother and less dry.

What you can do for yourself: Skin cancer is preventable. Get serious about sun exposure. Question the claims being made by so-called beauty-enhancing skin-care products. Ask yourself if they're really worth the money and better than a less expensive and simpler regime.

OUR SKIN, OUR BODY'S LARGEST ORGAN

Our skin is our body's largest organ, the one that's most visible and the one through which we connect with the outside world through the sensation of touch. Through our skin we feel temperature, pain, pleasure, pressure, tickling and itching.

The skin's most important function, however, is to protect the internal organs from injury, the harmful rays of sunlight, dehydration and life-threatening infections from agents such as bacteria. The skin helps keep body temperature constant: if the body gets hot it is cooled off by sweat glands and blood vessels that dilate or widen to dissipate the heat; if the body gets cold, the blood vessels in the skin constrict or narrow in order to retain or conserve the body's heat more efficiently.

The skin is composed of a thin outer layer called the epidermis. This surface skin comprises approximately ten layers of cells which are constantly being replaced by fresh cells from the bottom of the epidermis. The process usually takes about 25 days. Below the epidermis is a thicker inner layer called the dermis. Beneath this is the fat layer.

SKIN CANCER: YOU CAN REDUCE YOUR RISKS GREATLY

PART ONE

The facts: why skin cancer is a women's health issue

- The Canadian Dermatology Association estimates that in 1995, 60,000 Canadians got skin cancer.
- Rates for the most common skin cancers have at least doubled in North America since the 1970s.
- A decade ago, skin cancer was unusual in people under the age of 40; today, it is not uncommon to find the disease in someone in their twenties.
- People born in the mid-1970s have a lifetime risk of one in 12 of developing skin cancer.
- A child born today has a one in seven risk of developing the disease.
- Female baby boomers have a higher incidence of basal cell carcinoma than their male counterparts, according to a 1994 report in the *Medical Post*.
- The incidence of melanoma has doubled in the past 15 years.
- Melanoma is slightly more common in women than men.

WHAT IS SKIN CANCER?

Skin cancer is a type of cancer that begins with the uncontrolled growth of cells in one of the layers of the skin. It is the most common form of cancer found in humans: one in every three new cancers is a skin cancer.

There are several kinds of skin cancers. Basal cell carcinoma and squamous cell carcinoma are the most common forms; they are disfiguring and painful, but usually don't kill. Melanoma (it means black tumor) is the type of skin cancer responsible for the majority of skin cancer deaths in Canada.

What causes skin cancer, and who's at risk?

Sun exposure is the major cause of all types of skin cancer, says Vancouver dermatologist Dr. Roberta Ongley. "An ounce of prevention is really worth a pound of cure when it comes to skin cancer."

Ultraviolet radiation (uv rays) is a natural part of the sun's energy that reaches the earth's surface. These rays have three different wavelengths: uvc are the shortest and do not reach the earth's suface; uvb are medium wavelengths that cause skin to burn and may cause cancer; uva rays are the largest of the wavelengths and cause skin to age and wrinkle while also damaging its support structure.

Because the ozone layer is thinning, you are exposed to increased daily dosages of uv radiation when you spend more time outdoors.

uv radiation not only damages your skin, it can also decrease your body's ability to fight disease, and it can damage your eyes, which may lead to cataracts.

Research suggests that several blistering sunburns during childhood or teen years (when 75 percent of lifetime sun exposure occurs) may play a significant role in the later development of melanoma, the most serious type of skin cancer. The cumulative effect of sunlight is important: the more sun you get, the more likely you are to develop skin cancer. And your skin colour affects your susceptibility. "You inherit your skin type," notes Dr. Ongley, "and that will determine how you react to the sun. If you're a blue-eyed fair-haired Celt, then you've inherited skin that tends to be much more sensitive to the sun."

There are common sun myths: that a tan is healthy (not true, it's a sign of skin damage); that people with dark skin have built-in protection from the sun (again, untrue – while blue-eyed fair-haired women may be more vulnerable, people with dark skin also get skin cancer); that you will not sunburn while you're swimming (not only can the sun's rays penetrate under water, but radiation penetrates deeper into the skin when it's wet); and that glass protects you from ultraviolet rays (not true).

One of the biggest myths is that lots of sunshine is terrific for kids. Actually, one of the best things we can do for our kids is to get them into the shade. Babies burn more easily because the outermost layer of their skin is thinner. Remember, one blistering sunburn doubles a child's lifetime risk of skin cancer.

As Dr. Ongley says, women at greatest risk include fair-skinned people, who burn easily and rarely tan. Fair-skinned people often can't produce enough melanin (a pigment which filters out some of the damaging radiation) and so have less protection for their skin. Women who work outdoors – for example, gardeners, farmers and construction workers – are also at increased risk. And anyone who regularly plays a sport outdoors should ensure they wear sunscreen and cover up.

PART TWO

Your guide to skin health

SAVE YOUR SKIN: 10 WAYS TO PROTECT YOURSELF FROM THE SUN

1. Keep sun exposure to a minimum, especially between 11:00 a.m. and 4:00 p.m., when the sun's rays are strongest.
2. Wear a hat – and choose your hat carefully.
    *   Check the fabric of the hat and hold it up to the sun or light bulb: if the light can't get through it, neither can UV rays.
    *   Straw hats may let light through and not be the best choice.
    *   Baseball caps often don't shield the back of the neck, ears or cheeks; flat caps provide little protection for the face or neck.
    *   Wide-brimmed hats (7.5 cm or more) reduce the UV danger by stopping up to 75 percent of the UV rays from reaching our eyes.
    *   Legionnaire-type hats (with a long flap in the back) protect the neck, ears and side of the face.
3. Wear loose-fitting, long-sleeved shirts and other protective clothing. The rule of thumb about fabrics: if it's sheer enough to see through, the sun's rays will also get through.
4. Wear sunglasses that state 100 percent UV protection or UV400.
5. Use a sunscreen liberally and reapply it every two hours when working, playing or exercising outdoors. Some sunscreen tips:
    *   Sunscreens are classed by Health Canada as a drug and are required to carry a drug identification number on the label. Read and follow the directions carefully.
    *   Sunscreens with an SPF (Sun Protection Factor) of 15 or more are recommended because they screen out as much as possible of the sun's harmful UVA and UVB rays.
    *   Suncreens should be fragrance-free and water-resistant.
    *   Apply sunscreens 30 to 60 minutes before going out in the sun and before you apply other creams such as moisturizers.
    *   Sunscreens should not be used to increase your time in the sun but rather to protect you when you cannot avoid being in the sun.
    *   Protect your lips, tips of your ears and earlobes with a sun block containing zinc oxide.

6. Beware of clouds: the sun can penetrate light cloud cover, fog and also haze.

7. Remember that sand, snow and concrete can reflect up to 80 percent of the sun's damaging rays.

8. Don't be fooled by indoor tanning devices. They claim safe tans, but you can still get a serious burn through prolonged use of ultraviolet A (UVA) sunbeds or lamps. In fact, the amount of UVA emitted by these tanning devices can be up to twice as much as that found in natural sunlight.

9. Sun tips for babies and children:
   - Keep babies under a year old out of direct sunlight. Be sure they're completely covered: long pants, long-sleeved shirts, brimmed hats.
   - Children over the age of six months can wear a sunscreen; choose a milky lotion for young children. Sunscreens containing alcohol may burn or sting a child's skin or eyes. Also apply an SPF (Sun Protection Factor) 15 lip balm to children's lips.

10. Travel tips: Be aware of how the sun impacts on your location. For instance, the closer you are to the equator, the greater the strength of UV rays that reach the earth. Sun rays are also more dangerous in the mountains because of the higher altitude.

HOW SUNSCREENS WORK

Most sunscreens work by absorbing ultraviolet rays. That is what para-aminobenzoic acid (PABA), one of the common ingredients found in sun-screen products, does. The Canadian Dermatology Association has a committee that examines sunscreens on the market. Those that they feel are good blocking agents are given a stamp of approval. So look for the Canadian Dermatology Association approval on your product. Also make sure your sunscreen has an SPF of 15 or more (the higher the number, the better the protection; for example, 15 SPF means the sunscreen provides 15 times your natural UVB protection) and that it contains ingredients that will block both UVA and UVB rays: two very good blocking agents are titanium dioxide (which reflect the sun's rays) and Parsol (which absorbs throughout the UVA spectrum).

Learn the Early Warning Signs of Skin Cancer

Everyone should do a mole check on herself and her children. The Canadian Dermatolgy Association recommends an annual mole check along with your yearly physical exam. "You should really examine your body the way you do with your regular breast self-exam," says Dr. Roberta Ongley. In other words, a mole check should be part of your self-examination ritual.

Most of us have moles, blemishes and other dermal imperfections. But when it comes to cancer of the skin, here are the warning signs to watch for:

- A skin growth that increases in size and appears pearly, tan, brown, black, or multicoloured.
- A mole, birthmark or beauty mark that changes color, increases in size or thickness, changes in texture or has an irregular outline.
- A spot or growth that continues to itch, crust, scab, bleed or hurt.
- An open sore on the skin that persists for more than four weeks without healing, or one that heals and then reopens.

Learn the Early Warning Signs of Melanoma

- Darkening of an existing mole.
- An increase in the size of a mole.
- Irregularity of margins and an elevation of the mole.
- Additional changes in the color of the mole (perhaps it develops a reddish or bluish tinge).
- Sometimes, there may be bleeding, particularly after a minor injury to the mole.
- Itching and scaling of the mole area may also develop.

The sun aggravates skin cancer in moles, says Dr. Roberta Ongley. "But you can also have a mole not exposed to the sun that can go wrong. If you have a lot of moles, you shouldn't be sunbathing because sunbathing tends to increase that risk."

Treating Skin Cancer: Many Reasons for Optimism

The good news: Almost all skin cancers are preventable. And most skin cancers, including melanoma, are curable if treated at an early stage.

A diagnosis of skin cancer is usually made through a biopsy performed under local anesthesia in a doctor's office.

If you're diagnosed with skin cancer, consider asking your physician the following questions (taken from *Everyone's Guide to Cancer Therapy*, edited by Dr. Richard Hasselback, Somerville House):

- What are the most important things I can do to lower my risk of getting skin cancers?
- Will my physician be carefully and regularly examining all my skin surface to look for any premalignant and malignant lesions?
- Has the biopsy been reviewed by a pathologist with special training in skin tumors?
- Which method of treatment will give me the best results?
- What is the chance of recurrence or spread with this lesion and your recommended treatment?

Skin cancer is treated by many methods, including surgery to remove the cancer and a small area of normal skin. For deep melanomas, local lymph nodes may also be removed along with the surface area of the skin.

PROFILE

Lynn Williams – being fit doesn't mean being cancer-free.

Most skin cancers are preventable, says Canadian middle-distance runner Lynn Williams who found out the hard way.

Her good-news story is this: incredibly fit and drug-clean (she has often publicly supported the drug testing of athletes), Williams, who lives in Vancouver, is a Commonwealth gold and Olympic bronze medalist who has run (and won) countless races around the world.

Her bad-news story is this: during a meet in Japan five years ago, her husband (Canadian male running champ Paul Williams) pointed out a dark spot on her shoulder. It turned out to be malignant melanoma. As an athlete, she was in tune with her body and looked after herself well. "But all those years that I was out training in the sun, I just didn't worry about whether I wore a sunscreen or not," says the mother of two young sons who has now retired from competitive sports.

Williams trained in California during winter months so she was out in the sun more than most Canadians. Like the rest of us snowbirds, a winter vacation in the southern sun was something she looked forward to. Born in

Saskatchewan, she spent her childhood summers "putting on the oil and just frying."

Williams, now healthy, no longer competes, but works hard delivering her protect-yourself-against-the-sun message for the Canadian Dermatology Association.

If she were training now, she says she undoubtedly would follow the guidelines set by the Canadian Dermatology Association, for which she has been a spokesperson.

PSORIASIS: A NEW LOOK AT AN OLD CONDITION

WHAT IS PSORIASIS?

Psoriasis is a noncontagious, chronic skin condition which presents as thick, red or silvery scaly patches on the skin. It's unsightly, often itchy (the name of the condition is derived from the Greek word *psora*, meaning itch) and ranges from being a small, dry, scaly patch to an alarming and disabling condition that can cover the whole body.

PART ONE

The facts: why psoriasis is a women's health issue

Almost one million Canadians suffer from psoriasis. It can occur in babies, though it most often starts in the teens and thirties. It commonly occurs on pressure areas of the skin, such as the hips, knees, lower back, buttocks, back of the head and elbows.

There are various types of psoriasis, each with its own unique profile. No matter the type, what actually happens in the skin is this: normally, our skin replaces its surface every 25 days; with psoriasis, the process of skin renewal speeds up and occurs ten times faster than normal, with the result that patches and scales form because the old skin doesn't shed as quickly as new skin develops.

A recent Canadian survey revealed that 74 percent of people with psoriasis reported that it affected their lives. Discomfort and pain were not as difficult to cope with as embarassment, self-consciousness and the reaction of others, the survey said. Many people reported being called lepers, being refused haircuts and manicures and being asked to leave swimming pools.

Peer support is absolutely crucial, says Dee Taylor, who's had the condition since childhood. "Some doctors still have the attitude, 'Look, it's not going to kill you so live with it.'"

PART TWO

Your guide to treating psoriasis

WHAT CAUSES PSORIASIS?

The cause of psoriasis is unknown. There are, however, several recognized triggers that can aggravate the condition and promote flare-ups. These include strep throat, surgery, sunburn, hormonal changes, skin irritations, alchohol, emotional stress and certain medications such as beta blockers (used for high blood pressure) and lithium (used for the treatment of manic-depression).

A genetic predisposition to the disease has been identified. Some people who suffer from psoriasis remember a grandparent, aunt or cousin who had it. If one parent has psoriasis, there is a 30 percent chances a child will develop the condition. But it can also skip a generation. Rheumatologists say there is a connection between psoriasis and arthritis: approximately 5 percent of psoriasis patients develop arthritis.

HOW IS PSORIASIS TREATED?

The bottom line for psoriasis sufferers is, unfortunately, pessimistic. Why? Because nobody has found a definitive cure. For this reason, it can be an isolating, frustrating disease.

The most common treatments are topical steroids, anthralin, tar and short-wave ultraviolet light rays (UVB). Recently, dermatologists have recommended a new treatment based on a natural Vitamin D derivative (available by prescription).

Other treatments can be everything from iffy to smelly, and from time-consuming to downright dangerous if not carefully monitored. They range from coal tar to cyclosporine, from Vitamin A derivatives to anti-cancer medication. Some patients have reported trying mayonnaise, honey, even deer fat.

Dee Taylor – a walking encyclopedia

Getting rejected from elementary school for her unsightly psoriasis didn't keep Dee Taylor off the stage. When she got a part in a musical in Montreal, her doctor cooperated and kept her dancing nightly by helping her choose the right makeup coverup. But as upbeat and optimistic as Taylor is, she doesn't pretend to put a happy face on the condition that has challenged her physically since childhood and on several occasions has kept her hospitalized.

Taylor grew up in Newfoundland in the 1950s. It was difficult to get a correct diagnosis, she says: "Nobody knew what it was or what to do about it. The only treatment at the time was a primitive tar treatment and it burned. I remember, at six years of age, standing in the kitchen and having this tar all over me and being fanned all over with newspapers."

In those days, everyone was supposed to look perfect and be flawless, Taylor says of her childhood. "So what could you do but try to hide it?" Trying didn't stop her school from asking her to stay home, however. "Today, a child who is told she can't go to school because of the way she looks is protected by law," Taylor says.

Over the years, Taylor, who now lives in Burlington, Ontario, has improvised various ways to be kinder to her body. While treating Taylor daily, an observant physiotherapist noticed how Taylor had made the clinic's sterile treatment room more hospitable through art posters she had purchased herself. The physiotherapist realized that her patient was a walking encyclopedia of tips for living with her psoriasis. "Why not share your knowledge," she encouraged Taylor, who, as a result, now gives numerous workshops and has recorded a self-help audiotape entitled Coming Out of Your Shell: Living with Psoriasis.

Taylor's tips can benefit people living with various skin conditions:

- Wear clothing made from natural fibres rather than synthetics. Natural fibres allow the skin to breathe and also are absorbent.
- Take a warm, not hot, bath or shower daily to help remove the top layers of plaques on the skin if you have psoriasis; use mild body soap and mild or natural shampoos only.

- Wear a loose bathrobe or old cotton shirt for about 20 minutes after applying thick prescription creams and before dressing, to prevent clothing from sticking to the skin.
- Buy long cotton underwear or pant liners to protect legs from wool pants.
- Use thin plastic gloves when applying hair mousse or spray.
- Wear cotton gloves underneath thin plastic gloves when handling vegetables in the kitchen or working in the garden, as the cotton will prevent hands from perspiring.
- Apply moisturizer or oil immediately after bathing to seal water into the skin.
- Try using a paint roller, or the back of a long, large spoon or soup ladle, to apply moisturizer to difficult-to-reach areas such as the center of the back.

YOUR SKIN: ARE SKIN-CARE PRODUCTS NECESSARY?

PART ONE

The facts: Canadian women spend millions of dollars on skin-care products

Women's concern about how their skin looks has created a multimillion-dollar market for skin-care products. But do these products really work?

Dermatologists say that unless you have very dry skin, any soap will do to clean the skin. Most are also wary of claims that astringent closes the skin's pores, and many dermatologists consider expensive creams a waste of money. "We see the occasional allergy to skin-care products and cosmetics, but my concern is more that I think there are a lot of false expectations," says Dr. Roberta Ongley. "People tend to spend a lot of money on dreams, a product they think will make them look 16 again. Nothing does, of course. Cosmetics, as products according to Canadian law, are not allowed to alter the structure of the skin. If they did that, they'd have to be classified as a drug, not a cosmetic."

"I always tell patients to treat their skin a little like ivy – it thrives on a little neglect," says Dr. Ongley. "Overdoing creates more problems than underdoing."

Soaps, Moisturizers, Creams and Lotions: How to Choose

Study the following guidelines to choose the best soap and skin-care products to suit your skin and your budget:

- For very dry skin, try the mild superfatted soaps such as Dove or Neutragena. Some women with dry skin don't ever use soap, only water, when washing their face.
- Experiment with cheaper brands of creams, oils and lotions. And remember, any cream or oil that holds moisture in the skin does the job better when you apply it to damp skin.
- Your face has many oil glands around the forehead, nose and chin. In the winter, cheeks are prone to dryness. Lips are especially sensitive to low humidity and should be protected by a lip balm that traps moisture in. Petroleum jelly (Vaseline) does nicely – and is very inexpensive.
- Elbows, knees and feet have thick skin. Bumping, rubbing and walking cause an excessive buildup of thick, dead skin cells, so rich moisturizers are best.
- The secret moisturizer recommended by many dermatologists is plain old petroleum jelly. But since it doesn't feel very pleasant on your skin, you might try equally inexpensive alternatives – cocoa butter or mineral oil.
- The latest buzzwords in skin moisturizers are antioxidants and alpha hydroxy acids (AHAS).

What are antioxidants?

They include Vitamin E, beta carotene and Vitamin C. Experts agree they are beneficial when taken orally; as to their efficacy when applied as a moisturizing ingredient to the skin, the jury is still out.

What are AHAS?

AHAS are alpha hydroxy acids. They claim to minimize skin damage such as sun spots (age spots). Dermatologists say what AHAS really do is act like mini-peels by removing the superficial layers of the skin. "They're good when indicated," explains Dr. Ben Fisher, a dermatologist at Toronto's Wellesley Hospital. "But they will actually dry out the skin."

- Certain face creams may provoke allergic reactions: always try a new lotion or cream on a small patch of skin in order to determine how you'll react to it before applying larger amounts.

- A good lotion contains one or more of these ingredients: urea, silicone or lanolin. "If it's called a lotion, it's got more water content than a cream," says Dr. Fisher. "It usually contains some type of an oil like a lanolin, a mineral oil, or even a fancy oil such as a Vitamin E (there's no proof it's really better)."
- When a patch test comes as part of the instructions, do it! If your skin is sensitive or if you have allergies, try your own patch test with new products: dab a bit of the cream or lotion on your forearm and cover it with a bandage. Repeat daily for three or four days, then wait 24 hours. If you don't have a reaction, you can probably use the product. Try this with new makeup and perfumes, too.
- If a product you're used to using on your skin or scalp says "new and improved," try the patch test: the remade version may contain an irritant that the old version didn't.
- Facials may do more for your psyche than for your skin. "I don't think they really do anything," says Dr. Roberta Ongley. "They're more a feel-good kind of thing and there's nothing wrong with that."

PART TWO

A guide to skin-care

Dry Skin 1: If It's February in Canada, Your Hands Show it First

If it's winter in Canada, you probably have dry skin.

Hands are especially prone to dry winter skin because they have thin skin and fewer oil glands; dry patches, even tiny cracks that become painfully inflamed, can easily develop.

Here are some ways to protect yourself from chapped hands:

- When washing your hands, use a mild soap and apply moisturizer while your skin is still a little damp.
- Toners, peels and facial scrubs can be harsh on your skin, so if your skin tends to dryness during the winter, stop using them.
- Hot water for washing is not recommended by dermatologists. The best temperature for your skin is warm water. Even better, suggest some dermatologists, bathe or shower once every couple of days instead of daily. Cut down on or eliminate bubble baths and bath oils as they can not only trigger skin irritations but also provoke urinary tract infections in children, especially girls.

- By all means try rubber gloves (with a cotton lining) when washing dishes or using cleaners. Give your hands a light application of moisturizer when you take off the gloves as the sudden air contact may contribute to dryness.
- For dryness, choose creams over lotions; creams have more of an oil content and stop the evaporation of water from your skin.
- Buy a humidifier or put a shallow pan of water in each room of the house to moisturize the air in winter.

DRY SKIN 2: IF IT'S FEBRUARY IN CANADA, YOUR FEET ARE A MESS

We're good to our feet in summer, but, come winter, we barely see them. Good advice comes from Scholl, a specialty footwear and foot-care products retailer.

Here's their advice about how to keep feet healthy and cozy throughout winter:

- Warm winter footwear can be a breeding ground for bacteria. Wash and deodorize feet daily. Use an antibacteria spray or powder to refresh and protect feet and footwear.
- Because feet spend most of the time covered, it's important to dry them thoroughly between the toes to prevent moisture and bacteria build-up.
- Avoid sprinkling powder between the toes, where it can become trapped and cause infection.
- Treat your feet to a warm footbath with soothing oils. Avoid soaking feet in salt-based solutions, however, since these can have a drying effect on the skin.
- Callus build-up tends to increase during winter, so use a natural pumice stone to slough off dead skin regularly.
- Moisturize feet daily to prevent dry, cracked skin.
- Keep toenails properly trimmed.
- If possible, choose natural fibres (cotton and wool socks) to keep feet the warmest in cold weather.
- To warm the feet, briskly rub bare feet with a towel, then soak them for a few minutes in lukewarm water – never hot water.
- Leather and suede will keep your feet warmer than synthetic materials. Leather's ability to breathe helps insulate feet, keeping them warm and dry in winter and cool and dry in summer.
- When shopping for boots, never assume your shoe size is also your boot size. Always try on footwear near the end of the day when your feet are at their largest.
- When shopping for boots, take along the appropriate foot coverings, such as

heavy socks or linings, to ensure the correct sizing. Keep in mind that thick pile lining will eventually flatten with wear, allowing more room.

MOISTURIZERS: THERE'S NO MAGIC FORMULA

Despite all their fancy claims, moisturizers are water-based lotions that work on the skin's surface to relieve the tightness and flakiness that is central to dry skin; they don't penetrate the skin at all, nor can they slow the aging process.

There are two categories of moisturizers. The first, emollients, act as an oily barrier to the skin's surface, sealing in moisture. The most common of these are mineral oil, lanolin and petroleum jelly. The second, humectants, attract and hold water on your skin's surface. They include urea, lactic acid and glycerin.

As a rule, the simpler the mositurizer the better, as the more additives there are to the product's basic formula, the greater the chance you may find it irritating to your skin.

CAN YOU HAVE STRESSED-OUT SKIN?

I didn't believe my dermatologist who told me that an emotional shock can both trigger a skin problem and clear it up. But then I read about a dermatologist psychiatrist who told a meeting of the American Psychiatric Association that the skin can indeed be a psychosomatic battlefield. Dr. Carolyn Koblenzer told *Psychology Today* that the skin and brain are intimately connected. Dermatitis, eczema and chronic acne can be triggered by stress. (And when you don't know the cause of your outbreak, the stress increases.)

Ask any teen about the connection between pimples and first dates, and blemishes and exams. "Some people have skin that is more responsive to their emotions," says Dr. Roberta Ongley. "They tend to be most responsive to things like acne. One theory is that when you're under real stress it alters your testosterone level, which is a real trigger for acne. Stress can affect psoriasis, eczema and itchy skin conditions in people who are prone to it."

There is circumstantial anecdotal evidence for a variety of skin-and-emotion connections, Ongley says, "but for acne there is actually a physiological basis."

IS IT DERMATITIS OR IS IT ECZEMA?

Skin outbreaks happen for different reasons, but chronic dry skin can lead to dermatitis, a condition in which the skin becomes not only dry, but also inflamed or itchy, with crusty patches or cracks. The terms dermatitis and eczema are often used

interchangeably. Some dermatitis is caused by direct contact with a long list of substances that may include metals such as nickel, rubber, certain fabrics, laundry products, perfumes, or makeup.

Dermatitis occurs either because a noxious substance touches the skin repeatedly (for example, washing dishes without protective gloves), or because you become
sensitive to a certain substance (such as gold). While most people consider nickel the
culprit in contact dermititis, gold got the "allergen of the year" award at a 1994 meeting of the American Contact Dermatitis Society in Boston. Gold allergies affect
mostly women and are second only to nickel in causing contact dermatitis.

Spots on the body that are affected include contact sites, but also eyelids, probably because eyelid skin is very sensitive. Mild dermatitis may be treated by using a 0.5
percent over-the-counter hydrocortisone topical ointment, cream or lotion. For
more severe cases, or if the condition persists, consult a dermatologist.

Be Smart with Body Art

The current body-piercing, tattooing and branding fads have made health authorities consider regulating an industry that uses instruments which have the potential
to cause harm. Today, piercing is done on every conceivable body part, including
lips, tongues, navels, eyebrows and genitals. Using instruments that are poorly steril-
ized can accelerate the spread of AIDS and hepatitis B. Be aware, too, that nickel allergies and scar tissues can develop in some people who pierce their ears and other
body parts. Make sure that anytime you have your skin pierced for cosmetic reasons,
you have it done by a reputable practitioner. (Since body piercing parlours are not
licensed, it is "buyer beware.")

Sun Spots

They appear on the forehead and the backs of hands and arms and are called age spots
by some, adult freckles by others, liver spots by our grandmothers. They have nothing
to do with your liver; they do happen as you age but not when you're aged. So they
really should be called sun spots, for that's what they really are. There are lightening
agents found in pharmacies under the names of Neostrata HQ and Eldopaque.

Wrinkles? Relax!

You can't change your wrinkles, so try changing your attitude about them. Instead of
thinking of them as age lines, think of them as experience lines. "There are the wrin-

kles you develop as a result of muscle action – laugh lines, for example," explains Dr. Roberta Ongley. "Those are gradually built into our skin by our muscles over the years and we have earned them. Then there are finer lines; most of those are the result of our skin's exposure to the sun."

PART THREE

Your guide to skin resources

ORGANIZATIONS

The following groups provide educational materials on everything from how to protect against skin cancer to coping with psoriasis:

Canadian Cosmetic Toiletry & Fragrance Association, 5090 Explorer Dr., Ste. 510, Mississauga, Ontario L4W 4T9 (905) 629-0111.

Canadian Psoriasis Foundation, 1306 Wellington, Ste. 500A, Ottawa, Ontario KLY 3B2 (613) 728-4000 or 1-800-265-0926.

Canadian Dermatology Association, 774 Echo Dr., Ste. 521, Ottawa, Ontario K1S 5N8 (613) 730-6262.

BOOKS/PAMPHLETS

The following, recommended by experts and sources used in this chapter, will give you information on a particular skin problem or will help you become more savvy about skin care in general:

A Consumer's Dictionary of Cosmetic Ingredients, Ruth Winter, M.S. (Crown Trade Paperbacks, Inc., 1995).

Coming Out of Your Shell,: A Guide to Living with Psoriasis (produced by Leo Laboratories, published by Kerbel Communications Incorporated). To order, call (905) 427-8828 or 1-800-263-4218.

Don't Go to the Cosmetics Counter Without Me: An Eyeopening Guide to Brand Name Cosmetics, Paula Begoun (Beginning Press, 1994).

Young As You Look: Medical and Natural Alternatives to Improve Your Appearance, Dr. Don Groot and Patricia Johnston (InForum Publishing, 1993). Available from 11523–100 Ave., Ste. 207, Edmonton, Alberta T5K 0J8.

CHAPTER 13

HEADACHES: TAMING YOUR TRIGGERS

Why is this a women's health issue? Tension headaches affect close to one out of three Canadians. And migraine headaches affect and disable 3.2 million Canadians, most of them women.

What you can do for yourself? Learn what your headache triggers are and learn how to manage your migraine.

ARE THERE MANY DIFFERENT KINDS OF HEADACHES?

Yes. One book lists more than 15 types, not including those that are life-threatening or migraines. Perhaps the most common is the tension-type or muscle-contraction headache often described as a tight tension at the back of the neck or a squeezing pain across the forehead or back of the head. Emotional stress and tight muscles may play a role in triggering these headaches.

Migraines are severe headaches which may include any or all of the following: moderate to severe one-sided or bilateral head pain; nausea; sensitivity to light or sound. In some people, migraines are preceded by an "aura" or temporary visual hallucination, such as seeing zigzag lines across a visual field.

PART ONE

The facts: why headaches are a women's health issue

"Life's a headache" is a cute bumper sticker. Not quite so cute if you're among the 29.5 percent of Canadian men and women who suffer from tension headaches. And not cute at all if you're one of the 3.2 million Canadians who suffer from migraines – most of them women.

Tension-type headaches are not physiologically harmful, they can be debilitating as well. So much so, that the cost of lost productivity each year in North America from all types of headaches is estimated at half a billion dollars. That's a lot of money, but it's only a fraction of what North Americans spend annually on over-the-counter painkillers.

Migraines cost the Canadian economy a loss in workplace productivity in the range of $486 million annually. According to Valerie South, author of *Migraine* (1994), twice as many women as men, worldwide, suffer from migraines.

South, a former executive director of The Migraine Foundation and a migraine sufferer herself, says that although hormones don't actually cause migraines in women, the typical monthly fluctuations of female hormones can trigger migraine attacks in women who are predisposed to them.

According to The Migraine Foundation, migraine hits women the hardest between the ages of 25 and 44. Migraines can start at any age, however: some women report migraines beginning at menopause, when estrogen levels drop; others report migraines after they've been placed on hormone replacement therapy.

Here are some additional facts on women and migraines from The Migraine Foundation:

- The tendency towards migraine is frequently inherited; 56 percent of migraine sufferers have a close blood relative with migraine, and 65 percent of the time that relative is their mother.
- In one study, 25 percent of women suffered from one or more attacks per week, and 35 percent had one to three severe attacks per month. Another study showed that in 77 percent of cases, the migraine sufferer's most recent attack affected her normal routine.
- Migraine sufferers for whom hormones are a factor began having migraines either at puberty or in their twenties.
- Migraines associated with the menstrual period tend to occur at the same time monthly, be it mid-cycle with ovulation or at the beginning or end of a period.

- Hormone-triggered migraines are often worse in the first trimester of pregnancy, but tend to ease off during the second and third trimesters. (Non-drug strategies are usually recommended for controlling attacks.)
- Medications containing hormones (such as birth control pills, hormone replacement therapy or medications used in treating endometriosis) may contribute to or alleviate migraines. Women on these medications should report any changes in attacks to their doctors immediately. Some migraine sufferers on oral estrogen report better success using a transdermal skin patch.

MIGRAINE SUFFERERS SPEAK OUT: LEARN TO TAKE CARE OF YOURSELF

Learning to take care of yourself can't be emphasized enough, particularly for women who are busy taking care of others, says Maureen Robertson, a certified neuroscience nurse specialist and cofounder of the Headache Society of Southern Alberta. Robertson's women patients have learned to have a baby-sitter on call and some meals in their freezer in case a migraine strikes.

Vancouver neurologist Dr. Gillian Gibson agrees. She knows from personal experience how the stresses created by juggling the demands of home and work can trigger migraines. Her migraine attacks have become more severe since her two children were born.

Gibson told *Headlines*, The Migraine Foundation's newsletter, that her headaches have made it easier to recognize and understand her patients' symptoms. "All migraine sufferers know how difficult it is to describe to a non-sufferer what a migraine feels like and how incapacitating it can be," she said.

Gibson practises what she preaches about lifestyle changes. One bad migraine year convinced her to commit to daily exercise. Today, Gibson's daily regime includes running, fitness classes, aerobics or cycling. Exercise has made a significant difference, she says.

"People used to suffer headaches in silence," says Maureen Robertson. "They didn't talk about their headaches and they tried coping on their own." Times have changed. Now when the Headache Society of Southern Alberta gives public education forums, the forums attract crowds of more than 400 people. "These people learn from each other," says Roberston. "They say, 'It's amazing, all these people have headaches, too.' We tell them, 'There are things you can do for yourself.' They learn they can take some control."

PART TWO

Take charge of your headaches: a personal guide

If you suffer from headaches, it's important to become knowledgeable about headaches and to take charge of your own care.

1. The First Step Towards Headache Management: Consult With Your Doctor

- Tell your doctor about the kinds of headaches you have – when they occur, how frequently, the site of the pain and whether the pain is throbbing, stabbing, dull or pressure-like.

    Keeping a headache diary helps. You should also note what kind of pain relief you've tried and how successful you've been with it.
- Choose your doctor carefully. If your doctor isn't particularly interested or open to helping you cope with your headaches, says *Migraine* author Valerie South, find one who is. Your doctor may then conduct tests such as a neurological exam, possibly even a CAT scan, to rule out other serious health problems (aneurysm, brain tumor, infection).

2. Coping With Headaches: How Successful Are Pills?

Most headache sufferers agree that matching the pill to the pain is not as easy as television commercials imply. And trying to find the right formula can be frustrating, not to mention a waste of money if the pills you choose do nothing for you. Unfortunately, most sufferers only find out what works and what doesn't through trial and error.

Frequently used nonprescription headache medications

1. ASA or acetylsalicylic acid can be useful to some, but should be avoided by people with certain health problems such as bleeding disorders, peptic ulcers and ASA-sensitive asthma.
2. Acetaminophen is the most frequently recommended and used nonprescription pain reliever. It has similar pain-relieving properties to ASA but does not cause as much stomach upset in some people; however, it doesn't have ASA's anti-inflammatory properties.

3. Ibuprofen is one of Canada's newer headache remedies; it's a nonsteroidal anti-inflammatory agent that apparently blocks the production of pain producers in the body.

Frequently prescribed headache medications

A 1990 survey indicated that 44 percent of migraine sufferers received prescription medications from their physicians.

These prescribed drugs include:
- anti-inflammatories;
- a wide range of painkillers;
- migraine-specific symptomatic medications, the newest of which is sumatriptan.

Preventive medication sometimes prescribed include:
- beta blockers;
- calcium channel blockers;
- antiserotonin agents.

Pills: The Downside

Although pain management through pills can be an important weapon in a person's headache-fighting arsenal, experts realize that pills may be abused. Moreover, pills may be the source of rebound or medication-induced headaches; this can happen when even the mildest forms of pain relievers (as few as two or three over-the-counter pain relievers, three or four days a week) are taken on a regular basis.

3. BEYOND PILLS: RELAXATION TECHNIQUES AND COMPLEMENTARY THERAPIES

If you have severe headache disorders, many health care professionals say it's probably unrealistic to expect complete control with nonpharmacalogical techniques. But there are some therapies you can try to supplement your pain control or to try to ward off a headache when you feel one coming on. Even if your headache isn't caused by tension, learning to control the tension that invariably comes with a headache is bound to help you relax more and thus deal with the pain better.

- *Regular exercise*
You've heard the old expression, "There's nothing like a good walk to clear the head."

While exercise doesn't cure a headache, regular exercise helps you feel fitter and can help you to cope better. Some migraine sufferers report that regular exercise both decreases the severity and the number of migraine attacks.

• *Massage*
Regular massage helps keep back and neck muscles smooth and supple. Some specialty massages like shiatsu work on pressure points and may help relieve headaches in some people.

• *Yoga*
Stretching exercises, deep breathing and a general appreciation of calm are all cornerstones of yoga and may mean fewer headaches, particularly those caused by tension or stress.

• *Biofeedback*
Some studies show biofeedback to be as effective as some drug therapies. Biofeedback instructors teach you how to control your body's physical response to stress. This approach can be very effective in preventing or alleviating headaches by training the brain to lessen the severity of the fight-or-flight response.

Biofeedback works this way: patients are hooked up to a machine that measures your body's physiological variables (this is the bio part), in the case of headaches, muscle tension. The machine's readouts report on whether the tension is increasing or decreasing, depending on what you do (this is the feedback part). You, the patient, try to alter (in the case of headache tension, decrease) the level of tension by focusing on the painful or tense area and using whatever internal focusing, imaging or relaxing techniques that enable you to take control, and change your level, of tension. When successful, this method relaxes muscles, reduces anxiety and may contribute to pain relief.

4. THE NEW TREND IN HEADACHE MANAGEMENT: IDENTIFY YOUR TRIGGERS

Over the past decade, there's been a shift from relying on medication only, to headache management through identifying triggers and making lifestyle changes.

a. Identify Your Triggers

What are the most common headache triggers?
- Headaches are frequently triggered by certain foods or beverages (anything from chocolate to coffee, aspartame to alchohol, bologna to bananas)
- Sleep changes: some people feel especially frustrated because their headaches seem to hit on weekends, spoiling their days off. These headaches occur as a result of sleep changes (you may sleep more on weekends, and deviating from your sleep schedule can bring on a headache).
- Caffeine withdrawal: if you're a four-cups-a-day woman at the office and switch to one morning coffee on weekends, don't be surprised if the result is a headache.
- Stress: the definition of stress is mercurial. Sometimes time "off" can be more stressful than a regular busy workday.
- Certain fragrances or smells: some headache sufferers report that particular odours – anything from flowers to fresh paint – are definite triggers. Some churches and fitness clubs (for example, the fitness centre at Nova Scotia's Mount Saint Vincent University) are now fragrance-free because some members have reported that perfumes and scented personal products (including shampoos and clothes cleaned with certain fabric softeners) can bring on headaches as well as other illnesses.
- Weather: A high humidex discomfort index during the summer is a big culprit. So are drizzly skies or rapid changes in barometric pressure. Calgary, with its rapid barometric changes, seems to be a migraine-prone city: a study done by Calgary neurologist Dr. W. J. Becker asked sufferers to keep headache diaries and found a distinct correlation between weather and headaches. Biometeorology is the study of the impact of weather on health: in Canada, CANMED-METNET is the organization currently exploring this connection.
- Loud noise or bright or flashing lights: these can bring on headaches in some people, particularly those who are light- or sound-sensitive.
- Hormone fluctuations: some women report more headaches after menopause when estrogen levels fall to an all-time low; others report fewer headaches.
- Medications: certain medications can trigger headaches. Ask your pharmacist about the side effects your medication may cause.
- Rebound headache: taking regular medication for headache pain, whether it's a prescription drug or an over-the-counter remedy, can cause rebound headache – the drug-equivalent to caffeine withdrawal.

Remember: different people have different triggers. To figure out what yours are, you have to do a little sleuthing.

It's worth the effort. Because by figuring out your triggers (keeping a headache diary is one way to do this), you may be able to change your pattern of headaches, lessen their severity, manage them better or even eliminate them entirely if your headache disorder is relatively mild.

Identifying your triggers is only the first step, notes Maureen Robertson. Next, "you have to be motivated to avoid those triggers," she says. If you're a chocoholic, it's hard to say no when the dessert being offered is triple-fudge mousse.

Triggers are especially important to migraine sufferers because research shows that migraines are usually set off by something specific, such as weather and stress.

But, to confuse the issue, many migraine attacks appear to be spontaneous. And, to further confuse the issue, spontaneous migraines may involve unrecognized triggers. And then there are combination triggers: a number of triggers that add up to produce a migraine. For example, under normal circumstances, you may tolerate a little chocolate. But if you are short of sleep, stressed or if there's been a recent weather change, the chocolate may trigger a migraine. Ditto for a glass of wine.

Unfortunately, if you are prone to migraines, simply avoiding your triggers may not be enough. You may need other therapies or medications.

5. MANAGING YOUR MIGRAINES

Although there are some pretty good over-the-counter and prescription pain "breakers," the key to migraine control is learning how to manage it yourself. At the top of The Migraine Foundation's list of coping strategies are avoiding your triggers and maintaining overall good health through a balance of moderate exercise, proper rest and good nutrition. Other suggestions for migraineurs (people with migraines) from the foundation:

- On the road, always carry polarized sunglasses to protect yourself from the sun's glare on snow, water, sand or streets.
- Try substituting dimmer-switches for standard light switches; you may appreciate being able to diminish the glare from lights when you feel an attack coming on.
- If paint is your headache trigger, make alternative living arrangements any time you paint in your home.
- If you work in a noisy environment, try earplugs. Earplugs or curtains made of heavy material can reduce the noise coming in from the street at home.
- Take a break from work. Even getting up to stretch, or answering a phone call

while standing, will help stave off tense muscles. In her excellent book *Migraine*, Valerie South suggests you keep a mirror near your desk "so you can monitor your facial expression every so often." If you don't see a relaxed, friendly face, stopping to smile and relaxing the jaw may crack the facial tension which may have triggered a headache.

- When possible, a brisk walk around the block does wonders. Migraine sufferers claim a breath of fresh air helps a lot, particularly when you work in today's closed-air or poorly ventilated office towers.
- Some migraineurs suggest avoiding sports that involve bending or stooping in a head-down position. A brisk 20- to 30-minute walk three or four times a week is great.
- Keep a regular eating pattern because skipping meals can trigger a headache. If caffeine hinders rather than helps your headache, switch to herbal teas.
- Drugstore-purchased cold-gel packs may help. Good comfort spots include the temple, the forehead, behind the neck and around the wrists. Bags of frozen vegetables also do the trick.

6. FIVE HEADACHES NOT TO IGNORE

Fewer than 10 percent of headaches are caused by serious underlying medical conditions such as an aneurysm, brain tumor or infection. However, all severe or recurring headaches should be checked out by a doctor. And there are times when you should seek immediate medical attention for a headache. These include:

1. Any severe headache that occurs for the first time as an adult that is markedly different from any headaches you have had in the past.

2. A thunderclap of a headache that's worse than anything you've ever experienced. It can happen at rest or during exertion and may or may not be accompanied by behavioural or memory changes, a decreased level of consciousness or seizure.

3. If your headache worsens over a period of hours, worsens when you cough or strain and is a headache different from those you usually get.

4. Headaches accompanied by other symptoms such as a stiff neck, persistent fever or vomiting, or neurological changes such as numbness, clumsiness, visual or speech disturbances or memory loss.

5. A headache that follows any kind of head injury, bump or whiplash.

Valerie South – the key to taking control is self-education

Toronto mother and former nurse Valerie South learned about headache triggers at the young age of 20 when she was first diagnosed with migraines. A nursing student at the time, she found the shift work caused sleep-pattern disturbances which, in turn, triggered migraines. Like millions of other sufferers, South's migraines can be preceded by auras and problems of vision such as seeing a checkerboard pattern or scrambling letters while reading a sign. About 20 percent of migraineurs experience an aura before they experience other migraine symptoms such as nausea or extreme sensitivity to light or noise.

South's way of mastering her headaches was to throw herself into the world of migraines. In 1989, she joined the Toronto Hospital as a project coordinator during a migraine study the hospital was doing. Then, after a stint as a volunteer with The Migraine Foundation, she eventually became its executive director, had November named Migraine Month and began an information line which handles in excess of 5,000 calls from across the country.

Empowering was a word South used before it came into vogue: it was always her belief that self-education was the key to taking control and becoming a migraine manager. South's migraines subsided during her first pregnancy. She also credits lifestyle changes such as a healthier diet and regular sleeping habits.

Over the years, South has learned practically all there is to know about migraines. She knows the latest word on what's available prescription-wise and she's also up on complementary therapies such as acupuncture and chiropractic care. If it's home remedies you're interested in, South can tell you the advantages of ginger and water or the pros and cons of feverfew, a plant from the chrysanthemum family.

And, between babies and migraines, South wrote the excellent and informative book *Migraine*, quoted earlier.

Barbara Pan – "just get over it" isn't good enough

Shouldering a heavy load at university while being a single mother with two young children wasn't the only challenge in Barbara Pan's life. The Calgary archeologist also suffered migraines, sometimes as many as two a week. "Exam time was a juggling challenge," she says. "When the stress was off, my head would explode."

Pan says she used to consider her head pain as "just bad headaches." She wasn't diagnosed with migraines until seven years ago. But her experiences in living with migraine taught her that you can't expect a quick fix when it comes to living with a chronic condition: "In the end, you have to assume responsibility for your own health management."

Pan believes we all need to listen to our bodies and learn to recognize the stressors that make us unwell. But the president of the Headache Society of Southern Alberta also believes that migraines have been downplayed in terms of their severity and the impact they have on people's lives. "The textbooks say migraines affect work, but I've spoken to people who've made actual career changes and choices because of their headaches. It's a chronic disability that makes you feel like you're living your life under a shadow. There's a reluctance to schedule events, everything from a bike ride with your child to attending a friend's wedding," Pan says.

Pan thinks that women with migraines are too often dismissed by physicians as either weak, or Type A personalities, or hypochondriacs. Friends and colleagues who don't understand headaches often regard a woman with a migraine as someone who has failed to deal with stress appropriately.

There's a lot of work to be done to sensitize the public to migraines, Pan believes. "Just get over it" is an attitude she's often heard articulated or implied. When a husband recently referred to his wife's serious migraines as "her little headaches," her jaw dropped.

Unlike a broken arm, you can't see someone's migraine. Pan says she now hears of teenage girls who, a generation ago, might have said they had their period to get out of gym class now use migraine as an excuse. That's something migraine sufferers are saddened to hear, but it only strengthens Pan's resolve that more education is needed: "You don't understand migraine unless you understand the feeling of wanting to scream at the person next to you for peeling a banana," she quips. Women with migraines need to learn about looking after themselves, she says: "If you have to sacrifice eight to 24 hours once a week to your headache, you usually take it from yourself rather than from your family or your work. Then life becomes playing a constant game of catch-up." Her own ways of taking care of herself: "I draw a bath, put a bag of frozen peas on my head, sip some tea, then try to sleep."

PART THREE

Your guide to headache resources

ORGANIZATIONS

Contact the following groups for information on headaches and/or to find the support group nearest you.

The Headache Society of Southern Alberta, Calgary General Hospital, Bow Valley Centre, M6-012, 841 Centre Ave. E., Calgary, Alberta T2E 0A1 (403) 268-9287.

The Migraine Association of Canada, 120 Carlton St., Ste. 210, Toronto, Ontario M5A 4K2 (416) 920-4916; 1-800-663-3557; 24-hour info line (416) 920-4917.

BOOKS/PAMPHLETS/
NEWSLETTERS/VIDEOS

While most of the following focus on migraines, they all address tension and other headaches in lesser detail:

Headache Relief, Alan M. Rapoport, M.D., and Fred. D. Sheftell, M.D. (Fireside Books, 1991).
Headlines: Canada's Migraine Newsletter; and *Living with Migraine* and *Taking Action Against Migraine* are two pamphlets available from The Migraine Association of Canada, 120 Carlton St., Ste. 210, Toronto, Ontario M5A 4K2 (416) 920-4916; 1-800-663-3557; 24-hour info line (416) 920-4917.

How To Manage Your Migraine, a 20-minute video available from The Migraine Association of Canada (see address above).

Migraine, Valerie South (Key Porter Books, 1994).

CHAPTER 14

EATING DISORDERS: LEARNING TO LIKE YOURSELF JUST THE WAY YOU ARE

Why is this a women's health issue? One-third of Canadian women feel they're overweight even though their weight is within a healthy range. And 90 percent of persons with potentially life-threatening eating disorders are women.

What can you do for yourself: Learn to like yourself just the way you are, recognize the signs of eating disorders, and get help if you think you need it.

What is an Eating Disorder?

There are actually two "disorders" – anorexia nervosa and bulimia nervosa. These two disorders are both extreme expressions of a range of emotional, weight and food issues. Both are characterized by an inappropriate preoccupation with weight and body shape, persistent dieting, abnormal eating behaviours and obsessive weight control.

Anorexia nervosa
Anorexia nervosa is an obsession with thinness to the point of self-starvation. Fifteen percent of people with anorexia are in danger of dying from their condition. The main symptom is a significant weight loss – 15 percent or more of one's original weight. Some women lose so much weight that they stop menstruating – a definite sign that the body is losing essential stores of fat.

Symptoms may start with the person narrowing her food choices – for example, choosing nothing with even a trace of fat – which inevitably leads to a longer list of forbidden foods. Withdrawal from social occasions, mood swings, depression, irritability, difficulty concentrating and a morbid fear of fatness develops. The illness is further characterized by an increase in physical activity, a resetting of weight-loss goals downward and weighing of oneself several times each day.

By being able to control their eating, anorexics begin to falsely believe they are in control of their lives. But their behaviour masks their real feelings of inferiority and sets in motion a state of starvation whereby their illness takes on a life of its own.

Bulimia Nervosa

Bulimia nervosa is identified by cycles of bingeing and purging through self-inflicted vomiting, laxatives, diuretics, exercise or fasting. Bulimics force themselves to vomit so often that they may have calluses on their knuckles as a result of forcing their fingers into their throats to make themselves vomit. Bulimics characteristically have a frenzied attitude towards their food: they may consume as many as 5,000 to 10,000 calories in a matter of minutes or hours. Their binges occur several times a week or even daily.

Bulimics can appear outwardly healthy. Although sometimes they are under- or overweight, they often are of average weight. Their normal appearance, added to the fact that most bulimics guard their secret and shame very well, make the condition difficult to diagnose. Princess Diana is the most famous recent example of a normal-weight bulimic (after counselling, she has recovered).

Fifty percent of patients who develop anorexia will go on to develop bulimia, says Dr. Allan Kaplan, a psychiatrist who heads the Toronto Hospital's Eating Disorder Programme. "A vicious cycle occurs where the bingeing and purging increases depression as patients feel more and more out of control. These persons then increase their food restriction even more in the hope of gaining control, only to fuel the binge eating and purging."

PART ONE

Why eating disorders are an issue in our body-obsessed society

The shape and size of our bodies is an obsession for many Canadian women. According to Statistics Canada, more than one-third of Canadian women whose weights are within a healthy range believe themselves to be overweight. The obsession with body image can affect women of any age, but the number of young women it harms statistically outweighs other ages; eating disorders affect one in nine women in Canada, most of them between the ages of 14 and 25.

One Stanford University study found that the majority of women surveyed felt worse about their bodies and appearance after reading fashion magazines. The reason? The magazines' unrealistic standards of beauty.

"Happiness is measured by the size of your heart, not the size of your dress," says Karin Davis, who has spoken often on the subject of redefining beauty for young women. Davis, a recovering anorexic, believes too many young women repeatedly try to reach an impossible physical state of being.

Body image is a complex issue. "Part of growing up in this culture as a female is you learn to feel bad about your body," says Carla Rice, a body image consultant at the Regional Women's Health Centre at Women's College Hospital in Toronto. "It doesn't matter what the beauty ideal is, you learn your lack of value – or your value – lies in how you look."

In earlier times, extra pounds and voluptuous curves were considered a mark of beauty. Too bad that counts for nothing to today's women, Rice observes. "Over the years we've gone from breasts to no breasts, from muscles to the waif look. It really doesn't matter what's in and what's not because we learn not to feel comfortable or attractive in our bodies." Teens are especially vulnerable to the social messages that skinny is beautiful.

Parents have an important role to play in preventing eating disorders in their daughters. Ann Kerr, coordinator of group therapy for Toronto Hospital's Eating Disorder Programme and assistant professor in the University of Toronto's psychiatry department, encourages parents to raise anti-diet kids who are as adamant about not dieting as they are about not smoking. "I'd like to see the day kids say, 'You gotta be kidding. Me, diet? I like myself just as I am,'" says Kerr.

Each of us struggles with body image daily. We can work together to prevent body damage, however. For starters, there's more to good health than the size of your jeans or the number on your bathroom scale. Staying healthy is a worthwhile goal, but for some women striving for perfection can overshadow getting healthy.

WHAT CAUSES EATING DISORDERS?

Dr. Allan Kaplan believes that body-image disorders are multifaceted: "One can't say they are totally caused by the culture, or solely caused by a neurochemical problem; there is no one cause. Rather these conditions are mutidetermined." But, he cautions, "not everyone who's conscious of their weight or is on a fitness regimen is at risk of developing a body-image disorder."

Experts say there are four core issues that affect eating disorders: self-esteem, separation, sexuality and control.

1. *Low self-esteem*

Women with eating disorders invariably have low self-esteem, says Dr. Kaplan. "In addition, a child who has a difficult time experiencing herself as separate from her parents is vulnerable." But the reasons one teen girl falls prey to an eating disorder while the other does not, are more complex than that. "Persons who do *not* suffer from an eating disorder, diet as a response to external pressures," Kaplan explains.

2. *A need to try to fix something inside oneself*

"For a person with an eating disorder, dieting is a response to some internal psychopathology," Dr. Kaplan says. "They are trying to fix themselves by changing their bodies." A person without an eating disorder may decide she wants to wear a skimpier swimsuit, so she goes on a diet. She loses some weight and then, at some point, she begins to feel faint, she can't sleep, she's irritable. Her friends say to her, "You look awful." So she says to herself, "This is nuts. I feel awful. I'm defeating my purpose." She stops dieting. She may have a number of these cycles, but she does not get an eating disorder.

3. *A fragile sense of self*

The young woman who develops an eating disorder does so because she is vulnerable on many levels. She undoubtedly has a fragile sense of self: she may feel like a leaf tossed about in the wind. Perhaps she was a chubby kid and was exposed to the cruel taunting of her peers. Perhaps she had a diabetic father or an overweight mother who was preoccupied with dieting and weight control.

4. *A possible history of abuse*

A person with an eating disorder may have been sexually abused. She may experience conflicts over her sexuality and have trouble accepting herself as a mature sexual being because she experiences her body as alien and as something to be controlled. She may have come from a family in which someone had a history of substance abuse.

5. *Unrealistic expectations*

A woman with an eating disorder may have come from a family where unrealistic expectations are the norm: perhaps her parents were exercise obsessed, or she may have been pushed into activities where low weights are crucial – ballet, gymnastics or figure skating. "The more the above kinds of forces are present, the more vulnerable the person becomes to developing an eating disorder," Kaplan says. People with eating disorders experience body distortion; that is, they overestimate their size and perceive their shape to be something other than it is. The self-denial and self-discipline that they perceive to be desirable in order to control their bodies are really a form of self-punishment.

PART TWO

Your guide to a healthy body image

LEARN TO RECOGNIZE THE EARLY SIGNS OF AN EATING DISORDER

Here are warning signs of an eating disorder:
- A preoccupation with food and weight (excessive dieting, counting calories, weighing oneself several times daily).
- Claims of feeling fat when weight is normal or even low. Body distortion is common to people with eating disorders.
- Guilt and shame about eating, not wanting to eat in front of others.
- Evidence of bingeing, hoarding of food, use of laxatives, emetics, purgatives.
- Excessive exercise, primarily to lose weight, not to get healthy or fit.
- Emotional changes such as moodiness, depression or social withdrawal.
- An overconcern about one's appearance.
- An oversensitivity to criticism of any kind.
- A need for perfection, an inflexibility, a thinking in extremes such as, 'If I'm not thin, then I'll be obese.'

LEARN HOW TO HELP A FRIEND OR RELATIVE WITH EARLY WARNING SIGNS OF AN EATING DISORDER

Once you identify the early warning signs of a friend's eating disorder, "you need to know what to do with that information," says Merryl Bear, director of the Toronto-based National Eating Disorder Information Centre. "There has to be call to action."

Here's what you can do if you spot the warning signs in a friend, daughter or colleague:
- Examine your own motives: "Ask yourself, 'Is this my issue that I'm projecting on this person or is it really her problem?' It may be an eating problem, may be not," cautions Merryl Bear.

- Talk to a counsellor, doctor or nurse about your concerns. Only approach the person you suspect if you feel there's actual evidence of an eating disorder.
- Watch your words: in your talks with the person, don't focus on body size. Say, 'I notice you're not eating well and I wondered if something is wrong.' Don't say, 'You're so thin! Why don't you eat!' "Focusing on weight and shape is a red flag," says Bear. Express your concern for her well-being without commenting on her appearance.
- Be supportive. When your friend insists she is too fat, you can say, 'No, you're not.' Encourage her to get help, Ann Kerr advises. Give her information on eating disorders and nutrition.
- Don't use mealtime as a tool to try to influence someone with an eating disorder. "You can be supportive and a friend, but you can't make her eat," says Kerr. Trying to do so may only perpetuate her eating disorder. Food should never be presented in a battlefield power-struggle fashion. After all, says Dr. Kaplan, "Food and eating should be like breathing. It should just happen."
- Be a good role model: "Parents may sometimes act out their own weight problems onto their children," says Carla Rice. "Young girls watch their mothers around food. And some mothers can overtly influence their daughter's weight by rewarding good weight." Today, there are dieting parents and dieting children, observes Ann Kerr. We are the first generation to be so fat- and calorie-conscious and it may be backfiring on us, she says.
- Educate yourself: become informed so that you can accept the illness in your friend or in a family member. Have patience and accept that she needs help. Denial is the cornerstone of an eating disorder, so don't be surprised if you're rejected by the person at first. After all, admitting to an eating disorder is as frightening as giving up the behaviour that goes along with it.

LEARN HOW TO LOVE YOUR BODY AND GET HEALTHY

Preoccupation with weight and size isn't something limited to teenage women. So whatever your age, here are ways to get healthy while learning to love your body:
- Learn about healthy weight.

    Healthy weight is a range of weights that is just right for your frame size and body composition. Along with emotional well-being and healthy bones, heart and blood, a healthy weight is one component of optimal health. Don't compare your body to your friends' bodies. Everyone is different and teens especially can have growth spurts that temporarily put them in a different weight range from their peers.

- Know and accept your body type.

  Genetics, not what you eat, defines your body type more than anything else. Generally speaking, there are three body types. Endomorph bodies tend to have an average to large frame with a higher proportion of body fat; they have soft, round bodies with large hips. Ectomorph defines the long, lean body with a light frame composed of little muscle or fat. Mesomorph is a muscular body type with narrow hips and broad shoulders.

- Learn about "set point," your own unique weight.

  While magazine articles promise to get rid of fat cells, the truth is that the body tends to maintain a certain weight that is determined by one's genetically coded "set point," something addressed several years ago by Janet Polivy, a University of Toronto researcher. Just as the body fights to maintain a healthy body temperature set point, so it fights to make up the calories needed for its weight set point.

- Throw away your Barbie doll.

  Did you know that two Barbies are sold every second around the world? When you translate Barbie's measurements into real body measurements, they're 40, 18, 32. As impossible as those measurements are to attain in real life, the Barbie-doll ideal – a woman who's thin, lean, yet large-breasted – is desperately sought by many women through dieting and cosmetic surgery.

- Get rid of your fat prejudice.

  Toronto's Jackqueline Hope, a successful and beautiful large-size model, has often said that society thinks of overweight women as unkempt and un-groomed. The owner of Big, Bold and Beautiful, a boutique and mail order business specializing in great large-size clothing for women, Hope says large men in the corporate world are viewed as being powerful and in control, whereas large women in business have to try twice as hard to prove themselves.

  In countless studies, some obese people have been shown to eat the same as or less than people of average weight. Despite the fact that obese people have to deal with tremendous social pressures, they are no more emotionally disturbed, nor happier, than people of normal weight. The risks of being seriously overweight are the same as the risks of being seriously underweight.

- Join the anti-diet movement.

  In North American society, more people diet than don't. This despite statistics that show that 95 percent of dieters regain their lost weight within five years. "I think that abnormal eating has become the norm," says Merryl Bear. "We talk about normal dieters as opposed to people with eating disorders, but diets in themselves are not normal." Eating properly and exercising regularly should help you reach and maintain a healthy weight.

- Consider starting a support group in your school or community. Such programs do exist, but not in enough schools. This is one curriculum addition worth lobbying for.

  Contact school board trustees, curriculum superintendents, day school teachers and principals, and urge them to include image/self-esteem programs in the school curriculum.

SPECIAL PLACES IN CANADA THAT TREAT EATING DISORDERS

Programs for treating eating disorders are few and far between and waiting lists are common. But Canada has two very special places, one of international repute and the other newly created and in the process of taking root.

In the West, Victoria's Montreux Clinic has gained international status for its work with severe eating disorder cases. Director Peggy Claud-Pierre describes her patients as women who are special, sensitive and intelligent individuals. Montreux Clinic measures its success as total recovery, a return to normality in all aspects of life. Unlike some other treatment programs, Montreux does not feel that a patient must be motivated or compliant in order to be treated. In fact, it bases its treatment on an intensive one-on-one 24-hour-per-day supportive environment that ensures a unique measure of patient safety and security.

Sheena's Place, a new information and resource centre in Toronto, was begun by the Toronto Sun Publishing Corporation in response to the death of Sheena Carpenter, the daughter of a Sun employee. Sheena, who died at age 22 weighing 50 pounds, battled anorexia for years. When she was 14, a modelling agency told her that her face was too fat. Her mother, Lynn Carpenter, teamed up with Sun employee Jane Fenton, who had her own struggles with eating disorders, and Trudy Eagan, the Sun's vice president of corporate affairs, to raise awareness about eating disorders and to found Sheena's Place.

PROFILE

Karin Davis – accept yourself as you are

"People say to you, 'Oh, you've lost ten pounds. Congratulations!' You say to yourself, 'I look good, but I'm starving.'" Toronto's Karin Davis fought her own eating disorder for over a decade. It started while Davis was in high school. "I used to think, 'It's not happening to me.' I threw myself into everything, was a straight A student and Athlete of the Year," she says.

When I interviewed her a few years ago, Davis was speaking about "body pride"and was taking that message to elementary and high school students. Here's what she had to say: "What you hear and see about being thin is false. Beauty truly is skin deep. If you can find things you're good at rather than wearing a mini, you become a beautiful person in your own way."

Davis notes that the average North American fashion model is five foot eight inches and 115 pounds, yet the average North American woman is five foot three inches and 144 pounds. "Look through a fashion magazine today," she says, "supermodels who are considered beautiful are unusually tall and severely underweight. You flip through the pages of magazines and see clothes on bodies with no breasts, their ribs sticking out and their shoulders pointed." Super-thin is equated with super beauty and super success.

It's self-image, not body image, that counts most, Davis believes. "I didn't want to grow up. I wanted the fat on my body to go away. I was fighting my body. Today, I advocate not dieting, and healthy eating along with moderate exercise. But loving yourself and accepting who you are is what I advocate above all."

Kaca Henley – helping larger women blossom

One size fits all is a sham, says Kaca Henley, a Toronto facilitator who dispels common fallacies about fat and weight through her You•Nique seminars aimed at the 25 percent of adult women who are larger than the norm. Henley is one of them, and at age 60, she's learned to live with the enemy in her battle with the bulge. A former translator of fiction, Henley now devotes her time to helping large women claim their value and worth through dynamic interactive seminars and audiotapes.

"All her life, the larger woman has received overt and covert messages that she is out of control, that she doesn't measure up," Henley says. "She is brainwashed to believe that the only way to become okay is to become someone she is not, to restrict and punish herself for being bad." Henley's seminars share coping mechanisms while building strategies that help reprogram the messages women send themselves in a society like ours, where being fat is like having leprosy. "I come in with a quiver full of arrows – bootstraps we can pull ourselves up by," Henley says.

Neither a therapy nor a weight-loss program that offers quick fixes, Henley's You•Nique is nonetheless a special sort of self-help group. "Today, women want and need ways to feel worthy and to reward themselves as they grow and develop," Henley says. Changing attitudes and helping larger women blossom is her goal. In the groups she's run, something exceptional happens, she says, "because we give ourselves something that few of us have ever received – unconditional acceptance."

PART THREE

Your guide to eating disorders resources

ORGANIZATIONS

The following organizations raise awareness of body-image disorders through education; they're part of a cross-Canada network that can help people with eating disorders find support groups or therapeutic programs. Some, like the Canadian Association for the Advancement of Women and Sport and Physical Activity (CAAWS), have done research papers on the subject and work to fight against body-image disorders in their particular fields. A word of warning: sometimes, programs offered may change according to resources and volunteers available, so you'll have to do some investigating on your own.

Eating Disorder Resource Centre of British Columbia, St. Paul's Hospital, 1081 Burrard St., Vancouver, British Columbia V6Z 1Y6 (604) 631-5313; (outside lower mainland) 1-800-665-1822.

Montreux Counselling Centre, PO Box 5460, Victoria, British Columbia V8R 6S4 (604) 598-3066.

Vancouver Women's Health Collective, 1675 West 8th Ave., Ste. 219, Vancouver, British Columbia V6J 1V2 (604) 736-4234.

Women's Psychological Services, 1405 2nd Street S.W., Calgary, Alberta T2R 0W7 (403) 228-5594.

Calgary Women's Health Collective, 223 12th Ave., S.W., Ste. 315, Calgary, Alberta T2R 0G9 (403) 262-5563.

Eating Disorder Clinic, 771 Bannatyne, Winnipeg, Manitoba R3N 3N4 (204) 787-3482.

BANA (Bulimia Anorexia Nervosa Association) has books, articles, pamphlets, audiovisual material on eating disorders. BANA, c/o Mary Kay Lucier, University of Windsor, Psychological Services, Windsor, Ontario N9B 3P4 (519) 253-7545.

Body Pride, 7B Pleasant Blvd., Ste. 1015, Toronto, Ontario M4T 1K2 (416) 486-3710.

National Eating Disorders Information Centre (NEDIC), The Toronto Hospital, Toronto General Division, 200 Elizabeth St., #CW 2-332, Toronto, Ontario M5G 2C4 (416) 340-4156.

Sheena's Place: An Eating Disorders Resource Centre, 87 Spadina Rd., Toronto, Ontario M5R 2T1 (416) 927-8900.

Canadian Association for the Advancement of Women and Sport and Physical Activity (CAAWS),

1600 James Naismith Dr., Gloucester, Ontario K1B 5N4 (613)-748-5793.

Eating Disorder Support Group, 4071 4th Ave., Whitehorse, Yukon Territory Y1A 1H3 (403) 667-2970.

Eating Disorders Unit, Douglas Hospital, 6605 LaSalle Blvd., Verdun, Quebec H4H 1R3 (514) 761-6131, ext. 2985.

Eating Disorder Program, Victoria General Hospital, 1278 Tower Rd., Halifax, Nova Scotia B3H 2Y9 (902) 428-2287.

Eating Disorder Resource Centre, YWCA of Moncton, 35 Highfield St., Moncton, New Brunswick E1C 5N1 (506) 855-4349.

PEI Self-Help Clearinghouse, Box 785, Charlottetown, PEI C1A 7L9 (902) 628-1648 1-800-682-1648.

General Hospital, Psychology Department, Leonard A. Miller Centre, 100 Forest Rd., St. John's, Newfoundland A1A 1E5 (709) 737-6150.

Books/Videos

The following, recommended by the National Eating Disorders Information Centre (NEDIC), provide an excellent introduction to the complex subject of women and body image:

A Hunger So Wide and So Deep: American Women Speak Out on Eating Problems, Becky W. Thompson (University of Minnesota Press, 1994).

Backlash: The Undeclared War Against American Women, Susan Faludi (Crown Publishing, 1991).

Consuming Passions: Feminist Approaches to Weight Preoccupation and Eating Disorders, Catrina Brown and Karin Jasper (Second City Press, 1993).

Getting Beyond Weight: Women Helping Women, Catrina Brown (Women's Health Clinic, 1988). Available from Women's Health Clinic, 419 Graham Ave., 3rd Flr., Winnipeg, Manitoba R3C 0M3 (204) 947-1517; TTY (204) 956-0385.

Never Too Thin, Eva Szekely (Women's Press, 1988).

Reviving Ophelia: Saving the Selves of Adolescent Girls, Mary Pipher, Ph.D., 1994

The Beauty Myth: How Images of Beauty Are Used Against Women, Naomi Wolf (William Morrow, 1990).

Understanding and Overcoming an Eating Disorder, a resource kit from the Eating Disorder Resource Centre of British Columbia, St. Paul's Hospital, 1081 Burrard St., Vancouver, British Columbia V6Z 1Y6 (604) 631-5313; (outside lower mainland) 1-800-665-1822.

The Famine Within, a 60-minute video; distributor, McNabb and Connolly (905) 278-0566.

Killing Us Softly, a 30-minute video, National Film Board 1-800-267-7710.

CHAPTER 15

PREVENTING OSTEOPOROSIS: BUILDING THE BEST BONES

Why is this a women's health issue? 2.5 million Canadian women are at risk of developing this potentially life-threatening disease.

What you can do for yourself: Stock up on calcium in your teens, twenties and beyond – and do regular weight-bearing exercise.

WHAT IS OSTEOPOROSIS?

Osteoporosis is a porous bone disease, characterized by low bone mass and an increased susceptibility to fractures. It is a serious disease that causes bones to become so thin and brittle that they can fracture very easily, often without trauma. In advanced stages of the disease, bones resemble a laced honeycomb. The disease causes severe pain, deformity, disability, even death.

PART ONE

The facts: why osteoporosis is a women's issue

Osteoporosis affects 1 million Canadian women. According to some estimates, one in four women over the age of 50 and one in two over the age of 70 develop the disease. But it can strike at any age: bone loss starts as early as age 30 to 35. Small amounts of bone are lost and replaced throughout our lives, but the older we get the less bone replaces that which is lost.

Osteoporosis is a subject that is addressed often in newspaper columns dealing with seniors' issues. But it should be an issue for women of all ages – in particular, mothers and their teenage daughters. "It's in your teens and twenties that you need to be getting in your calcium," says Dr. Rick Adachi, director of the Rheumatic Disease Unit at Hamilton's St. Joseph's Hospital and professor of medicine at McMaster University. "The more bone you get in the bank, the more you can afford to lose in later life."

To some extent, however, losing bone is a consequence of aging: you've probably noticed that your parents or grandparents seemed to shrink in height as they aged. The reason? Our bones gradually become thinner, lose mass and become more fragile.

It's not unusual to hear of people with osteoporosis breaking a bone by sneezing, giving a strong hug, lifting a heavy bag of groceries or engaging in some other activity most of us consider nonthreatening. Osteoporosis can rob a woman of her independence – especially in Canada, where slippery ice and snow are with us almost half the year and osteoporosis can make vulnerable women shut-ins. Women who've experienced fractures know how difficult getting around can be, and women with the disease who've broken a bone once are justifiably frightened of falling.

THE BAD NEWS FOR WOMEN ABOUT OSTEOPOROSIS

Calcium is essential to building strong bones and 78 percent of calcium's sources come from milk and milk products. But women of every age are flunking their calcium tests. Dr. Rick Adachi says that many young women, concerned with body image and weight, forgo their calcium because by cutting down on dairy foods, women can maintain the low-fat (less than 30 percent) diet recommended to manage cholesterol and protect against some cancers.

Knowing about osteoporosis risk factors does not always affect young women's behaviour. In one study of college-aged women, even women who correctly identified a lack of calcium as an osteoporosis risk factor were no more likely to make sure they consumed adequate calcium than women who had a lower awareness of the disease.

THE GOOD NEWS FOR WOMEN ABOUT OSTEOPOROSIS

1. *An Innovative Physiotherapy Program at Toronto's Queen Elizabeth Hospital Shows Positive Results*

About 225 women with osteoporosis come to the Prevention and Rehabilitation of Osteoporosis (PRO) program at Toronto's Queen Elizabeth Hospital each week.

There, they do a series of stretching, walking and weight-bearing exercises while receiving sound information on lifestyle changes. "Our program at the hospital is grassroots," says Jean Drumm, the hospital's physiotherapy manager. "It's been tremendously successful in terms of social integration, in terms of getting women to manage their own pain and, ultimately, in managing their own disease. I really believe in physical rehabilitation and therapy because it's such a natural process and because it's so empowering to the individual."

Dr. Joan Harrison, who started the PRO program and is now retired, is looked upon by many as "the mother of osteoporosis." In 1962, when Harrison joined the team at Queen Elizabeth Hospital, osteoporosis was being neglected as an issue: "What many physicians felt at the time was that it was a problem we didn't know the cause of and a problem we didn't have any solutions for, and that it was probably due to the aging process. I didn't think that was good enough. I felt nobody was concerned with the disease and it was time somebody was."

In 1983, Harrison, whose background is in metabolic bone disease, decided that some form of rehabilitation for osteoporotic patients would be a good thing. At the time, it was feared that exercise might cause even more fractures, but Harrison believed that some sort of physiotherapy was needed and that patients should do the exercises along with their peers so as to encourage a peer-support system and to protect against the depression that having the disease often brought.

Four years after the program started, it was declared a success. "I'm still much more positive about it than some of my colleagues," Harrison said. "I do believe it's much more possible to improve bone mass than others think it is. But even if you can't improve bone mass in the elderly, an exercise program does improve muscle tone and muscle strength. This helps people to be steadier so as not to fall. Also, good muscle tone reduces the force on bone, so that if a person falls they're less likely to twist and jar."

Harrison almost believes more in the link between exercise and strong bones than in the current preoccupation with calcium and strong bones. "Calcium and hormone replacement are being pushed right now. There's a lot of talk and theory and we really don't know. But we do know that young people who are better fit have better bones. The evidence of the need to keep using your bone is strong. I think that should be pushed a great deal more."

2. *A New Study Shows How Weight Training Builds Bone Density*

In a February 1995 issue of the *Journal of the American Medical Association*, it was reported that a 45-minute workout using various weight-lifting machines twice a week had more benefits than estrogen replacement therapy in preventing osteoporosis. Mirian Nelson of Tufts University in Boston was the lead author of a recent study that followed 39 women aged 50 to 70; none of the women took ERT or were on other treatments for osteoporosis. The 20 women in the study who pumped iron for one year increased their bone density by 1 percent; those who didn't lift weights actually lost 2.5 percent of their bone density by the end of the year.

PART TWO

Your guide to healthy bones

1. What Are the Symptoms of Osteoporosis?

Unfortunately, the symptoms of osteoporosis are silent. Often, pain is not present at the outset. Loss of height or broken bones may be the first signs.

One major symptom of advanced osteoporosis is something called a dowager's hump – a curving of the spine caused when the cervical vertebrae fracture and collapse. Other signs of advanced osteoporosis are a loss of height of more than one inch, a broken wrist, hip or rib, and back pain (mainly in the mid to lower spine).

2. How Do You Know If You're at Risk of Developing Osteoporosis?

The most accurate test for predicting the disease, reports the Osteoporosis Society of Canada, is through a painless noninvasive procedure called a bone scan. Bone densitometry is used to measure the amount of bone in the lower spine and hip: you lie on a table and a machine scans your body for a few minutes. Unfortunately, not all communities have this machine, which is similar to an X ray machine. You may want to bring this to the attention of your local politician or hospital (What a great idea for a fund-raising project!).

The calcaneal ultrasound unit, small enough to fit into a suitcase and as simple for the patient as having her foot measured for shoes, is the newest way to measure bone density. At $40,000, the machine is thousands of dollars cheaper than the scanner mentioned above (which costs about $500,000) and so may be affordable to many smaller communities. In addition, these so-called heel ultrasound assessments take about two minutes, as compared to the 20 to 40 minutes required to have your bone density assessed by the larger body scanners.

Learn the Risk Factors of Osteoporosis

If you check yes to four or more of the following risk factors, experts say you are in a higher category of risk.

- Do you have a history of fractures in members of your family?
- Do you have an estrogen deficiency?

Dr. Rick Adachi says that hormone replacement therapy brings good results: "Even the person who is fractured can benefit from estrogen therapy and will reduce their risk of further fractures by up to 40 percent." However, hormone replacement therapy (HRT) is not recommended for all women, particularly women with a history of breast cancer or recent thrombophlebitis. Discuss HRT with your doctor.

Studies are currently being done on new bisphosphonate agents as treatment for both primary and secondary osteoporosis; some of these drugs (such as alendronate) are about 95 percent effective in osteoporosis and are being looked at as possible alternatives to hormone replacement therapy.

- Do you have a small stature and thin bones? Small women, in particular, are at risk.
- Are you Eurasian or Caucasian?

    Research suggests these races seem more at risk.
- Do you drink alcohol or coffee in excess?
- Do you use thyroid, corticosteroids, anticonvulsant or anticoagulant medications?
- Is your diet deficient in calcium and/or Vitamin D?
- Is your lifestyle sedentary?

    Preventing the disease depends on weight-bearing exercise such as walking, skating, skiing, running, dancing, tennis and golfing. The more work a bone has to do, the stronger it becomes.
- Is osteoporosis part of your father's health history?

    A study of more than 800 women at the University of California School of Medicine, San Diego, suggests that paternal history is an additional risk factor that women and their doctors should consider.
- Have you had your ovaries removed, or entered early menopause (before the age of 45)?
- Are you small-boned and underweight?

    Osteoporosis patients tend to be thinner; some experts believe that a few more pounds may be a protective factor and that being underweight puts a person at greater risk.
- Are you postmenopausal and take high doses of thyroid hormone?

Check with your doctor to make sure you have your thyroid levels examined (a simple blood test does this). Test results may indicate to your doctor
that the strength of the hormone you're taking needs adjusting.

Women taking high levels of thyroid replacement hormone should ask
their doctors about bone-density testing. Getting a base-line reading may be
worthwhile; that way, when you have another bone-density test done years
from now, you'll be able to compare the two. (A bone-density test is fast and
painless.)

3. Learn How to Prevent Osteoporosis

A. Make Sure You're Absorbing Enough Calcium

An adequate intake of calcium over your lifespan is essential to preventing osteoporosis. But calcium's connection to building strong bones can be complex. For
example, the calcium in some vegetables and fruits such as spinach, strawberries and
rhubarb, although high, is not absorbed well by our bodies.

To benefit from calcium, the body must also have enough Vitamin D, because
Vitamin D helps the body use calcium. Milk is an excellent source of Vitamin D. But
Vitamin D is also produced by your body through exposure to the sun on your
hands and face (a minimum of 15 minutes of sunlight a day is necessary). So if you
spend no time in the sun or don't drink enough milk, you should talk to your doctor
or dietitian about a multivitamin that contains Vitamin D. (To make matters even
more confusing, you must remember, too, that Vitamin D can be harmful if taken in
excess. Check with your physician.)

One solution to calcium deficiency is simply to make sure you're eating a balanced diet. Another way to ensure you are ingesting sufficient amounts of calcium is
to talk to your physician or nutritionist about taking calcium supplements. Request
supplements that are easily absorbed (your body can't use calcium until it's
absorbed) and that contain the most elemental calcium.

The Osteoporosis Society of Canada suggests the following tips for choosing calcium supplements:
- Check the label for the amount of "elemental" calcium. When deciding on your
  intake, count only the amount of elemental calcium, not the weight of each
  tablet.
- Again, read the label: avoid taking calcium that comes from bone meal, fossil
  shell or dolomite; these may be contaminated with toxic metals such as lead.

Some tips about taking calcium supplements:
- Try to not take calcium and bulk-forming laxatives together, because the laxatives interfere with the calcium absorption. Increase your calcium intake if bulk-forming laxatives are used regularly.
- Try to take calcium supplements at the same times each day. For best absorption, take them at mealtimes and bedtime rather than all at once.
- Check with your doctor to make sure you're getting the right amount of calcium – that it is neither too much nor too little.
- When taking calcium supplements, drink plenty of fluids, including at least six to eight glasses of water a day.

Recommended Daily Amounts of Calcium

1,000 mg if you're premenopausal; 1,200 mg if you're pregnant or breastfeeding; 1,000 to 1,500 mg if you're postmenopausal.

Great Natural Food Sources of Calcium

About three glasses of milk contain 1,000 mg of calcium. Skim milk contains a little more calcium than whole milk. If you're lactose intolerant, try a lactose-reduced milk or ask your doctor about tablets for lactose-intolerant persons.

Other sources of calcium:

1.5 oz of Edam, Swiss, cheddar or Gouda cheese (about 300 mg)

7 medium sardines with bones (about 300 mg)

1 cup yogurt (about 300 mg)

1/2 cup almonds (about 200 mg)

1 cup baked beans (about 150 mg)

1/2 cup broccoli (about 50 mg)

B. Start a Walking Program

There's a solid link between weight-bearing exercises and strong bones. One great way to prevent osteoporosis is to start a walking program. Here's how, but remember to discuss any new exercise program with your doctor before you begin:
- Start your walking program slowly and build up gradually.
- Start with a simple warmup and some stretches.
- Walk for ten minutes every other day at the beginning of your program. Do this for a week, then increase the length of the walks by three to five minutes a week as long as you're comfortable doing so.
- Try the talk test: if you can talk while you walk, you're probably fine; if you're

breathless, you are probably working too hard.

· If you have chest pain or any discomfort while doing this activity, stop immediately and get medical attention.

· Muscle soreness is to be expected and lasts a few days; if it lasts longer, ease up.

· If you take time off for illness or vacations, start your activity again, but at a lower level.

· Make your goal 30 to 45 minutes daily. The distance you cover is more important than your speed.

C. Take Common-Sense Precautions

Osteoporosis causes fractures, which in turn cost our health care system millions of dollars a year. Anyone with risk factors should be aware of environmental factors that can increase the risk of falls. Loose rugs, improper eyeglasses and houses where there are broken steps or dark hallways can all precipitate falls.

Taking medications such as tranquilizers and sleeping pills also can cause unsteadiness. Buying a good pair of shoes (shoes that support your feet; fit your feet in length, width and in the toes; and have heels that are a comfortable height and soles that are non-slip), having your house safety-checked and investing in a cane or walker if you need these aids are all ways to ensure you're ready and steady.

PROFILE

Eleanor Mills and the boney express

"You can be well with osteoporosis," says 80-year-old Eleanor Mills of Toronto. "But the lifestyle you need to lead as part of the treatment is one of exercise." Mills knows of what she speaks. This remarkable woman has not only lived with advanced osteoporosis for 15 years, she's also started a movement that's raised Canadian women's awareness of the debilitating disease.

At age 65, Mills was changing arms with a bag of groceries when she heard a crushing sound. "I was so unaware of osteoporosis at the time, I thought, 'Well, isn't that extraordinary!' I had bought a new Laura Ashley dress and it had been midcalf. After that incident, I put on the dress and it was down to my ankles." Her vertebrae had collapsed and she had shrunk.

Not yet in too much pain, the former social worker and mother of two eventually had her condition diagnosed. But by 1982, after several more fractures (including one during which she had simply lifted a potted geranium), Mills was in excrutiating pain, so much so that she could barely teeter across a room. Her bone mass had slumped down to 46 percent: "I felt like a Dresden cup," she told me.

As part of her therapy over the years, Mills took part in several programs, including the Prevention and Rehabilitation of Osteoporosis program set up by Dr. Joan Harrison at Queen Elizabeth Hospital in Toronto. That essential physiotherapy, coupled with the purchase of a walker chair, gave Mills a new life and a renewed sense of purpose. "Walking with a cane is for nobody," says Mills, who has a so-called dowager's hump as a result of the disease and therefore can't straighten up. "With these seat walkers, the weight is on the wheels rather than on you." That first day, she walked 100 yards with the device. "I was so taken with the success of the walker that when I sped around the room, I said to myself, 'I feel as if I could walk to Vancouver.'"

Within three months, Mills was walking eight miles or 13 km a day. And by the next summer, she had formed The Boney Express, The Osteoporosis Canada Walk (she went to Vancouver and 140 other cities) to raise awareness and funds for the debilitating disease. "In Quebec, one woman was so enthralled that a bent old lady was doing this that she pressed some friendship rings on me." Every time Mills looks at those rings, she thinks of the women that she met.

"Several of them called me a role model and I guess that's what I am. I have the energy and the sense of duty to my community," she says. And she's living proof that you can take charge of your health, even when it seems to be taking charge of you! Slowly, her bone mass began to reverse, so that today, tests show that her bone mass has risen to around 70 percent. "I have had a lot wrong with me but I can't waste time on things that have happened," Mills says when asked about her upbeat approach to life. "I don't let the past haunt the future. You need energy to be negative, so why not transfer that energy to be positive!"

PART THREE

Your guide to osteoporosis resources

ORGANIZATIONS

Check with the following provincial or national organizations to obtain educational materials and information regarding osteoporosis. Some hospitals offer educational seminars and/or preventive programs or clinics. Check with your local hospital to see if and when such programs run.

British Columbia's Women's Hospital and Health Centre, 4500 Oak St., Vancouver, British Columbia V5H 3N1 (604) 875-2424.

Osteoporosis Society of Canada, 33 Laird Dr., Toronto, Ontario M4G 3S9 (416) 696-2663; Osteoporosis Society's Osteoporosis Bilingual Menopause Information Line, 1-800-463-6842. Regional Osteoporosis Society offices: British Columbia – 2110 West 12th Ave., Vancouver, British Columbia V6K 2N2 (604) 731-4997; Saskatchewan – Box 99, Royal Univeristy Hospital, Saskatoon, Saskatchewan S7N 0W8 (306) 933-2663; Quebec – PO Box 2170, Avenue Lincoln, Ste. #201, Montreal Quebec H3H 2N5 (514) 935-3726 or (in Quebec only) 1-800-977-1778.

OSTOP Ottawa – The Osteoporosis Self-Help Group, Good Companions Centre, 670 Albert St., Ottawa, Ontario K1R 6L2 (613) 563-9660.

Osteoporosis Society of Canada's Women Against Osteoporosis – A Support and Referral Group, 12966 Keele St., King City, Ontario L7B 1H8 (905) 833-3026.

BOOKS/PAMPHLETS/VIDEOS

The following have been recommended by osteoporosis experts and/or are published by the Osteoporosis Society of Canada:

The 150 Most-Asked Questions About Osteoporosis, Ruth Jacobowitz (Hearst Books, 1993).

Osteopororsis: The Long Road Back: One Woman's Story, Pamela Horner (University of Ottawa Press, 1989).

Preventing & Reversing Osteoporosis: Every Women's Essential Guide, Alan R. Gaby (Prima Publishing, 1993).

The Osteoporosis Book, Gwen Ellert and Dr. John Wade (Trelle Enterprises, 1993). Also available through the Osteoprorosis Society of Canada or by mail from publisher at 2577 Willow St., Ste. 202, Vancouver, British Columbia V5Z 3N8 (604) 943-0996.

Osteoporosis Basic Exercise Program, a 64-minute video, available through the Osteoporosis Society of Canada.

The following educational pamphlets are all available from the Osteoporosis Society of Canada, 33 Laird Dr., Toronto, Ontario M4G 3S9 (416) 696-2663. For large orders, however, call the number that follows the title of the publication: *Building Better Bones*, Osteoporosis Society of Canada, 1-800-463-6842; *An Appetite for Good Health*, Dairy Farmers Canada, 1-800-361-4632; *Calcium Calculator*, Dairy Farmers of Ontario, (905) 821-8970; *Enjoying Life Through Menopause*, Wyeth-Ayerst Canada Inc., 1-800-268-1946; *Osteoporosis: Your Prevention Guide*, Proctor & Gamble Pharmaceuticals, 1-800-265-8676.

CHAPTER 16

MENOPAUSE: POWER-SURGING INTO THE YEAR 2000

Why is this a women's health issue? By the year 2000, approximately four million Canadian women will be in their menopausal or postmenopausal years.

What you can do for yourself: Become aware of your body's changes, choose treatments appropriate to your needs and risks and think of midlife as your best years yet.

WHAT IS MENOPAUSE?

The word *menopause* comes from Greek: *meno*, or month, pertains to the monthly menses; *pause* comes from the Greek verb "to halt." In other words, menopause literally means a woman's last menstrual period. Menopause represents the end of a woman's reproductive life. The average age of menopause today is 51; by age 55, 95 percent of Canadian women have entered menopause.

PART ONE

The facts: What every woman should know about menopause

After centuries in the closet, menopause is only now being talked about. Why the change? For two reasons – because there are so many ways of handling menopause now, and because so many Canadian women are either in it or about to go through it:

in 1994, an estimated four million Canadian women, aged 45 and over, were in their menopausal years; by 2011, that number will increase to six million, an estimated 20 percent of our population.

In 1900, the average life expectancy of Canadian women was 48 – only one year longer than the average age of menopause at the time – 47). In 1986, the average life expectancy of Canadian women was 78 and the average age of menopause, 51.

"As our life expectency goes up, we assume we're going to spend those extra years on the tennis court rather than in a nursing home," says Dr. Jennifer Blake, chief of obstetrics and gynecology at Chedoke-McMaster Hospitals in Hamilton. "But independent life expectancy is something different. What's new is our expectation of not only prolonged life, but prolonged, productive postmenopausal years."

A November 1994 issue of *Fortune* magazine pointed out that corporations will have to address the needs of an entire generation of working women coming up to their change of life. Some gynecologists say that working women are frankly embarrassed to have menopausal hot flashes in the middle of a boardroom presentation. Uncomfortable, yes – but embarrassing? It's likely that working women who enter menopause over the next decade won't tolerate the openly dismissive attitude corporate North America has shown to older women in the past. Menopause may be the end of our periods, but it is not the end of the road. Old attitudes die hard, but they *will* die.

The midlife woman is a vital woman who has forged her individuality over decades. She's gone through many stages and transitions. Her menopause is yet another passage. Chances are, her menopausal symptoms will be as unique as she is. I remember author Betty Friedan, addressing an audience during a lecture on aging, giving her view of menopause: "I had a hot flash – once – in my sixties," she mused. Her point was that every woman's menopause is unique.

Hot flashes get a lot of press but they may not be the defining issue of *your* menopause. And your way of handling this change of life may not work for your sister, colleague or best friend. You may mourn the loss of your childbearing years – or you may be thankful they've come to an end. You may feel a little blue as an empty-nester – or experience a sweet rush of freedom like never before. You may choose hormonal treatment, vitamin supplements, herbal therapies, a combination of these or other things – or no treatment at all. You have many, many choices.

QUESTIONS, CONTROVERSY AND DEBATE

THE CONTINUING DEBATE: SHOULD WOMEN TREAT MENOPAUSE MEDICALLY OR APPROACH IT NATURALLY?

Menopause itself is not the problem. The problem, when there is one, is our lack of information and our lack of confidence in choosing what is best for ourselves.

To illustrate our current crisis of confidence in menopause treatment, let me tell you about a workshop I attended in March 1994: at the start of the evening, the four women who were to speak walked on stage in single file. Three of the women were wearing business suits and sensible pumps; the fourth came out shoeless, and wearing a flowing robe. A woman beside me in the audience tapped her friend and said what we were all thinking: "Guess which one's the herbalist!"

Susun Weed, the shoeless, long-tressed herbalist, may have seemed out of place, but she was in touch with her audience. Instead of delivering her speech at the podium like the others, she sang it. Her poetic song compared hot flashes to power surges that would enable women to change the world. She thumbed her nose at the gynecologist on the panel who was there to represent traditional medicine and its approach to the change.

Weed struck a chord with the women in the audience, regardless of whether or not they were into complementary therapies or not. She tapped into the fact that women are wary of taking hormones. Many women remember the seventies when high doses of hormones in birth control pills were linked to a risk of strokes and high blood pressure. Though the hormones used for menopause are of much lower dosages than even today's birth control pills, the way that the medical profession has medicalized menopause in the nineties has made some women so cautious that they have rejected hormones in favour of questionable alternative therapies. ("At least doctors have gone to medical school," Janine O'Leary Cobb, publisher of a Montreal-based menopause newsletter, told her audience during the symposium. "In alternative medicine, virtually anybody can hang out a shingle.") Nonetheless, Weed got a rousing round of applause for an anti-hormone replacement therapy comment which she delivered with a message about how menopause can give women newfound power: "If I were a man who knew that 100 million women in the next ten years would go into menopause, I would definitely try to drug them into submission."

Despite the documented benefits of hormone replacement therapy (HRT), it's estimated that only 11 to 15 percent of postmenopausal women across Canada are taking HRT. "HRT is not an easy choice because all the answers are not in," says Dr.

Jennifer Blake, who reminds women that no choice is totally without risk.

If there's one time in your life when you truly are in charge, it's during your peri-menopausal and menopausal years. In the last five years or so, a ton of information about the change has become available to anyone who wants to do a little research for herself. If there's one thing we hear over and over again from experts, it's the necessi-ty for women to weigh their options and arrive at a decision that best suits them. It may be hormone replacement therapy, but it may not be.

Montreal's Janine O'Leary Cobb, author and publisher of *A Friend Indeed*, a menopause newsletter, has often said she'd like to "close the gap a little" between the biomedical model that says menopause should be medically managed and the com-plementary model that says menopause is a natural occurrence. The gap that now exists, she says, is wider than any French-English gulf that she's ever experienced liv-ing in the city of Two Solitudes.

O'Leary Cobb disagrees with the attitude of the Society of Obstetricians and Gynecologists of Canada (SOGC), which in May 1994 issued its Canadian Menopause Consensus, a statement recommending that hormone replacement therapy be urged for all women. "I take issue with this," Cobb told a Toronto forum on menopause in March 1995. "Some women should take hormones, but some needn't."

Vancouver endocrinologist Dr. Jerilyn Prior says our whole attitude to menopause as a disease of deficiency should shift towards an acceptance of it as a stage in life. After all, Prior says, our hormone levels fluctuate throughout life and at menopause drop to levels similar to those during childhood, yet we don't think of childhood as a disease of deficiency. Prior would like to see menopause regarded as normal "since all women go through it." Prior believes that hormones should only be prescribed if a woman has bone loss or troubling vasomotor symptoms (hot flashes).

Obviously menopause is not a new phenomenon. But in the early sixties, Brooklyn gynecologist Robert Wilson began to praise the benefits of estrogen as a therapy that could not only save women from the ravages of this so-called deficiency but, when given to premenopausal women, could even prevent menopause. This assertion – that menopause deprives women of their "womanliness" – has reverber-ated through the subsequent thirty years: even today, medical literature talks of senile vaginas and a deficiency of hormones. Some doctors will still tell you that when the body's estrogen is shut off, a woman comes as close as she can to being a man. "It's implied that every midlife woman is in need of medication. This implies that menopause is not normal," Janine O'Leary Cobb, author of *Understanding Menopause* (1993), says. Today, thankfully, most women would interpret any doctor's antimenopause statement as a gender putdown. But as Cobb remarks, "Is it any won-der women worry about menopause?"

THE PROS AND CONS OF HRT

Hormone replacement therapy is more than 50 years old in Canada. Originally, it was administered to alleviate symptoms associated with menopause, symptoms that included hot flashes, vaginal atrophy and depression. But the treatment fell out of favour in the sixties because of reports that it increased the incidence of endometrial cancer. In the seventies and eighties, HRT came back in vogue because progestin, when given along with the estrogen, was found to protect against that cancer. In the eighties, HRT became popular again because of its effectiveness in preventing bone loss associated with osteoporosis; however, it subsequently became suspect when some studies showed a possible link between estrogen replacement therapy and breast cancer. In the nineties, the breast cancer risk has again resurfaced (one study in 1995 revealed that women who took HRT increased their breast cancer risk by 40 percent).

Many physicians feel that the benefits of estrogen replacement therapy still outweigh the risks, and there's considerable excitement over studies that have shown that HRT is good not only for bones but for hearts, as well: estrogen, even when combined with progestin, reduces the relative risk of heart disease in women – in some studies by as much as 50 percent. Recent studies also suggest that estrogen therapy decreases colon cancer risk.

Dr. Wendy Wolfman, a Toronto Hospital gynecologist, is an HRT advocate. She explains that HRT benefits the heart by reducing total cholesterol, by increasing the body's high density lipoproteins (HDLs) and by its direct action on the actual heart vessels. According to the Society of Obstetricians and Gynecologists of Canada's Canadian Menopause Consensus, the benefits of HRT greatly outweigh the risks. Cardiovascular disease (CVD) is the leading cause of female deaths, the society points out: it accounts for 41 percent of all deaths in women, more than all deaths due to cancer. Estrogen deficiency, it reported, is a major cause of CVD in post-menopausal women and estrogen replacement (including the addition of recommended low dosages of progestin) shows a protective effect against CVD. The report adds that contrary to prior beliefs, the beneficial effects of HRT should not be withheld from smokers or women who have diabetes, hypertension, angina or a history of coronary thrombosis. Primary studies also suggest that estrogen may be safe for women with localized breast cancer – after a period of being cancer-free.

All of the above adds up to what sounds like an irrefutable argument in favour of HRT. However, the most effective type of hormonal regimen is under debate. Consider the following:

When it comes to HRT's heart protection factors, many of the studies referred to were done on conjugated equine estrogen/0.625 dosage (an oral estrogen prepara-tion in Canada available under the brand name Premarin). Says the SOGC's Canadian Menopause Consensus report: "The literature since the 1980s is replete with short term studies of hormone replacement regimens. Only a few clinical trials have lasted for more than 24 months duration and there is a paucity of randomized prospective controlled trials. Although it is possible to infer from this literature that hormone replacement therapy does confer benefits to the postmenopausal woman, it is not yet possible to state with authority the optimal type, dosage, duration, and route of administration of hormone preparations."

So there you go – HRT is good, but some types are of more benefit than others. And therein lies the confusion: should you take an oral or transdermal (skin patch) hormone; what dosage, what type of regimen and for how long should you take it? Any HRT regimen, the committee concludes, should be tailored to the needs of the individual.

Dr. Jennifer Blake believes that women should make their decision regarding HRT based on education. Healthy skepticism is good, she says. As the old saying goes, there's lies, damned lies and statistics, so don't make your choices based entirely on those statistics. Look at the data to see what's being compared to what, Blake advises, before you swallow it whole hog.

That's good advice, considering two conflicting studies in 1995 on HRT and breast cancer: one study said HRT increased your risk; another study, released a few weeks later, said it did not.

THE BENEFITS OF HRT

Two Approaches: Symptom Relief versus Health Promotion

When physicians recommend HRT, they use one of two very different approaches. In the past, they prescribed the treatment to relieve the uncomfortable symptoms of menopause. This "disease model" argues that if something is wrong (hot flashes, for instance), doctors should try to fix it by prescribing estrogen. Today, physicians are more likely to prescribe HRT to promote health than to relieve symptoms. HRT, many feel, spells prevention of disease. Its benefits may show up 20 years down the road when women have less heart disease and stronger bones.

In the end, HRT may be like seat belts: they protect us, even save our lives if we're in a car crash, but do little or nothing for us if we're accident-free. "Calling it preven-tion doesn't make it prevention," says menopause health educator Janine O'Leary

Cobb. "If we want to prevent heart disease and osteoporosis, the best attitude to have is to watch your diet and to exercise."

The Debate Continues . . .

Are We Cheering for the Wrong Hormone?

Because it protects both heart and bones, estrogen has been the queen of hormones in the nineties. But in hormone replacement therapy, progestin is taken along with the estrogen in order to shed the uterus lining and thus prevent uterine cancer. Progestin is a category of hormones that includes progesterone and synthetic progesterone, and one menopausal specialist thinks it may be even more important than estrogen. Vancouver endocrinologist Dr. Jerilyn Prior believes that if hormone therapy is indicated at menopause, progesterone, not estrogen, is the hormone we should be telling women about. Progesterone levels drop even more than estrogen levels once the ovaries stop functioning, she says. Given as therapy to postmenopausal women, progesterone relieves hot flashes and is good for bone growth. She'd like to see more women talk to their doctors about progesterone, though she admits that most doctors today seem to be backing the estrogen establishment. Some of her patients are on continuous progesterone: 10 mg of medroxyprogesterone (one of the most common of which is Provera) per day controls vasomotor symptoms, prevents vaginal atrophy in women of normal weight and promotes new bone formation. And there's no cancer risk.

Menopause and Culture

As we begin to realize how narrow our own view is, we're becoming more interested in how other cultures perceive menopause. In North America, where agism is rampant, a menopausal woman is portrayed as unattractive, unstable, irrational, less useful to the workforce (if not society at large) and nonsexual. But in other cultures, women become more powerful and their status in the community is elevated following menopause.

During a visit to Africa, Dr. Jennifer Blake noticed an attitude about menopause not prevalent in North America. "It's great," an African woman in midlife told her. "It's when you get to join the elders and get to be a man." Blake interpreted that statement as the woman feeling a sense of recognition and achievement. In other words, some doors close, but others open.

In some parts of South America, the oldest woman is the wise woman and head of her household. In Navajo culture, postmenopausal women can become spiritual leaders and healers. In some parts of the Middle East, women are finally allowed to lower their veils after menopause.

One of the most interesting explorations of cultural attitudes towards menopause came about through the Regional Women's Health Centre of Women's College Hospital in Toronto. There, the centre's Gail Weber coordinated a team that looked at menopause in six ethnocultural communities in the city. These included women from the Afghan, Caribbean, South Asian, Spanish-speaking and Somali communities, as well as a group of women who were born in Canada. Her findings were published in a book entitled *Celebrating Women, Aging and Cultural Diversity*.

"Menopause was experienced by all the women in all the cultural groups as a natural transition, a phase of life that was, for the most part, acceptable," Weber wrote in her book. "The women of the ethno-cultural communities seemed to express less anxiety about growing older and the effects this had on their physical person." Some of the specific findings:

- The Afghan community's women talked about menopause's benefits: according to Islamic law, women are forbidden to go to prayers or to fast during their menstrual periods. So menopause made them feel they could take more of a part in the spiritual life of the community.
- Somali women regarded menopause as freedom not only from menstruation but also from the traditional roles of child bearing and childraising. As well, menopause meant they could stop wearing the veil, since its purpose in Islamic tradition is to preserve modesty and protect women.
- Women from Caribbean cultures saw midlife as an age associated with privilege, wisdom and respect. Because most families expect their elderly to live with them rather than in a nursing home, there's a feeling of belonging to a family long after you've mothered your own children.

PART TWO

Your guide to menopause resources

WHAT YOU SHOULD KNOW ABOUT MENOPAUSE AND ESTROGEN

A baby girl is born with one to two million eggs, Dr. Wendy Wolfman, a Toronto Hospital gynecologist, told a March 1994 awareness-raising workshop on menopause in Toronto. "By the time she hits puberty, there are about 400,000 eggs left." And by menopause, there are no eggs left.

Estrogen, a hormone produced primarily in the ovaries, declines rapidly when women reach their late forties and early fifties. Estrogen affects every organ in the body – the heart, bones and even the vagina. "At the time of menopause, all the body's organs show changes because the estrogen just isn't there," says Wolfman.

CUTTING THROUGH THE HRT MAZE

When HRT Is Prescribed – and When It Is Not

Despite the current applause for HRT, physicians agree that it's not for everyone. Your doctor may not prescribe HRT if you have:

- a history of unexplained vaginal bleeding;
- active liver disease;
- breast cancer;
- thrombosis;
- migraine headaches;
- gallbladder disease.

Just looking at the list of precautions doctors must advise their patients of before prescribing hormones suggests they are not safe, Janine O'Leary Cobb says. So, under what circumstances should your doctor prescribe them for you?

Dr. Wendy Wolfman's recommendations on when HRT should be prescribed:

- after a woman has had no period for five months;
- after her physician takes a complete medical history;
- after her physician does a physical that includes an examination of the thyroid and maybe even a pelvic ultrasound.

Is HRT for You? Questions to Ask your Physician:

- Am I at any risk for heart disease, osteoporosis, breast cancer, ovarian cancer or stroke, given my personal and family medical history?
- Will HRT change my risk of developing the above? If so, how?
- Which of the following tests (mammogram, Pap smear, cholesterol levels, bone density scan, vaginal ultrasound) – and which others – do you feel are necessary before we determine whether HRT is appropriate for me? How often will these tests be repeated and why?
- Do I need both estrogen and progesterone? What about androgen, the male sex hormone? (Sometimes HRT contains male hormones, which may be prescribed

to improve your libido. Too much androgen hormone, however, can make you develop male features such as a deeper voice and an increase in body hair.)

- What exactly are the side effects and benefits of each of the prescribed hormones?
- Which method (pills, patches, injections) do you prefer and why?
- I am a smoker, so will HRT benefit me and, if so, how? Or will estrogen's protective action be countered by my smoking?
- How will HRT affect my depression, sleep, energy, sex drive, weight, mood?
- How long do I need to take HRT in order for it to be truly effective?
- What are my risks or benefits in not choosing HRT?
- What are some of the alternatives available to me?
- Can I go on and off hormone therapy, and if so will I lose the protection from bone loss or heart disease?

THE DIFFERENT FORMS OF HRT

You can take estrogen in several forms: pills, patches or vaginal creams. There are also several progesterone preparations available, including synthetic progestins (such as Provera) and natural source oral micronized progesterone (such as Prometrium). There are also a couple of different ways you can take HRT: Estrogen tablets come in dosages of 0.3, 0.625, 0.9 and 1.25 mg (0.625 seems to be the dosage most commonly prescribed). Skin patches which are changed twice weekly contain either four or eight mg of estrogen.

We now know that when we take progesterone along with estrogen, the risk of cancer to the uterus is eliminated because the uterine lining is shed through an induced period. There are several different ways to take the combination therapy. For instance, some women take their estrogen pill daily from day one to day 25, and take the progesterone pill daily from day 14 to 25. They then stop both pills while they bleed, then begin the same cycle again the first of the next month. Other women take one estrogen pill and one progestin pill daily, the progestin counteracting the estrogen with the result that no uterine lining is built up and therefore no withdrawal bleeding is experienced. Discuss these and other possible options with your doctor.

The Natural Route: It *IS* an Option

Although menopause spokesperson Janine O'Leary Cobb does not dismiss HRT as an option for menopausal women, she believes that women should start with much less potent treatments, see whether they suit them and, if they do not, work their way up from there. Hormone therapy is a powerful treatment, she says. She challenges traditional medicine's approach to alleviating menopausal problems, aches and pains solely through drug therapy.

Above all, information seeking is preferable to passive prescription taking, says Cobb. Got hot flashes? "Get a fan. Or dress in layers."

Only 2 percent of Canadian doctors present natural options as strategies for dealing with menopause, Cobb says. Compare this to Britain where four out of ten physicians refer patients to homeopathy, which is covered by their health plan. "Here, we have assumed a narrow attitude," she says. Moreover, many of the complaints we associate with menopause may not be menopause at all. For instance, fatigue, joint pains and irritability were also complaints of middle-aged men in many surveys, Cobb noted. "I would argue that most women in menopause need reassurance and support more than they need a prescription."

"Menopause is not change; menopause is not transformation," says herbalist Susun Weed. According to the herbalist, change and transformation are not strong enough terms. She likens what happens in menopause to a caterpillar cocooning, then emerging a butterfly. "Menopause is metamorphosis!" Weed says.

Weed believes that menopause is a three-stage process of cocooning, meltdown and the emergence of ourselves in a changed state. The hot flash is the archetypal symbol of menopause: "Here's your body forcing you to do things differently. You have the right to take time for yourself," she says. "What menopause gives us is a full stop so we can craft, if we choose to, not the last third of our lives but the last half of our lives."

The following are some nonmedical options for managing menopausal symptoms:

- Dress in layers so you can remove some clothing if you feel overheated during the day.
- Use a lubricating cream such as K-Y jelly, Astroglyde or Replens for vaginal dryness. Keeping sex alive (with a partner or through masturbation) also helps keep natural moisture levels in the vagina while maintaining pelvic muscle tone.
- Try Vitamin E: some women report that a supplement of this vitamin reduces the severity of hot flashes. Talk to your doctor about the appropriate dosage.
- Although there's little scientific data to support herbal remedies, they are a postmenopausal choice for 15 percent of North American women. So-called remedies for hot flashes include evening primrose oil, the Chinese herb ginseng, and dong quai, a root famous in Chinese medicine.

What's a Hot Flash?

They've been called power surges, but women who experience hot flashes of volcanic intensity hardly feel powerful. Some women call them the acne of midlife; some women don't get them at all. But what actually happens in a hot flash?

"The hot flash has actually been measured," says Dr. Jennifer Blake. "It's a physical event." What happens is this: a sudden drop in your body's estrogen levels results in your body's thermostat being thrown out of kilter and wrongly sensing that you're cold; the result is, your brain sends out messages to warm up your body by constricting blood vessels in your skin in order to elevate your temperature. But since you weren't really cold, your body quickly tries to reverse the process by reopening the blood vessels in an attempt to cool itself down. The result is a rush of blood to the top of your body – a hot flash in which the upper torso and face may flush and sweat breaks out.

Hot flashes last from several seconds to several minutes; they can occur rarely or as often as every 30 minutes. Some women feel them so intensely that their hot flashes interfere with sleep. These women wake up with night sweats and may be forced to change their nightgowns and even bedsheets.

Hot flashes aren't harmful, but they can be disturbing and disorienting. The best advice? Consider the list below.

How to handle the hot flash: a herbalist's approach
- Exercise more.
- Turn down your room temperature.
- Try decaffeinated coffees and teas.
- Use a fan.
- Dress in layers.
- Chart your flashes by noting what sets them off: time of day, foods, beverages or moods.
- Consider biofeedback.
- Drink herbal teas. Red clover, fennel and sarsaparilla are good for hot flashes and sweats.
- Try tepid showers to bring down body temperature.
- Certain prescription drugs can trigger hot flashes; if you suspect this is the case, discuss possible alternatives with your doctor.

COPING NATURALLY WITH SLEEPLESSNESS AND FATIGUE

To foster better sleep patterns, work on your sleep hygiene:
- Go to bed and get up at the same time each day.
- If you wake up at night and can't fall back to sleep within 20 minutes, get up, read or have a cup of warm milk – then try to go back to sleep again 20 minutes later.
- To help manage the fatigue or irritability that sometimes comes with menopause, try taking some time out each day just for yourself.
- Exercise daily (but not just before bed, as you may feel overstimulated and unable to sleep).
- To help with depression, seek out women friends to talk to, or see a therapist.
- Enrol in a yoga course and learn a variety of relaxation techniques.

MENOPAUSE AND INCONTINENCE: THE LAST TABOO

Adult diapers are a product that you didn't see in television commercials or magazine ads ten years ago. With our aging population, the product is a very necessary one. Incontinence, however, doesn't just happen to babies and seniors. Statistics show that incontinence affects about 37 percent of women over the age of 60.

Many doctors advise patients with this problem to try Kegel exercises. Developed by Dr. Arnold Kegel in the forties and designed to strengthen all the pelvic muscles, they can be done anywhere – at a desk, in the car or at the movies. As with all exercises, start slowly and build up to the recommended number of times. The great thing about these pelvic exercises, which tone up the sphincter muscles surrounding the urogenital tract, is that they not only help stress incontinence but also enhance sexual pleasure:

Kegel Exercises for the Pelvic Muscles

Step #1: Identify the muscle groups around your vagina and urethra and tighten them, as if you were trying to stop the flow of urine. Squeeze these muscles for three seconds, then relax. Repeat ten times; do three sets of ten each day.
Step #2: Alternately squeeze the muscles around your vagina and urethra and release them, rapidly, ten times. Do three sets of ten each day.

Being upfront with your doctor is the first step to managing or curing incontinence. Estrogen therapy is sometimes advised, and surgery may be appropriate as a last resort. If the condition persists, your family physician may want to refer you to a urologist who specializes in female bladder problems.

PART THREE

Your guide to menopause resources

INFORMATION AND SUPPORT GROUPS

There are many excellent groups across the country, each of them offering information and support. If you're interested in creating an information session for a group of women on the subject of menopause, contact these groups for suggestions; some of these groups provide speakers.

Vancouver Women's Health Collective, 1675 West 8th Ave., Ste. 219, Vancouver, British Columbia V6J 1V2 (604) 736-4234.

Menopause and You, 4120–125 St., Edmonton, Alberta T6J 2A3 (403) 436-7164.

Menopause/Women and Aging, Women's Health Clinic, 419 Graham Ave., 3rd Flr., Winnipeg, Manitoba R3C 0M3 (204) 947-1517; TTY (204) 956-0385.

Artificial Premature Menopause Support Group, Women's Health Centre, St. Joseph's Health Centre, 60 The Queensway, M6R 1B5 Toronto, Ontario (416) 530-6388.

Older Women's Network, 427 Bloor St. E., Ste. B4, Toronto, Ontario M5S 1X7 (416) 924-4188.

The Mature Women's Clinic, 90 Eglinton Ave. E., Ste. 402, Toronto, Ontario M4P 2Y3 (416) 489-2106.

Menopause Support Group, c/o Planned Parenthood, 203 Merrymeeting Rd., St. John's, Newfoundland A1C 2W6 (709) 579-1009.

Menopause: E-mail support network. MENOPAUS@PSUHMC.MARICOPA.EDU

BOOKS/NEWSLETTERS/ AUDIOS/VIDEOS

There's no scarcity of information on the menopausal years. And with the first of the baby boomers having recently reached the age of 50, expect more materials to flood the market. Some favourites:

Menopause, a Well Woman Book (Montreal Health Press, 1990).

A Friend Indeed: A Newsletter For Women in the

Prime of Life, Box 515, Place du Parc Station, Montreal, Quebec H2W 2P1 (514) 843-5730.

Celebrating Women, Aging and Cultural Diversity: A Handbook for the Community, Gail Weber (Regional Women's Health Centre, Women's College Hospital and Riverdale Immigrant Women's Centre, Toronto, 1994).

Is It Hot in Here? (PEI Women's Network, 1991). A booklet published by the Women's Network of Prince Edward Island, available from Box 233, Charlottetown, Prince Edward Island C1A 7K4 (902) 368-5040.

Menopause Naturally, Dr. Sadja Greenwood, M.D. (Volcano Press, 1992). For order information, call (209) 296-3445.

Menopause: The Complete Practical Guide to Managing Your Life and Maintaining Physical and Emotional Well-Being, Dr. Miriam Stoppard (Random House, 1994).

New Passages: Mapping Your Life Across Time, Gail Sheehy (Random House, 1995).

Take Charge of Your Body, (5th ed.), Carolyn DeMarco (Well Woman Press, 1994).

The Silent Passage: Menopause, Gail Sheehy (Random House, 1992).

Turning Points: The Myths and Realities of Menopause, C. Sue Furman (Oxford University Press, 1995).

Understanding Menopause, Janine O'Leary Cobb (Key Porter Books, 1993).

The Change, Germaine Greer (Knopf, 1992).

Red Hot Mamas: Coming Into Our Own At Fifty, Colette Dowling (Bantam, 1996).

Is It Hot in Here? a 37-minute video directed by Laura Alper and Haida Paul, National Film Board.

The Best Time of My Life. A video directed by Patricia Watson, the National Film Board, 1985.

Turning Fifty. A movie directed by Helen Roy, Video Femmes, Quebec, 1986.

CHAPTER 17

WOMEN AND ARTHRITIS: ON THE PATH TO SELF-MANAGEMENT

Why is this a women's health issue? Arthritis and related disorders affect three to four million Canadians. And women are affected more often than men.

What you can do for yourself: Early intervention is crucial to prevent or slow down disability and deformity. Learn to listen to your body and, if you suspect arthritis, get a proper diagnosis. If you have osteoarthritis (the wear-and-tear disease), limit your exercise to halt further deterioration. If your doctor has diagnosed this or other forms of arthritis, make sure you learn all you can about your disease. Then find the best way to manage your particular type of arthritis to keep body damage at a minimum and make the most of life.

WHAT IS ARTHRITIS?

Arthritis is a disorder of the musculoskeletal system in which there is inflammation of a joint, characterized by pain, swelling and stiffness. It is really the name for joint disease from a number of causes. Arthritis is not a single disorder. It can involve one or many joints; its pain can be anything from mild to severe; and it can range from having merely a nuisance effect to causing deformity.

PART ONE

The facts: why arthritis is a women's issue

Arthritis disables more Canadians than high blood pressure, respiratory conditions, visual impairment and spinal cord trauma combined. Arthritis and related disorders are the second most frequent reason for prescription and nonprescription drug use, after medications for high blood pressure and colds or flu. It hits men and women of all ages. If all adult Canadians disabled by arthritis moved to the same location, they would make up Canada's tenth largest city, roughly the same number of people as the entire population of British Columbia. But of the 115 or more types of arthritis, women are affected much more than men in at least three types – rheumatoid arthritis (RA), fibromyalgia and lupus. Women comprise more than 60 percent of rheumatoid arthritis cases; 90 percent of fibromyalgia cases; and 90 percent of lupus cases. Scleroderma, a rare form of arthritis, affects 15 times more women than men.

Despite this, little is known about the cause of arthritis. And there is still no cure.

Why the gender differences? Researchers are beginning to look for answers by studying the link between hormones and certain autoimmune diseases such as RA and lupus. "Estrogen turns on the immune system while testosterone turns it off," says Dr. Edward Keystone, chief of the Rheumatic Disease Unit at Wellesley Hospital and director of Advanced Therapeutic Studies, the Arthritis and Autoimmunity Research Centre. "Women tend to have higher antibody levels in general than men. They have more gamma globulin than men so their immune systems seem more prone to aggravation than do men's – and estrogens can do that."

The hormone connection explains why, after menopause, lupus quiets down in many women. Research also shows that women with lupus have lower levels of androgen (a male hormone) than the general population of women. Other findings show that women with RA tend to go into remission during pregnancy and that oral contraceptives may protect women predisposed to RA. (On the other hand, oral contraceptives may prove to be detrimental to women with lupus.) Hormones, then, are a significant part of the arthritis puzzle. However, until we know more about how androgens and estrogens control immune function, there is no way to turn that knowledge into practical treatment.

PART TWO

Your guide to arthritis

UNDERSTANDING ARTHRITIS

Arthritis is a component of many diseases: it can be present in everything from pso-riasis to gout. Experts define it as redness, heat, pain and swelling in a joint. Joints are the parts of our body that allow us to bend, sit, kick, kneel, reach and grasp. If they didn't move properly, it would be impossible to write, dance, jog, type or turn our heads to see who is behind us. The joint capsule covers the place where any two bones come together to enable us to move: tendons, ligaments and muscles make up the supporting structures around these bones.

On the inner surface of the joint, there is a lining that provides nutrition for the joint. The two bones have a cartilage cap over them so that the surface is smooth. In a healthy joint, there is very little friction when that joint is used and virtually no heat generated as a result. With arthritis, however, there is inflammation and the cells release chemicals that cause damage to the tissue, including the cartilage and the bone. But arthritis is not just a wear-and-tear disease. In fact, it is a collection of more than 115 different afflictions, most of which involve painful swelling in the joints – usually the toes, fingers, knees, elbows, wrists and hips.

This chapter addresses the common forms of arthritis that affect mostly women. Because each of the different forms has different suspected causes, it's vital that you find out which one you have. Early intervention can slow degeneration and even pre-vent deformity. And since suspected causes may be anything from an infection, to wear and tear, to a genetic predisposition, identifying the type of arthritis is key to getting the right kind of treatment.

CAN YOU PREVENT ARTHRITIS?

Not necessarily. Only osteoarthritis (OA), the wear-and-tear arthritis, can be pre-vented or slowed down by limiting movement: joggers, skaters and dancers can experience OA at a fairly young age (former National Ballet star Kevin Pugh was forced to end his career at age 31 due to the disease – performing 33 leaps each time he danced his role in *Sleeping Beauty* did nothing for his knees!). But you needn't be a finely tuned athlete to experience OA: anyone whose joints have undergone great duress (either from movement through activity or as a result of bearing too much body weight) can suffer from OA.

COMMON FORMS OF ARTHRITIS THAT AFFECT WOMEN

Osteoarthritis

Osteoarthritis (OA) is the most common form of arthritis. It occurs in one in ten people; three million Canadians go to the doctor with the disease annually.

Osteoarthritis is caused by a deterioration of the bone cartilage: it is a chronic wear-and-tear disease. It can affect the knees, hips, neck, back, big toe, thumb joint and end joint of the fingers.

The loss of cartilage causes pain and inflammation. And the disease exacerbates itself: the loss of cartilage means the joints have less protection, which causes more wear and tear, and more cartilage damage. The final result can be bone grinding on bone and actual destruction of the joint's function.

The symptoms of osteoarthritis include:
- pain, aches and morning stiffness;
- creaky bones;
- pain, swelling and stiffness in one or more joints.

Treatment for osteoarthritis includes:
- painkillers and anti-inflammatory drugs;
- heat treatments;
- physiotherapy;
- Patients who are overweight are advised to lose weight for symptom relief;
- Since wear and tear is what this disease is about, patients are advised to do some exercise such as swimming or walking, but not in excess;
- In serious cases, OA may require hip or knee replacements. Hip joint replacement is an increasingly common response to severe arthritis and is being performed on people in their forties, fifties and sixties as well as on the elderly. In this operation, all or part of a diseased hip joint is replaced with an artificial hip joint made from a metal ball and shaft, which fit into a metal or plastic socket. Results are remarkably successful: mobility may be restored to people previously incapacitated by stiffness and pain.

Rheumatoid arthritis

About 250,000 Canadians are affected by rheumatoid arthritis (RA): it occurs in one in every 100 people. It is a woman's disease, affecting women two to three times as much as men.

"Rheumatoid arthritis causes the most crippling, the most deformity, and the most impairment of any arthritis," rheumatologist Dr. Arthur Bookman explained at a seminar on the subject held at Toronto Hospital in the summer of 1995. "It occurs in the childbearing years so has a great implication in the ability to bear and care for a child, the ability to partake in a marriage and the ability to partake in life."

RA is an autoimmune disorder in which the immune system attacks the body's own tissue. RA occurs when a membrane lining the joints produces autoantibodies that attack and damage the joints.

Eventually, these antibodies attack the cartilage (a smooth glistening substance that caps the joint bones and allows bones to move one on the other without friction); then the ligaments that support the joint are loosened and the bones begin to painfully rub one against the other.

"This disease runs the entire gamut from being mild to severe," Dr. Bookman points out. Eventually tendons can rupture, muscles can waste and the joints start to move in directions they are not meant to, he explains. "Virtually 100 percent of patients who have true RA develop joint damage. The only thing that's left to be determined is how severe the joint damage will be. In 10 percent of the cases, the joint damage is profound and it leaves people with a major loss in their ability to function. With early intervention we hope to prevent these 10 percent of patients from being debilitated."

Early intervention is the key. The reason: early intervention may prevent joint damage. Because RA is an autoimmune disease, other organs can also be affected – the skin, the eyes, the lungs, the heart, the nerves, even the thyroid.

Obtaining a proper diagnosis, therefore, is crucial. One way of diagnosing RA is through a blood test: about 75% of RA patients have blood that tests positive for RA.

Symptoms of RA include:
- swollen, red, warm, painful and stiff joints (fingers, wrists, toes, ankles, knees, neck or shoulders can be affected);
- mild fever along with generalized aches and pains;
- marked morning stiffness; unlike osteoarthritis, the wear-and-tear disease in which stiffness may be associated with use of a particular joint, patients with RA find they're extremely stiff the first hour or two after rising;

- joint inflammation that flares up suddenly. "The disease follows a course very often of exacerbation and remission," says Dr. Bookman. "A flare-up and a settling. We don't know what causes this."

Treatment for RA includes:
- drugs (see below);
- physiotherapy (see below);
- occupational therapy (see below);
- surgery.

Drugs include:
- nonsteroidal anti-inflammatory drugs for pain and stiffness;
- drugs such as antimalarials or gold to arrest progress of the disease;
- immunosuppressant drugs and corticosteroids.

Nonsteroidal anti-inflammatory drugs can cause gastrointestinal problems, some of them serious (including ulcers, perforation or bleeding). Taking a medication to protect against ulcers may be advisable, particularly for high-risk patients.

Physiotherapy for RA patients is important to help relieve the pain and stiffness. In contrast to OA patients who are advised to limit movement, RA sufferers are often advised to keep moving: they often feel better when they move.

Occupational therapy can help people learn new techniques for managing their everyday lives. Montreal's Diane Archambault learned how to reorganize her apartment to provide a compact sewing centre which she could comfortably access from her wheelchair. Since she makes all her own clothes, she made sure that her dressmaking tools are ones that make her life easier as an RA patient. Her sharp, lightweight scissors have wide handles adapted to her needs, and she has a 60-cm-long metal rod with a nonslip grip at one end and a magnet at the other to allow her to easily pick up pins and needles dropped on the floor.

Lupus

Lupus or systemic lupus erythematosus is an autoimmune illness that attacks women nine times more often than men. Its symptoms are many and may include red, tender, swollen joints; skin roughness and rashes; sun sensitivity; and oral ulcers.

What happens in lupus is this: the immune system goes into overdrive. For some people the disease is a mere annoyance with the occasional flare-up; but in its most serious form, lupus can be life-threatening and can cause serious kidney and other organ damage, which is treated with certain chemotherapies similar to those used to combat cancer.

"When I was in medical school, we were told the incidence of lupus was one per 100,000," says Dr. Daphna Gladman, a rheumatologist and leading lupus expert at Toronto's Wellesley Hospital. "Now we know it's one per 1,000. That's 100 times less than breast cancer, which has a one in ten risk. So some people say, well, lupus isn't so important then. But it is a chronic disease and unlike, say, breast cancer, you can't get rid of it – nor does it get rid of you. It also takes its toll because it affects not only the patient, but her family and society."

The symptoms of lupus

For the disease to be classified as lupus, the patient has to meet at least four of eleven criteria. These may include:

- photosensitivity;
- a classic butterfly rash that spreads over the cheeks and bridge of the nose (in 1851 a French dermatologist described this rash as wolflike, hence the name lupus);
- hair loss;
- mouth sores;
- weakness or fatigue;
- arthritis (that is, already having another form of arthritis).

Four of the criteria are confirmed by lab analysis. The lab analyses done are:

- blood tests to provide platelet counts; and
- urinalysis to determine kidney function.

The treatment of lupus

Since there is no cure, the goal of treatment is to reduce inflammation and to alleviate symptoms. To do this, there's a whole arsenal of drugs available beginning with non-steroidal anti-inflammatory drugs for joint pain, corticosteroid drugs for fever and neurological symptoms and antimalarial drugs to limit skin rash. In severe cases, immunosuppressant drugs (called "the big guns") are used. Lupus patients learn to avoid the sun (the sun can make symptoms worse in some sufferers) and become more attuned to their bodies: becoming overtired or overexerting oneself, particularly when you experience a flare-up, only taxes the immune system.

Scleroderma

Scleroderma is a rare systemic autoimmune condition that affects many organs and tissues in the body. It's 15 times more common in women than men and it's most likely to appear between the ages of 40 and 60. Like lupus, it is an autoimmune disorder in which the body's immune system goes into overdrive and attacks its own tissues and organs.

Scleroderma causes the skin to become hardened and thickened, tight and bound. Scleroderma can affect the blood vessels, the joints and the gastrointestinal tract. Symptoms range from mild to severe. One common symptom is called Raynaud's phenomenon in which the fingers become white and painful upon exposure to the cold. Scleroderma can be life-threatening, particularly when degeneration is rapid; it can lead to kidney, heart or respiratory failure.

The treatment of scleroderma

Though there is no cure, treatment can relieve symptoms. Physiotherapy is often recommended for joint stiffness. High blood pressure, one of the symptoms, may be treated with drugs. In severe cases, life-sustaining treatment is necessary (such as dialysis for kidney failure).

Fibromyalgia

Fibromyalgia is a syndrome that includes muscle and joint pain without joint swelling.

Patients often experience more pain in damp weather. Sleep disturbances are also common; depression may be present. Though women who contract the disease tend to have a history of good health, their life changes dramatically when they begin to suffer from fibromyalgia. They become plagued by fatigue; they also experience stiffness or are in constant pain particularly around certain tender points on the body.

Fibromyalgia is a very misunderstood condition. Many physicians consider it a psychosomatic illness. In Chapter 19, you'll see that fibromyalgia is one of a group of illnesses currently being studied by various medical specialists interested in a cluster of illnesses special to women and previously ignored by many in the medical community.

Treatment for fibromyalgia

A physician who is sensitive to this disease would first rule out any immune disorders. Stiffness and muscle soreness may be treated with anti-inflammatory drugs;

some people feel better on low-dose antidepressants. Once a comfort level is achieved, the next goal is to establish a regular low-impact exercise program. Consultation with the experts at a sleep clinic may also be advised to rule out serious sleep disturbances.

ALTERNATIVE CURES FOR ARTHRITIS: CAN THEY HARM YOU?

The lure of a cure for arthritis represents billions of dollars in the marketplace. Arthritis sufferers are pitched everything from copper bracelets to WD-40, a metal rust protector. Arthritis experts tend to view both as a waste of money. The former probably does no harm and some people feel it works; but the latter can cause severe allergic reaction and inflammation of the lungs when inhaled.

Some arthritis sufferers claim that certain diets send their arthritis into remission. But there is no scientific evidence to suggest any diet other than a healthy balanced one is consistently helpful to arthritic patients. Herbal remedies (aloe vera is one) often claim to cure arthritis, but no herbal cure has ever been confirmed and some can do more harm than good. Other popular but questionable alternatives include bee venom and vitamin megadoses.

The Arthritis Society reports that the annual public donations in North America to arthritis research (about $20 million) is about 1 percent of what is spent on questionable arthritis remedies. Why do people continue to buy unproven remedies? According to The Arthritis Society, alternative medicines and therapies that promise to empower patients attract persons facing a progressively debilitating illness.

So, what's the harm, patients often ask. Well, besides being a waste of money, concentrating on questionable medicines and therapies may encourage you to ignore your medically prescribed treatment. As a result, your disease may progress at a faster rate. And since questionable remedies haven't been scientifically tested, they may be harmful to your health. Moreover, if you abandon your treatment and your visits to the doctor, there's no way to tell (objectively) whether you're getting better or not.

LEARNING TO HELP YOURSELF: A SAFE ALTERNATIVE

Every province now offers the six-week course called the Arthritis Self-Management Program (ASMP). Trained volunteer leaders often suffer from the same arthritic conditions as the participants, so their empathy comes from firsthand experience with the frustrations of the disease. As well as providing information about arthritis and commonly prescribed medications, ASMP covers relaxation and pain management, exercise and getting the most from the doctor-patient relationship. In addition, there's the benefit of sharing experiences and solutions. Whether it's a tip on making a cup of tea without adding stress to your wrist or discovering a new assistive device to help your reach, participants come away having learned a lot. Best of all, most say they feel more in control of their arthritis, instead of the arthritis controlling them.

PROFILE

Barbara Brunton – support is survival

Scarborough, Ontario's Barbara Brunton has encountered some pretty serious challenges in the decade since she was diagnosed with rheumatoid arthritis. Along with the disabling disfigurement the disease caused in her hands, the excruciating pain sometimes took her to the emergency department of her local hospital. She was also getting hot angry skin spots, anemia, diverticulitis and a septic toe.

When Brunton got an additional diagnosis of lupus, instead of feeling pushed over the edge, she pulled herself together and joined a support group. "For me, it was survival," she says. "The thought of not being able to work anymore or not being around people would kill me."

Brunton went on to work as a volunteer for The Arthritis Society. Then, when the society asked her to work on their Arthritis Bell Canada Support and Information Line (ABSIL), Brunton became a paid employee. Who better to staff an information and support line than someone living with the same illness as the callers? Calls to ABSIL have quadrupled since it began a few years ago.

In the beginning, Brunton says her diagnosis seemed like a life sentence. "You do have to readjust and give up a lifestyle you once knew," she says, explaining that she learned a lot through social workers and physiotherapists who worked with her to help her adjust, both emotionally and physically, to a new life. Today, instead of cooking complex recipes with 25 ingredients, she makes simpler meals. "I have a major hand-and-foot deformity and can't easily lift a bowl, scrape it up and pour out the batter. So that kind of cooking is out for me now. I eat fruit instead."

Though her doctor told her she'd never work again, Brunton didn't believe him. "I said, 'You just watch!'" In her role with ABSIL, she tries to help others find the spirit to keep on going and growing. "If their pilot light is out, I try to light it," she says.

PROFILE

Sheila Billing – "I am a person beyond my disease"

Former Miss Toronto Sheila Billing credits her career as a child model, actress, singer, dancer and fifties beauty queen for helping her get past her pain. Though she has lived with rheumatoid arthritis for the past 22 years, it has only been in the past two years that she's stopped practising her craft as a television makeup artist.

Looking good has always been important, and it still is: "If a woman looks good, she is going to feel good about herself," says Billing, who is writing a book on her craft. "I am a person beyond my disease. I can do everything, just about everything." Renoir [the artist] strapped paintbrushes to his arms during his last arthritic years, says Billing: "When I learned that, I found it inspirational."

Billing swims three times a week because she feels no pain in water. She looks at her life as a half-full vessel and feels blessed living in a city with accessible heated pools. "I find the movement keeps me out of a wheelchair," she says. (She does use a scooter or a cane sometimes to help her get along.) "I am always out and about. I am rarely home."

Billing has empathy for other sufferers, but she also feels that too many people dwell on their diseases. Her think-positive philosophy has been passed down from her mother who spent the last ten years of her life in a wheelchair. "Mom's favourite saying was this: 'There are two men in prison looking out from behind bars. One sees mud and one sees stars.' Now, what is it you want to see?"

PART THREE

Your guide to arthritis support and services resources

INFORMATION, SUPPORT GROUPS, AND HOTLINES

The Arthritis Society, through its provincial chapters, offers both excellent educational materials and a wide range of wonderful programs such as the Arthritis Self-Management Program; plus, the Arthritis hotline now offers support and information across the country.

Arthritis Bell Support and Information Line (ABSIL): ON (416) 967-5679, 1-800-361-1112. BC/YT (604) 871-4537, 1-800-667-2847; AB/NT (403) 228-2571, 1-800-667-0097; SK (306) 352-3312, 1-800-667-0097; MB (204) 942-4892; PQ (514) 846-8840; NB (506) 457-1652; NS/PE (902) 429-7025, 1-800-565-2873; NF (709) 368-8190.

The Arthritis Society: National Office/Ontario Division, 250 Bloor St. E., Ste. 901, Toronto, ON M4W 3P2 (416) 967-1414. Provincial chapters: NF: Box 522, Stn. C. St. John's, NF A1C 5K4 (709) 579-8190. PE: 109 Heath Ave., Sherwood, PE C1A 6Z3 (902) 887-3524. NS: 5516 Spring Garden Rd., Halifax, NS B3J 1G6 (902) 429-7025. NB: 65 Brunswick St., Fredericton, NB E3B 1G5 (506) 452-7191. PQ: 2155 rue Guy, Ste. 1120, Montreal, PQ H3H 2R9 (514) 846-8840. MB: 386 Broadway Ave., Ste. 105, Winnipeg, MB R3C 3R6 (204) 942-4892. SK: 2078 Halifax St., Regina, SK S4P 1T7 (306) 352-3312. AB: 301, 1301-8th St. S.W., Calgary, AB T2R 1B7 (403) 228-2571. BC/YT: 895 West 10th Ave., Vancouver, BC V5Z 1L7 (604) 879-7511.

NEWSLETTERS/BOOKS/VIDEOS

Arthritis News, National Office, The Arthritis Society, 250 Bloor St. E. Ste. 901, Toronto, ON M4W 3P2.

The "Be" Attitudes – Keys to Healing from Within, 120-minute video from the Ontario Fibromyalgia Association, c/o The Arthritis Society, 250 Bloor St. E., Ste. 901, Toronto, ON M4W 3P2 (416) 967-1414, 1-800-361-1112.

INFORMATION AND SUPPORT SERVICES

Lupus Canada, 635–6 Ave. S.W., #040, Calgary, AB T2P 0T5.

Lupus Erythematosus Society of Alberta, Edmonton Chapter, 6235-103 St., Ste. 133, Edmonton, AB T6E 5H6 (403) 435-5067.

The Lupus Society of Hamilton, Jackson Station, PO Box 57414, Hamilton, ON L8P 4X2 (905) 527-2252.

BOOKS AND NEWSLETTERS

TLC: *Taking Life as a Challenge: A Newsletter for Teens with Lupus,* Joanne McCarthy, 3262 Ivernia Rd., Mississauga, ON L4Y 3E8.

CHAPTER 18

WOMEN AND DISABILITIES: HEALTH MEANS ACCESS AND ACCEPTANCE

Why is this a women's health issue? More than two million Canadian women experience mild to severe disabilities, and countless others will experience either a short- or long-term disability sometime in their lives.

What you can do for yourself: Learning what support and information services are available in your community can help you learn to manage your own disability better. Actively support other women with disabilities by campaigning for accessibility to places and services.

WHAT IS A DISABILITY?

The dictionary definition of the word implies a loss of power or ability in a physical or mental sense. It's important to distinguish between sickness and disability: a person who is disabled is not necessarily sick. She probably requires the same health care as a nondisabled woman; at the same time, certain aspects of her disability may require that she see a specialist or have a particular kind of treatment at some time in her life. Many people consider disability to be part of a continuum from ability to disability on which all of us find ourselves at different points in our lives. Whether we are born with a disability, develop a disability from an accident or disease as a child or an adult or whether it is the chronic disability some of us will experience as we age (bring out those reading glasses!), many women will have the experience of being disabled at some point in their lives.

PART ONE

The facts: why disability is a women's issue

Statistics Canada figures from 1991 report 4.2 million Canadians (about 16 percent of the population) experience mild through severe disabilities; of that number, roughly half, or more than two million, are women. Disabilities cover a wide range of experiences, from being sight-impaired to paraplegic. But you don't have to be permanently disabled to experience what disabled people have to cope with daily. Just break an ankle one winter and end up with your leg in a cast up to your knee, and you'll have an idea of how different and complex life can be. Everything, from walking with crutches on snow-covered sidewalks to your daily shower or bath, requires you to learn new ways of coping. When you're on crutches, you consider accessibility to restaurants as much as you consider the menu; stay on crutches long enough and you have to consider other ways of maintaining physical fitness when jogging, cycling or walking isn't an option.

Any temporary experience that renders us disabled only serves to remind us how vast the world of disabilities really is. Some people are obviously, visibly disabled: they are wheelchair-bound, missing a limb or obviously sight-impaired. Other disabilities are not so obvious and include everything from the child with a learning disability to a senior who has lost her speech because of a stroke. That's why, in speaking about people with disabilities, DAWN (The Disabled Women's Network) included the following frames of reference in their 1993 guide for health care professionals:

Non-visible disabilities
Examples include diabetes and epilepsy.
Mobility disabilities
These include a wide range of disabilities where mobility is restricted. Examples include cerebral palsy, paraplegia or quadriplegia, muscular dystrophy.
Deaf, deafened or hard-of-hearing disability
Visual disability
Persons who are blind or have limited vision.
Mental health disability
Persons with a psychiatric illness.
Learning disability
Examples include dyslexia (a reading disorder), hyperlexia (a perceptual learning problem) and dysgraphia (a writing disorder).

Environmental disability

Persons with extreme allergies to elements in the environment. Examples include peanut butter allergy, hypersensitivity to certain chemicals used in cleaning agents, paint or carpeting.

THE GOOD NEWS ABOUT WOMEN AND DISABILITIES

1. *Disability activists have accomplished a lot over the past decade*

The tenacious efforts of disability activists over the past ten years have reaped many rewards. These have included:

- changes in legislation relating to discrimination against people with disabilities;
- accessible transportation systems in most major cities;
- an increase in the number of public buildings which have been "retro-fitted" with wheelchair ramps and other means for allowing access to people with disabilities;
- a heightened awareness of the need to provide services such as sign-language interpretation at public events and closed captioning on television and in movies;
- the gradual inclusion of people with disabilities in mainstream media and in advertising.

To those without disabilities, these may seem tremendous accomplishments – and indeed they are. But to those who live with a disability and who must navigate the physical and social landscape every day, it seems we've only scratched the surface of the changes that are needed.

2. *DAWN and the Feminist Disability Movement*

A feminist disability movement has gradually emerged over the past ten years from two other movements – the women's movement and the disability rights movement. Over the years, women with disabilities have come together to talk about the issues they share and to plan strategies for change. Many were and continue to be active as feminists and as disability rights activists, but they joined together under this new banner because they felt that the women's movement was not looking at their unique needs as women with disabilities and the disability activists were not considering that gender also plays a role in access and public perception.

In 1985, a grassroots group called DAWN (Disabled Women's Network Canada) was formed to provide a source of support and information for women with disabilities and to lobby for change in areas that matter to them. Now there are about two dozen DAWN chapters across the country. Two issues high on DAWN's agenda since its inception are the health needs of disabled women and the treatment of disabled women by the health care system.

3. *Health Canada and DAWN: a Joint Self-Help and Awareness-Raising Project*
Between 1990 and 1994, Health Canada funded a unique project in Ontario in which members of DAWN organized a provincewide self-help network in addition to working at educating health care providers about health issues for women with disabilities. In the process, many women with disabilities across the province (and beyond, since their materials were circulated widely across Canada) came to know more about health issues for women with disabilities and about the resources available to them. Some of the educational resources that resulted from the project are listed at the end of this chapter.

The evaluators of the DAWN project learned some things that are important to our discussion of health issues for women with disabilities:

- Women with disabilities change their attitudes about their role in health care when they have the chance to talk with other women, when they are encouraged to increase their self-esteem and when they are provided with information about their bodies and preventive health care.
- Health care providers need women with disabilities to educate them about the specific needs of women with disabilities. They need to challenge the myth that the disability changes the health need.

The project produced a range of useful health resources and initiated productive discussion around the ways in which the "helping" professions need to reexamine some of their views about women with disabilities.

The Bad News for Women With Disabilities

1. *Women With Disabilities Are Put on Display in the Name of Medical Education*
Girls born with disabilities learn from a very young age to put up with being paraded around for doctors in the name of medical education. Toronto counsellor and disabled feminist Francine Odette notes that if a body doesn't "measure up," we learn pretty quickly what our culture wants from women. She elaborates: "We may have been asked to strip, walk back and forth in front of complete strangers so they can get a better view of what the physical 'problem' is, or to manually manipulate our limbs to determine flexibility and dexterity. Today, pictures or videos are taken of us and

used as educational tools for future doctors, with little thought given to our needs to have control over what happens to our bodies or who sees us."

Being paraded around as Exhibit A can have a lasting effect on the self-esteem of disabled girls and women. Says Odette: "Women with disabilities living in this society are not exempt from the influence of messages that attempt to dictate what is desirable and what is not in a woman. These messages are often internalized, and have an impact on how we see ourselves."

2. *Women with Disabilities Can Experience Related Problems.*
a. *Women with disabilities frequently experience isolation, abandonment and poverty.* In Canada, long winters, inadequate access and cutbacks to transportation systems to help people with disabilities go places mean that some disabled women may face lengthy periods of physical isolation. The stresses and strains of coping with a newly diagnosed disability can result in a relationship breakdown, particularly if the male partner feels burdened by his partner's new needs and is unwilling to be supportive or to adapt to required changes in their lifestyle. Statistics Canada's 1991 Health and Activity Limitation Survey notes that the median employment income for a disabled woman in Canada is only $8,360.
b. *Women with disabilities frequently develop mental health problems.* The stress of isolation along with their ongoing struggles to navigate inaccessible landscapes and live with poverty, can make women with disabilities especially vulnerable to mental health problems. A recent study of suicide and abuse among women with disabilities conducted by DAWN Canada, found that an alarming 58.7 percent of 381 respondents reported that they had thought about killing themselves at some time. Many of these women suffered from sexual, emotional or financial abuse.

QUESTIONS, CONTROVERSY AND DEBATE

1. THE DISABLED LABEL: MORE THAN ONE WAY TO LOOK AT IT

Most women with disabilities just want to have access to places and things the same way that those without disabilities do, and not to be viewed by others as needing help or pity. Nevertheless, there are two distinct attitudes held by disabled women:

The first is held by disabled women who do not wish to be identified as disabled. They feel that the label separates them from others and categorizes them as "different." Even some women with a visible disability feel this way.

The second is held by disabled women who are proud to be disabled and want to pass on this sense of pride to young girls with disabilities. These women are vocal and politically active about disability issues and work for improved awareness and services for women with disabilities.

2. IS SHE SICK OR IS SHE DISABLED?

We live in a society which tends to consider only one aspect of disability – the medical side. In a culture consumed with finding "cures," many people with disabilities are viewed by others as "sick" and needing to be "cured." However, it is important to distinguish between sickness and disability. A person who is disabled is not necessarily sick. In fact, most women with disabilities are quite healthy and require the same health care as nondisabled women – although certain aspects of their disability may require them to see specialists or take special treatments at different times in their lives. In *Women With Disabilities: A Guide for Health Care Professionals*, one disabled woman involved with DAWN Ontario put it very well: "Doctors often relate all illness or problems to my disability even though it may be gallstones or a cold." (On the other hand, some women with disabilities may be so focused on medically tending to their disability that they ignore other health needs. One woman with multiple sclerosis told me how, after years of tending to the medical needs surrounding her disability, she realized that she had never taken the time to have a mammogram – yet her mother had died from breast cancer!)

3. THE QUESTION OF ACCESSIBILITY

The question of access is one of the most critical health care issues for women with disabilities. Health care facilities and health-related events for women are sometimes set up or planned without consideration for the needs of many women.

Access for the Disabled: a List

- wheelchair ramps;
- accessible washrooms and elevators;
- telephones equipped with telecommunications devices for deaf women;
- the provision of sign-language interpretation;
- literature printed in large type or made available on tape for women with visual disabilities;
- the provision of attendant care for those who require it (if a woman who needs

help with feeding attends an all-day seminar, she would be entitled to have someone there to help her at mealtimes).

All of the above are necessities for women with disabilities. If an office is not equipped with a TTY (telecommunications device for deaf persons built into a telephone), a deaf or hard-of-hearing woman must go through a second party to make or change her own appointments or get confidential information there. If a doctor's office or birth control clinic is not equipped with a height-adjustable examining table which can be lowered and raised, women with mobility disabilities may find it extremely difficult, if not impossible, to have a Pap test, be fitted for a diaphragm or have a proper internal examination.

Barriers to Access: a Counter-list

Barriers to access can be subtle. They can include:
- Attitude: a health care worker becomes impatient or patronizing with a woman whose speech is difficult to understand; and
- Structure: inflexible medical-appointment schedules may not consider the extra time needed by a woman who requires more time to dress and undress because of her disability.

Disability activists have argued that issues such as accessibility should not be viewed as an "add-on" to existing services, or be treated as a huge sacrifice on the part of the service provider. As Pat Israel, a disabled feminist, commented, "Accessibility is not just a special service for disabled persons. Women with baby carriages, seniors – everyone benefits from accessible facilities and accessible attitudes."

More Barriers to Access: Denying Disabled Women a Sexual Identity

"Society believes that lack of physical attractiveness, as defined by the dominant culture, hampers our ability to be intimate," says Francine Odette. For most women with disabilities, this perceived inability to be intimate is just that, says Odette: a perception. That false perception colours the way many health and social service providers approach women with disabilities. Some, assuming the disabled person is not intimate or sexual, do not speak to them about birth control, or discuss any concerns they may have about sexuality or sexually transmitted diseases.

This lack of appropriate care can have serious consequences, sometimes fatal ones. It can mean women with disabilities are less knowledgeable about available

contraception. And it can also mean they may not be protected from sexually transmitted diseases, including life-threatening ones such as AIDS.

4. BIRTH CONTROL, NEW REPRODUCTIVE TECHNOLOGIES AND DISABLED WOMEN

There are risks associated with some forms of birth control and reproductive drugs that are specific to disabled women.

Women with certain disabilities may be at risk when taking some forms of birth control and other reproductive drugs (for example, infertility drugs, hormone replacement therapy). Although this area has not been well researched, we do know the following:

- Blood clots can form more easily in women with limited mobility, and estrogen is known to promote the formation of blood clots.
- Birth control devices that require a certain degree of manual dexterity – for example, a diaphragm – may not be appropriate for women with limited move-ment in their hands. Special attention to unique needs such as these should be common knowledge amongst doctors and birth control counsellors. Unfortunately, this information is not found in medical curricula. However, a growing body of information now exists for health care providers who wish to become more knowledgeable about this and other health issues for women with disabilities, and make their practices more accessible (See Resources sec-tion at the end of this chapter).

There are questions associated with the new reproductive technologies that are specific to disabled women.

One health care issue that has a high profile with women's disability rights activists
and groups is the new reproductive technologies. Although these reproductive technologies – such as in vitro fertilization and donor insemination – are often profiled
in the media as panaceas for infertile couples, many women with disabilities take a
slightly different view.

On the one hand, some of the technologies have allowed some women with
disabilities to become pregnant. But some of the technologies pose significant
ethical problems for people with disabilities. Prenatal diagnostic tests (including
amniocentesis, and chorionic villi sampling) are used, as Vancouver-based DAWN
Canada president Eileen O'Brien notes, "to determine whether the fetus is "abnor-

mal"... [and are] performed on women to facilitate the elimination of the "wrong" kind of fetus within the first few months of pregnancy." Many disabled feminists, while not opposing a woman's right to choose, are asking hard and serious questions about what these technologies represent for people with disabilities.

Women with disabilities who wish to be mothers speak of the importance this role has in their lives, particularly if they have spent much of their adolescence and young adulthood fighting the stereotype that they are asexual or incapable of reproducing. Pat Israel, in an address to the Toronto Women's Health Network, pointed out: "It is amazing that any disabled women do have children considering what they have to go through. When disabled women get pregnant, many people around them may be negative. Her doctor may try to pressure her into having an abortion. Her family and her spouse's family may show their displeasure openly. Often the only people who are happy about the pregnancy are the disabled woman and her partner and... friends with disabilities."

PROFILE

Bonnie Klein – when you get old prematurely, you have to reinvent yourself

Not all disabled women were born that way. In 1987, award-winning Canadian documentary filmmaker, Bonnie Klein (*Not a Love Story: A Film About Pornography,* made in 1981) suffered a severe stroke at the age of 46. It left her temporarily paralysed and unable to breathe on her own.

After many months of determination and rehabilitation, she regained some movement and the ability to speak, less one vocal chord. Today, she gets around her home city of Vancouver with a scooter she calls Gladys. She has transformed her own misfortune into a tremendous gain for society by choosing to write and go public about learning to live with a disability. To speak to the world about her experience of becoming disabled as an adult, she has moved from film to radio and print. She is also writing a book about her experience. In an article in the December 1992 issue of *Ms. Magazine,* Klein writes about how profoundly the experience has changed her life: "I learned to rest. In my prestroke life, this was never easy for me, juggling the three F's: family, filmmaking and feminism. Now I have no choice. My body's messages are non-negotiable." Like others before her, she notes how drastically life's priorities have changed: "I have to ration my energy. I have no time to waste on bullshit, but I do have time to smell the flowers."

Klein quotes American disability activist Jennifer Yen Wood, who became disabled as an adult: "When you have a traumatic injury or a stroke, it's just getting old prematurely – you go from one life into another one compared to your chronological peers . . . you lose the culture of your peers, so you have to invent one for yourself." Klein speaks of her own stroke as having brought her "a preview of aging," and given her "a telescope on aging."

Klein points out that many of us are afraid of disability. If we are not disabled, we look away from it, in horror or in fear, averting our eyes "in polite embarrassment." For Klein, it was other disabled women, in particular the Disabled Women's Network, who helped her to come to terms with her disability. Although she received "first-class traditional medical rehabilitation" after her stroke, she says that "the real progress and learning came from outside the medical establishment. The most important resource for women with disabilities and their health," she adds, "is to meet other women with disabilities. But peer support is not seen as part of the health care system; it's only seen as an adjunct to it."

Today, Klein is a strong advocate for the payment of disabled people as experts. Like others, she argues that they are the best people to be working with other people with disabilities. She also feels very strongly that it's important "not to give up. There's no gain in accepting, before you need to, that you can't do something."

PROFILE

Linda Crabtree – it's OK to be disabled

It's hard to believe that artist, writer, publisher, editor, designer, entrepreneur, lecturer, counsellor and Order of Canada recipient Linda Crabtree ever felt suicidal. But ten years ago, when she finally faced up to her disability, she says she felt "totally useless." Her disability, which she had ignored for decades, was getting the best of her: Crabtree has Charcot-Marie-Tooth Disease in which her muscles have atrophied from non-use, her thumbs don't work the way they used to and there are other medical complications as well. As she explains it:

"The message from the brain is not able to get through to the nerves properly." After her disability forced her to end a lifelong newspaper career, Crabtree, who lives in St. Catharines, Ontario, fell into a deep depression.

Crabtree's mother quietly but persistently kept showing her books about people who had come through the worst of times and thrived. Eventually, Crabtree got herself a scooter and set her sights on a psychology degree: "My first day back at school was my first day on my scooter. I ran into walls because I literally didn't know how to stop," she told me. In her second year of school, she wrote to newspapers across the country asking readers who had the same disease to contact her. Over 300 did, all of them wanting to talk. So Crabtree started the Charcot-Marie-Tooth Disease newsletter which today reaches 2,500 families in 44 countries; it helps all of them to keep in touch with the latest in research and communicate with others who have the neuromuscular syndrome.

After she completed her psychology degree, Crabtree became an accredited rehab worker. And in between those challenges, she designed and built herself a new house – a one-storey structure that wraps around a goldfish pond and outdoor oasis where she can combine her office and her home. Because she spends much of her time indoors, she had the house designed for 100 percent accessibility with skylights throughout, a total of 14. The walls are covered with Crabtree the artist's works: batiks, collages and watercolours (I call her a closet Martha Stewart: she even makes her own Christmas cards).

As if those accomplishments weren't enough, Crabtree also launched a unique newsletter on sexuality, sex, self-esteem and disability. "We are tired of hearing people saying things like, 'Oh, look at that poor dear in a wheelchair wearing her low-cut dress.' When I see a sexy disabled person I say, 'Great!' Until now, the subject of sex and disability has simply been a closed shop." But just because something is wrong on the outside doesn't mean there are no sexual feelings inside, she says. "It's time for an attitude change." After several years developing the newsletter, Crabtree has handed over the publishing of the newsletter, which is called It's Okay!, to friend Susan Wheeler who now publishes it (Write to Sureen Publishing, Box 23102, 124 Welland Ave., St. Catharines, Ontario L2R 7P6).

Now Crabtree is onto another project: planning a resort for people with disabilities. With her energy, however, I just know she'll be the last one to relax and enjoy it. Consider what she's accomplished over a few years: she's started a newsletter, received an honourary doctorate AND the Order of Canada, and she's become a member of Canada's Women's Inventor Project for her invention of the "butt brush," a hygiene tool for disabled persons.

Crabtree's role model is Albert Einstein. When asked what he was interested in, he said: "Everything! I just do what I gotta do!"

PART TWO

Your guide to resources for women with disabilities

ORGANIZATIONS

The following groups will bring you up to speed on disability issues in the areas of education and integration as well as in legal and advocacy issues. Some offer additional support through regular newsletters and/or published materials. Each can help you find the nearest disability support network in your community.

Canadian Abilities Foundation, 489 College St., Ste. 501, Toronto, Ontario M6G 1A5 (416) 923-9848.

Canadian Association for Community Living (CACL), 4700 Keele St., Kinsman Building, North York, Ontario M3J 1P3 (416) 661-9611.

Canadian Association of Independent Living Centres (CAILC), 350 Sparks St., 10th Flr., Ottawa, Ontario K1R 7S8 (613) 563-2581.

Canadian Disability Rights Council (CDRC) 208-428 Portage Ave., Ste. 208, Winnipeg, Manitoba R3C 0E2 (204) 943-4787.

Canadian National Institute for the Blind (CNIB) 1929 Bayview Ave., Toronto, Ontario M4G 3E8 (416) 486-2500.

Council of Canadians with Disabilities, 294 Portage Ave., Ste. 926, Winnipeg, Manitoba R3C 0B9 (204) 947-0303.

DAWN Canada, 3637 Cambie St., Ste. 408 Vancouver, British Columbia V5Z 2X3.
(Check your telephone book or contact DAWN Canada for the DAWN chapter nearest you).

North American Chronic Pain Association of Canada (NACPAC), 6 Handel Ct., Brampton, Ontario L6S 1Y4 (905) 793-5230.

People First of Canada, 489 College St., Ste. 308, Toronto, Ontario M6G 1A5 (416) 920-9530.

AboutFace, 99 Crowns Lane, 3rd Flr., Toronto, Ontario M5R 3P4 (416) 944-FACE or 1-800-665-FACE.

Canadian Association of Captioning Consumers, 443 Reynolds St., Oakville, Ontario L6J 3M5 (905) 338-1246 (Voice/TTY).

Canadian Paraplegic Association, 1101 Prince of Wales Dr., Ste. 320, Ottawa, Ontario K2C 3W7 (613) 723-1033.

NEWSLETTERS/MAGAZINES/ REPORTS

Captioning Today: Canada's Captioning News Magazine. Published by Canadian Association of Captioning Consumers, 443 Reynolds St., Oakville, Ontario L6J 3M5 (905) 338-1246 (Voice/TTY).

Abilities, Canadian quarterly magazine for people with disabilities, published by the Canadian Abilities Foundation, 444 Yonge St., Toronto, Ontario M5B 2H4.

"*It's Okay.*" A newsletter on sexuality and disability. Published by Sureen Publishing, Box 23102, 124 Welland Ave., St. Catharines, Ontario L2R 7P6.

Meeting Our Needs: Access Manual for Transition Houses, Shirley Masuda and Jillian Riddington, DAWN Canada, 1992.

CMT. A newsletter for people with Charcot-Marie-Tooth Disease. 1 Springbank Dr., St. Catharines, Ontario L2S 2K1 (905) 687-3630.

Resourceful Woman. A newsletter published by the Health Resource Centre for Women with Disabilities at the Rehabilitation Institute of Chicago, 345 E. Superior St., Ste. 681, Chicago, Illinois, 60611.

Staying Healthy in the Nineties: Women with Disabilities Talk About Health Care, Fran Odette (DAWN Toronto, 1994).

Table Manners: A Guide to the Pelvic Examination for Disabled Women and Health Care Providers. A brochure available from Planned Parenthood Alameda-San Francisco, 815 Eddy St., Ste. 300, San Francisco, California 94109.

The Baby Challenge: Handbook of Pregnancy for Women with a Physical Disability, Mukti Jane Campion (Tavistock Routledge, 1990).

The Only Parent in the Neighbourhood: Mothering and Women with Disabilities. Position Paper No. 3, prepared for DAWN Canada by Jillian Riddington, 1989.

The Health and Disabled Women Project: A Symposium for Change, Anne Rochon Ford, ed. (DAWN Toronto, 1993).

Violence Against Women with Disabilities: Practical Considerations for Health Care Professionals. A booklet prepared by and available from DAWN Toronto, 180 Dundas St. W., Ste. 210, Toronto, Ontario M5G 1Z8.

"Women and Disability." Special issue of *Canadian Woman Studies,* Summer 1993, Vol. 13, No. 4. (Back issues of the journal available by writing: Canadian Woman Studies, 212 Founders College, York University, 4700 Keele St., North York, Ontario, M3J 1P3).

BOOKS/AUDIOS/VIDEOS

Steps to Access Social Services: A Practical Guide to Social Services. Available through Sureen Publishing, PO Box 23101, 124 Welland Ave., St. Catharines, Ontario L2R 7T6.

Toward Intimacy. A video directed by Debbie McGee. Available from the National Film Board.

Cabin Fever. A 48-min. video written and directed by Deborah Shames (415) 332-8191

Special Edition for Disabled People. A catalogue listing sex aids, publications and booklets. The Lawrence Research Group, PO Box 31039, San Francisco, California 94131, 1-800-242-2823.

"Bonnie and Gladys." A series of four programs prepared by Bonnie Klein which aired on CBC radio's Morningside, November 4-10, 1994. A set of audiocassette tapes is available from CBC Radioworks Dept. for $32 plus tax. (416) 205-6161.

Toward Intimacy. A film on sexuality and disabled women by the National Film Board. Videocassette available for loan or purchase from NFB Audio-Visual Library, 1-800-267-7710.

CHAPTER 19

CFITS: ACKNOWLEDGING ILLNESSES WOMEN HAVE BEEN TOLD ARE "ALL IN YOUR HEAD"

Why is this a women's health issue? This group of disorders, which includes chronic fatigue syndrome, fibromyalgia, irritable bowel syndrome, interstitial cystitis and temporomandibular joint syndrome are overrepresented in women. Many doctors dismiss the concerns of women suffering from these disorders.

What you can do for yourself: Learn all you can, find a doctor who listens and get the best help either in the form of medication, therapy, peer support or all three.

PART ONE

The facts: why CFITS is a women's issue

Five little words that make women see red are "It's all in your head." Yet these words have been heard by millions of women in doctors' offices around the world for generations. In the past, many diseases were labelled psychosomatic. But more and more today, the thinking goes this way: whether or not the origin of a condition is psychogenic (that is, originating in the mind) matters little because the pain, discomfort and anxiety felt by the patient are very real indeed. By now, most of us realize that putting on a stiff upper lip in the face of pain or discomfort (even if no organic cause can be found) is of little use long-term: while many of us can get through a meeting or special engagement by moving that discomfort and pain to the back burner of our minds, we are nonetheless worn down by it if the pain or discomfort is chronic.

In the past, some physicians have been frustrated by patients for whom no organic cause of pain can be found and for whom, therefore, determining treatment is difficult. Moreover, none of these disorders is life-threatening. Since fatigue is an underlying symptom in all these disorders, it's hard for doctors to separate normal everyday fatigue from fatigue symptomatic of a disorder: after all, some might say, who today is not fatigued? Some physicians send their patients from specialist to specialist in an attempt to put a name to the condition that plagues them. Some physicians actually believe that these patients have been misdiagnosed and will be properly treated by the next specialist they see. But other physicians decide that these patients are milking our medical system: why spend money investigating an illness that is in someone's head, they ask. It is true that the cost to treat a nonspecific chronic disease is enormous to both the medical system and the economy at large; however, that is no reason to dismiss these ailments as insignificant.

Thankfully, there are a growing number of doctors in Canada who are interested in working with patients who suffer from these disorders, which include chronic fatigue syndrome, fybromyalgia, irritable bowel syndrome, interstitial cystitis, and temporomandibular joint syndrome. The majority of patients who suffer from these disorders are women. In 1994 in Toronto, a group of doctors interested in helping patients with these disorders pledged to meet on a regular basis to share what each had learned from their patients and the different disorders – which they call CFITs, after the first initial of the five disorders.

What exactly are these conditions, their symptoms and treatments? And how are doctors and patients finally getting a handle on them? Let's look at each of the five.

PART TWO

Your guide to CFITS

CHRONIC FATIGUE SYNDROME (CFS)

The *C* in CFITs, chronic fatigue syndrome (CFS) affects 1 to 2 percent of the population. It is also known as myalgic encephalomyelitis, according to the Myalgic Encephalomyelitis Association of Canada (M.E. Canada). Its main identifying characteristic is in its name – chronic fatigue that is both unexplained and unrelieved by rest and that continues for at least six months. Four or more of the following symptoms must accompany the chronic fatigue for the condition to be identified as CFS:

- memory or concentration problems;

- a sore throat;
- tender lymph nodes;
- multi-joint pain but without joint swelling or redness;
- muscle pain;
- headaches;
- nonrefreshing sleep;
- fatigue that lasts about 24 hours after exercise.

Seventy percent of CFS patients are women; 10 percent are teens and children. Alberta's 18-year-old Melanie Crooker, who has suffered from CFS since she was 12, explained how she felt in a 1995 article in the *Edmonton Journal*. She described her sensitivity to light and noise and her chronic exhaustion and headaches. Frustration was part of her history because it wasn't until a few years ago that her illness was finally diagnosed properly: up until then, she had been told by doctors that she had allergies.

Sometimes CFS is confused with fibromyalgia (the F in CFIT s) because there are several characteristics common to both. In one study, the two disorders shared nine out of ten criteria. The main difference between the two ailments is that patients with fibromyalgia report more muscular and joint pain, while CFS patients report a greater amount of fatigue as well as other accompanying symptoms.

Dr. Carolyn DeMarco, author, educator and general practitioner, points out that CFS patients may need counselling for depression. They may also be helped with cognitive therapy to alter their beliefs about illness, as well as a gentle exercise program, a good diet and even some massage. Sometimes low-dose antidepressants are prescribed.

As with all CFIT s, one of the first steps to healing and managing CFS is to find a sympathetic doctor who believes that CFS is legitimate.

FIBROMYALGIA

The F in CFIT s, figromyalgia is a soft-tissue disorder that used to be called fibrositis. Fibromyalgia affects 2 to 3 percent of the population and is really a collection of symptoms that can include aches and pains, and tenderness in at least 11 of 18 identified tender spots on specific sites of the body. Persons with fibromyalgia tend to hurt all over.

Some experts call the disorder a subgroup of arthritis; many rheumatologists regularly see patients with fibromyalgia, some of whom have been wrongly diagnosed with rheumatoid arthritis. Other symptoms can include headaches, morning stiffness, fatigue, an intolerance to cold or damp weather, a feeling of restlessness in the limbs and either irritable bowels or bladder syndrome.

One of the distinguishing features of fibromyalgia is a disturbance in sleep patterns. Tina Harvey, program director of M.E. Canada, describes the sleep disorder in the 1995 winter issue of *The Messenger*, the organization's newsletter: "In many fibromyalgia patients, their delta sleep is broken by bursts of alpha waves (awake-like brain activity). This results in people with fibromyalgia awakening feeling sore all over and being more tired than when they went to bed."

Sleep researcher Dr. Harvey Moldofsky of Toronto Hospital/Western Hospital Division says that unrefreshing sleep is tied in some way to the syndrome of fibromyalgia. And he adds: "Fibromyalgia is a gender-specific disorder. More than 80 percent of the people are women. This is a women's health issue."

The average age of women with fibromyalgia is 39, Dr. Moldofsky says. These women report that for much of their lives they felt fine and were relatively healthy. Often, women will say that things changed after their children were born. So one of the questions being asked today is whether women develop the disorder as a result of experiencing years of interrupted sleep as mothers getting up to care for young children. Dr. Moldofsky suggests that as well as giving their patients a psychological and physical function exam, doctors should ask patients with suspected fibromyalgia to keep a sleep diary. "These patients need help with sleep," he says. "Today, we are into a famine of time." Women are the prime sufferers, he says. Women with families have two jobs – only one of which they get paid to do.

Treatment includes establishing a good sleep habit, which may be achieved by avoiding caffeine, tobacco, alcohol, bedtime snacks and napping. Exercise is important too, though fibromyalgia patients usually report pain after exercising: walking, aquatics and any other exercise that can gradually improve cardiovascular fitness with the least amount of muscle resistance is often recommended.

IRRITABLE BOWEL SYNDROME (IBS)

Irritable bowel syndrome (the I in CFITs) affects close to three million Canadians, most of them women. Yet the disorder is dismissed by many physicians. Symptoms include bloating, persistent abdominal cramps, flatulence and diarrhea, none of which are rooted in any organic reason. Some doctors say they see it in women who have the "superwoman syndrome." Others explain it more simply as people with gut reactors who can inherit the tendency towards a hypersensitive gastrointestinal tract.

Dr. Brenda Toner, a psychologist at Toronto's Clarke Institute of Psychiatry and head of its Women's Mental Health program, told the *Toronto Sun* that IBS has to "come out of the closet." Too many people are embarrassed to talk about their "gut reactions," especially when those gut reactions include bloating and diarrhea. She describes IBS as a very real, complex, physical, emotional and psychosocial condition. Helping patients learn to relax and turn off chronic tension is her approach to treatment.

INTERSTITIAL CYSTITIS (IC)

Interstitial cystitis (another I disorder under the CFIT s umbrella) is a bladder disorder that can cause severe pain and causes a desire for frequent urination – sometimes up to 60 times a day. It is believed that Napoleon suffered from it. However, 90 percent of IC patients are women. An estimated 50,000 Canadians are affected.

IC patients suffer frustration along with pain, notes Sheila Holmes, vice president of the Interstitial Cystitis Association of Canada. Since the classic symptoms are similar to those common to urinary tract infections, doctors often react by having patients' urine analyzed. In IC, however, standard urine cultures are negative, and patients don't respond to antibiotics. The result is that women are overprescribed antibiotics, or told to drink lots of cranberry juice (helpful for common bladder infections but not IC) or, once again, are told the disease is all in their heads.

Some doctors consider interstitial cystitis a disease of postmenopausal women. But younger women get it, too. Other doctors persist in believing IC doesn't exist at all. The only true diagnosis can be made with a cystoscopy (an examination of the inside of the bladder done with a lighted tube), a procedure that must be performed under anesthesia. People with IC usually have tiny hemorrhages or ulcers that dot the bladder wall.

The cause of the disease is unknown. Theories range from its being an autoimmune disorder to its being infection-based. Treatments vary, and may include dietary changes, antihistamines or antidepressants. Surgery is a last resort.

TEMPOROMANDIBULAR JOINT SYNDROME (TMJ)

Temporomandibular Joint Syndrome (the T in CFIT s) is a condition in which the temporomandibular joint – located where the jawbone is connected to the headbone – becomes inflamed and swollen. The condition can also send pain to the neck, shoulder, head and even teeth. There may be tenderness or spasms. Sometimes the disorder can create a clicking sound when you open and close your jaw.

Determining who treats TMJ can be a conundrum: orthodontists sometimes claim the disorder as their area; some rheumatologists say it may be associated with arthritis; and some family physicians suggest the sinuses might be involved.

Stress can induce this dysfunction: if you keep a mirror handy near your work-space, you can easily monitor yourself to see if your teeth are clenched or your jaw is tense. Sometimes, wearing a special mouth-guard appliance designed by an ortho-dontist can realign your jaw and may relieve some pain. Biofeedback, facial exercises and counselling also may be advised. Often, a support group can help its members cope with facial pain, so talk to your physician or dentist about helping you find such a group – or about starting one of your own.

WHAT'S THE FUTURE FOR CFITS DISORDERS?

Support or information groups have been crucial in helping put all CFITs disorders on the medical map. "Having someone to talk to that knows what it is, is the most important element," Sheila Holmes says. Members can compare notes, share stories, and research information about each disorder in the CFITs family. Raising aware-ness, and ultimately raising funds for research into the disorder, is part of the educa-tional aspect of such groups and associations.

"What all these [disorders] have in common is that they are overrepresented in women," says Dr. Susan Abbey, a psychiatrist at Toronto Hospital who meets with other physicians interested in CFITs. "For all of them, the underlying pathophysiolo-gy is poorly understood. The disorders are extremely disabling – women are missing an awful lot of work. Many of them end up on short-term disability, so these disor-ders cost a lot to the system."

Abbey and her colleagues see a connection between these disorders and women's mental health. At one end of the spectrum are the symptoms and at the other end are the depression and anxiety associated with having the disorder. "The problem comes in as a what-came-first-the-chicken-or-the-egg-type question," Abbey explains. "Some people say these are just anxious and depressed women – so why spend money investigating their problems? But women with these problems may feel they are being devalued and that they are not being listened to or taken seriously." Doctors admit that there still are not very good treatments for any of the CFITs disorders.

Current treatment for all these disorders includes some medication and some therapy. Current research into CFITs includes exploring their connection to sera-tonin metabolism levels. The brain chemical serotonin is a neurotransmitter related to mood; studies suggest that a drop in serotonin contributes to depression.

But where does that leave patients now? "I see [CFITs sufferers] walking down the road carrying two heavy suitcases," Abbey says. "In one suitcase, there is the biology of the problem, the associated pain, the virus, the accident, or whatever else there is. In the other suitcase, there is the secondary stuff – the sleep disturbances, the interruptions in one's interpersonal relationships, the anxiety, the depression. We do not at the present time have good treatments for suitcase number one. But we have a ton of good treatments for suitcase number two."

PART THREE

Your guide to CFITS *resources*

CHRONIC FATIGUE

Environmental Medicine Clinic, Victoria General Hospital, 1278 Power Rd., Halifax, Nova Scotia B3H 2Y9 (902) 428-2110.

M.E. Support Group, 9303 - 107th Ave., Fort St. John, British Columbia V1J 2P2 (604) 787-1178.

M.E. Society of Edmonton, Box 465, 10405 Jasper Ave., Ste. 21, Edmonton, Alberta T5J 3S2 (403) 944-0809.

M.E. Association of Ontario, 90 Sheppard Ave. E., Ste. 108, North York, Ontario M2N 3A1 (416) 222-8820.

M.E. Society of Edmonton, University of Alberta Hospital, 8440 112 St., Edmonton, Alberta T6G 2B7 (403) 492-8822; 24-hour info line: (403) 988-3443.

M.E. Society of Calgary, Box 30402, 1323N - 6455 Macleod Trail S.W., Calgary, Alberta T2H 2W2 (403) 248-7773.

Nightingale Research Foundation (NFR), 383 Danforth Ave., Ottawa, Ontario K2A 0E1 (613) 728-9643.

Sleep and Snoring Institute, 4869 Dundas St. W., Ste. 202, Islington, Ontario M9A 1A4 (416) 241-6121.

The M.E. Association of Canada (Myalgic Encephalomyelitis or Chronic Fatigue Immune Dysfunction Syndrome), 246 Queen St., Ste. 400, Ottawa, Ontario K1P 5E4 (613) 563-1565.

BOOKS

Hope and Help for Chronic Fatigue Syndrome, Karyn Feidan (Prentice Hall, 1992).

Living With Chronic Fatigue, Susan Conan (Taylor Publishing, 1990).

M.E (Chronic Fatigure Syndrome) and the Healer Within, Nick Bamforth (Amethyst Books, 1993).

Recovering from Chronic Fatigue Syndrome, William Collinge (The Body Press, 1993).

Running on Empty, Katrina H. Berne (Hunter House Publishing, 1992).

Sleep, Dr. Paul Caldwell (Key Porter Books, 1995)

The Messenger. A newsletter published by M.E. Canada, 246 Queen St., Ste. 400, Ottawa, Ontario K1P 5E4 (613) 563-1565.

The Alchemy of Illness, Kat Duff (Pantheon Books).

The Doctor's Guide to Chronic Fatigue Syndrome, Dr. David S. Bell (Addison-Wesley)

The Canary and Chronic Fatigue, Majid Ali, M.D. (Life Span Press)

Women and Fatigue, H. Atkinson (Pocket Books, 1985).

FYBROMYALGIA

Arthritis Bell Support and Information Line (ABSIL): (416) 967-5679, 1-800-361-1112 (Ontario only). Hours of operation, 10:00 a.m.–4:00 p.m., Monday through Friday.

The Arthritis Society: National Office/Ontario

Division, 250 Bloor St. E., Ste. 901, Toronto, Ontario M4W 3P2 (416) 967-1414. Provincial chapters: Newfoundland: Box 522, Stn. C., St. John's, Newfoundland A1C 5K4 Prince Edward Island: 109 Heath Ave., Sherwood, PEI C1A 6Z3 Nova Scotia: 5516 Spring Garden Rd., Halifax, Nova Scotia B3J 1G6. New Brunswick: 65 Brunswick St., Fredericton, New Brunswick E3B 1G5. Quebec: 2075 University St., Ste. 1206, Montreal, Quebec H3A 2L1. Manitoba: 386 Broadway Ave., Ste. 105, Winnipeg, Manitoba R3C 3R6. Saskatchewan: 2078 Halifax St., Regina, Saskatchewan S4P 1T7. Alberta: 1301-8th St. S.W., Ste. 301, Calgary, Alberta/ Northwest Territories T2R 1B7. British Columbia/Yukon: 895 West 10th Ave., Vancouver, British Columbia V5Z 1L7.

Ontario Fibromyalgia Association, c/o The Arthritis Society, 250 Bloor St. E., Ste. 901, Toronto, Ontario M4W 3P2 (416) 967-1414 or 1-800-361-1112 (Ontario only).

BOOKS/PROGRAMS/VIDEOS

Arthritis Self-Management Program: A six-week program, operating throughout Ontario, with the focus on coping skills for people suffering from arthritis, lupus and fibromyalgia.

Fibromyalgia: Face to Face. A 14-min. video, available from the Ontario Fibromyalgia Association for $19.95. Profiles of research doctors and people successfully coping with this syndrome.

Fibromyalgia: Fighting Back and Coping with Fibromyalgia. Two booklets, $6.95 each, LRH Publications, PO Box 8, Stn. Q, Toronto, Ontario. M4T 2L7.

Tender Points. Newsletter of the Ontario Fibromyalgia Association. 250 Bloor St. E., Ste. 901, Toronto, Ontario M4W 3P2 (416) 967-1414.

The "Be" Attitudes – Keys to Healing from Within. A 120-min. video. $15 from the Ontario Fibromyalgia Association. 250 Bloor St. E., Ste. 901, Toronto, Ontario M4W 3P2 (416) 967-1414.

OTHER SUPPORT AND INFORMATION

Crohn's and Colitis Foundation of Canada, 21 St. Clair Ave. E., Ste. 301, Toronto, Ontario M4T 1L9 (416) 920-5035; 1-800-387-1479.

If This Is a Test, Have I Passed Yet? Living with Inflammatory Bowel Disease, Ferne Sherkin-Langer (Macmillan Canada, 1994).

Interstitial Cystitis Association (ICA), Box 5814, Stn. A, Toronto, Ontario M5W 1P2 (416) 920-8986.

TO 2000 AND BEYOND: TAKING CHARGE, BY TAKING CARE

Knowledge is power. I believe that's the key to taking charge of our health both today and tomorrow. Consider two major diseases, cancer and heart disease, and think about how far we've come in our knowledge about them since the fifties. In the fifties, a diagnosis of cancer was often considered to be a death sentence. The disease wasn't talked about openly; people who had it were avoided; and support groups for them or their families didn't even exist. And heart disease? It was considered an unfortunate but predictable and often inevitable result of the aging process. We simply didn't understand heart attacks; frequently, the first indication of heart disease was sudden death.

Today, we have a fairly good grasp of cancer at the molecular level and, while treatment can be difficult, there are many effective treatments and millions of people now recover to live cancer-free lives. Daily, we hear about studies and breakthroughs in the ongoing war against this dreadful illness. We've also seen a dramatic change in the diagnosis and treatment of heart disease. Do you remember when the *last* thing a heart attack patient was advised to do was to get into better physical shape? And who, in the fifties, thought that what they ate might affect their cardiovascular health? Now we know many ways to protect against heart disease through modifying our lifestyle. More important, we now know and accept that heart disease doesn't just happen to men but is the number-one killer of women!

Modern medicine has extended the length of our life *and* it has expanded our expectations about good health. Decades ago, good health basically meant living disease-free. Today, we expect much more. For most of us, enjoying good health includes being disease-free plus a fair level of satisfaction with our social, sexual, occupational and personal existence. Quality of life counts, and feeling a sense of control is important (whether we're sick or well!). A 1995 nationwide survey by Toronto's Women's College Hospital reported that 77 percent of Canadian women define being healthy as extending beyond just the physical; 63 percent included mental health and a good mental outlook as part of their wellness definition. Good health also depends on being in a healthy environment (safe water, clean air and adequate sewage disposal), as well as having access to medical care – things that as Canadians, many of us have taken for granted.

The future promises even more dramatic changes in medicine and health care. And these changes will mean that we as health consumers have a crucial role to play. The World Health Organization defines health promotion as the process of enabling people to increase their control over their health while at the same time improving their health. When it comes to women's health, the changes are particularly welcome after centuries of paternalistic medicine in which women were powerless and were expected to be passive consumers. It's often said that women's health today has become the new women's movement, one which doesn't depend on being a feminist or a traditionalist, one which accepts no political boundaries and one which has no barriers of class, colour or age.

But what do all these changes mean to you, one Canadian woman?

Chances are, you are the gatekeeper of your family's health. We know that women don't just take care of themselves. Their circle of care may include children, partner and aging parents. We also know that women tend to live longer than men. In fact, a woman who reaches age 50 today (and remains free of cancer and heart disease) can expect to live to be 92. All these reasons only underline why learning to become advocates for ourselves and others is a skill worth acquiring at any age.

We know that doctors don't have the time they used to have to spend with patients. If we want the best care possible for ourselves and our families, we'll need easy-to-access educational materials to help us become smarter health care consumers. One important way to give something (while getting something in return) is to join or support a health association or foundation that focuses on women's research issues or education on a specific health issue. Examples include The Heart and Stroke Foundation of Ontario's Women's Initiative, The Osteoporosis Society of Canada, The Genesis Foundation, or the Migraine Association. Or start your own educational or fundraising group: that's what back-sufferer Judylaine Fine did with the Back Association of Canada, an educational and support group for people with back problems. Recently, cookbook author Rose Reisman founded The National Breast Cancer Fund, which will receive profits from her cookbook sales for research and educational projects accross the country. A shift of power from health care providers to consumers means that we're going to be expected to do more for ourselves – to take charge and take responsibility for our own care. Moreover, the many advances in medicine (from genetic testing to reproductive technologies to the newest drugs to fight everything from depression to breast cancer) mean that consumers have some homework to do before determining whether or not to participate in medicine's new frontiers.

We are learning that prevention is the key to maximizing our health and minimizing the drain on the health care system. Health care spending is taking an increasingly larger share of our gross domestic product – about 9.9 percent in 1991 compared to 7.5 percent in 1971. There is plenty you can do to take better care of yourself and your family, from practising nutritional good sense, to making good health care choices in everything from ensuring you have your regular checkups, to doing monthly breast self-examinations and practising safe sex. You *can* change your lifestyle for optimum health. You and your doctor can work together to find ways to help you stop smoking, cut down on alcohol and caffeine, eat better, manage stress and benefit from exercise.

Now, and in the future, you can also get the most out of your health by being an informed consumer, learning about the warning signs of major diseases, and being proactive about your health. If you are diagnosed with a particular disease or condition, do ask your doctor questions – and find out what you can do on your own as well. Remember, any Canadian has the right to refuse treatment or to ask that treatment be withdrawn. You also have the right to ask questions and to learn all you can beforehand about any treatment being offered.

Share health information you've learned and the experiences you've lived, with others. That's what Monica Wright-Roberts did when she published *Side By Side*, a handbook for breast cancer caregivers. When Roberts was experiencing the worst of her own breast cancer treatment, an old friend became a fairy godmother and arranged for a team of round-the-clock caregivers who would take turns helping Roberts, a single mom with two school-aged kids, through her difficult months. One person picked up and returned library books, another provided casseroles, still another took the kids to their skating lessons. Some of the people involved were close friends, others were practically strangers. Roberts wrote her handbook to show caregivers how such a system might work for them.

If no information or support group exists for your type of condition, consider starting one yourself. A group of Collingwood, Ontario, women started a Women's Health Interest Group so they could bring women's health education to their own community. Public health nurses and local doctors give presentations on subjects of interest; the female members fill in the gaps with a lot of research and information sharing. Remember, bibliotherapy can be the best therapy possible!

A word of caution, however. Although this book is all about encouraging women to play a more active role in their health, remember that bad things can and do happen to good people. "We are mere mortals; we're not bionic," Dr. Carolyn Bennett, a Toronto family physician says. We do get sick and our bodies can betray us, sometimes no matter how well we look after ourselves. There may be times when getting sick is simply beyond our control.

That old cliché about living life to the fullest every day may be the best advice, after all. Bennett (and countless others, myself included) believes that, as women, we must learn to prioritize: "There are things that consume energy and things that create energy. I hope every one of us will start to say no to some of those things that consume energy and are not really necessary. We must draw some of those boundaries."

Put another way, the things that matter most should never be at the mercy of the things that matter least. I hope that this book will help you to take charge and take care – and to put first things first. And that first is you and your health – so that you can live to the fullest the life you so richly deserve.

BMI CHART

Nutrition Services, Ottawa-Carleton Health Department, 1987. Revised.

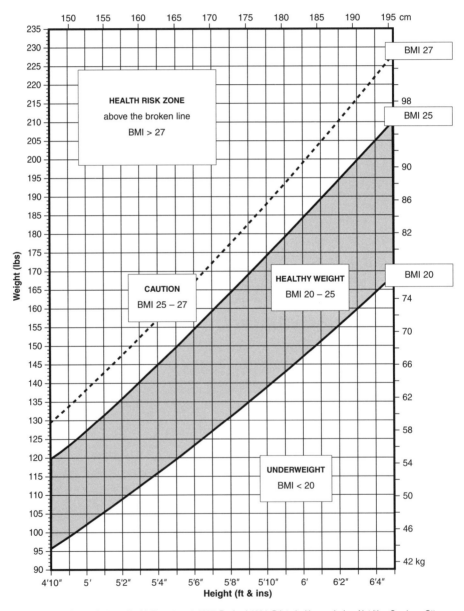

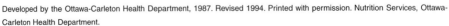

Developed by the Ottawa-Carleton Health Department, 1987. Revised 1994. Printed with permission. Nutrition Services, Ottawa-Carleton Health Department.

CANADA'S FOOD GUIDE TO HEALTHY EATING

Grain Products
Choose whole grain and enriched products more often.

Vegetables & Fruit
Choose dark green and orange vegetables and orange fruit more often.

Milk Products
Choose lower-fat milk products more often.

Meat & Alternatives
Choose leaner meats, poultry and fish, as well as dried peas, beans and lentils more often.

INDEX